Religion and Society in Early Modern Europe

Religion and Society in Early Modern Europe 1500–1800

Edited by

KASPAR von GREYERZ

THE GERMAN HISTORICAL INSTITUTE

GEORGE ALLEN & UNWIN
London
Boston   Sydney

George Allen & Unwin (Publishers) Ltd,
40 Museum Street, London WC1A 1LU, UK

George Allen & Unwin (Publishers) Ltd,
Park Lane, Hemel Hempstead, Herts HP2 4TE, UK

Allen & Unwin, Inc.,
Fifty Cross Street, Winchester, Mass 01890, USA

George Allen & Unwin Australia Pty Ltd,
8 Napier Street, North Sydney, NSW 2060, Australia

First published in 1984

British Library Cataloguing in Publication Data
    Religion and society in early modern Europe 1500–1800.
1. Civilization, Modern   2. Church history
I. Greyerz, Kaspar von   II. German Historical
Institute
940.2   CB358
ISBN 0–04–940078–9

Library of Congress Cataloging in Publication Data
    Main entry under title:
    Religion and society in early modern Europe, 1500–1800.
Includes index.
1. Europe—Church history—Addresses, essays, lectures,
2. Europe—Religion—Addresses, essays, lectures.
I. Greyerz, Kaspar von.
BR735.R43   1984   209'.4   84-12291
ISBN 0–04–940078–9 (alk. paper)

Set in 10 on 11 point Times by Setrite Ltd, Hong Kong,
and printed in Great Britain by Mackays of Chatham

Contents

Part Five   Historiography, Sacred or Profane?

Foreword

The German Historical Institute considers that one of its main duties lies in the promotion of co-operation between British and German historical scholarship and, indeed, with scholars from other countries as well. Historical research should no longer be pursued within the narrow confines of national historiographies as has been the case for a long time in the past. International academic conferences, the proceedings of which are subsequently published, appear to be a suitable way to bring together scholars from different national backgrounds and with different methodological outlooks. This is true in particular of the theme to which this volume of essays is devoted, namely, popular religious attitudes during the sixteenth, seventeenth and eighteenth centuries. Whilst in Great Britain and, more particularly, in France pioneering research has been undertaken in the history of popular as opposed to official religious attitudes and modes of conduct, research in the Federal Republic of Germany has only recently begun to pay closer attention to these problems. It appears, none the less, that important work has been done which is relevant to this theme, although the scholars in question more often than not worked in relative isolation from each other. Bringing these trends of research together and presenting them to a wider audience alongside one another would appear to be a useful way to cross-breed historical research in this field.

Considerations of this nature induced the German Historical Institute to arrange an international conference on popular religion and its relationship to the religious attitudes of the dominant elites.[1] It took place from 12 to 14 November 1981 in the Herzog August Bibliothek in Wolfenbüttel which is a renowned research centre for early modern European history and which also administers an invaluable collection of early printed books and pamphlets collected by the Dukes of Brunswick since the late sixteenth century. The collection of essays published in this volume is based upon the papers presented to this conference although in many cases they have been subject to substantial revision and extension in order to take up the numerous suggestions made during the debates. Their theme is not limited only to popular religion and its contrast to the religious culture of the learned elites; they also discuss many of the wider social and political dimensions of religion from the late Middle Ages until the beginning of the Industrial Revolution. In their entirety they cover a wide field and can be considered a good sample of the different approaches in contemporary historical research to the problems of popular religion. They provide the reader with up-to-date information about current trends of research in this field and it is hoped that they will be of some use to him in his own work. The volume, furthermore, allows comparisons to be made between the different methodological approaches to this theme which in turn will not fail to generate future research.

At this point we should like to express our thanks to the Director of the Herzog August Bibliothek Wolfenbüttel, Professor Dr Paul Raabe, as well as to Professor Walther Killy and Dr Sabine Solf who made it possible for the conference to be held at Wolfenbüttel in a most stimulating atmosphere. Thanks should also be extended to all the members of the German Historical Institute London who prepared the groundwork for the conference and typed and retyped the manuscripts. Particular thanks go to the translators who rendered the often difficult texts into readable English, as well as to Professor A. G. Dickens, Drs Peter Burke, Michael Hunter and Bob Scribner and Ms Lyndal Roper for their invaluable assistance in the editing of the translations. Last but not least thanks have to go to Dr von Greyerz who was largely responsible for arranging the original conference and for editing the essays assembled in this volume.

London, 22 February 1984   *Wolfgang J. Mommsen*

Note

1   See the conference report by Kaspar von Greyerz in *Bulletin of the German Historical Institute London*, no. 10 (Spring 1982), pp. 3–11.

*Religion and Society in Early
Modern Europe*

Introduction

Kaspar von Greyerz

Contemporaries of these seemingly secular 1980s often are too quick in associating the notion of religion solely with 'church' or even with 'sects'; some of the readers of this volume may therefore wonder why this book has not been given a different title. Why 'Religion and Society'?

A cursory perusal of the following pages may thus leave the non-specialist reader rather puzzled. What has religion to do with animals and alehouses, calendrical cycles and civic rituals, or for that matter with courts, crime and chastity and indeed with sexual symbolism and behaviour?

The fact is that religion was an all-pervasive force in pre-industrial society, by far transcending the life of the church. All those interested in the history of early modern Europe cannot ignore this fact with impunity. Admittedly, it has now become fashionable to drive home this message. To a large extent, this stands to reason, for 'religion' has long been a quasi-monopoly of church history and comparative religion. The *social* history of religion attempts to supplement these approaches. Rather than concentrating on the various aspects of established and institutionalised religion alone, its aim is the historical study of religion within society as a whole.[1]

Despite the relative newness of the field concerned, research carried out within it has proved excitingly, and to some extent, confusingly, prolific. There is a wealth of burgeoning (interdisciplinary) ramifications that are currently being pursued. No attempt could be made to cover all of them here, notably such concerns as the study of witchcraft and its persecution,[2] of the changing attitudes towards death,[3] and of religious iconography which has only just begun to attract the interest of the social historian,[4] although several authors represented here touch upon some of these offshoots.[5] However, it is hoped that the essays assembled here will convey an impression of the innovative approaches and the lively debates which have stimulated recent work and continue to invigorate current research in the social history of early modern religion.

With the exception of Richard Trexler's concluding essay, the contributions incorporated into this volume have been grouped under four different headings which categorise major foci and concerns of current research. In the following pages a brief outline of these concerns will be given with reference to the essays assembled here.

(1) Religion as a Cultural Phenomenon

The most common denominator among social historians of religion is their general agreement that religion must be explained and understood as a cultural phenomenon. The influence which social and cultural anthropology continue to exert on their research accounts for a good measure of this consensus. Among others, the British social anthropologist E. E. Evans-Pritchard, whose influence is apparent in Keith Thomas's pioneering study on *Religion and the Decline of Magic* (1971), has argued that 'religion, whatever else it may be, is a social phenomenon', and that 'we have to account for religious facts in terms of the totality of the culture and society in which they are found'.[6] His American colleague Clifford Geertz likewise describes 'religion as a cultural system'.[7] This view of religion is thus implicitly linked with the idea of a cultural order,[8] in which are distinguished sacred and profane times, places and objects.

Beyond this point, however, there still is some disagreement among social historians of religion, as among anthropologists and historians in general, on how 'culture' should be understood and defined.[9] There are obvious differences fraught with important implications between an essentially descriptive definition of culture as, for example, 'a system of shared meanings, attitudes and values, and the symbolic forms (performances, artefacts) in which they are expressed or embodied',[10] and an explanatory (in this case, Gramscian) understanding of culture as 'the common sense or way of life of a particular class, group or social category, the complex of ideologies that are actually *adopted* as moral preferences or principles of life'.[11]

Moreover, such differences can be the result of the varying degree of exposure to modern social and/or cultural anthropology of different historiographical traditions to which present-day scholars are explicitly or implicitly committed. A comparative assessment of the respective understanding of 'culture' in the contributions of Bob Scribner and Hartmut Lehmann, or of Peter Burke and Robert Muchembled, to this volume could illustrate this point. While much recent Anglo-American research in the field is based on an 'extended' and instrumentalised notion of 'culture', many French and especially German social historians continue to adhere to a 'restricted' concept, which incorporates the old dichotomy between 'culture' and 'civilisation'.[12] Here we have what Peter Burke has recently termed the 'high and the low road'.[13] Taking the 'high road', and thus opting essentially for a bird's-eye view in the study of religion within early modern society as a whole, is not without its problems, because – as Richard Trexler observes below – this can lead to viewing 'the "false religion" of the people . . . as dangerous to "true religion", but even more to "civilisation"'.

A second area of disagreement or diversity among social historians of religion has to do with how one views the relationship between culture and society. Should culture be seen as a product and projection of the social sphere, or vice versa? Or is there a kind of dialectical relationship between the two spheres? These questions are intrinsically linked with a basic conceptual problem, which, as has rightly been observed, 'is one of the many issues in the history of society which are not amenable to actual evidence':[14] should religion be approached as a set of beliefs or as a set of practices? Among the authors represented here Richard Trexler is the only one who explicitly opts for one approach at the exclusion of the other. He asserts that 'religion must be founded upon the study of behaviour if that study hopes to examine all social groups without a priori psychological assumptions. The task is not to dismiss ideas, but to gain the behavioural foundation to begin to understand them.' In complex societies, he adds, 'beliefs exist only in performance'.

This quotation points to a third issue at stake in the context of the theme of this volume: whether cultural and religious facts should be interpreted only in terms of the structural framework to which they belong.[15] The functionalist or structuralist 'anthropologising' of history is fraught with particular problems related to change over time.[16] Among the articles in this volume several demonstrate that the important debate (1975) between Hildred Geertz and Keith Thomas regarding the latter's treatment of 'religion' and 'magic' in *Religion and the Decline of Magic* is still very much alive. It surfaces notably in R. Trexler's and B. Scribner's contributions.

K. Thomas was criticised for suggesting 'that beliefs are to be understood primarily in terms of the needs which they serve, and that these needs are assumed to be individual and, in the final analysis, psychological'.[17] There can be no question that Thomas only partially heeded E. E. Evans-Pritchard's justified attack on B. Malinowski's time-honoured theory of religion as emotional need-fulfilment.[18] As Evans-Pritchard observes, 'the acquisitions of rites and beliefs precedes the emotions which are said to accompany them later in adult life'.[19] However, by the very nature of this process rites and beliefs acquire meaning and, thus, become amenable to change with respect to both form and function.[20] Thus, if K. Thomas 'sympathizes' with his critic 'in her suspicion of any shallow functionalist attempt to treat popular beliefs as simple defenses against anxiety, vain compensations for technological inadequacies', he is surely right to point out at the same time 'that the historian would be ill-advised to separate such beliefs from their social and technological context'.[21] How this is done by the historian of religion depends, in the last resort, on his or her conception of the relationship between the sacred and profane.[22] John Bossy's scepticism (as expressed during the Wolfenbüttel conference) regarding Bob Scribner's and Hermann Hörger's suggestion of close links between Catholic rituals and contemporary calendrical cycles shows that there is yet little general agreement about the admissibility of such historical references.[23]

All this goes to show that obvious hermeneutical problems are involved in the historical study of religion and that the social historian of religion would be ill advised to cast away all hermeneutical concerns in favour of an exclusively analytical approach.[24] Here lies the prime importance of Richard Trexler's attempt in his concluding essay 'to critique the language and concepts we use to study past religion by relating them to our own corporate identity'. It is for the reader to judge whether the remedy he suggests, the use of a 'language of profanation' by the historian of religion, can success-fully eliminate the hermeneutical problems which normally confront us, and whether we can abandon all psychological categorisations in favour of a sociological approach.

A fourth area, finally, where there is yet little consensus among social historians of the early modern period, pertains to the usefulness of differentiating between a learned and/or elite culture and religion and a popular culture and religion. A comparison between R. Trexler's and J. Wirth's contributions to this volume and some of the other articles assembled here could illustrate this point.

Even in the French *histoire des mentalités*-tradition, which has been preoccupied with the study of popular culture for some time, there has always been a certain amount of individual variation regarding the relationship between popular and learned culture and religion.[25] It is certainly true that a good part of recent French history of the late medieval and early modern periods, including such different works as, for example, Roland Mousnier's studies on the 'société des ordres' of the ancien régime,[26] Robert Mandrou's research on the 'historical psychology' of France during the early modern period[27] and Emmanuel Le Roy Ladurie's book on the fourteenth-century Cathar community of Montaillou,[28] cannot be spared the criticism that it tends to neglect social and cultural tensions and conflicts. On the other hand, we should not underestimate the problems inherent in a strong emphasis on the opposition between popular and learned culture and religion. First, this can lead to a misjudgement as to the existence of different cultural levels within popular culture itself.[29] Secondly, it leaves little room for an appreciation of cases of interpenetration of both cultures and religions. Peter Burke's essay in this volume, emphasising the negotiations which took place between 'centre' and 'periphery' regarding the canonisation of Counter-Reformation saints, provides a good illustration of this. I am not sure, therefore, whether we should go along with Carlo Ginzburg's denial that 'popular culture exists outside the act that suppresses it'.[30]

(2)   The Reform of Popular Culture and Religion

The Protestant Reformation and Catholic Counter-Reformation of the sixteenth century had important repercussions for the relationship between learned and popular culture and religion. The resulting process of change has been called an attempt at 'reform of popular culture', as Peter Burke describes it, 'the systematic attempt by some of the educated . . . to change the attitudes and values of the rest of the population, or as the Victorians used to say, to "improve" them'.[31] The Reformation and Counter-Reformation resulted in an effort launched by church and state to impose upon the laity a more rational faith and a more rigorous moral discipline. Manifestations of traditional popular culture, such as carnivals, charivaris, and so on,[32] increasingly became subject to restrictions. The activities of confraternities, a traditional link between parish and community, were abolished by the Reformation and severely curtailed through the Counter-Reformation. The latter process is vividly described and analysed by Jean-Pierre Gutton in this volume.

In a well-known, if still not uncontroversial, study on *Le Sentiment religieux en Flandre à la fin du Moyen Age* (Paris, 1963), Jacques Toussaert argues that the population of Flanders in the fifteenth century adhered to predominantly pre-Christian and even pagan beliefs. Since then, not least under Toussaert's influence, Jean Delumeau has developed the thesis that the two reformations – Protestant and Catholic – constituted 'two complementary aspects of the same process of christianisation' which began in the sixteenth century.[33] He dismisses the notion of 'medieval Christianity' as a legend – at least as far as the level of popular beliefs is concerned – and views both reformations as massive missionary onslaughts by the two churches aiming at the conversion of the masses. As a result, the de-christianisation of the eighteenth century, whose widespread grassroots nature Michel Vovelle has established for southern France,[34] assumes under Delumeau's pen the form of a mere abandonment of conformism, facilitated by the increasing laxity of the control hitherto exercised by the Tridentine church.[35]

Michel Vovelle's essay in this collection offers a more complex view of the situation prevailing in late eighteenth-century France in distinguishing between two parallel popular movements of resistance against, and promotion of, dechristianisation. The widespread popular campaign of the Year II in favour of dechristianisation, he argues, must be seen as both the last significant expression of traditional popular culture and as this culture's revenge for the disciplinary constraints it had suffered under the Tridentine conquest.

A more recent and more pointed version of Delumeau's thesis is that of the 'acculturation' of the masses by the church and state of the Tridentine period, as developed by Robert Muchembled and restated in his contribution to this volume.[36] This interpretation sharply opposes learned and popular culture and religion. It has obvious merits,[37] but tends to over-emphasise the rift between a learned and written and a popular and oral culture[38] and to suggest that this popular oral culture was by definition 'primitive' in nature, as if the growth of literacy during the seventeenth and eighteenth centuries helped to replace ignorance with knowledge.[39] As Jean Wirth observes in his critique of this thesis in his contribution below,[40] it also tends to oversimplify the nature of popular religion.

In the universe of the popular masses, writes Jean Delumeau, 'nothing is [seen as] natural, certainly not illness and death. Primitive man, because he is rather inapt to analyse, differentiates badly between the visible and invisible, the part and the whole . . .'[41] By extension, this has led to a view of early modern popular culture and religion as essentially static. However, there can be no doubt that 'the idea of an unchanging popular culture is a myth',[42] and that Marc Bloch's 'regressive method' has rendered a disservice in this respect to the *histoire des mentalités*-tradition.[43]

Christina Larner is surely right in suggesting 'that there was more than one level of popular belief, that popular belief could vary from region to region, and that popular belief, like learned belief, was not static. Where there is more than one cultural level these will always interact.'[44]

Hermann Hörger, in fact, has argued that rather than to try to 'acculturise' their peasant flock, Upper Bavarian prelates of the seventeenth century chose to introduce elements of popular *mentalité* into official ecclesiastical liturgy.[45] In his present contribution he makes a similar point.

In a recent article Bob Scribner contrasts the 'acculturation thesis' with German evidence and points to 'a continual struggle to "christianise" the countryside in Germany extending back well before the fifteenth century. This struggle involved a high degree of two-way flow between rural religion and "orthodox" Christianity, resulting in a deeper absorption of Christian elements than Muchembled admits for France.' Not unlike H. Hörger, Scribner suggests that 'part of this two-way flow resulted in an "acculturation" of Christianity by popular rural religion'.[46]

The theme of the interaction between different cultural levels is pursued in this volume by Peter Burke. He views the Counter-Reformation canonisations of the period 1588 to 1746 as the result of a process of negotiation between centre (in this case, the Roman curia) and periphery, or between central and local religion, or between learned and popular culture.

If early modern popular culture should thus not be seen as something static as opposed to a dynamic learned culture of clergy, lawyers and statesmen, this does not necessarily mean that these two cultures evolved in the same rhythm, as Jean Wirth suggests in his critique of the acculturation thesis. The problem of the 'Gleichzeitigkeit des Ungleichzeitigen',[47] that is, of the different 'timetables' of concurrently existing popular and learned cultures, as argued by Robert Muchembled in this collection, is a very real one, even though further studies may find that there were in fact more than just two different 'timetables'.

Perhaps the most problematic aspect of the concepts of 'christianisation' and 'acculturation' is the fact that they rest on an historical approach which is concerned with 'establishing the boundary between superstition and the religion of sacrament and spirit'. By opting for such an approach, as Natalie Z. Davis has observed, the social historian of religion limits his or her own possibilities of appreciating 'the meaning, modes and uses of popular religion to peasants and city dwellers'.[48] It is mainly due to this approach that Jean Delumeau and Robert Muchembled tend to neglect the question of the actual efficacy of the Tridentine onslaught.[49]

Jean-Pierre Gutton argues in his contribution to this volume that on the level of the *Lyonnais* village the Counter-Reformation resulted – paradoxically – in the secularisation of communal life, and that the 'christianisation' thesis may thus well be a *question mal posée*. Similar conclusions have recently been drawn for the Tridentine period in a study of marital litigation in the Upper German diocese of Constance.[50] Bob Scribner's conclusions in his contribution below likewise point in this direction. However, unlike J.-P. Gutton, Scribner, in pinpointing 'an important element of crypto-materialism' in pre-industrial popular belief, seems to suggest that there was a kind of inner secularising dynamic inherent to this popular belief, which was little affected by such changes as the Protestant and Catholic reformations.

On more general grounds, Martin Ingram observes in his article that an all too single-minded insistence on the theme of the 'reform of popular culture and religion' 'may obscure the importance . . . of unspectacular orthodoxy'. Primarily addressed to British local historians, this caveat would scarcely fit the context of German research, where the 'unspectacular orthodoxy' of the laity has long been an all too widely shared assumption of historians of the Reformation and Counter-Reformation periods.

Klaus Deppermann's important suggestion in this collection that early sixteenth-century Anabaptism may have been far more widespread than we have so far assumed, provides a welcome challenge to that assumption. Deppermann also establishes once again that the German and Swiss Reformation, particularly in its urban setting, was from the beginning marked by clericalism – a development which the secular authorities encouraged.[51] To a certain extent this relativises Jean Wirth's critique of Pierre Chaunu, although it is fair to add that Deppermann does not set out to corroborate Chaunu's rather one-sided view of humanist reformers.

(3) Religion and Social Control

Although the notion of 'social control' has proved a useful analytical tool for historians of the early modern period, there is as yet no general agreement about its precise meaning among sociologists.[52] In the most general sense the notion points to cultural norms, values and institutions, which shape, influence and regulate the behaviour of individuals and groups.[53] In the context discussed here, social control also aimed at shaping 'belief': the process of enforcing norms within a population went hand in hand with an attempt to secure 'interior assent by means which may or must include the instilling of guilt'.[54]

Again this points to the problem already discussed above of whether the social historian should treat religion as practice and/or belief. While it is possible within the limits imposed by the available source material for the historian of the early modern period to gauge the efficacy of social control exerted over the people by church, state and community as far as 'behaviour' is concerned, it is very difficult to determine whether this social control actually succeeded in doing more 'than [to] superimpose a mental automatism on the behavioural automatisms of the code of external practice'.[55] Or, to take Margaret Spufford's poignant remarks concerning the villagers of seventeenth-century Cambridgeshire: 'Amongst them were presumably some who went to church, not solely because worship was required of them by ecclesiastical law, but because they had a meaningful faith. But this faith has no history.'[56]

However, M. Spufford's own and other more recent research have shown that it is possible to bridge this gap at least partially, in respect of belief rather than faith, through an analysis of preambles of testaments and last wills.[57] This is also how Gerald Strauss's argument in his contribution to this volume could, at least partially, be verified at the grassroots level.[58]

Gerald Strauss's recent work has had the merit of drawing attention to the neglected connection between education and social control in the German Reformation.[59] Including his contribution to the present collection, this has chiefly dwelt on the written word as a vehicle for indoctrination. It is important to note, however, that in 1530 Luther recommended the creation of an illustrated Bible for the laity.[60] This points to an aspect of sixteenth- and seventeenth-century education and indoctrination which clearly calls for increased interest from the social historian, although I scarcely need to add that it is extremely difficult to assess the actual effect of this form of indoctrination.[61]

Unlike Gerald Strauss, who mainly analyses the effects of social control, Bruce Lenman and Mary Fulbrook[62] look at the preconditions of hierarchically imposed social control. In a remarkably similar way they both insist on the consensus among the power-bearers and governors in church and state of seventeenth-century England, Scotland, Württemberg and Prussia as a necessary condition for a policy of imposing godly discipline and religious conformity. The advent of religious toleration during the seventeenth century in the states concerned thus appears as a result of the breakdown of social control, that is, as an essentially reluctant concession on the part of the secular and ecclesiastical hierarchies to their own increasing lack of inner cohesion. Clearly, then, early modern religious toleration was not the result of an independently formulated, or even enlightened, policy.[63]

Martin Scharfe's contribution deals in part with the distant heirs of the Anabaptists discussed by Klaus Deppermann. It concentrates on an assessment of cases of deviation from hierarchically imposed norms of social and religious conformity. These were strictly enforced in the eighteenth-century Württemberg village by the *Kirchenkonvent* (village consistory). Scharfe provides important insights into how a policy of enforcing religious conformity was continuously pursued by the representatives of the established church at the local level at a time when cases of deviation had ceased to attract the undivided attention of the state's administration, unless they assumed distinctly 'political' proportions.[64] In pointing to a time-lag between centre and periphery regarding the late eighteenth-century shift from religious to more secularised forms of social control, Scharfe's contribution thus emphasises the importance of the local historical approach to the problem of social control. This is pursued notably by Jean-Pierre Gutton and Martin Ingram in this collection. They demonstrate that only at the local level is it possible to assess the important aspects of *informal* social control.[65]

(4)   Religion and the Community

The context of 'religion and the community' has a far wider thematic framework here than in current historical village studies. The latter have become something of a testing-ground for the application of anthropological approaches to history:[66] the examples of Montaillou, Terling and Neckarshausen are cases in point.[67]

Martin Ingram's contribution is a good example of the community study approach. He discusses the recent findings of K. Wrightson and D. Levine on 'poverty and piety' in Terling (Essex)[68] in comparison with his own work on Keevil in Wiltshire – a county with notably less Puritan activity at the local level than Essex. This discussion permits a thorough assessment of what the 'reform of popular culture and religion' and 'social control' looked like from the local environment of the English parish and community. M. Ingram's contribution thus contrasts and complements some of the discussion taken up in more broadly conceived articles by other authors of this volume.

John Bossy explores in his contribution, as in some of his earlier work,[69] the role of kinship in late medieval and early modern Christianity as an essential component of 'community'. He rejects a functional understanding of godparenthood as (profane) patronage and insists on the essentially sacred nature of the institution. Bossy's essay reveals a conception of the sacred in its relationship to the profane, which clearly differs from that proposed by Hermann Hörger,[70] although both essays have in common a judicious use of research on baptismal names.

Hermann Hörger's exploration of Upper Bavarian rural religion of the early modern period, and especially of the links between official ecclesiastical liturgy and the agrarian calendrical cycles, shares much with Bob Scribner's understanding of the sacred as experienced within the profane, in and through the concerns of daily life.

Like John Bossy's, Jean-Pierre Gutton's contribution provides an example of how the Counter-Reformation attempted to transform communal life. He highlights the fact that this was linked with severe restrictions which the Tridentine church and its local representatives, the *curés*, imposed on the traditional framework of popular culture, for example, on confraternities, *royaumes*, or *reinages* and on the abbeys of village youth. Gutton demonstrates how the application of such measures in the villages of the *Lyonnais* resulted, rather paradoxically, in a laicisation of village life. This has obvious implications for the discussion of the concept of 'christianisation'.[71]

It is important that we also include under the heading of 'religion and the community' studies on urban religion,[72] lest we neglect the important insights comparative examination of works on rural and urban culture and religion can offer to the social historian.[73] My own paper in this volume tries to draw attention to this point, although, unlike community studies, it is not concerned with a specific town, but rather with autobiographical evidence covering aspects of the religious practice and belief of the German and Swiss Protestant urban middle and upper classes of the sixteenth and seventeenth centuries. This evidence demonstrates how the Reformation changed the prevailing sense of 'community' in that traditional religion took on distinctly more individualised forms and functions.

Notes: Introduction

1 On the concept of 'social history' see, for example, J. Kocka, 'Sozialgeschichte: Begriff-Entwicklung-Probleme', in id., *Sozialgeschichte* (Göttingen, 1977), pp. 48–111; B. Scribner, 'Is there a social history of the Reformation?', *Social History*, Vol. IV (January 1977), pp. 483–505; T. A. Brady, 'Social history', in S. E. Ozment (ed.), *Reformation Europe: A Guide to Research* (St Louis, Miss., 1982), pp. 161–81; W. Schieder, 'Religion in the social history of the modern world: a new perspective', *European Studies Review*, Vol. XII (1982), pp. 289–99.

2   Among the numerous recent works see, for example, S. Clark, 'Inversion, misrule, and the meaning of witchcraft', *Past and Present*, Vol. LXXXVII (May 1980), pp. 98–127; M.-S. Dupont-Bouchat *et al.*, *Prophètes et sorciers dans les Pays-Bas, XVIe–XVIIIe siècle* (Paris, 1978); R. Muchembled, *Les Derniers Bûchers: Un village de Flandre et ses sorcières sous Louis XIV* (Paris, 1981); H. Lehmann, 'Hexenverfolgungen und Hexenprozesse im alten Reich zwischen Reformation und Aufklärung', *Jahrbuch des Instituts für deutsche Geschichte*, Vol. VII (1978), pp. 13–70; D. Unverhau, *Von Toverschen und Kunsthfruwen in Schleswig, 1548–1557* (Schleswig, 1980); G. Henningsen, *The Witches' Advocate: Basque Witchcraft and the Spanish Inquisition* (Reno, Nev., 1980). For recent attempts at a synthesis, see J. Delumeau, *La Peur en occident, XIVe–XVIIIe siècles* (Paris, 1978), pp. 346–88; and C. Larner, 'Crimen exceptum? The crime of witchcraft in Europe', in V. A. C. Gatrell, B. Lenman and G. Parker (eds), *Crime and the Law: The Social History of Crime in Western Europe since 1500* (London, 1980), pp. 49–75. The most recent survey is by H. C. E. Midelfort, 'Witchcraft, magic and the occult', in Ozment, *Reformation Europe*, pp. 183–209.
3   Recent research is reviewed by M. Vovelle, 'Encore la mort: un peu plus qu'une mode?', *Annales E.S.C.*, Vol. XXXVII (March–April 1982), pp. 276–87.
4   On its importance see, for example, the pertinent comments by F. Rapp, *L'Église et la vie religieuse à la fin du Moyen Age*, Nouvelle Clio, Vol. XXV, 2nd edn (Paris, 1980), pp. 140–2. cf. also n. 60 below.
5   In particular, see the passages dealing with iconography and iconoclasm in the contributions by H. Hörger, B. Scribner, R. Trexler and J. Wirth, and with witchcraft in R. Muchembled's paper.
6   E. E. Evans-Pritchard, *Theories of Primitive Religion* (Oxford, 1965), pp. 111–112.
7   In M. Banton (ed.), *Anthropological Approaches to the Study of Religion*, ASA Monographs, Vol. III (London, 1966), pp. 1–46.
8   On this notion, see I.-N. Greverus, *Kultur und Alltagswelt: Eine Einführung in Fragen der Kulturanthropologie*, Beck'sche Schwarze Reihe, Vol. CLXXXII (Munich, 1978), p. 36.
9   See the wide variety of definitions accounted for by A. L. Kroeber and C. Kluckhohn, *Culture: A Critical Review of Concepts and Definitions*, new edn (New York, 1963).
10 P. Burke, *Popular Culture in Early Modern Europe* (New York, 1978), prologue.
11 R. Johnson, 'Three problematics: elements of a theory of working-class culture', in J. Clarke *et al.* (eds), *Working Class Culture: Studies in History and Theory* (London, 1979), pp. 201–37, esp. p. 234.
12 See the discussion of the 'extended' and 'restricted' concepts of 'culture' in Greverus, *Kultur und Alltagswelt*, pp. 53–6. Regarding the time-lag in the development of a German social history of religion, see the recent comments by R. J. Evans, 'Religion and society in modern Germany', *European Studies Review*, Vol. XII (1982), pp. 249–88, esp. pp. 252–3, and by Schieder, 'Religion in the social history', cited n. 1 above.
13 P. Burke, 'The high road and the low road: approaches to early modern France', *Historical Journal*, Vol. XXIV, no. 3 (1981), pp. 731–8.
14 Larner, 'Crimen exceptum?', cited n. 2 above, p. 66. See also ibid., p. 74, for pertinent comments on the bearing witchcraft evidence can have for the discussion of this problem. cf. also my comments below on 'The Reform of Popular Culture and Religion'.
15 Compare, for example, Stuart Clark's structural-linguistic approach to sixteenth-century demonology with Christina Larner's attempt to interpret European witchcraft persecutions in terms of the 'labelling theory' of deviance. Both articles are cited in n. 2 above.
16 See A. Macfarlane, 'History, anthropology and the study of communities', *Social History*, Vol. I (May 1977), pp. 631–52, esp. p. 640. cf. also R. Koselleck, 'Wozu noch Historie?', in J. Rüsen and H. M. Baumgartner (eds), *Geschichte und Theorie: Umrisse einer Historik* (Frankfurt/M., 1976), pp. 17–35, esp. pp. 31–2.
17 H. Geertz, 'An anthropology of religion and magic, I', *Journal of Interdisciplinary History*, Vol. VI, no. 1 (Summer 1975), pp. 71–89, esp. p. 77.
18 Evans-Pritchard, *Theories*, pp. 39–40.
19 ibid., p. 46.
20 See V. Drehsen and H. J. Helle, 'Religiosität und Bewusstsein: Ansätze zu einer wissenssoziologischen Typologie von Sinnsystemen', in W. Fischer and W. Marhold (eds), *Religionssoziologie als Wissenssoziologie* (Stuttgart, Berlin, Cologne and Mainz, 1978),

pp. 38–51, esp. pp. 45–9. On 'myth, rite and function', see C. Ginzburg, 'Charivari, associations juvéniles, chasse sauvage', in J. Le Goff and J.-C. Schmitt (eds), *Le Charivari: Actes de la table ronde organisée à Paris (25–27 avril 1977),* Civilisations et Sociétés, Vol. LXVII (Paris, The Hague and New York, 1981), pp. 131–40. On the 'meaning' of cultural and religious action, cf. also P. Burke, 'Oblique approaches to the history of popular culture', in C. W. E. Bigsby (ed.), *Approaches to Popular Culture* (London, 1976), pp. 66–84, esp. p. 80; R. W. Scribner, *For the Sake of Simple Folk: Popular Propaganda for the German Reformation*, Cambridge Studies in Oral and Literate Culture, Vol. II (Cambridge, 1981), p. 95.

21 K. Thomas, 'An anthropology of religion and magic, II', *Journal of Interdisciplinary History*, Vol. VI, no. 1 (Summer 1975), pp. 91–109, esp. p. 101. For general comments related to this issue, cf. also W. J. Mommsen, *Geschichtswissenschaft jenseits des Historismus* (Düsseldorf, 1971), p. 45.

22 See notably Bob Scribner's discussion of some of these problems in his contribution below.

23 On the specific question at stake, cf. also A. Macfarlane, *The Family Life of Ralph Josselin, a Seventeenth-Century Clergyman* (Cambridge, 1970), p. 181n. See also Scribner's and Hörger's replies to John Bossy in their respective contributions below.

24 A debatable procedure recently recommended by R. van Dülmen, 'Religionsgeschichte in der historischen Sozialforschung', *Geschichte und Gesellschaft*, Vol. VI, no. 1 (1980), pp. 36–59, esp. p. 36; compare this with R. Rürup's appropriate comments in 'Zur Einführung', in id. (ed.), *Historische Sozialwissenschaft: Beiträge zur Einführung in die Forschungspraxis* (Göttingen, 1977), pp. 5–15, esp. p. 7.

25 Witness, for example, the differing interpretations in M. Vovelle's seminal study on *Piété baroque et déchristianisation en Provence au XVIIIe siècle* (Paris, 1973) – relative autonomy of popular culture – and R. Mandrou, *De la culture populaire aux XVIIe et XVIIIe siècles: La Bibliothèque Bleue de Troyes* (Paris, 1964) – a popular culture largely shaped 'from above'. For criticism of the latter interpretation represented by R. Mandrou, G. Bollème and others, cf. Burke, *Popular Culture*, p. 72; and especially C. Ginzburg, *The Cheese and the Worms: The Cosmos of a Sixteenth-Century Miller*, trans. J. and A. Tedeschi (London and Henley, 1980), pp. xvii and xxiii.

26 A. Ariazza, 'Mousnier and Barber: the theoretical underpinning of the "Society of Orders" in early modern Europe', *Past and Present*, Vol. LXXXIX (November 1980), pp. 39–57, and the bibliography provided there.

27 Cf. notably R. Mandrou, *Introduction à la France moderne, 1500–1640*, 2nd edn (Paris, 1974).

28 *Montaillou: Village occitan, de 1294 à 1324* (Paris, 1975).

29 Cf. Richard Trexler's criticism in his contribution to this collection of Carlo Ginzburg's view that the sixteenth-century Friuli miller Domenico Scandella called Menocchio was a genuine representative of peasant culture and religion. Menocchio is the *dramatis persona* in Ginzburg's *The Cheese and the Worms*, cited n. 25 above.

30 ibid., p. xvii.

31 Burke, *Popular Culture*, p. 207.

32 G. Strauss, *Luther's House of Learning: Indoctrination of the Young in the German Reformation* (Baltimore, Md., and London, 1978), pp. 223–46 and 300–8; T. Robisheaux, 'Peasants and pastors: rural youth control and the Reformation in Hohenlohe, 1540–1680', *Social History*, Vol. VI, no. 3 (October 1981), pp. 281–300; Scribner, *For the Sake of Simple Folk*, pp. 71–3; Le Goff and Schmitt, *Le Charivari*, notably the contributions by A. Burguière, N. Z. Davis, R. Muchembled and M. Ingram; P. Clark, 'The alehouse and the alternative society', in D. Pennington and K. Thomas (eds), *Puritans and Revolutionaries: Essays in Seventeenth-Century History Presented to Christopher Hill* (Oxford, 1978), pp. 47–72, esp. pp. 61–2; J. Bossy, 'The Counter-Reformation and the People of Catholic Europe', *Past and Present*, Vol. XLVII (May 1970), pp. 51–70; W. Reinhard, 'Gegenreformation als Modernisierung? Prolegomena zu einer Theorie des konfessionellen Zeitalters', *Archive for Reformation History*, Vol. LXVIII (1977), pp. 226–52. cf. also several of the contributions to this volume.

33 J. Delumeau, *Le Catholicisme entre Luther et Voltaire*, Nouvelle Clio, Vol. XXXbis, 2nd edn (Paris, 1979). The quotation is on pp. 5–6.

34 Vovelle, *Piété Baroque*.

35 Delumeau, *Le Catholicisme*, pp. 318 ff.
36 Cf. also R. Muchembled, *Culture populaire et culture des élites dans la France moderne (XVe–XVIIIe siècles)* (Paris, 1978), and his other works listed in the notes to his contribution.
37 See the recent critical assessment by P. Burke, 'A question of acculturation?', in *Scienze, Credenze Occulte, Livelli di Cultura: Convegno Internazionale di Studi (Firenze, 26–30 giugno 1980)* (Florence, 1982), pp. 197–204.
38 Cf. Michael Hunter's comments on 'atheism and orthodoxy' in id., *Science and Society in Restoration England* (Cambridge, 1981), pp. 162 ff.: a case in point that learned culture, like that of the masses, was far from being monolithic.
39 A pertinent critique of such a view can be found in E. Hinrichs, *Einführung in die Geschichte der Frühen Neuzeit* (Munich, 1980), pp. 102–3.
40 Contrary to Jean Wirth, I would consider Robert Muchembled as the current main exponent of the 'acculturation' thesis. R. Muchembled's rebuttal at the Wolfenbüttel conference (see the reference to my report in Wolfgang J. Mommsen's Foreword) consisted essentially of two points. First, he made it clear that he applies the 'acculturation' concept only to the period starting c.1560, that is, to the Counter-Reformation period and the formation of the absolutist state. Secondly, he drew attention to the 'fundamental philosophical differences' between his own evolutionist position and J. Wirth's 'fixisme religieux'. Commenting specifically on J. Wirth's conclusions, he pointed out (1) that he considers seventeenth-century popular *mentalité* as different, but by no means as 'retarded' when comparing it to that of the elites; (2) that fifteenth- and sixteenth-century society is 'une société poly-segmentaire'; (3) that he has made it sufficiently clear in his work that the process of acculturation could and did, on occasion, have very negative effects.
41 Delumeau, *Le Catholicisme*, pp. 249–50.
42 P. Burke, 'Oblique approaches', cited n. 20 above, pp. 69–84. The quotation is on p. 81.
43 For the commitment of French historians of this 'school' to Marc Bloch's method, see P. Ariès, *L'Enfant et la vie familiale sous l'Ancien Régime*, abridged edn, Éditions du Seuil (Paris, 1973), p. 26; J. Delumeau, *Le Catholicisme*, p. 203.
44 C. Larner, 'Crimen exceptum?', cited n. 2 above, p. 64. A similar point is made by J. Wirth in his contribution to this collection.
45 H. Hörger, *Kirche, Dorfreligion und bäuerliche Gesellschaft...*, pt 1, Studien zur altbayerischen Kirchengeschichte, Vol. V (Munich, 1978), p. 185.
46 B. Scribner, 'Religion, society and culture: reorientating the Reformation', *History Workshop*, Vol. XIV (Autumn 1982), pp. 2–22, esp. p. 14.
47 This is the title very appropriately given to the German edition of five articles on Italian history, ed. and trans. by E. Maek-Gérard, ed. Suhrkamp, no. 991 (Frankfurt/M., 1980). cf. also Greverus, *Kultur und Alltagswelt*, pp. 52–3.
48 N. Z. Davis, 'Some tasks and themes in the study of popular religion', in C. Trinkhaus and H. A. Oberman (eds), *The Pursuit of Holiness in Late Medieval and Renaissance Religion*, Studies in Medieval and Reformation Thought, Vol. X (Leiden, 1974), pp. 307–36, esp. pp. 307–9. For similar comments, cf. also R. Trexler's contribution to this volume.
49 However, it must be pointed out that, although it is neglected, this problem is not entirely ignored. See, for example, R. Muchembled, 'The witches of Cambrésis: the acculturation of the rural world in the sixteenth and seventeenth centuries', in J. Obelkevich (ed.), *Religion and the People, 800–1700* (Chapel Hill, NC, 1979), pp. 221–76, esp. pp. 254–5, where Muchembled argues that 'the acculturation of the countryside has never been complete' in Cambrésis.
50 T. M. Safley, 'Marital litigation in the diocese of Constance, 1551–1620', *The Sixteenth Century Journal*, Vol. XII, no. 2 (1981), pp. 61–77, esp. pp. 76–7.
51 Cf. also H. A. Oberman, *Werden und Wertung der Reformation* (Tübingen, 1977), pp. 352–7 (English version: *Masters of the Reformation: The Emergence of a New Intellectual Climate in Europe*, trans. D. Martin, Cambridge, 1981).
52 See C. K. Watkins, *Social Control*, Aspects of modern sociology: Social processes (London and New York, 1975); M. Janowitz, 'Wissenschaftshistorischer Überlick zur Entwicklung des Grundbegriffs "Soziale Kontrolle"', *Kölner Zeitschrift für Soziologie und Sozialpsychologie*, Vol. XXV (1973), pp. 499–514.
53 B. Scribner, 'Sozialkontrolle und die Möglichkeit einer städtischen Reformation', in

B. Moeller (ed.), *Stadt und Kirche im 16. Jahrhundert*, Schriften des Vereins für Reformationsgeschichte, no. 190 (Gütersloh, 1978), pp. 57–65, esp. p. 57.

54 J. Bossy's summary of T. Tentler's usage: see J. Bossy, 'Holiness and society', *Past and Present*, Vol. LXXV (May 1977), pp. 119–37, esp. pp. 127–8.

55 Bossy, 'The Counter-Reformation', cited n. 32 above.

56 M. Spufford, *Contrasting Communities: English Villagers in the Sixteenth and Seventeenth Centuries* (Cambridge, 1974), p. 319.

57 ibid., pp. 320–44, and notably Martin Ingram's paper below. The pioneering study in this field is, of course, M. Vovelle, *Piété Baroque*, cited n. 25 above. Bernard Vogler (University of Strasburg) is currently running a long-term quantitative research project on Alsatian wills from the period 1648–1789; cf. B. Vogler, 'L'histoire moderne en Alsace: un bilan des recherches effectuées depuis 1968', *Revue d'Alsace*, Vol. CV (1979), pp. 75–94, esp. pp. 75 and 83–4.

58 This summarises some of the comments made during the discussion at the Wolfenbüttel conference. Additional information on Bible ownership, as Martin Ingram demonstrates below, could be gained from an analysis of inventories of personal property drawn up after death. cf. also P. Clark, *English Provincial Society from the Reformation to the Revolution: Religion, Politics and Society in Kent, 1500–1600* (Hassocks, 1977), p. 210. Research on book ownership in sixteenth- and seventeenth-century Germany is currently being carried out by Erdmann Weyrauch (Wolfenbüttel).

59 G. Strauss, 'Success and failure in the German Reformation', *Past and Present*, Vol. LXVII (May 1975), pp. 30–63; and id., *Luther's House of Learning*. For a discussion of Strauss's research in a comparative context, see G. Parker, 'An educational revolution? The growth of literacy and schooling in early modern Europe', *Tijdschrift voor geschiedenis*, Vol. XCIII, no. 2 (1980), pp. 210–220.

60 R. Engelsing, *Analphabetentum und Lektüre: Zur Sozialgeschichte des Lesens in Deutschland zwischen feudaler und industrieller Gesellschaft* (Stuttgart, 1973), p. 23. For Luther's reliance on religious imagery as a vehicle of communication, see the suggestive remarks in J. Wirth, *Luther: Étude d'histoire religieuse*, Travaux d'histoire éthico-politique, Vol. XXXVI (Geneva, 1981), pp. 105–16; and id., 'Le dogme en image: Luther et l'iconographie', *Revue de l'Art* (1981), pp. 9–23. cf. also C. D. Andersson, 'Religiöse Bilder Cranachs im Dienste der Reformation', in L. W. Spitz *et al.* (eds), *Humanismus und Reformation als kulturelle Kräfte in der deutschen Geschichte*, Veröffentlichungen der Historischen Kommission zu Berlin, Vol. LI (Berlin and New York, 1981), pp. 43–79.

61 On popular pictorial propaganda for the German Reformation, see now Scribner, *For the Sake of Simple Folk*.

62 Cf. also M. Fulbrook, 'Religion, revolution and absolutist rule in Germany and England', *European Studies Review*, Vol. XII, no. 3 (July 1982), pp. 301–21.

63 This is why H. R. Guggisberg, in the discussion of M. Fulbrook's paper during the Wolfenbüttel conference, put particular emphasis on the differentiation between the notions of 'religious toleration' and 'religious liberty'. In slight contradiction to part of B. Lenman's and M. Fulbrook's arguments, he added that an important turning-point was reached in many European countries in about 1560/70, when rulers realised that religious toleration could under certain circumstances be useful and profitable to the state. See H. R. Guggisberg, 'Wandel der Argumente für religiöse Toleranz und Glaubensfreiheit im 16. und 17. Jahrhundert', in H. Lutz (ed.), *Zur Geschichte der Toleranz und Religionsfreiheit*, Wege der Forschung, Vol. CCXLVI (Darmstadt, 1977), pp. 455–81.

64 A different, and more debatable, point was made by C. Köhle-Hezinger in an unpublished conference paper on 'Religion in bäuerlichen Gemeinden: Wegbereiter der Industrialisierung' presented to the fifth meeting of the SSRC Research Seminar Group in modern German social history, University of East Anglia, 7–8 January 1981. See my conference report in *Social History*, Vol. VII, no. 2 (1982), pp. 205–10, esp. pp. 209–10, and especially the extended discussion by R. J. Evans, 'Religion and society in modern Germany', cited n. 12 above, pp. 263–70.

65 On this question, cf. the instructive comments by J. A. Sharpe, 'Enforcing the law in the seventeenth-century village', in Gatrell *et al.*, *Crime and the Law*, pp. 97–119, esp. pp. 117–18.

66 Cf. A. Macfarlane, 'History, anthropology and the study of communities', *Social History*,

Vol. I, no. 5 (May 1977), pp. 631–52; and C. Calhoun, 'History, anthropology and the study of communities: some problems in Macfarlane's proposal', *Social History*, Vol. II, no. 3 (October 1978), pp. 363–73, and especially A. Macfarlane, S. Harrison and C. Jardine, *Reconstructing Historical Communities* (Cambridge, 1977).

67   Le Roy Ladurie, *Montaillou*; K. Wrightson and D. Levine, *Poverty and Piety in an English Village: Terling, 1525–1700*, Studies in Social Discontinuity (New York, San Francisco and London, 1979); on Neckarshausen, see D. Sabean, 'Verwandtschaft und Familie in einem württembergischen Dorf 1500 bis 1870: einige methodische Überlegungen', in W. Conze (ed.), *Sozialgeschichte der Familie in der Neuzeit Europas* (Stuttgart, 1962), pp. 231–46, and id., 'Unehelichkeit: Ein Aspekt sozialer Reproduktion kleinbäuerlicher Produzenten. Zu einer Analyse dörflicher Quellen um 1800', in R. M. Berdahl *et al.*, *Klassen und Kultur: Sozialanthropologische Perspektiven in der Geschichtsschreibung* (Frankfurt/M., 1982), pp. 54–76.

68   Wrightson and Levine, *Poverty and Piety*.

69   See his own notes, as well as the articles cited nn. 32 and 54 above.

70   cf. the brief discussion of this point above under 'Religion as a Cultural Phenomenon'.

71   See the discussion above.

72   See, for example, N. Z. Davis's pioneering work on sixteenth-century Lyons in id., *Society and Culture in Early Modern France* (Stanford, Calif., 1975); id., 'The sacred and the body social in sixteenth-century Lyon', *Past and Present*, Vol. XC (1981), pp. 40–70; P. Benedict, *Rouen during the Wars of Religion* (Cambridge, 1981); R. Trexler, *Public Life in Renaissance Florence*, Studies in Social Discontinuity (New York and London, 1980).

73   See the pertinent remarks on this problem in K. Deppermann's and J.-P. Gutton's contributions to this volume. cf. also Y. Castan, 'Mentalités rurale et urbaine à la fin de l'Ancien Régime dans le ressort du Parlement de Toulouse d'après les sacs à procès criminels, 1730–1790', in F. Billaçois *et al.*, *Crimes et criminalités en France sous l'Ancien Régime*, Cahiers des Annales, Vol. XXXIII (Paris, 1971), pp. 109–86.

Part One

Religion as a Cultural Phenomenon

1 Cosmic Order and Daily Life: Sacred and Secular in Pre-Industrial German Society

BOB SCRIBNER

In this essay I want to describe some aspects of what I call an 'economy of the sacred', and to offer some comments on how it was perceived to operate in pre-industrial Germany. Let me state the assumptions on which the main discussion will rest. The most important is that it is manifestations of the sacred within the profane world which provide, for the religious mentality, a principle of order. Such 'manifestations of the sacred' enable people to establish relations with the sacred and to create from them a form of 'cosmic order'. This cosmic order encompasses human relationships with the sacred, with other persons and with the natural world.[1] Relations with the sacred are ordered through a patterned sequence of human action towards the sacred in space and time, expressed, for example, through acts of worship or more elaborately through a cycle of ritual. Relations with other persons are ordered by recognising and responding to elements of the sacred in human relationships, what John Bossy has called 'piety'.[2] Relations with the natural world are ordered by seeing it as dependent in its contingency on the sustaining power of the sacred, which must be invoked to set right any disorder which may appear in the world. We can thus speak of an 'economy of the sacred', of an ordered structure of relationships with the sacred, encompassing persons, places, times and things.[3]

I want to make three other preliminary points. The first is that this concept of an 'economy of the sacred' does not depend on any radical division of reality into two clearly identifiable realms, the sacred and the profane. Rather, it assumes that the sacred is always experienced from *within* the profane; it is always manifested as a historical fact, within some historical situation. Such manifestations occur as a state or condition conferred on things otherwise regarded as profane, revealing themselves through rites, myths, sacred objects, holy persons, animals, or plants. Religion is the response made to such manifestations of the sacred, which always depend on human response for their existence.[4]

Secondly, it is an essential characteristic of the sacred that it displays extraordinary and extraordinarily effective power. This power is an integral part of the 'economy of the sacred', and it is something to which religious persons have always sought access for its ability to control the profane world. It is also the reason for the fear and awe with which the sacred is regarded. When the sacred manifests itself within the profane world, it does so as a radically different order of being, indeed, for religious thought, the ultimate order of being. To be raised to this order and at one with it represents 'salvation'.[5]

Thirdly, manifestations of the sacred and of sacred power, because they are always historically located, display great variety and can be very transient. Indeed, it is of the essence of the sacred that it is unconditioned by time, place and person, and so can reveal itself capriciously. This can lead to quite dramatic changes in religion. For someone with a new perception of the sacred, old manifestations can become obstacles to expressing the new mode of religious experience. They then become idols, fake and misleading manifestations. The most dramatic example is found in the Protestant rejection of images.[6]

Let me turn now to the 'economy of the sacred' in our period of discussion. It was closely correlated with two modes of secular life, with social reproduction in the household and in the community, and with biological reproduction in animal and plant life. In both areas sacred meaning was imparted by ritual cycles, which sought to invoke divine power and blessing in constituting and reconstituting social and biological life. This ordering process occurred through two major cycles, the individual life-cycle and the annual calendrical cycle.[7] There is no need to linger over the 'rites of passage' involved in the former, for their general characteristics are well known. These established and re-established relations between the individual and the community, declaring them to be 'holy'. John Bossy has called attention to the role of baptism and marriage as ritual actions linking kinship groups, while Natalie Davis has pointed out how funeral rites, as 'rites of separation', reordered social relationships among the survivors, and incorporated the deceased into the 'extended age group' of the departed, a group which continued to have collective relationships with the living.[8]

The calendrical cycle saw a more complex range of ritual ordering. First, there was the annual sequence of great church feasts, all of which fell in the first half of the calendar year, between Christmas and midsummer. All of these feasts provided a framework for human relations with the sacred, their liturgies being designed to express the mysteries of Christian belief, to honour God and to sanctify the participants. However, there were many others, extra-liturgical or para-liturgical in nature, which were concerned with social relationships. The *Flurritt* (or boundary ride), the Corpus Christi procession or the St John's day fire were all designed to redraw community boundaries and to reaffirm communal solidarity.[9] Others were intended ritually to purify the community, as in Leipzig, where there was a *Hurenumzug* (procession of whores) each year at Carnival time to free the city from threat of plague; or in Augsburg, where there was a ritual expulsion of prostitutes on St Gallus' day each year.[10] There were other rituals designed to order the rhythms of biological reproductive life, by invoking divine blessing on human, animal and agrarian fertility. These often clustered in small ritual cycles concerned with fertility, the needs of primary production and the vagaries of the weather.

A good example is the cycle surrounding the feast of the Purification of the Virgin on 2 February. Liturgically, it is a feast of purity and virginity, the day on which candles are blessed which symbolise both the purity of the Virgin and the light of the world to which she has given birth, that is,

Christ. The feast falls forty days after Christmas, and marks the turning-point from winter towards the onset of spring. It is the day on which winter work such as spinning is given up in favour of outdoor work in fields and gardens, made possible by the lengthening light. Hence the aptness of the feast as a feast of light and illumination growing out of darkness. The weather on that day is held to indicate the prospects for the coming growing season for grain, vines and flax. However, it does not stand alone as a celebration of new light and new life, but is preceded and followed by a number of other feasts which celebrate the same phenomenon.[11]

The cycle begins on 20 January, the feast of Fabian and Sebastian, a day on which new sap is rising in the trees, so that no wood is cut from a tree after that date to avoid 'bleeding' of the sap.[12] On 21 January, St Agnes' day, a lamb, a symbol of new spring life is brought into church and blessed with holy water. The following day, 22 January, is St Vincent's day, after which no vine is cut to prevent 'bleeding'. An experienced vintner can tell from the state of the sap on St Vincent's day what the effects of the spring on the vines might be.[13] St Vincent shares with St Paul, the feast of whose conversion is next in the sequence on 25 January, the reputation of a weather prophet, for the prospects for springtime weather can be read from the weather on both feasts.[14] By 1 February the emphasis has shifted from new sap to new light. This day is the feast of St Bridget, who is a personification of light, being depicted with a flame above her head, a suitable introduction to the feast of the Purification or *Lichtmess* (Candlemas).[15]

The day following the Purification, 3 February, is St Blasius' day, on which horses and cattle were given Blasius-water before the church as a protection against future sickness.[16] The same applied to St Agatha, 5 February, on which blessed bread, the *Agathabrot*, was distributed for the health of man and beast. Also on this blessings against fire were given, another variant of the theme of light, here as fire kept within proper bounds.[17] On 6 February was the feast of St Dorothea, who promised protection against frost on tender new plants, for her legend told how she produced fruit and flowers during frost.[18] There is then a gap until St Valentine's day on 14 February, a feast of mating, but also another celebration of new light, for in his legend he gave sight to a blind girl to prove that the Christian God brought illumination to those who believed in him.[19] This cycle of incipient springtime, growing light and hope for fertility is closed by the feast of *Cathedra Petri* on 22 February, on which grazing oats for cattle were sometimes blessed, and the last day for gathering dead wood which has fallen from the trees in the winter and which is used as tinder during spring and summer.[20]

We could point to other similar ritual cycles during the year which sought to invoke divine blessing on the material world – for example, the summer cycle around the Rogation Days[21] – but space does not permit closer description. I now want to turn to a group of objects which play an important part in such rituals, the so-called sacramentals. Sacramentals provide an important link through which ritual actions were made effective in the more mundane areas of daily life. In the broader sense, sacramentals include numerous minor rites and benedictions, often associated with processions and exorcisms. In the narrower sense, they are a class of blessed objects whose efficacy, unlike that of the sacraments, was not automatic, but which depended on the dispositions of the user. Like the sacraments, however, they depended for their power on the blessing of a priest.[22] The sacraments were manifestations of the sacred *par excellence*, for they guaranteed divine favour *ex opere operato*, independently of the disposition of the minister, but they were linked to the high points of the individual life-cycle, and one alone, the eucharist, provided grace for daily needs, either on its own or within the ritual of the mass.[23] But the eucharist was limited and localised, either being consumed on reception or reserved in church.[24] Its use in dealing with the problems of daily life, if it was not to be sacrilegious, was confined to the priest. (There were, admittedly, numerous popular usages attached to the eucharist and the mass which still conformed to what was considered permissible by the church.) However, sacramentals could be taken away and used as the individual desired. Whereas sacraments usually took place inside a church, under the eye of the priest, sacramentals were used everywhere in the wider community – in the household, in stables, barns, fields and gardens – and the uses to which they were put resided in the hands of the laity.[25]

Let us take the example of the candles associated with the celebration of the Purification of the Virgin. On this day various sizes of candles were brought to be blessed during the liturgy. Heads of households brought large house candles, women and young girls slim tapers, boys brought 'penny candles', and a large quantity of small candles was also piled up in baskets before the altar. Some of these blessed candles were later used at home for devotional purposes. The large house candle, symbolising Christ the Light of the World, was lit at a death-bed or carried behind the bier at funerals, while the penny candles were lit for family devotions at All Souls' or during Advent. They were also used as a form of protective magic. The large house candle was lit during bad weather, to invoke protection against hail, storms and evil spirits, and in Bavaria one could purchase at *Lichtmess* special black 'rain- or storm-candles' to use for this purpose. The wax tapers of the women were used at childbirth, placed by the hands and feet of the woman in labour and by the utensils, to keep evil spirits from mother and child.[26]

Similar use was made of the palms blessed on Palm Sunday or the fragrant herbs blessed on the feast of the Assumption. The palm was laid on the hearth fire during summer storms to invoke protection over the house, while the herbs blessed on Assumption day were used to protect houses, barns, livestock and crops against fire, storms and lightning. They were stuck in sown fields and thrown in the hearth fire. They were also used as medicine for sick cattle, carried as talismans against danger, laid in the bed of newly baptised children and stuck under pillows to ward off witches.[27]

The wider range of sacramentals – the various rites and benedictions so excellently described by Adolf Franz – served the same purpose of removing or preventing disorder in the natural world, especially the agrarian and pastoral world. They provided blessings against sickness, cold, famine, fire, flood and pestilence. They included conjurations for the expulsion of all kinds of creature harmful to crops – birds, rodents, insects, locusts, or worms – and for the protection of humans and animals in their dwelling places.[28] Sacramentals were closely linked to the church's liturgy, for the benedictions usually took place during, or in conjunction with, a liturgical celebration of more regular kind. This was the case with 'holy water', either the more usual form of water, blessed every Sunday by the curate immediately after early mass, or the more special water blessed on the feasts of St Blasius, St Stephen, St Anthony, St Anne, Blessed Peter Martyr, and even Ignatius Loyola.[29]

Other means of creating 'sacred order' in daily life fell completely outside the scope of normal church life, and became a kind of do-it-yourself means of access to sacred power. We could mention various magical uses made of the consecrated communion bread,[30] but I want to concentrate here on formulae for private conjurations. These were transmitted largely by oral communication, but are well attested in manuscripts of the fifteenth and sixteenth centuries, and they began to appear in various printed collections from the seventeenth century onwards.[31]

Private conjuration formulae deal with the entire range of difficulties and tribulations of daily life: human and animal sicknesses of all kinds (from nose-bleeds to dysentery), wounds, injuries, possible danger from enemies or from mere mischance, homicide, fire, theft and the attacks of evil spirits and witches. There are formulae for success in court cases, for the protection of cattle driven out to pasture after winter folding, for the increase of newly sown seed, for good fortune during the coming day, for safety while travelling, for invulnerability against bullet, knife, sword, or the attacks of wild animals, for the recovery of lost or stolen objects, and even for invisibility.[32]

The conjurations sometimes take the form of simple prayers, others are ritual formulae, involving threefold repetition and signs of the cross, and occasionally the use of some object such as a juniper branch. They usually invoke the Trinity, the life, suffering and death of Christ, the Virgin (often in allusion to legends from her life or that of Christ), various apostles or archangels, or the saints (but less frequently than one might expect!). Occasionally they conjure the Devil, sometimes they use magical incantations. They are akin to sacramentals in their wider application, providing a means whereby ordinary folk could invoke sacred power to create order in the daily life of an agrarian and pastoral society. They differ from sacramentals in being immediately accessible, relying only on individual memory and desire to put them into practice.[33]

The three categories I have described stand at different points on a double spectrum: that ranging from communal to individual attempts to invoke sacred power; and that ranging from clerical/ecclesiastical/liturgical actions to purely lay and extra-ecclesial. The whole field of activities involved in the 'economy of the sacred', with its different modalities and forms, is too complex to discuss within the framework of this paper, and I have chosen these three categories more to illustrate the nature of ordering ritual. For the remainder of the paper I want to consider the processes by which such ordering rituals appear to work.

The first way of regarding them is to see them as supplicatory: they appeal to God as Creator, to Christ as Lord, or to the Trinity to bless objects so that they might become a means of benefit for those using them. Such expressions are common in liturgical formulae, as in the exorcism of palms in the 1487 Augsburg Ritual Book, which invokes God's blessing on all who carry the blessed palms and on all places to which they are taken. The formula makes it clear that only a symbolic connection is intended, by praying that what is indicated in bodily form may be spiritually effective.[34] Sometimes, however, there is a more direct connection, for the blessing imparts a kind of sacrality or sacred power to the objects involved. The formulae in these cases ask that the objects might become a means of protection for those using them. The protection envisaged is spiritual, material and psychic. Protection is invoked 'for the good of body and soul', and against the 'dreams and fantasms caused by the tricks of the Devil'.[35]

Indeed, the no less common feature of these benedictions and conjurations, which appears as often as the more purely spiritual process, is that they were predominantly apotropaic, that is, concerned with protective magic. As in the weekly consecration of holy water, alongside the invocation of divine blessing, there is the exorcism of various evil spirits. These could range from the 'wickedness, cunning and tricks of the Devil', over demons, fallen angels and impure spirits, to dreams, 'fantastic images', 'all kinds of monsters', the wandering spirits of the damned and the souls of the untimely deceased and unburied.[36] Sometimes this is close to animism, to the belief that such spirits reside in inanimate objects and have to be driven out for the bodily and spiritual well-being of those using the objects.[37] At other times, it is simply a matter of counteracting the power of demonic spirits abroad in the world, who are able to plague mankind by psychic causality (the dreams and fantasms caused by the tricks of the Devil), or by physical causality, in the cases where thunder, storms, hail, or lightning were believed to be the work of demons.[38] The formula for blessing holy water on Sundays in the 1487 Augsburg Ritual Book sums all this up neatly. It invokes a blessing, through Christ the Lord, that whoever is touched or sprinkled by the water will be free from all uncleanness and all attacks of evil spirits, and that all places in which it is sprinkled 'will be preserved from all uncleanness, freed from harm, nor will any pestilent spirit nor any injurious air reside there'.[39]

It was this twofold apotropaic character which formed the basis of numerous popular beliefs about the curative and protective powers of holy water: it healed sickness, protected from wolves cattle that drank it, and protected from worms the plants and seedlings over which it was sprinkled.[40] At the heart of such practices was a belief in an inherent physical power imparted by the blessing, expressed in the formulae by terms such as *per virtutem, per vim benedictionis, per gratiam benedictionis*.[41] The same is true of most of the other ritual blessings conducted by the church – blessings of palms, candles, herbs, various kinds of water, blessed bread, wine, salt, beer, cattle, grain and seed, granaries, threshing floors, hearths and homes.[42] There is certainly a good deal of ambivalence about the nature of the efficacy involved. Theologians such as Bonaventure and Suarez opposed the idea that it was physical efficacy; rather, it was spiritual efficacy, based on the prayers of the church.[43] But there are numerous formulae for benedictions which can only be understood in terms of physical efficacy. A ritual book published in 1520 by Thomas Wolf of Basle gives a formula for blessing salt and water to sprinkle on grain, aimed at keeping birds and worms away from it when used as seed. Another formula for blessing grazing oats on St Stephen's day prays that the cattle who feed on them will be protected from all danger throughout the coming year.[44]

The variations of spiritual, psychic and physical efficacy that can be found throughout the ritual books is reflected fairly accurately by the fifteenth-century writer Turrecremata, who summed up in ten points the efficacy of holy water. Four of its effects were spiritual or moral: recalling the heart from earthly things, remitting venial sin, as preparation for prayer or for doing good works. Two were psychic or psychological: purifying the mind from fantasies and driving out impure spirits. The last four were a matter of direct physical efficacy: removing infertility in humans and animals, encouraging fertility in all earthly things, repelling pestilence and protecting against sickness.[45]

Much the same notion of the physical efficacy of sacred power is associated with a range of popular beliefs attached to the eucharist. Objects laid under the altar while mass was being celebrated acquired healing power. Looking into the chalice after mass was held to be a cure for jaundice. The altar cloth and the corporal on which the consecrated host had been placed during the celebration were also held to have healing power. The former could cure epileptics and the possessed, the latter was good for eye illness. The consecrated host was held to be effective in extinguishing fires, and the corporal also acquired this power through its contact with the eucharist. There were similar beliefs about the curative power of the water and wine used to wash out the chalice after mass, and stroking with the priest's fingers after this ablution was held to protect from bodily evil. Belief in the enormous power of the eucharist formed the basis for its use in weather blessings, undertaken at times of storms or severe hail. The sacrament was carried outside, held up to the heavens with a threefold sign of the cross, and the clouds enjoined to disperse in the name of Christ.[46]

Private conjurations display the same concern with physical efficacy, mostly invoking the power of God as Creator or Christ as Saviour. Sometimes these are merely prayers, Christ being asked to stand by the suppliant. But sometimes it is the power of Christ's sacred blood, his five wounds or his cross that are invoked: these are such powerful aids to human salvation that they must surely be of assistance in lesser, worldly tribulations.[47] This is close to sympathetic magic, for example, where Christ's miracles are invoked to still a fire, or where his patience is invoked to tame oxen or unbroken horses: 'Oxen, bear the yoke and be patient, as Christ was patient.'[48] Sometimes it is the sacred bond among Christians, created by eating Christ's flesh and drinking his blood, that is invoked, as it is in a conjuration used against someone from whom one fears harm.[49]

These conjuration formulae also presuppose demonic or diabolical causality in creating disorder in the world, disorder which must be countered by invoking the greater power of the divine. In the introduction to one of the more commonly reprinted collections from the end of the early modern period the example of Job is cited to prove that God can permit the devil to wreak harm in the world. But his works can be countered by conjurations, for Christ himself commanded: 'do all that you do in the name of God the Father, the Son and the Holy Spirit, so that the devil shall have no power over you'.[50] Clearly, what removes these conjurations from the realm of merely supplicatory prayer into the realm of magic is the belief that humans can instrumentally apply sacred power to their own personal situations. The links are cosmological, involving the belief that the functioning of the material world was dependent on sacred power, which intervened to ensure the flourishing of material creation under the forms of human, animal, or agricultural reproduction, especially by driving out demonic and diabolical forces that harmed such reproduction. However, in sacramentals and private conjurations, this cosmology is strongly anthropocentric, allowing for human agents to act as channels and directors of sacred power.

In a sense, these conjurations represent a kind of popular Catholic version of the priesthood of all believers, for they are seen to work virtually *ex opere operato*. This was doubtless a result of the ill-defined theological understanding of sacramentals, which usually contained blessings and conjurations. But we find the first systematic discussion of sacramentals only during the Counter-Reformation, with Bellarmine and Suarez.[51] Although the official view of the church was that sacramentals did not automatically guarantee divine grace, but depended on the disposition of those using them, there seems to have been a widespread popular tendency to use them as though they did.[52] Certainly, the act of blessing and exorcism by a priest, which emphasised the expulsion of evil spirits and the infusion of divine 'virtue', could easily lead to a blurring of that distinction. Even Bellarmine admitted that it was 'probable' that sacramentals could work *ex opere operato*.[53] Even where no explicit theological support was given to any magical understanding of sacramentals and their power, this may have influenced the popular outlook hardly at all, especially when a preacher as renowned as Geyler von Kaisersberg could recommend their use as a form of counter-magic.[54]

I have emphasised the affinity between sacramentals and private conjurations because both exemplify an essentially sacramental view of the world. This leads to my last major point, the way in which the sacred is manifest in and through the profane. There was clearly present in pre-industrial popular belief an important element of crypto-materialism. This had three observable strands: a pragmatic, inner-worldly understanding of the efficacy of sacred power; the development of a sensual connection with sacred objects; and a materialist conception of the workings of the sacred.

The pragmatic understanding of the efficacy of sacred power can be explained by what the folklorist Max Rumpf called the contractual nature of human relationships with the sacred. Rumpf pointed out that God was seen as a genuine *Bauerngott*, a powerful ruler over weather and fertility. Relations between God and the agricultural producer rested on a strong sense of mutuality: God was accorded all that belonged to him in worship and honour; he provided in turn his blessing and protection. In this economy of divine–human relations Rumpf saw an Old Testament style of covenant, an agreed bargain involving a near-legal sense of obligation. Once struck, the agreement demands loyalty from both sides, who must fulfil it mutually out of justice. Failure to do so from either side arouses just anger.[55]

Rumpf's argument is supported by the common view of the early modern period that disorder in the natural world was a sign of divine anger at human failure to keep God's command. Seen from the human side of the agreement, it is also supported by what we know of attitudes towards the saints, who were regarded polytheistically as providers of sacred power. Those who fulfilled their role as intercessors and protectors were venerated; those who did not were mocked and abused. St Urban, the patron saint of vintners, for example, was invoked in Germany to provide clement weather for the vine-harvest. If the weather on St Urban's day was fine, this was taken as a token of a good harvest and he was honoured; if it was bad, his image was unceremoniously thrown in the mud.[56] Much the same custom was used in Bavaria with the image of St Leonhard, the patron saint of cattle, and Florence with the image of Our Lady of Impruneta, a local rain-deity.[57]

For the same reason, I suspect, the demonic was not regarded by the laity with the same abhorrence as it was by the clergy or theologian. Rather, it was an alternative means of access to efficacious sacred power. Thus, one turned to the professional magician or sorcerer, folk who knew how to deal with spirits or demons and their power. It is also seen in cases where weather bells were blessed in the name of the divinity, and when this brought little success, they were re-blessed in the name of the devil. The apparent indifference to theological disapproval in such an act shows an ambivalence about the nature of the sacred, exemplified in those circumstances where saints were regarded as malevolent, as working evil on humans.[58] Here the test applied seems to have been that of pragmatic efficacy.

The sensual connection with sacred objects is exemplified in the psychic effects of conjurations, and was singled out for comment by Huizinga. He saw it as symptomatic of the decline of a genuinely spiritual attitude to religion in favour of an emotional sensibility too preoccupied with outward appearances.[59] A. L. Meyer called this *die heilbringende Schau* (salvific display), a desire to have the mysteries of religion made visible, presented to the bodily eye, rather than just apprehended through an inner vision. It led, he argued, to demands to see the host displayed at the moment of consecration, and afterwards put on display in a monstrance. In its most intense form, an emotional link was set up between the object and the viewer, such that the object 'made present the holy'. For example, by looking at the Cloth of St Veronica, one received both spiritual and physical healing. The church compromised with the attitude in as far as it stressed the importance of viewing holy objects at pilgrimage sites and other cultic places.[60]

In the art of the pre-Reformation period this effect was achieved, as

Michael Baxandall has shown, through an excessive emphasis on the materiality of images, in many cases seeking to arouse sensuous emotions that were more worldly than religious.[61] The very materiality of the image encouraged the viewer to see it as pure object, as mere material. The worldly nature of the emotions aroused led religious reformers to condemn the role of images in popular belief as pure idolatry, as the worshipping of paint, wood and stone. The central issue on which the question of images and image-worship turned was that for the believer in images, the image had 'valid, participatory intelligence'; for the iconomach, it was an idol, 'pure object, without spirit, without efficacy'. The logical development of this latter view was iconoclasm, the smashing of images to prove that they had no sacred power. But even independently of religious reformers, many folk were quite aware of the materialist basis of the image-cult, and images that 'failed' were often smashed in the same way.[62]

The materialist conception of the workings of the sacred can be seen at its most striking in the eucharist and the miracles associated with it. Two attempts to express the doctrine of the Real Presence for the theologically uneducated were the popular depictions known as *The Host-Mill* and *Christ in the Wine-Press*. In the first, Christ is fed into the hopper of a mill, and host-breads emerge where the flour would normally appear. In the second, the suffering Christ is crushed in a wine-press and blood flows out, like the juice of pressed grapes, into a chalice. This grossly materialistic representation was matched by a spate of host miracles in the later Middle Ages, which asserted the truth of the Real Presence through stories of host-breads turning to real flesh, of hosts bleeding and suffering all-too-human wounds, and of wine in chalices turning into real blood.[63]

I want to make just three brief points in conclusion. The ways in which the sacred was experienced in and through the secular make it very difficult to distinguish between 'religion' and 'magic' in pre-Reformation religion. The penumbra in which spiritual and material conceptions of the sacred, or spiritual, and physical understandings of its efficacy were intermingled was too broad. Churchmen and theologians attempted to label certain practices as 'superstitious', but the church's commitment to a sacramental view of religion made any hard and fast distinction between 'religion' and 'magic' almost impossible. It was left to the Reformation, with its radically different understanding of the sacred, to achieve that distinction, with a firm break between the sacred and the secular worlds.

Secondly, given the role of pre-Reformation religion in creating cosmic order in the daily life of an agrarian society, the Reformation attempt to 'purify' religion faced an equally impossible task. It had to shatter an entire world-view, to effect a change in popular understanding of moral, psychic and physical causality. We should not be surprised to find that its success was rather limited. Within its own terms, it changed views largely only of the physical efficacy of the sacred, not of its psychic or moral efficacy.[64]

Thirdly, the emergence of less sacramental (or, if one will, 'superstitious') views of the world may not, in any case, have depended on the success of the Reformation's new theological perceptions of the nature of the sacred. A world-view with such a pragmatic understanding of the efficacy of the sacred, which sees it as something already inner-worldly, may not need to experience any great intellectual or scientific revolution to break the nexus between natural and supernatural. It may be enough to discover other means to order the natural world, without resorting to sacred intervention. Changes in material standards of life, in agricultural techniques, in hygiene and public health, and even in the means of compensation for material loss (for example, through the rise of insurance), may be sufficient to explain the retreat of the sacred from its role in creating cosmic order, without any great shift in theological attitudes. There is no sudden shift from one form of belief to another; rather, the sacred is no longer regarded as a workable means of effectively ordering the profane world.[65] This need not involve a loss of belief in the sacred, so much as a limitation of its field of activity. Such a hypothesis, properly tested by further research, may explain the rise of 'secularisation' in those societies or part-societies which remained relatively 'immobile', retaining a basically 'peasant mentality' and pattern of belief, untouched by the reforming efforts of social or intellectual elites.

Notes: Chapter 1

1 The concept of 'manifestations of the sacred' I have taken from M. Eliade, *Patterns in Comparative Religion* (New York, 1958), pp. 1–3; see also the discussion in S. S. Acquaviva, *The Decline of the Sacred in Industrial Society* (Oxford, 1979), ch. 1; the theme of the sacred ordering human relationships is suggested by the work of John Bossy, 'Blood and baptism: kinship, community and Christianity in Western Europe from the fourteenth to the seventeenth centuries', in *Sanctity and Secularity. Studies in Church History*, Vol. X, ed. D. Baker (Oxford, 1973), pp. 129–43; id., 'Holiness and society', *Past and Present*, Vol. LXXV (1977), pp. 119–37, esp. pp. 129 ff.; id., 'The social history of confession in the age of the Reformation', *Trans. Royal Hist. Soc.*, Vol. XXV (1975), pp. 21–38; the ordering of the natural world is suggested by A. Franz, *Die kirchlichen Benediktionen im deutschen Mittelalter*, 2 vols (Freiburg/Br., 1909), and it is also a major theme in W. A. Christian, Jr, *Local Religion in Sixteenth-Century Spain* (Princeton, NJ, 1981), esp. ch. 5.

2 Bossy, 'Holiness and society', p. 129.

3 On the notion of 'order' used here see Natalie Davis, 'Some tasks and themes in the study of popular religion', in C. Trinkaus and H. A. Oberman (eds), *The Pursuit of Holiness in Late Medieval and Renaissance Religion* (Leiden, 1974), p. 312.

4 Eliade, *Patterns*, p. 2. I do not wish to suggest that the sacred is created *by* such relationships; the description attempted here is intended to be independent of any judgements about the a priori or derived nature of such phenomena. It is sufficient to state that for the religious mentality, such relations between the sacred and the profane always have ontological status.

5 Eliade, *Patterns*, p. 17.

6 ibid., p. 25.

7 For this distinction, L. A. Veit, *Volksfrommes Brauchtum und Kirche im deutschen Mittelalter* (Freiburg/Br., 1936), pts II and III.

8 On 'rites of passage', there has been nothing in the early modern period to match van Gennep's original anthropological sketch, *The Rites of Passage* (London, 1960), but see Veit, *Volksfrommes Brauchtum*, pp. 141–209 on 'Lebensringe'; see also Bossy, 'Blood and baptism', pp. 131, 134; Davis, 'Some tasks and themes', pp. 326 ff.

9 On the *Flurritt* and Corpus Christi, K. S. Kramer, *Bauer und Bürger im nachmittelalterlichen Unterfranken* (Würzburg, 1957), pp. 115–16; on St John's day fire, H. Bächtold-Stäubli (ed.), *Handwörterbuch des deutschen Aberglaubens*, 12 vols (Berlin/Leipzig, 1927–42), Vol. IV, p. 734; see also Franz, *Die kirchlichen Benediktionen*,

Vol. II, p. 72; L. Eisenhofer, *Handbuch der katholischen Liturgik*, 2 vols (Freiburg/Br., 1932–3), Vol. I, pp. 562–3.

10   On the Leipzig *Hurenumzug*, D. Peifer, *Lipsia seu originum lipsiensium libri IV* (Leipzig, 1689), p. 312; C. F. Flogel, *Geschichte des Groteskekomischen* (Liegnitz and Leipzig, 1788), p. 221. On the Augsburg expulsions on St Galli, Archivar Buff, 'Verbrechen und Verbrecher zu Augsburg in der zweiten Hälfte des 14. Jhts', *Zeitschrift des historischen Vereins für Schwaben und Neuburg*, Vol. IV (1878), pp. 189, 200; I. Bloch, *Die Prostitution*, Vol. I (Berlin, 1912), p. 708. The Leipzig expulsions involved other marginal elements, but prostitutes played the major role. I am grateful to Lyndal Roper for much valuable information on the latter.

11   On the feast of the Purification, see J. H. Albers, *Festpostille und Festchronik* (Stuttgart, 1907), pp. 84–91; Bächthold-Stäubli, *Handwörterbuch*, Vol. V, pp. 1261–9, esp. pp. 1266–7; Eisenhofer, *Handbuch*, Vol. I, pp. 582–6. John Bossy's expression of 'extreme scepticism' (in the discussion of Hermann Hörger's paper) that there was any link between the liturgical cycle and the cycles of the seasonal year is only possible by taking the narrowest view of the liturgy and ignoring all the other resonances that liturgical feasts had for most people, clerical and lay alike. Liturgicists may have held to distinctly spiritual interpretations of feasts, but I doubt whether these alone formed the common view of what was acted out on such days. I have discussed some aspects of the question in an article on 'Ritual and popular belief in Catholic Germany in the sixteenth century', forthcoming in *Journal of Ecclesiastical History*.

12   Bächthold-Stäubli, *Handwörterbuch*, Vol. II, p. 1110.

13   On St Agnes' day, Bächthold-Stäubli, *Handwörterbuch*, Vol. I, p. 214; M. Buchberger (ed.), *Lexikon für Theologie und Kirche*, 10 vols (Freiburg/Br., 1957–65), Vol. I, pp. 196–7; K. Künstle, *Ikonographie der Heiligen* (Freiburg/Br., 1926), pp. 39–42. St Agnes' day was also believed to be the day on which the first larks appeared, and on which the bees swarmed, Bächthold-Stäubli, ibid. On St Vincent's day, Albers, *Festpostille*, pp. 67–72; *Lexikon für Theologie und Kirche*, Vol. X, p. 803.

14   St Vincent's day was taken as midwinter's day, and so as the turning-point towards spring, *Lexikon für Theologie und Kirche*, Vol. X, p. 803; so was *Pauli Bekehrung*, Bächthold-Stäubli, *Handwörterbuch*, Vol. VI, pp. 1463–4, and so a day on which many customs stressed *Bekehrung* by turning around or inverting.

15   On St Bridget, Bächthold-Stäubli, *Handwörterbuch*, Vol. I, p. 1577.

16   On Blasius-water, Eisenhofer, *Handbuch*, Vol. I, pp. 583, 586, 588; Franz, *Die kirchlichen Benediktionen*, Vol. I, p. 459. Candles were also used on this day.

17   Bächthold-Stäubli, *Handwörterbuch*, Vol. I, pp. 209–10; Franz, *Die kirchlichen Benediktionen*, Vol. I, p. 272. *Agathabrot* was mentioned in 1516 by Geiler von Kaisersberg as good for protection against fire, ibid.

18   Künstle, *Ikonographie*, pp. 187–8; L. Reau, *Iconographie de l'art chrétien*, Vol. III (Paris, 1958), pp. 403–4. St Dorothea was therefore the patron saint of gardeners.

19   Bächthold-Stäubli, *Handwörterbuch*, Vol. VIII, p. 1503. Other days in this cycle considered favourable for mating were St Vincent's day and Cathedra Petri, ibid., Vol. IX, p. 236.

20   Bächthold-Stäubli, *Handwörterbuch*, Vol. VI, pp. 1531–6. This day counts as the first day of spring. Here it should be noted that before the introduction of the Gregorian calendar in 1582, these days fell ten days later than they do now, so accentuating their role as harbingers of spring.

21   On Rogation Days and their associated *Bittprozessionen*, Eisenhofer, *Handbuch*, Vol. I, pp. 556–7. I have discussed them at greater length in 'Ritual and popular belief' (see n. 11 above).

22   On sacramentals in general, Franz, *Die kirchlichen Benediktionen*, Vol. I, pp. 10–37.

23   Franz, ibid., Vol. I, p. 37, argues that the sacramentals stood on the periphery of religious life, while the sacraments stood at its centre. While this might be theologically true, it does not seem to be the case in terms of *frequency of use*. Only two, confession and the eucharist, were received regularly, the former usually once a year, the latter at most twice or three times a year. Attendance at mass was much more frequent, certainly, but the use made of the sacramentals in daily life would have made them the commonest means of access to the sacred. On confession, see Bossy, 'The social history of confession', p. 24; on

the eucharist and mass attendance, J. Toussaert, *Le Sentiment religieux en Flandre à la fin du Moyen-Age* (Paris, 1963), pp. 127–36, 161–96.

24 For this reason, L. Rothkrug, *Religious Practices and Collective Perceptions: Hidden Homologies in the Renaissance and Reformation* (*Historical Reflections*, Vol. VII, No. 1, Waterloo, Ontario, 1980), p. 27, speaks of the eucharist as a special kind of relic with a 'sacred locus'.

25 Franz, *Die kirchlichen Benediktionen*, Vol. I, p. 624; M. Rumpf, *Das gemeine Volk*, Vol. II of *Religiöse Volkskunde* (Stuttgart, 1933), p. 33: Veit, *Volksfrommes Brauchtum*, pp. 62–75.

26 On the candles at *Lichtmess*, Eisenhofer, *Handbuch*, Vol. I, pp. 583, 585; Franz, *Die kirchlichen Benediktionen*, Vol. I, p. 456; Bächthold-Stäubli, *Handwörterbuch*, Vol. V, pp. 1262, 1682; see also Vol. I, p. 1414.

27 On blessed palms, Franz, *Die kirchlichen Benediktionen*, Vol. I, p. 481; Eisenhofer, *Handbuch*, Vol. I, pp. 509–10; on herbs blessed at Assumption, Franz, ibid., p. 407; Eisenhofer, ibid., pp. 595–6.

28 See Franz, *Die kirchlichen Benediktionen*, Vol. I, p. 624, on the 'almost exclusively agrarian' uses of sacramentals.

29 On holy water, Franz, ibid., pp. 201–20; Eisenhofer, *Handbuch*, Vol. I, pp. 304–8.

30 See P. Browe, 'Die Eucharistie als Zaubermittel im Mittelalter', *Archiv für Kulturgeschichte*, Vol. XX (1930), pp. 134–54; A. Franz, *Die Messe im deutschen Mittelalter* (Freiburg/Br., 1902), pp. 87–9.

31 I have chosen the word 'conjuration' to describe what are called variously in German *Beschwörungen, Besprechungen, Segen* or *Zaubersprüche*. A common English term for these is 'spell', sometimes 'charm', see, e.g., K. Thomas, *Religion and the Decline of Magic* (Harmondsworth, 1973), pp. 46–7, 211–14. The word used is less important than the conceptual distinctions to be observed in the discussion. *Beschwörung* is taken to involve the summoning up of a higher sacred power against its will, and so is a matter of contest; *Segen* and *Besprechungen* do not involve personal conflict with the power called upon. See Bächthold-Stäubli, *Handwörterbuch*, Vol. I, p. 1110. *Zaubersprüche* sometimes involve the use of magical objects, but I have usually avoided including these in the discussion. A second point of importance is the provenance of these conjurations. Manuscript sources are either monastic or medical (in *Arzneibücher*), visitation records or court records (hearings for witchcraft and sorcery); printed records from the sixteenth and seventeenth centuries are *Arzneibücher*, magical handbooks, collections of conjurations, sometimes broadsheets, published by both Catholic and Protestant clergymen: see Bächthold-Stäubli, *Handwörterbuch*, Vol. VII, p. 1587; G. Müller, 'Zaubersprüche und Segen aus sächsischen Visitationsakten', *Neues Archiv für sächsische Geschichte und Altertumskunde*, Vol. IX (1888), pp. 334–7; S. Singer, 'Segen und Gebräuche des xvii. Jhts. aus der Schweiz', *Zeitschrift des Vereins für Volkskunde* (abbrev. *ZsVfVK*), Vol. IV (1894), pp. 447–51 (extracts from a collection published in Zürich in 1646 by the pastor of Meilen, near Zürich, Rudolf Gwerb). From the eighteenth century (until the twentieth) they appeared in printed collections, which enjoyed great popularity in the rural population: see F. Losch, 'Deutsche Segen, Heil- und Bannsprüche', *Württembergische Vierteljahrshefte für Landesgeschichte*, Vol. XIII (1890), pp. 157–258; A. Spamer, *Romanusbüchlein: Historisch-philologischer Kommentar zu einem deutschen Zauberbuch* (Berlin, 1958). It has been argued that they descend from the clergy, over the nobility and urban classes, until they finally reach the rural lower classes in the nineteenth century, during the period of their ossification: see Bächthold-Stäubli, *Handwörterbuch*, Vol. VII, p. 1587. However, there is far too much evidence of non-clerical origins in non-Christian forms of magic, as well as in popular healing: see O. Ebermann, *Blut- und Wundsegen in ihrer Entwicklung dargestellt*, Palaestra XXIV (Berlin, 1903); and I. Hampp, *Beschwörung, Segen, Gebet: Untersuchung zum Zauberspruch aus dem Bereich der Volksheilkunde* (Stuttgart, 1961). There is also clear evidence from the Middle Ages that they were used by layfolk: Bächthold-Stäubli, *Handwörterbuch*, p. 1603; Ebermann, *Blut- und Wundsegen*, pp. 134–8. Whether they were the exclusive preserve of sorcerers or cunning folk is more difficult to determine, but there seems to be prima facie evidence for regarding them as I have here, as means available to private individuals to apply sacred power to the problems of daily life, without denying the other aspects of their usage or development. The entire

subject requires much closer detailed attention than is possible in the scope of a paper such as this, but it illustrates effectively the complexity of the whole problem of the 'popular' and 'learned', lay and clerical dimensions in religion of this period. For further bibliography and discussion see Bächthold-Stäubli, *Handwörterbuch*, Vol. I, pp. 1109–29 (*Beschwörung*), 1157–72 (*Besprechung*); Vol. VII, pp. 1582–1620 (*Segen*); and the works of Ebermann, Hampp and Spamer, cited above.

32 As far as possible, I have drawn this enumeration from sixteenth-century examples, occasionally from seventeenth or fourteenth-fifteenth: see C. Bartsch, 'Zauber und Segen', *Zeitschrift für deutsche Mythologie und Sittenkunde*, Vol. III (1855), pp. 318–34; J. Bolte, 'Deutsche Sagen des 16. Jhts.', *ZsVfVK*, Vol. XIV (1904), pp. 435–8; W. Crecelius, 'Alte Segensformeln', *Zeitschrift für deutsche Mythologie und Sittenkunde*, Vol. I (1853), pp. 277–80; Müller, 'Zaubersprüche' (see n. 31 above); O. Schülte, 'Zaubersegen des 16. Jhts. aus dem Orgichtboecke im Braunschweiger Stadtarchiv', *ZsVfVK*, Vol. XV (1905), pp. 180–1; Singer, 'Segen und Gebräuche', cited n. 31 above; K. Weinhold, 'Zwei Bienensegen', *ZsVfVK*, Vol. II (1892), p. 86; O. v. Singerle, 'Segen und Heilmittel aus einer Wolfsthurner Hs. des xvi. Jhts.', *ZsVfVK*, Vol. I (1891), pp. 172–7, 315–24.

33 On the difference between conjurations and prayers, see Hampp, *Beschwörung, Segen, Gebet*, pp. 136–40, but she is incorrect to argue that *Segen* are directed at 'good' powers, *Zaubersprüche* at 'bad'. On the oral nature of the formulae, it has been argued that they do not belong to oral tradition since the exact words of the formulae are so important that written transmission is essential, see Bächthold-Stäubli, *Handwörterbuch*, Vol. VII, p. 1587. However, their nature as formulae is exactly what makes them suitable for oral transmission (expecially in rhymed form) by the non-literate, who are recognised to have possessed highly developed powers of memory: see J. Vansina, *Oral Tradition. A Study in Historical Methodology* (Harmondsworth, 1973), pp. 4, 146.

34 *Obsequiale secundum diocesis Augustensis* (E. Radoldt, Augsburg, 1487), British Library, IA 6652, fol. XII: *ut quod populus tuus tua veneratione hodierna die agit, hoc spiritualiter summa devocione perficiat.*

35 E. Bartsch, *Die Sachbeschwörungen der römischen Liturgie* (Münster, 1967), pp. 339–40; Eisenhofer, *Handbuch*, Vol. I, pp. 304 ff.

36 Franz, *Die kirchlichen Benediktionen*, Vol. I, pp. 154–92 *passim*. On apotropaic power, see Eisenhofer, *Handbuch*, pp. 585 (*Lichtmess*), 596 (*Kräuterweihe*); and Bächthold-Stäubli, *Handwörterbuch*, Vol. I, pp. 129–50 (*Abwehrzauber*), especially the fourth category, directed against demons and evil spirits.

37 On animism, Bächthold-Stäubli, *Handwörterbuch*, Vol. I, pp. 439–47, esp. pp. 440–3.

38 On medieval views on the powers of demons, see Franz, *Die kirchlichen Benediktionen*, Vol. II, pp. 19–37, 514–28. Geiler von Kaisersberg laid great emphasis on the psychic power of demons to plague humans through *Teufelsgespenster*: see A. Stöber, *Zur Geschichte des Volks-Aberglaubens am Anfang des 16. Jhts: Aus der Emeis von Dr. Johann Geiler von Kaisersberg* (Basle, 1875), pp. 25–6; but Geiler also believed that the Devil could wreak physical harm, p. 37.

39 *Obsequiale*, fol. IV: *et quicquid ex eo tactum vel respersum fuerit, careat omni immundicia, omnique impignatione spirtualis nequicie, per Christum dominum nostrum ... ut quicquid in domibus vel locis fidelium hec unda resperserit careat omnia immundicia liberatur a noxa, non illic resideat spiritus pestilens, non aura corrumpens.*

40 Franz, *Die kirchlichen Benediktionen*, Vol. I, p. 109; Eisenhofer, *Handbuch*, Vol. I, p. 304.

41 Franz, *Die kirchlichen Benediktionen*, Vol. I, p. 33.

42 The enumeration is taken from an *Agenda sive benedictionale commune* (Thomas Wolf, Basle, 1520), a ritual book which does not seem to have been tied to the practice of any single diocese, and which contains the largest collections of such blessings.

43 Franz, *Die kirchlichen Benediktionen*, Vol. I, p. 30. Even the more recent Catholic commentators are ambiguous on this: see F. Probst, *Kirchliche Benediktionen und ihre Verwaltung* (Tübingen, 1857), pp. 49–60.

44 *Agenda sive benedictionale commune*, fols XLVII[v], XLVIII[v]. On the blessing of grazing oats on St Stephen's day, see Franz, *Die kirchlichen Benediktionen*, Vol. I, pp. 381–8; Vol. II, pp. 9–12.

45 Franz, *Die kirchlichen Benediktionen*, Vol. I, pp. 118–19; see also Luther's comments in the Weimar edition (*WA*) of his works: *WA*, Vol. I, pp. 670–3.

46 Franz, *Die Messe*, pp. 87–9, 94–7; Browe, 'Die Eucharistie als Zaubermittel', cited n. 30 above, p. 138; P. Browe, *Die Verehrung der Eucharistie im Mittelalter* (Munich, 1933), pp. 123–6.

47 See, for example, the formulae in a mid-eighteenth-century manuscript, Losch, 'Deutsche Segen, Heil- und Bannsprüche', cited n. 31 above, pp. 158–64. See also Hampp, *Beschwörung, Segen, Gebet*, pp. 158–63.

48 Losch, ibid., p. 175, no. 72 (from an early nineteenth-century collection). On sympathetic magic, see also Bächthold-Stäubli, *Handwörterbuch*, Vol. VIII, pp. 627–8.

49 Losch, ibid., p. 178, no. 88 (from an early nineteenth-century collection). This conjuration appears to have been somewhat unusual, for I have not been able to find any earlier examples of a similar usage.

50 Losch, ibid., p. 165, from *Die Egyptischen Geheimnisse des Albertus Magnus*, which began to circulate in the early nineteenth century, although the provenance is fairly uncertain and unresearched; see Spamer, *Romanusbüchlein*, pp. 21, 39–40.

51 Franz, *Die kirchlichen Benediktionen*, Vol. I, p. 12; Probst, *Kirchliche Benediktionen*, pp. 1, 53 ff.

52 Franz, ibid., Vol. I, pp. 12 ff.; Probst, ibid., pp. 53–60.

53 Franz, ibid., Vol. I, p. 18.

54 Stöber, *Zur Geschichte des Volks-Aberglaubens*, pp. 52–7. However, Geiler took pains to point out that the efficacy of these *sacramentalische Dinge* depended on the power of belief: *Dass wasser* [i.e. holy water] *wirckt nicht das du über dich besprengt, aber die andacht und die meinung die du hast, und der glaub in dem du das wasser nimmest. So wirckt es nit allein in deinem glauben, da hilfft auch der glaub der gantzen cristenheit und der heiligen vetter, die das geweicht wasser auf haben gesetzt,* ibid., p. 54.

55 Rumpf, *Das gemeine Volk*, pp. 27–9.

56 Sebastian Franck, *Weltbuch* (Tübingen, 1534), fol. LI. This was a south German custom, attested in Freiburg im Breisgau, and in Württemberg, A. Thomas, *Die Darstellung Christi in der Kelter* (Düsseldorf, 1936), pp. 32–4; as well as in Nuremberg, where it persisted until 1621, J. Dünninger and H. Schopf, *Bräuche und Feste im fränkischen Jahreslauf* (Kulmbach, 1971), pp. 78–81.

57 J. Grimm, *Deutsche Mythologie*, 4th edn, 3 vols (Berlin, 1875–8), Vol. II, p. 640n.; R. Trexler, 'Florentine religious experience: the sacred image', *Studies in the Renaissance*, Vol. XIX (1972), pp. 24–5.

58 R. Trexler, *Public Life in Renaissance Florence* (New York, 1980), p. 77.

59 J. Huizinga, *The Waning of the Middle Ages* (Harmondsworth, 1955), pp. 166–7.

60 A. L. Meyer, 'Die heilbringende Schau in Sitte und Kult', in *Heilige Überlieferung: Festschrift für I. Herwegen* (Münster, 1938), pp. 234–62.

61 M. Baxandall, *The Limewood Sculptors of Renaissance Germany* (London and New Haven, 1980), ch. 3, esp. p. 90.

62 Trexler, 'Florentine religious experience', cited n. 57 above, pp. 20, 27–9; see also his *Public Life in Renaissance Florence* (New York, 1980), pp. 118–28.

63 On these images, see E. Kirschbaum (ed.), *Lexikon der christlichen Ikonographie*, Vol. III (Freiburg/Br., 1968), p. 289 (on the host mill); A. Weckwerth, 'Christus in der Kelter: Ursprung und Wandlung eines Bildmotives', in *Beiträge zur Kunstgeschichte: Festschrift für H. R. Rosemann* (Munich, 1960), pp. 95–108, and Thomas, *Die Darstellung Christi in der Kelter*. On host-miracles, P. Browe, 'Die eucharistischen Verwandlungswunder des Mittelalters', *Römische Quartalschrift* (1929), pp. 137–69.

64 The preservation of belief in the moral efficacy of the sacred is seen in Reformation attitudes to omens, portents, natural disasters as signs of God's anger at human sinfulness; on psychic efficacy, see the continuing Reformation belief in a spirit world, and of course in the activities of the Devil.

65 On these points, see P. Burke, 'Religion and secularisation', in *New Cambridge Modern History*, Vol. XIII (Cambridge, 1979), p. 312; on the rise of insurance, Thomas, *Religion and the Decline of Magic*, pp. 779–82, and for a practical example, Rumpf, *Das gemeine Volk*, p. 98. I have slightly reworked this last point from the presentation in the Wolfenbüttel conference, where it was generally misunderstood. I wished to suggest that

'secularisation' may have spread *not only* through more secular ideas filtering down 'from above' (cf. the suggestions in A. D. Gilbert, *The Making of Post-Christian Britain*, London 1980, esp. ch. 2), *but also* through a form of conceptual drift from below. Underlying this idea was the distinction drawn by S. S. Acquaviva, *The Decline of the Sacred in Industrial Society* (London, 1979), p. 35, between *secularisation* as the decline of belief in the manipulatory value of sacred persons, places, things; and *desacralisation* as a change in the intensity and diffusion of the experience of the sacred.

2 The Cultural Importance of the Pious Middle Classes in Seventeenth-Century Protestant Society

HARTMUT LEHMANN, translated by Ian Waite

In a recently published study of European society in the early modern period, Richard van Dülmen refers to the way in which the leading classes of society became progressively more exclusive as a group, and describes how they exhibited a coincidence of interests common to their class which led to an accelerating polarisation between the common people and the aristocracy.[1] 'Just as European aristocratic culture with its rituals, social conventions, courtly ethos and cult of princes set itself apart from the cultural formation of the common people and the middle classes, so too did the local forms of popular culture with their language of symbolic gestures, simple rhetoric and magical-religious customs set itself apart.' Court culture, which reached its apogee in the seventeenth century, increasingly affected the middle classes. According to van Dülmen this process was so strong that, from the seventeenth century onwards, the urban middle classes lost their political and social independence.

This contribution is intended to disprove the thesis maintained by van Dülmen and others,[2] namely, that the middle classes did indeed lose their cultural independence in the seventeenth century. On the contrary, a section of the middle classes, which I shall call the 'pious middle classes' (*das fromme Bürgertum*), did manage to retain its cultural independence. I shall proceed as follows: first I shall describe the most important documents regarding this group, and then proceed to an analysis of their mentality. A discussion of the political and social background of their outlook will lead to the conclusion, where I shall assess the far-reaching intellectual and cultural influence of the pious middle classes.

I

The most important evidence for the religious life of the pious middle classes is to be found in the devotional literature of the age. This is at the same time the most important source for any attempts to research and describe their cultural role in society and history. In the narrowest sense of the word there were devotional books *per se*, such as Johann Arndt's *Bücher vom wahren Christentum*. In a wider sense, however, the devotional literature of the seventeenth century included hymns, funeral sermons, poems modelled on the Psalms, the so-called 'words of the dying' literature, as well as a considerable number of broadsheets on comets and religious poetry. Even without supplying series of statistics for the production and distribution of such literature,[3] it can be said that the production of such works reached its quantitative as well as qualitative apogee in the seventeenth century. The amount of devotional literature increased sharply after about 1580 and reached its first peak during the first decades of the seventeenth century. Production only began to ebb in the second third of the eighteenth century. Almost a quarter of the total books printed between the Reformation and the Enlightenment belong to this category of devotional literature. Moreover, their influence was not restricted to the printed word: funeral sermons were given in front of congregations; hymns were sung by congregations. We can, therefore, scarcely overestimate the importance of devotional literature in the period ranging from the late sixteenth to the early eighteenth century.

Devotional books, such as Valerius Herberger's *Evangelische Herzpostille* or Christian Scriver's *Seelenschatz*, were intended to comfort weak believers, bring certainty to the tempted and strength to the tired, and provide answers to those in need of them.[4] These books constantly reiterated the idea that it was possible, even in the most trying times, to lead a truly Christian life. From them one could learn what it was to be penitent and overcome sin. Johann Arndt and many others were quite explicit in their opinion that it was only those who were prepared to follow Christ unconditionally who would receive mercy at God's hands on Judgement Day.

As Winfried Zeller has shown, 'there are many and varied common aspects in terms of the history of piety as well as interconnections of a theological and literary kind' linking funeral sermons and devotional literature.[5] Rudolf Lenz and his colleagues have traced 240,000 funeral sermons in German for the period 1570 to 1770.[6] While not all of these share such aspects, it appears that the deceased tended to be presented to the congregation (and if the sermon was published, to the world at large) as a shining example of Christian living. Individual traits receded into the background. In Zeller's words, that which was important was 'what mattered for the cure of souls and all that went with it. The life and death of the deceased were used as instruments in the education to Christian maturity and right living.'[7] If we can rely on the figures we have, it appears that two-thirds of these stylised eulogies were of deceased persons who belonged to the middle and upper-middle classes.[8]

Like many funeral sermons, countless seventeenth-century hymns present us with the image of past generations of Christians who now belong to a 'higher order or community' to which all Christians strive.[9] In his song, composed in 1666, *Gib dich zufrieden und sei still*, Paul Gerhardt wrote:[10]

The day when God will free us from the snares of evil and the bonds of the flesh is at hand. Death will suddenly take us and free us all from the trials and tribulations of this life ... He [that is, Death] will lead us on to the legions of the faithful and elect, who, departed peacefully from this world, are now joyful in their contentment for they hear their own true foundation and corner-stone, the mouth from which the Word comes forth, speak. Be still and know!

(Prose translation of verse text)

In Johann Matthäus Meyfart's hymn *Jerusalem du hochgebaute Stadt* (1626) the eschatological presentation of death is even clearer:[11]

O Jerusalem, thou heavenly city, where I should love to be. My heart longs for thee so much that it has quite abandoned me. Now, far away, over the hills and valleys and over the wide open fields it races to leave this world.

When wilt thou come, thou longed for day, and more longed for, more beautiful moment, when I shall hand over my soul into God's good keeping, so that it will come softly to rest in the good new country?

Let me greet thee, O glorious citadel, open the gates of grace. How long I have longed for thee, before I could leave this evil life, this nothingness and receive from God the gift of eternity.

Which people, what hundreds can I see there? Christ the Lord has sent the best of those who were among the elect in this world to greet me. For I was in exile in this land of tears.

Great prophets and tall patriarchs and Christians together who bore the cross's yoke or the tyrant's pain when on earth, passed high above, as I watched, poised in honour, clad in clarity and surrounded with light.

When I do finally attain the heavenly paradise my sense will be filled with the greatest joy and my mouth with praises. There they sing Hallelujah in holiness and Hosanna to all eternity.

With joyful sound and fine instruments in countless choirs which make the room itself dance for joy (I see them there). A hundred thousand tongues and yet more voices go forth from the heavenly host as it sings now as it has done since the beginning.

(Prose translation of verse text)

The last words of the dying were highly praised by the living as a sort of spiritual testament, and written collections were frequently made.[12] Compositions based on the Psalms served to provide comfort or elevation in moments of deep trouble, or even in some cases 'to glorify this trouble as a spiritual trial', as a recent writer has expressed it.[13] Many seventeenth-century ballads and broadsheets on comets carried express warnings against falling into sin or disregarding God's commandments. Prayer collections, whether for all professions, classes, or even vicissitudes of life, were one in demanding from their readers penitence and conversion. Hymns and funeral sermons were dominated by the theme of death: *mors ultima linea rerum, mors ultima spes*.[14] As Ferdinand van Ingen has shown, the leitmotifs of German baroque poetry were *vanitas* and *memento mori*. In the works of Andreas Gryphius and his contemporaries one could read that life was short and all things pass away — death would come unexpectedly, relentlessly and unavoidably. Eternal things were more important than temporal things. Life should be arranged *sub specie aeterni*. In confessional poems of the seventeenth century heaven and hell were understood as real places of human experience, and the pains of hell or the joys of heaven as real possibilities of human experience.[15]

II

The Germanists have a legitimate interest in the study of the prosody and literary traditions inherent in devotional literature. What is noticeable, besides these literary aspects, is the primarily didactic intent of seventeenth-century devotional literature. Thus one should understand its statements as being fundamentally practical. Authors of devotional works place life and death firmly inside the course of the history of salvation. The *memento mori* was supposed to impose a strictly ethical style of life, whilst death became an integral part of one's existence. In other words, authors of devotional works used the fact of dying to proselytise and to convert the impious to a pious life by combining references to the eschatological context of human existence with exhortations to lead a better life.

It is scarcely necessary to point out that this strictly eschatological way of looking at things was equally as foreign to the culture of the courts as it was to the culture of the common person. Indeed the self-confidence of the pious middle classes was defined by its opposition to the court and to traditional popular culture. Pious folk considered court life to be sinful and reprehensible, and courtiers corrupt flatterers. Instead of the art of war and the construction of fortifications they praised the way of the inner life. God was their supreme Lord, and reading the Bible their *raison d'état*. Fashionable clothing and language were simply diabolically inspired temptations, just as were fireworks, illuminations, dancing and theatre. 'At court' was as much as to say 'in hell', as Helmuth Kiesel significantly called his literary critique of the court.[16] In the seventeenth century the pious middle classes were a self-reliant spiritual and cultural alternative to the world of the court and all that went with it.[17] The world of the common people was equally alien to them, being just as devoid of the strict morality and rigorous discipline to which they subjected themselves as it was of the eschatologically inspired criticism of the world.[18]

But the piety of which seventeenth-century authors spoke was not to be equated with political quietism or economic passivity. Of course they sought to diminish the importance of activities instrumental to worldly success by emphasising the superiority of the life to come, but fulfilment of God's commandments also consisted in living up to the expectations of one's station in life, and providing one's daily bread. In other words, they demanded an ethic of achievement in this life as a reflection of religiously desirable qualities such as love of order, punctuality, integrity and honesty, which were a necessary precondition of economic success.

One must also bear in mind that the religious renewal caused by the devotional literature was only partly contained within the church. Certainly hymns and funeral sermons were important in stimulating activities within the congregation. And funeral sermons were, of course, delivered before they were collected and printed. But even more important was the fact that devotional literature was directed towards a Christian readership so that the contact between an individual Christian and a clergyman was bypassed. 'The relationship between the devotional author and the Christian seeking advice was and remained anonymous.'[19] The result was a distinction between that which was associated with the church and piety. If we seek to define the pious middle classes in the seventeenth century, then we mean groupings within the church, but primarily groupings on the fringes of, and also outside, the established churches; all those Christians whose concern for salvation cut across confessional ties.[20]

The pious middle classes are not a homogenous social group. Their sociological spectrum ranges from pious artisans to devout patricians, village clergymen to Lutheran Superintendents. It includes members of the semi-literate classes as well as the learned. Consequently the term 'pious middle classes' can only be approximate, sociologically speaking, and I have used it for lack of a more suitable or precise expression.[21] Furthermore, one must bear in mind that the pious were only a part of their respective social groupings. They were united not by political privileges, social position, or economic interests, but by a common view of the world and the desire to play an active part in their own personal salvation.

III

Finally, we shall consider the political and social environment out of which the particular attitudes of the pious middle classes grew. We may also broach the subject of the spiritual, intellectual and cultural energy which their orientation and life-styles reveal. Towards the end of the sixteenth century a general deterioration in living conditions began in Europe. We should remember that after 1600 an economic depression set in, characterised as much by a series of bad harvests as by problems in trade. These difficulties were accompanied by growing social tensions, which erupted as local disturbances or fuelled civil wars. There were political conflicts which resulted in major wars in which thousands died and even more were made homeless. Much discussion still surrounds the question as to what had given rise to this situation.[22] More importantly, recent research shows beyond doubt that the prosperity and expansion of the sixteenth century was succeeded by a period of stagnation, depression and poverty which were only overcome by the post-1720 recovery.[23] However, 'emigration, death or revolt' were not the only options available to the people of that time, as has recently been asserted.[24] Devotional literature, which had become a vehicle for the pious middle classes, must rather be regarded as an additional impressive, as well as an effective, response to the grievous misery of the era. I am fully aware that such a psychological interpretation of this literature is not without speculation. Nevertheless there is a clear correlation between the rapid turnover of devotional literature and the decline in the conditions of life which people experienced at this time. What we want to examine is the relationship between the fears produced by the difficulties of the age and the guidelines for salvation provided by the authors of devotional works. It is my contention that when devotional authors referred to the better life beyond the grave, and called for a strictly ethical conduct of life, they were clearly helping the pious to cope with the difficulties of their era and contributed to their ability to overcome worries and fears. Seventeenth-century people did not, as is often asserted, only react to the fears that beset their lives by repressive behaviour or resorting to popular superstitions.[25] As the devotional literature shows, they also had the means to conquer their worries and fears on a spiritual level and progress to an ethically grounded and constructive way of conducting their daily lives.[26]

IV

One should not on this account ascribe only a negative function to the cultural importance of the pious middle classes. The pious person in the seventeenth century was not only someone who refused to be blinded by the brilliance of court life or even be taken in by it.[27] Their cultural achievement consisted in the development of their own view of the world and their own form of life. During the sixteenth century the church and its ministers had been responsible for the explanation of poverty and need, and for securing what Christians understood to be their eternal salvation. The state was responsible for looking after the church, and heads of households cared for their families' spiritual welfare. As things began to undergo great change at the beginning of the seventeenth century, these structures – it appears – declined in efficacy as aids to salvation. A proportion of pious Christians began to seek religious guidance from pious literature, whereas others, predominantly from among the educated, founded religious societies and yet others met in conventicles. Thus, as became clear during the seventeenth century, new and attractive means of lending religious certainty arose, which removed a good deal of the influence previously enjoyed by the church, the state and even the fathers of households. Later on in the seventeenth century the cultural energies of the pious middle classes were absorbed and, as a result, also impregnated by the great movements of religious renewal of this century: Puritanism, Jansenism and Pietism. Their moral and religious goals were often overshadowed, as in the Puritans' struggle against Anglicanism, the Jansenists' against the Jesuits and the Pietists' against orthodox Lutheranism. Many Puritans developed interests in natural philosophy. Jansenists were often attracted to philosophical questions, whilst Pietists were involved in reforming schools. All this tended to change and widen the attitudes which these people held. We should not forget, finally, that the influence of the pious middle classes can be felt in the secularisation of moral conceptions during the eighteenth century. Even figures of the Christian Enlightenment such as Christian Thomasius or Christian Wolff would be impossible to understand without accounting for the heritage of the pious middle classes of the seventeenth century.

It does not, therefore, appear to be too much to say that the cultural impulses which stemmed from the pious middle classes during the seventeenth century are no less important than the cultural activities of the upper classes.[28] Certainly, in baroque culture the seventeenth-century upper classes expressed themselves in a splendid manner. The painters, architects, stucco-workers, composers and musicians of the baroque era bequeathed cultural monuments of lasting value. However, there was often a great sterility and vacuity concealed behind the beautiful façades. Even amongst the pious middle classes we encounter narrow-mindedness, convention and cultural traditionalism, but, importantly, also the capacity for cultural innovation. We should not underestimate their cultural achievements: the separation of church-going and confessional differences from piety, the partial dissolution of the church's authority, the intense preoccupation and coming to terms with the idea of death, the assimilation of fears, the link established between observation of the present and the judgements they passed on their own times, the connection made between the history of salvation and the conduct of life, salvation and professional ethics. All this became part of seventeenth-century culture and had ramifications which extended far beyond the epoch and scope of the pious middle classes.

Notes: Chapter 2

1 R. van Dülmen, 'Formierung der europäischen Gesellschaft in der frühen Neuzeit', *Geschichte und Gesellschaft*, Vol. VII (1981), pp. 5−41. The succeeding references are to p. 26.
2 The following also postulate an increase in the differences between popular and elite cultures in the course of the early modern period: N. Z. Davis, *Society and Culture in Early Modern France* (Stanford, Calif., 1975); P. Burke, *Popular Culture in Early Modern Europe* (New York, 1978) (German trans.: *Helden, Schurken und Narren: Europäische Volkskultur in der frühen Neuzeit*, Stuttgart, 1981); C. Ginzburg, *Der Käse und die Würmer: Die Welt des Müllers um 1600* (Frankfurt, 1979); K. Wrightson and D. Levine, *Poverty and Piety in an English Village: Terling 1525−1700* (New York, 1979); R. Muchembled, 'Sorcellerie, culture populaire et christianisme au XVIe siècle, principalement en Flandre et Artois', *Annales E.S.C.*, Vol. XXVIII (1973), pp. 264−84; id., *Culture populaire et culture des élites dans la France moderne (XVe−XVIIe siècles)* (Paris, 1978); id., *La Sorcière au village (XVe−XVIIIe siècles)* (Paris, 1979). There are, however, important differences between these interpretations. P. Burke and Wrightson/ Levine emphasise the withdrawal of the upper classes from participation in the cultural activities of the people as the decisive development between the Reformation and the Enlightenment, whereas Muchembled singles out the oppression of popular culture by the elite as the important cultural development in the early modern period.
3 For a more detailed account, see H. Lehmann, *Das Zeitalter des Absolutismus* (Stuttgart, 1980), pp. 114−23.
4 See H. Beck, *Die Erbauungsliteratur der evangelischen Kirche Deutschlands* (Erlangen, 1883); id., *Die religiöse Volksliteratur der evangelischen Kirche Deutschlands in einem Abriss* (Gotha, 1891); C. Grosse, *Die alten Tröster: Ein Wegweiser in die Erbauungsliteratur der evangelisch-lutherischen Kirche des 16.−18. Jahrhunderts* (Hermannsburg, 1900); W. Koepp, *Johann Arndt: Eine Untersuchung über die Mystik im Luthertum* (Berlin, 1912).
5 'Leichenpredigt und Erbauungsliteratur', R. Lenz (ed.), in *Leichenpredigten als Quelle historischer Wissenschaften*, Vol. I (Cologne and Vienna, 1975), p. 66. For more detail on seventeenth-century funeral sermons, cf. also R. Mohr, *Protestantische Theologie und Frömmigkeit im Angesicht des Todes während des Barockzeitalters hauptsächlich aufgrund hessischer Leichenpredigten*, theol. diss. (Marburg, 1964); E. Winkler, *Die*

Leichenpredigt im deutschen Luthertum bis Spener (Munich, 1967).

6   R. Lenz (ed.), *Leichenpredigten: Eine Bestandsaufnahme; Bibliographie und Ergebnisse einer Umfrage* (Marburg, 1980).

7   Lenz, *Leichenpredigten*, Vol. I, pp. 67, 70. It seems to me to be mistaken to designate the particularly Christian outlook of funeral sermons as 'ideology', as F. Lerner does in 'Ideologie und Mentalität patrizischer Leichenpredigten', in *Leichenpredigten als Quelle historischer Wissenschaften*, Vol. II (Marburg, 1979), pp. 126–37. By doing so he does an injustice to the conviction of the preacher, who placed the deceased in a line with earlier witnesses to the faith, and he fails, with the concept of ideology, to grasp properly how the sermon was received by the congregation or later readers of the printed text.

8   R. Lenz, 'Vorkommen, Aufkommen und Verteilung der Leichenpredigten', in id. (ed.), *Studien zur deutschsprachigen Leichenpredigt der frühen Neuzeit* (Marburg, 1981), pp. 244, 248. According to Lenz, p. 248, seventeenth-century funeral sermons were 'a purely upper-class phenomenon in which university graduates are overrepresented'.

9   Zeller, in Lenz, *Leichenpredigten*, Vol. I, p. 68.

10 E. von Cranach-Sichart (ed.), *Wach auf mein Herz: Die Lieder des Paul Gerhardt; Vollständige Ausgabe* (Munich, 1949), p. 164.

11 'Tuba novissima', 1626. Cited from *Evangelisches Kirchengesangbuch* (Hamburg, 1956), pp. 319 ff.

12 See Zeller, in Lenz, *Leichenpredigten*, Vol. I, p. 68.

13 K.-P. Ewald, *Engagierte Dichtung im 17. Jahrhundert: Studie zur Dokumentation und funktionsanalytischen Bestimmung des 'Psalmdichtungsphänomens'* (Stuttgart, 1975), p. 19.

14 F. W. Wentzlaff-Eggebert, *Der triumphierende und der besiegte Tod in der Wort- und Bildkunst des Barock* (Berlin and New York, 1975), pp. 70–80.

15 See F. van Ingen, *Vanitas und memento mori in der deutschen Barocklyrik* (Groningen, 1966). Van Ingen writes (p. 354) that the *Bussdichtung* of the sixteenth to eighteenth centuries was marked by a massive fugue – first mounting, then declining – of poetry dealing in one way or other with the subject of death. cf. also H.-H. Krummacher, *Der junge Gryphius und die Tradition: Studien zu den Perikopensonetten und den Passionsliedern* (Munich, 1976); W. Rehm, *Der Todesgedanke in der deutschen Dichtung vom Mittelalter bis zur Romantik* (1928; repr. Darmstadt, 1967), pp. 189–243; W. Mauser, *Dichtung, Religion und Gesellschaft im 17. Jahrhundert: Die 'Sonnete' des Andreas Gryphius* (Munich, 1976); W. Vosskamp, *Zeit- und Geschichtsauffassung im 17. Jahrhundert bei Gryphius und Lohenstein* (Bonn, 1967).

16 'Bei Hof, bei Höll': Untersuchungen zur literarischen Hofkritik von Sebastian Brant bis Friedrich Schiller* (Tübingen, 1979), esp. pt 2/1 and 2.

17 Those who, like W. Flemming, *Deutsche Kultur im Zeitalter des Barocks* (1937; 2nd edn, Constance, 1960), place the pious in the category of 'baroque man' commit an error, if for no other reason than that the notion of 'baroque man' is itself not without problems.

18 Detailed studies are lacking here. The pious members of the middle classes evidently wanted nothing to do with popular astrology, accounts of curiosities, or proverbs and adventure stories, which played an important role in seventeenth-century popular literature. On popular culture in the seventeenth century, see, *inter alia*, Y.-M. Bercé, *Fête et révolte: Des mentalités populaires du XVIe au XVIIIe siècle* (Paris, 1976); G. Bollème, *La Bibliothèque bleue: La littérature 'populaire' en France du XVIe au XIXe siècle* (Paris, 1971); id., *Les Almanachs populaires aux XVIIe et XVIIIe siècles: Essai d'histoire sociale* (Paris and The Hague, 1969).

19 Lehmann, *Zeitalter des Absolutismus*, p. 122.

20 See also L. Kolakowski, *Chrétiens sans église: La conscience religieuse et le lien confessionel au XVIIe siècle* (Paris, 1969).

21 The pious as a tightly defined group are hard to fit into seventeenth-century society, which was divided into estates. The best description of the conceptions on order and the *Weltbild* of this society is E. Trunz, 'Der deutsche Späthumanismus um 1600 als Standeskultur', in R. Alewyn (ed.), *Deutsche Barockforschung: Dokumentation einer Epoche* (Cologne and Berlin, 1970), pp. 147–81; E. Trunz, 'Weltbild und Dichtung im deutschen Barock', in R. Alewyn (ed.), *Aus der Welt des Barock* (Stuttgart, 1957), pp. 1–35.

22 See Lehmann, *Zeitalter des Absolutismus*, pp. 105–14; T. Ashton (ed.), *Crisis in Europe*

1560–1660 (New York, 1965); G. Parker and L. M. Smith (eds), *The General Crisis of the Seventeenth Century* (London and Boston, Mass., 1975).

23   See especially P. Deyon and J. Jacquart (eds), *Les Hésitations de la croissance 1580–1740* (Paris, 1978).

24   G. Parker and L. M. Smith in the introduction to id., *The General Crisis*, p. 9.

25   J. Delumeau, *La Peur en occident* (Paris, 1978), is not, despite the wealth of material discussed, particularly useful or informative. Delumeau fails to take account of the consequences of the secular crisis of the seventeenth century. His distinctions between the various forms of fear, xenophobia and other forms of prejudice are too imprecise and he does not discuss non-repressive means of conquering fears, such as devotional literature and a heightened work ethic.

26   On the importance of the 'anxiety-factor' in the rise of Pietism, see H. Lehmann, ' "Absonderung" und "Gemeinschaft" im frühen Pietismus: Allgemeinhistorische und sozial-psychologische Überlegungen zur Entstehung und Entwicklung des Pietismus', *Pietismus und Neuzeit*, Vol. IV (1979), pp. 54–82.

27   If the pious middle classes refused to acclimatise themselves to courtly culture ('acculturation'), then the thesis (mentioned above, n. 2) of the growing polarisation in the course of the early modern period between the larger social groupings must be reconsidered.

28   This is certainly not the case among the lower classes. The more control the common person had to accept from above, the more he or she took refuge in a defensive cultural traditionalism.

Part Two

The Reform of Popular Culture and Religion

3 How To Be a Counter-Reformation Saint

PETER BURKE

I

A volume concerned with the ideas of the sacred and the profane would hardly be complete without some consideration of those holy people, the saints. In any case, saints are well worth the attention of historians because they are cultural indicators. Like other heroes, they reflect the values of the culture which sees them in a heroic light. As Western culture has changed over time, so have the kinds of people reverenced as saints: martyrs, ascetics, bishops, and so on. To complicate the story, the way in which saints are created has itself changed over the long term. It has always been the outcome of some sort of interaction between clergy and laity, centre and periphery, learned culture and popular culture, but at various times the balance of forces has shifted towards the centre. One of the periods in which this happened was the Counter-Reformation.

In the early church, sanctity was essentially an unofficial phenomenon, as it still is in Islam.[1] Some people became the object of cults after their deaths, and some of these cults spread outside their original locations. However, the process of saint-making gradually became more formal and more centralised. At the end of the eleventh century Pope Urban II emphasised the need for witnesses to the virtues and miracles of candidates for sanctity. In the thirteenth century Gregory IX formalised the rules of procedure in cases of canonisation. It was the same Gregory IX who set up the tribunal of the Inquisition. This was no coincidence: like a good lawyer, Gregory was concerned to define both saints and heretics, the opposite ends of the Christian scale. He used similar legal methods in both instances: trials. The trial for sanctity required witnesses; it required judges; and it required the notorious devil's advocate, the equivalent of counsel for the prosecution.[2]

However, side by side with the formally canonised saints, defined by the centre of religious authority, Rome, there survived informally chosen holy people, whose cult was local not universal and permitted not obligatory. It was a two-tier system, not unlike the dual structure of local and international trade. Holy people are not unique to Christianity. What does appear to be uniquely Christian, though, is the idea that saints are not only extremely virtuous people, but also efficacious mediators with God on behalf of the living; more powerful, more valuable dead than alive. This was, of course, an idea which came under fire at the Reformation. Erasmus, for example, pointed out that the veneration of the saints was 'not a great deal different from the superstitions of the ancients', such as sacrificing to

Hercules or Neptune.[3] Specific saints were identified with characters from classical myth: St George with Perseus, for example (since the cult of St George went back to 'time immemorial', he was exempt from the new strict verification procedures).

These criticisms worried the authorities, as can be seen from the discussion of the question of the saints at one of the last sessions at the Council of Trent. The fathers admitted that there had been abuses. However, the decree which emerged from the discussion reaffirmed the desirability of venerating the images and relics of the saints and of going on pilgrimage to their shrines. St George survived the criticisms of humanists and reformers and was not removed from the calendar till our own day. Changes were made, but they were limited ones.

In the first place, an attempt was made to emend the accepted accounts of the lives of the saints and to replace these accounts with something more reliable, judged by the criteria of humanist historical criticism. The most elaborate and systematic attempt at criticism and emendation was of course the work of the Bollandists in the seventeenth century, but the way had been shown by Erasmus himself in the life of St Jerome prefixed to his edition of Jerome's works.[4]

In the second place, the procedure for admitting new saints was tightened up. The last canonisations under the old regime were those of St Bruno (1514), St Francis de Paul (1519), St Benno and St Antonino of Florence (both 1523). There followed a hiatus of sixty-five years during which no more saints were canonised. It does not seem unreasonable to explain this hiatus in terms of a failure of nerve and to speak of a 'crisis of canonisation' at a time when, as we have seen, the very idea of a saint was under fire. In Lutheran Saxony, the canonisation of St Benno (a local worthy) was mockingly celebrated with a procession in which horses' bones figured as relics.[5] On the other hand, the Protestants developed the cult of their own holy people, notably the martyrs to Catholic persecution.[6] Thus the church authorities were placed in a dilemma. To create saints was to invite mockery, but to refrain from creating them was to yield the initiative in propaganda to the other side. The immediate response of the authorities was to do nothing. It was not until 1588, twenty-five years after the close of the Council of Trent, that saints began to be made again, starting with St Didacus, otherwise known as Diego of Alcala. There were only six formal canonisations in the sixteenth century, but there were twenty-four in the seventeenth century and twenty-nine in the eighteenth.[7]

The revival of saint-making was accompanied by an increase in the central control of the sacred, or of the right to define the sacred. 1588 was not only the year of the elevation of St Didacus but also that of the setting up of the Congregation of Sacred Rites and Ceremonies, a standing committee of cardinals whose responsibilities included canonisations. A treatise of 1610 affirmed that 'the authority to canonise saints belongs to the Roman pontiff alone'.[8] Saint-making procedures were made increasingly strict and formal by Pope Urban VIII in 1625 and 1634. The distinction between saints and the second-class *beati* was made sharper than it had been, and formal beatification was instituted. A fifty-year rule was introduced: in other words, proceedings for canonisation could not begin until fifty years after the death of the candidate for sanctity. This was a break with tradition. Carlo Borromeo, for example, had been canonised only twenty-six years after his death, and Filippo Neri twenty-seven years after (in Filippo's case, the canonisation process began within months of his death). The fifty-year rule was followed by another hiatus: there were no canonisations between 1629 und 1658. The final touches to the new system were added in 1734 by the canon lawyer Prospero Lambertini, later Benedict XIV.[9]

According to this system, sanctity was explicitly defined in terms of the Aristotelian-Thomist concept of a 'heroic' degree of virtue.[10] As for the procedures by which the possessors of this heroic virtue were recognised, they had become more 'bureaucratic', in Max Weber's sense of the term. The distinction between sacred and profane was made sharper than it had been, while recruitment procedures for the saints were made uniform and formal. In the trials for sanctity, the supernatural was defined, graded and labelled with increasing care. There was also an increase in the central control of the sacred, at the expense of local, unofficial, or 'wildcat' devotions. A papal monopoly of saint-making had effectively been declared. At a time of centralising monarchies, the next world was remade in the image of this one.[11]

These changes still did not mean that unofficial saints disappeared altogether, for the new rules were not made retroactive and the status of some individuals remained ambiguous – that of the plague-saint Roche, for example. His cult had spread widely in the later fifteenth century and popes had authorised confraternities and masses in his name. The Venetians made his cult official at the time of the great plague of 1576, during the hiatus in canonisations already discussed. However, this cult was hardly from time immemorial, since Roche had lived in the fourteenth century. He was an awkward case, as the popes recognised. According to the Venetian ambassador, Sixtus V meant 'either to canonise him or to obliterate him' (*o di canonizzarlo o di cancellarlo*), but in fact the pope died without having made his choice. Urban VIII authorised a special mass of St Roche, but even he, who defined so much, did not clear up the ambiguity of this saint's status.[12]

Local cults not only continued but also sprang up. Some were simply premature honours paid to those whose canonisation might reasonably be expected. In Milan, Carlo Borromeo was venerated before his canonisation in 1610, and scenes from his life were displayed in the cathedral. In similar fashion, at Antwerp, Rubens painted scenes of the miracles of Ignatius Loyola and Francis Xavier about 1617, although the two men did not become saints officially until 1622.[13] In 1631 the Venetians instituted an official cult of their former patriarch, Lorenzo Giustinian, who was not canonised until 1690.[14]

Other unofficial saints were less conventional. In Castille, Luisa de Carrión, who died in 1636, was treated as a saint and as a miracle worker at court as well as in popular circles, although the Inquisition accused her of imposture and even witchcraft.[15] In Naples, the fisherman turned rebel

Masaniello was treated as a saint after his murder in summer 1647. The hair of the corpse was torn out for relics; his name was added to the litany (*Sancte Masanalle, ora pro nobis*); there were stories of his miracles and it was believed that he would rise again.[16] Even in Rome itself, unofficial cults could still grow up. In 1648, for example, 'in the monastery of the Quattro Coronati, a nun called Sister Anna Maria died with the reputation of a saint, and her body was exposed to public view for three days'. The Franciscan Carlo da Sezze, who died in 1670, had lived in Rome with the reputation of a saint and was consulted on occasion by Pope Clement IX.[17]

However, people like this who died in the odour of sanctity could not be tried for fifty years, and if they failed, the cult would be suppressed. Many were examined, but few passed. There have been very few studies of the unsuccessful, despite the potential interest and importance of a historical sociology of failure.[18] The remainder of this paper will, therefore, be concerned with the successful, the happy few, the fifty-five individuals canonised between 1588, when the practice was revived, and 1767, which was followed by another hiatus, this time of forty years.[19]

II

That the prosopography of the saints might be of value for an under-standing of Catholic society is no new idea. A number of historians and sociologists have studied the changing social origins and career patterns of the saints as indicators – or even indices – of social and cultural trends.[20] They have pointed out the rise of martyrs in the sixteenth century and the rise of the middle class into sanctity in the eighteenth and nineteenth centuries.[21]

However, these historians and sociologists have not always been sufficiently conscious of a central problem of method, of the need to decide whether to treat the saints as witnesses to the values of the age in which they lived or the age in which they were canonised. In some cases, like those already mentioned of Carlo Borromeo and Filippo Neri, the problem is not acute, because they were canonised so quickly. On the other hand, several Counter-Reformation figures, now venerated as saints, received this title long after their deaths. John Berchmans, for example, died in 1621 and was canonised in 1888, while Peter Canisius died in 1597 but was not canonised until 1925. It is true that biographies of Canisius were published in 1614 and 1616 and that his beatification process lasted over 250 years, but if he is to be included as a Counter-Reformation saint, so should all those whose processes began in the period. They may, after all, be canonised one day. Conversely, among the saints canonised 1588–1767 were eight who died in the fifteenth century, six who died in the fourteenth century, four who died in the thirteenth century and one who died in the twelfth century.

Most students of the saints have assumed that they are witnesses to the age in which they lived. For a historian of mentalities, however, they have to be treated as witnesses to the age in which they were canonised; there is no other justification for confining oneself to this particular formally defined group.[22] It might also be worth looking at saints who were, one might say, 'reactivated' in the period, but since the criteria for reactivation are not likely to be precise, it may be more useful, in this brief sketch, to concentrate on the newly canonised alone, with the fifty-five saints formally canonised between 1588 and 1767. It might have been worth adding the formally beatified, of which there were forty-three between 1662 and 1767 (twenty-four individuals and the collective beatification of the nineteen martyrs of Gorkum).[23] However, sixteen of the individual *beati* were canonised later in our period, so the addition of this group would not affect the conclusions very much.

Since the total 'population' of the saints is so much less than one hundred, precise statistics will be of little use, let alone percentages. In any case, too much emphasis has been placed on 'objective' factors such as social origins and career patterns. As the Belgian sociologist Pierre Delooz has remarked, the saints have to be studied as part of the social history of perception. The objective factors will, therefore, be discussed only briefly here.

What kind of person had the best chance, during the Counter-Reformation, of achieving this particular form of upward mobility? Men had better chances than women: there were forty-three males to twelve females in the group. Italians (twenty-six saints) and Spaniards (seventeen) had better chances than anyone else (twelve altogether, comprising four French, three Poles, two Portuguese, one German, one Czech and one Peruvian). Nobles had better chances of becoming saints than commoners. At least twenty-six of the fifty-five saints were of noble origin, including some from leading families like the Borjas and the Gonzagas, while Elizabeth of Portugal was of royal blood. There is little or no precise information about the social origins of a number of the saints, but at least five were of peasant stock, while two more worked for a time as shepherds (Pascual Baylón and John of God) and one as a ploughman (Isidore). As for the 'middle classes', we know at least that John of the Cross was the son of a silk-weaver, Jean-François Régis the son of a merchant and Filippo Neri the son of a lawyer.

To have a good chance of becoming a saint it was better to be clerical than lay, and much better to be a member of a religious order than one of the secular clergy. Of our fifty-five individuals, only six were members of the laity (Isidore the ploughman, John of God, Francesca Ponziani, Elizabeth (Isabel) of Portugal, Caterina of Genoa and Margherita of Cortona), and of these, Margherita of Cortona was a member of the 'third order' of Franciscans, while John of God is associated with the Brothers Hospitallers and Francesca Ponziani with the Benedictines. Three of the fifty-five were lay brothers, on the margin between the lay and clerical worlds: Pascual Baylón, Felice of Cantalice and Serafino of Montegranaro. The secular clergy account for another eight of the fifty-five, making seventeen altogether who were not full members of religious orders.

Of the thirty-eight remaining saints, the Franciscans have the largest share, with one nun (Caterina of Bologna) and seven friars (Diego of Alcalá, Pedro of Alcántara, Giovanni Capistrano, Giacomo della Marca,

Francisco Solano, Pedro Regalado and Giuseppe of Copertino). Close behind came the Dominicans and the Jesuits. The Dominicans had three nuns (Rose of Lima, Agnese Segni and Caterina de'Ricci), and four friars (Hyacinth (Jacek), Raimondo Peñaforte, Luis Bertrán and Michele Ghislieri, better known as Pope Pius V). There were six Jesuits canonised in the period: Ignatius Loyola, Francis Xavier, Francisco Borja, Aloysius (Luigi) Gonzaga, Stanislas Kostka and Jean-François Régis. Then came the Carmelites, with two nuns (Teresa of Avila and Maria Maddalena de'Pazzi) and two friars (Andrea Corsini and John of the Cross). The Servites had three saints: a nun, Giuliana Falconieri, and two friars, Filippo Benizzi and Pellegrino Laziosi. The Capuchins had two saints, Fidelis of Sigmaringen and Giuseppe of Leonessa, not counting their two lay brothers, Felice and Serafino. The Theatines had two saints, Gaetano of Thiene and Andrea Avellino. There was one Benedictine (Juan of Sahagún), one Augustinian (Tomaso of Villanueva) and four saints who founded their own orders (Camillo de Lelis, Jeanne de Chantal, José de Calasanz and Girolamo Miani).

It is obvious enough that these fifty-five men and women were not a random sample of the Catholic population at large. However, the question remains, why these particular individuals achieved recognition rather than the many people of similar social background. It is not sufficient to say that they possessed 'heroic virtue': it is also necessary to discover who saw them as virtuous. There are two places to look for the answer to this question: at the grass roots, where a particular cult grew up, and at the centre, where it was made official.

To begin with the periphery. Delooz was surely right to view the problem of the saints as essentially one of collective representations, or the social history of perception. Some societies are, as he put it, 'programmed' to perceive sanctity, while others are not.[24] Italy and Spain were clearly programmed in this way. Saints were also perceived in stereotyped ways: there is a relatively small number of saintly roles, or routes to sanctity. It may be useful to draw up a typology and distinguish five main routes or roles.

The first is that of the founder of a religious order. No fewer than twelve out of our fifty-five fall into this class. Francesca Ponziani founded the Benedictine Oblates; Teresa of Avila the strict ('discalced') Carmelites; Ignatius Loyola founded the Jesuits. François de Sales and Jeanne de Chantal between them founded the Visitation nuns. Gaetano of Thiene was one of the founders of the Theatines. Vincent de Paul founded both the Congregation of the Mission and the Daughters of Charity. Camillo de Lelis founded the Camilliani, Girolamo Miani the Somaschi and José de Calasanz the Piarists. Filippo Neri is now regarded as the founder of the Oratorians, although he did not have a formal institution in mind, and, in a similar way, John of God may be described as the 'posthumous founder' of the Brothers Hospitallers.

A second important road to sanctity was that of the missionary. Nine of our fifty-five fall into this class, if we include an organiser of missions, Tomaso of Villanueva. Diego of Alcalá was a missionary in the Canaries;

Raimondo Peñaforte in North Africa; Francis Xavier in the Far East. Luis Bertrán and Francisco Solano both worked in Spanish America, in modern Colombia and in Peru respectively. Jean-François Régis tried to convert the Huguenots of the Cévennes, while Fidelis of Sigmaringen met his death on a mission to the Swiss. Giuseppe of Leonessa worked in Italy as well as outside Europe.

A third route to sanctity was that of charitable activity. There are seven obvious cases in the fifty-five, three women (Elizabeth of Portugal, Margherita of Cortona, Caterina of Genoa) and four men. Vincent de Paul's work among the galley-slaves is famous, and there was also John of God who worked among the sick in Granada; Camillo de Lelis; and José de Calasanz who set up schools for the poor.

A fourth route was that of the pastor, the good shepherd, with seven cases, of which the most famous is surely that of the model bishop of the Counter-Reformation, Carlo Borromeo, with François de Sales, Bishop of 'Geneva' (actually based at Annecy), close behind. The others are Pope Pius V; Turibio, Archbishop of Lima; Patriarch Lorenzo Giustinian; Jan Nepomuk, said to have been murdered for refusing to divulge the secrets of confession; and Tomaso of Villanueva, Archbishop of Valencia, who overlaps with the missionary group.

The fifth and last main route was that of the mystic or ecstatic, subject to trances, levitation, and so on. Again there are seven obvious cases, four women and three men. The women were Teresa of Avila (another overlap), Rose of Lima, Maria Maddalena de'Pazzi and Caterina de'Ricci, while the men were John of the Cross, Pedro Regalado and Giuseppe of Copertino. There were, of course, saints who did not fit any of these categories very well. Aloysius Gonzaga and Stanislas Kostka, for example, who were both Jesuit novices who lived ascetic lives and died young. Jan Kanty was a professor at Cracow. However, the five roles which have just been described seem the most important by far, although some omissions may seem surprising. These Counter-Reformation saints include no theologians, no equivalent of Thomas Aquinas (although Nicholas of Cusa was proposed for canonisation). Equally surprising is the relative lack of martyr-saints, in a period in which many people (some of whom have been canonised subsequently) did die for the Catholic faith, a period which did also reactivate the cult of the martyrs of the early church (encouraged by the discovery of the Roman catacombs at the end of the sixteenth century). Jan Nepomuk and Fidelis of Sigmaringen fall into the martyr category, while the nineteen martyrs of Gorkum, executed by the Calvinists, were beatified in 1675. That other martyrs were unofficially regarded as saints seems likely. A historian of the mission to Japan remarked that 'pour obéir au decret du Pape Urbain VIII, je déclare que s'il m'arrive de qualifier de Saints et de Martyrs ceux qui ont souffert la mort dans le Japon, je ne prétends point prévenir le jugement du Saint Siège: mais j'entends par le nom de Saints, des personnes signalées en vertu ...'[25] Was this a case of reluctant obedience?

The clustering of our fifty-five saints around five roles suggests that a key factor in the imputation of sanctity to an individual is the 'fit' between his or her career and the best-known stereotypes of sanctity. The process is, of course, circular or self-confirming. There are few lay saints, for example, because the stereotypes are biased in favour of the clergy and the stereotypes are biased partly because the clergy form the majority of saints. Individuals are matched with roles. They are perceived as similar to individuals who have already been recognised as saints. In some cases, the later saint consciously modelled himself or herself on an earlier figure. Maria Maddalena de'Pazzi and Rose of Lima are both said to have imitated Catherine of Siena, who was canonised in the fifteenth century. Carlo Borromeo is said to have modelled himself on St Ambrose, his great predecessor as Archbishop of Milan.[26] One may suspect that Filippo Neri, renowned for his gaiety and humility, was perceived as another St Francis; Francisco Borja, general of the Jesuits, as another St Ignatius; Ignatius himself as another St Dominic (another Spaniard who founded an order); and Aloysius Gonzaga, famed for his heroic degree of chastity, as another St Alexis. There were, of course, many lesser imitators of the saints. One of the main reasons for having saints, as the church officially saw it, was to provide models with which the faithful could identify.

In the imputation of sanctity, contiguity was important as well as similarity (or as Roman Jakobson would say, metonymy as well as metaphor).[27] The sacred seems to be contagious. At any rate, we find that Francis Xavier, Filippo Neri, Pius V and Felice of Cantalice were all associated with Ignatius Loyola; Felice of Cantalice, Camillo de Lelis, Maria Maddalena de'Pazzi and Caterina de'Ricci with Filippo Neri; Francisco Borja, Pedro of Alcantara and John of the Cross with Teresa of Avila; Andrea Avellino and Aloysius Gonzaga with Carlo Borromeo.[28]

So much for the growth of cults at the periphery. It remains to try to explain how and why certain cults were adopted by the centre and made official. The 'heroic virtue' of the candidates had to satisfy the examiners. To understand what happened it is not sufficient to study the trials themselves. One needs to remember, for example, that particular popes took a special interest in saint-making – Sixtus V, for example, whose recovery of nerve put the whole process back into motion in 1588; Paul V, who only canonised two saints himself but left five more cases pending, to be completed by Gregory XV; Clement X and Alexander VIII, who canonised five saints apiece; Benedict XIII, who canonised eight in one year; and Benedict XIV, who had written a treatise on the subject.[29] Papal interests also help to explain particular choices. Only one pope, Clement XI, canonised another, Pius V; but regional loyalties were extremely strong. The Roman Paul V canonised the Roman Francesca Ponziani. The Florentine Urban VIII canonised one Florentine, Andrea Corsini, and beatified another, Maria Maddalena de'Pazzi. The Venetian Alexander VIII canonised the Venetian Lorenzo Giustinian. Another Venetian, Clement XIII, canonised one Venetian, Girolamo Miani, and beatified another, Gregorio Barbarigo (who, like the pope, had been Bishop of Padua). In one case a process like the 'old school tie' loyalty seems to have been at work: Benedict XIV, an old pupil of the Somaschi, beatified the order's founder, Girolamo Miani. And Alexander VII, in spite of the fifty-year rule, canonised his old friend François de Sales.

The centre did not simply select from candidates presented by the periphery, but sometimes yielded to pressure. The religious orders were powerful pressure-groups and the high proportion of saints from their ranks has surely to be explained in these terms, among others.[30] Robert Bellarmine, for example, who was strategically placed at Rome, is said to have been responsible for the beatification of his fellow Jesuit, Ignatius. There were also pressures from rulers. If there was a 'Spanish preponderance' in the field of sanctity as in that of international relations, the two phenomena may not be unconnected. The first Counter-Reformation saint, Diego of Alcalà, was canonised following pressure from Philip II. Philip III pressed for Raimondo Peñaforte, Isidore and Carlo Borromeo. The bull canonising Ignatius refers to requests from both Philip II and Philip III.[31] Sigismund of Poland pressed successfully for the canonisation of Hyacinth and Louis XIII for Caterina of Genoa. Henri IV, Ferdinand II and Maximilian of Bavaria were other rulers who tried to exert pressure on behalf of particular candidates. As for Andrea Corsini, his case was urged by an alliance of his order, the Carmelites, the ruler of the region he came from, Tuscany, and his family.[32] For family pressure must not be forgotten: it was to the advantage of Carlo Borromeo that he had his nephew and successor, Federigo, to plead for him. Foreign visitors to Italy, including Burnet and Montesquieu, picked up gossip about Italian noble families paying large sums to have relatives canonised. 100,000 crowns was a figure quoted for Carlo Borromeo and 180,000 crowns for Andrea Corsini.[33]

Such stories do not have to be taken too literally. Suffice it to say, pending further research, that it is impossible to explain the achievement of sanctity entirely in terms of the qualities of the individual, or even by the qualities which the witnesses saw in each individual. The imputation of sainthood, like its converse, the imputation of heresy or witchcraft, should be seen as a process of interaction or 'negotiation' between centre and periphery, each with its own definition of the situation.[34] This process involved the official management of unofficial cults, which were, like religious visions, sometimes confirmed and sometimes suppressed.[35] It also involved the implantation of official cults in parts of the periphery other than the region where they first sprang up. The cults of Ignatius Loyola and Francis Xavier, for example, seem to have become part of German Catholic popular culture in the course of the seventeenth and eighteenth centuries, a process which involved their 'folklorisation' or assimilation to earlier local cults. Thus curative properties were now assigned to 'Ignatius water'.[36]

This process of negotiation deserves further study. Enough has been said here, perhaps, to suggest that saints are indeed cultural indicators, a sort of historical litmus paper sensitive to connections between religion and society.

Notes: Chapter 3

I should like to thank the audiences to whom drafts of this paper were read in Cambridge, Warwick and Wolfenbüttel for a number of helpful comments.

1 P. Brown, *The Cult of the Saints* (London, 1981); E. Gellner, *Saints of the Atlas* (London, 1969).

2　M. R. Toynbee, *St. Louis of Toulouse and the Process of Canonisation* (London, 1929); E. W. Kemp, *Canonisation and Authority in the Western Church* (Oxford, 1948); A. Vauchez, *La Sainteté en occident aux derniers siècles du moyen âge* (Rome, 1981).

3　Erasmus, *Enchiridion Militis Christiani*, in J. P. Dolan (ed.), *The Essential Erasmus* (New York, 1964), p. 60.

4　H. Delehaye, *L'Oeuvre des Bollandistes*, 2nd edn (Brussels, 1959); Erasmus's life of Jerome reprinted in his *Opuscula*, ed. W. K. Ferguson (The Hague, 1933).

5　K. H. Blaschke, *Sachsen im Zeitalter der Reformation* (Gütersloh, 1970), p. 116.

6　D. Kelley, *The Beginning of Ideology* (Cambridge, 1981), p. 121n., emphasises Protestant consciousness of this process. S. Bertelli, *Ribelli, libertini e ortodossi* (Florence, 1973), p. 59, emphasises Catholic consciousness of the need to respond.

7　I follow the list compiled by G. Löw from the archives of the Congregation of Rites, given in his article 'Canonizzazione' in *Enciclopedia Cattolica*, 12 vols (Rome, 1948–54). Slightly higher figures are given elsewhere, possibly by adding non-formal canonisations.

8　A. Rocca, *De canonizatione sanctorum* (Rome, 1610), p. 5.

9　P. Lambertini, *De canonisatione* (Rome, 1766). On Urban VIII, as on other popes of the period, the standard work is, of course, L. von Pastor's *Geschichte der Päpste*. The relevant volumes are XXI–XXXVII. I have used the English translation: *History of the Popes* (London, 1932–50). On Sixtus V, Vol. XXI, p. 138; on Clement VIII, Vol. XXIV, pp. 234 ff.; on Paul V, Vol. XXV, pp. 257 ff.; on Gregory XV,, Vol. XXVII, pp. 119 ff.; on Urban VIII, Vol. XXIX, pp. 8 ff.; on Alexander VII, Clement IX and Clement X, Vol. XXXI, pp. 128 ff., 338 ff., 468 ff.; on Alexander VIII, Vol. XXXII, p. 540; on Clement XI, Vol. XXXIII, pp. 343 ff.; on Benedict XIII and Clement XII, Vol. XXXIV, pp. 165 ff., 410 ff.; on Benedict XIV, Vol. XXXV, pp. 312 ff.; on Clement XIII, Vol. XXXVII, pp. 401 ff.

10　R. Hofmann, *Die heroische Tugend* (Munich, 1933); cf. R. De Maio, 'L'ideale eroico nei processi di canonizzazione della Contro-Riforma', *Ricerche di Storia Sociale e Religiosa*, Vol. II (1972), pp. 139–60.

11　For a development of Weber's ideas on religious power and legitimacy which emphasises the interaction between clergy and laity, see P. Bourdieu, 'Une interpretation de la théorie de la religion selon Max Weber', *Archives Européennes de Sociologie*, Vol. XII (1971), pp. 3–21.

12　*Bibliotheca Sanctorum*, 12 vols (Rome, 1961–70), s.v. 'Rocco'. Perhaps the most useful modern work of reference on the lives of saints.

13　R. Wittkower, *Art and Architecture in Italy 1600–1750* (Harmondsworth, 1958), p. 61; J. R. Martin, *The Ceiling Paintings for the Jesuit Church in Antwerp* (London and New York, 1968), pp. 29 ff. I should like to thank David Freedberg for bringing the point about Rubens to my attention.

14　A. Niero, 'I santi padroni', in S. Tramontin *et al.*, *Culto dei santi a Venezia* (Venice, 1965), pp. 77–95.

15　B. Bennassar *et al.*, *L'Inquisition espagnole* (Paris, 1979), p. 200, cf. pp. 208–9 and also W. Christian, *Local Religion in Sixteenth-Century Spain* (Princeton, NJ, 1981), p. 133.

16　Details and references in a forthcoming article in *Past and Present* by P. Burke, 'The Virgin of the Carmine and the Revolt of Masaniello'.

17　G. Gigli, *Diario romano* (1608–70), ed. G. Ricciotti (Rome, 1958), p. 311.

18　An exception: L. Ciamitti, 'Una santa di meno', *Quaderni Storici*, Vol. XLI (1979). In the same issue J. M. Sallmann, 'Il santo e le rappresentazioni di santità', notes the existence of about a hundred unsuccessful candidates in the Kingdom of Naples between 1550 and 1800.

19　For a full list from 1594 on, see Löw, 'Canonizzazione', cited n. 7 above.

20　G. G. Coulton, *The Medieval Village* (Cambridge, 1925), appendix 32; P. A. Sorokin, *Altruistic Love* (Boston, Mass., 1950), pt 2; K. George and C. H. George, 'Roman Catholic sainthood and social status', *Journal of Religion*, Vol. V (1953–4), reprinted in R. Bendix and S. M. Lipset (eds), *Class Status and Power*, 2nd edn (Glencoe, Ill., 1967), pp. 394–401; P. Delooz, *Sociologie et canonisations* (Liège and The Hague, 1969); D. Weinstein and R. M. Bell, 'Saints and society', *Memorie Domenicane* (1973); M. Goodich, 'A profile of thirteenth-century sainthood', *Comparative Studies in Society and History*, Vol. XVIII (1976), pp. 429–37; Vauchez, *La Sainteté en occident*;

W. O. Chadwick, *The Popes and European Revolution* (Oxford, 1981), pp. 81 ff. This essay was in proof before I was able to consult D. Weinstein and R. M. Bell, *Saints and Society* (Chicago and London, 1982) and S. Wilson (ed.), *Saints and their Cult* (Cambridge, 1983).

21 These points are made by Sorokin and George.

22 See Delooz (or his contribution in Wilson, ch. 6) and Weinstein and Bell, *Saints and Society*, pt 2.

23 *Enciclopedia Cattolica*, s.v. 'Beatificazione'.

24 Delooz, *Sociologie et canonisations*, p. 179.

25 P. Crasset, *Histoire de l'église du Japon* (Paris, 1715), preface.

26 V. Puccini, *Vita di M. M. Pazzi* (Florence, 1611), p. 1; G. B. Possevino, *Discorsi della vita di Carlo Borromeo* (Rome, 1591), p. 121; A. Valier, *Vita del beato Carlo Borromeo* (Milan, 1602), p. 53.

27 R. Jakobson, 'Two aspects of language', reprinted in his *Selected Writings*, Vol. II (The Hague and Paris, 1971), pp. 239–59.

28 Some of these associations are pointed out by De Maio, 'L' ideale eroico', cited n. 10 above.

29 See Pastor, *Geschichte der Päpste*.

30 Bertelli, *Ribelli*, p. 118. On orders as pressure groups in the late Middle Ages, Vauchez, *La Sainteté en occident*, pp. 131 ff.

31 F. Contelorus, *De canonizatione sanctorum* (Lyons, 1634), pp. 789 ff.

32 S. di S. Silverio, *Vita di S. Andrea Corsini* (Florence, 1683), pp. 54 ff.

33 G. Burnet, *Some Letters* (Amsterdam, 1686), p. 106.

34 On 'negotiation', F. Parkin, *Class Inequality and Political Order* (London, 1971), p. 92; R. Q. Gray, *The Labour Aristocracy of Victorian Edinburgh* (Oxford, 1976), ch. 7.

35 W. Christian, *Apparitions in Late Medieval Spain* (Princeton, NJ, 1981).

36 On 'Ignatius water', *Handwörterbuch des deutschen Aberglaubens*, Vol. IV (Berlin and Leipzig, 1931–2), p. 671. I should like to thank Bob Scribner for drawing my attention to this phenomenon. I have not been able to consult A. Schüller, 'Sankt Franciscus Xavier im Volksglauben', *Zeitschrift des Vereins für Rheinische Volkskunde* (1931), or H. Schauerte, *Die Volkstümliche Heiligenverehrung* (Münster, 1948).

4 Lay Judges and the Acculturation of the Masses (France and the Southern Low Countries, Sixteenth to Eighteenth Centuries)

ROBERT MUCHEMBLED, translated by
John Burke

In a recent study, I proposed that the concept of acculturation be used to describe and explain the immense endeavour by sixteenth- and seventeenth-century social, intellectual, political and religious elites to control and subject the masses in France and the Low Countries.[1] Among the numerous agents of that cultural conquest of the humble, a notable position was occupied by the lay judges. Bearers of an ideology heavily impregnated by Christianity, and in particular by the Counter-Reformation, they exercised acculturising functions in two principal areas: in the first place, they defined law and crime, that is, the Ideal City and the underworld of the outcasts; secondly, they played the role of cultural intermediaries at all levels of a judicial pyramid whose shadow extended more and more over the society of that time.

With the exception of village judges, municipal magistrates, or feudal knights of Flanders or Artois, for example, who came from rural areas and could not always read, sixteenth- and seventeenth-century magistrates partook of a new, almost closed, mental and cultural universe heavily marked by religion and by a sense of order. To be convinced of this, there is no need to undertake a painstaking study of the personnel of parliaments or sovereign courts,[2] nor of the striking personalities of the times – for example, Jean Bodin – nor even of the numerous legal commentators whose work achieved the dignity of print, such as Claude Le Brun De La Rochette's *Les Procès civiles et criminels* (Rouen, 1611).

Humbler magistrates were equally representative, not least in their ordinariness, of a group whose members differed from one another economically, but formed a very homogeneous team in ideological terms.

In effect, lawyers were formed by the universities and were cast in the successive moulds of the trivium, the quadrivium and the law. They were thus clerks by definition, and recorded this fact in codes of moral and religious behaviour which coloured their entire lives. They were also bookmen, eager to read and ready, at the slightest opportunity, to cite juridical works by ancient and modern authors. Consequently, they moved in a world of rules, precepts and sentences. They were unable to avoid fusing their lives and writings. As examples, the manuscript works of two Artesian jurists include a sufficient number of personal commentaries or digressions to enable the historian to understand the authors' ideology.

The first of these is the anonymous editor of a collection of criminal decrees from various courts in Artois in the sixteenth and first third of the seventeenth century.[3] He indicates that about 1616 he was advocate at Aire-sur-la-Lys, *échevin* at Arras and member of the Council of Artois. The second, Pierre Desmasures, Lord of Val Bernard, Bachelor of Law and *procureur général* of the county of Artois, is much better known.[4] He left a manuscript commentary on the *coutume générale* of Artois, which was completed towards 1638, and held authority until the end of the ancien régime,[5] as the many copies of the work demonstrate.

These two jurists, then, both subjects of the Spanish Crown before the French conquest of Artois and contemporaries of one another, were privileged witnesses to the 'Golden Age' of Catholicism in the southern Low Countries. They saw the Counter-Reformation develop and reaffirm the power of the prince, after the Wars of Religion in the second half of the sixteenth century. At their own level of authority and in areas under their jurisdiction, they recorded and disseminated the dominant ideas which laity and ecclesiastics imposed, in order to avoid contamination by the heretical United Provinces situated so near at hand. They hoped thus to steer clear of another 'revolution' like the one which shattered the unity of the Seventeen Provinces in 1579. Their thoughts, while not always new and original, at least constitute a coherent body, centred around complementary notions of obedience to God and to secular powers.

For Desmasures, who examines the crime of *lèse-majesté*, subjects must honour God, and, after Him, their king 'as the universal father of the country, legitimate prince and natural protector, keeper and guardian of the state and the republic'.[6] While commenting on the crime of larceny, the anonymous jurist makes clear the importance of the relation which exists in his mind and in those of his fellow creatures between God, nature and the powers which govern human society. For there exists a law of nature, which is 'a sovereign reason, situated in nature, which commands us to do good and prevents us from doing evil'. In other words, there is in man a law 'given to him by God to shape his life and form his morals'. Thus, if 'virtue is natural', 'vice is an odious adversary of nature, detestable to the universe'. The anonymous author adds that by misfortune Adam 'let himself be tricked and deceived by the imposture of Satan, principal enemy of nature'. Therefore criminal punishments have been invented. They are necessary, so that those who refuse to obey natural reason 'are constrained by fear of the punishment which the law has ordained for their faults'.[7]

Crimes are linked, according to these lawyers, to vice, the Devil and evil. Because of this, the mission of judges, like those of the king and established authorities, is profoundly moral. The anonymous Artesian then goes on to state 'the office of magistrate is the gift of God, a divinely ordained dignity so that human society may be kept, maintained and guarded in such good order that, all confusion avoided, everyone should be held and maintained in his position'. He adds, with a self-congratulatory flourish, that the magistrate stands in relation to human society as does the sun to the heavenly bodies.[8]

Of course, it is necessary to distinguish between the ideal and the real in reading such professions of faith. It is hardly surprising to find an old jurist, reflecting on the role he has played in society, or would perhaps like to have played, expressing judgements which value that role. But the discourse of Desmasures and his anonymous colleague must retain at least a fragment of truth. Common mental reflexes bound them. They distinguish two worlds, two camps, in the society of their times: one, superior, to which they belonged; the other, inferior, the confinement and control of which was their duty 'by nature'. In fact it is a commonplace that justice in the sixteenth and seventeenth centuries possessed clear class characteristics. A more detailed study, which it is not possible to provide here, would readily prove this. The anonymous author and Desmasures often speak in an offhand manner of their contempt for the 'vile populace', with their vulgar and scandalous morals. And each knows that criminal punishments vary according to many criteria, including the social origin of the culprit. Desmasures, for instance, calls for exemplary punishment in cases of inferiors insulting their superiors, failing which 'by the insolence and irreverence of a man of no substance, a person of quality would be attacked and insulted inopportunely, which would set a bad example'.[9]

In short, sixteenth- and seventeenth-century magistrates considered themselves invested with a quasi-divine mission and applied to human society a dualistic vision of the battle of good and evil, which had been forcefully reaffirmed by the Counter-Reformation. Their acculturising functions with regard to the masses proceeded from their social role and ideology.

The law underwent some important changes from the sixteenth century onwards. The common law (*coutumes*) began to be written down in France and the Low Countries. Criminal law was the object of important reforms, in 1539 and 1670 in France, and in 1570 in the Low Countries. In general, justice, which had been highly diffuse in the Middle Ages, was concentrated on diverse echelons in the hands of the officers of prince or king. A real judicial pyramid, imperfect, it is true, but more and more solid, began to appear. Judges and jurists defined precisely the boundaries of the Ideal City which they were duty-bound to defend against the hordes of besiegers – criminals and deviants of all descriptions. In the social arena, they tirelessly uprooted noxious weeds while defining new types of crime, or rather, reprimanding more ferociously than before certain anomalous modes of behaviour, in particular those pertaining to sexuality and superstition. Equally, the violence of the conflict led them to reinforce their real prestige and to pursue pitilessly any rejection of their authority. In these areas (which moreover were limitless) they worked steadily towards the acculturation of the masses, by spreading fear and making examples of offenders.

Historians of criminality have been much concerned to verify the hypothesis that in the sixteenth and seventeenth centuries crimes of violence decreased as crimes of theft increased. They have been less concerned with two other types of crime distinguished by authors of the early modern period: immorality, and the crime of human and divine *lèse-majesté*. Now at that time legal counsels and commentators were quite obsessed by sexual deviations, which they treated, in long chapters, with a kind of puzzled delectation.[10] As for crimes of *lèse-majesté*, they enabled the worst obsessions of the period to be defined and, by antithesis, they clarified the principal values held by ecclesiastic and lay elites.

It is doubtful whether sixteenth-century people so abruptly liberated themselves from sexual inhibitions that they committed an increasing number of crimes of this type. Nevertheless, the anonymous Artesian cited above devotes nearly a third of his manuscript to the presentation of provincial law on matters of immorality. He distinguishes lewdness, adultery, procuration, polygamy, debauchery ('which deflowers without force ...'), abduction, incest, sodomy, not forgetting hermaphroditism.[11] In fact, what had developed during the Middle Ages was rather repression than the crime itself. Since the Council of Trent, magistrates had become very aware of the problem of sexuality. The anonymous Artesian frequently cites the decrees of this Council. In the chapter he devotes to lewdness, for example, he recalls the prohibition of concubinage, directed at both married and unmarried men; or that prohibiting clerks to 'wallow in the filth of lewdness or in the sour lime of concubinage'. Then he comments:

> it is as feverish and furious a passion as carnal love, and very dangerous to him who lets himself be transported by it, for then where is he? He is no longer in control of himself, his body will undergo a thousand pains in the search for pleasure, his spirit will be racked a thousand times to serve his desire. Growing desire will turn into fury: as it is natural so also is it violent and common to all, whom it deranges by its action, uniting the fool and the wise man, man and beast, negating all wisdom, resolve, prudence, contemplation, and every operation of the soul.[12]

Whether it came from the pen of the anonymous magistrate or whether it had been copied from some literary source, this regular lay sermon against love and pleasure perfectly represents the Tridentine spirit as it issued from judges. The anonymous author makes clear once again that his preference leads to a morality of renunciation. 'Carnal pleasure is unsuitable for human nature', he writes, after having cited in support of his views Cicero and Pierre Charon. In conclusion he emphasises the necessity of knowing how the passions may be restrained, for it is 'an excellent thing to live by thrift, sobriety, temperance and in keeping to a golden mean'.[13]

The morality of the seventeenth-century 'honnête homme' flows from the pen of this jurist, who was directly influenced by the Council of Trent. Regarding debauchery, for example, the anonymous author refers to one of the rulings of the Council which defines lay celibacy as a state superior to marriage. In support of this decree he cites the writings of the Jesuit Théophile Bernardin. Then he personalises the issue: while marriages 'may be good and instituted by God himself, all the same, continence and virginity are more noble and excellent', he writes; and he further claims that such principles have guided his own judicial action, quoting a succession dispute settled by the Council of Artois, in which a testator demanded that his heir take an 'état honorable' to be eligible to inherit. 'In my opinion [*rapport*], it was judged that celibacy is not a favourable state if it is not followed by a simple vow of chastity, and that vow should be made known to people by outward action', he says. Finally, he refers to the works of Jean-Pierre Camus, Bishop of Belley, on marital continence, to conclude in a prophetic tone that 'to lie with a wife and do nothing, that is a miracle!'[14]

This example helps us to understand how and why judges became agents of the acculturation of the masses. The anonymous Artesian, quite as much as Desmasures, is profoundly influenced by the spirit of the Council of Trent. And he performs his office by trying to implement within society the principles of the Counter-Reformation. The chastity he advocates is certainly not part of the norm for the average Christian and rather forms part of the monastic ideal, or the path towards sanctity. Yet, this practitioner of law expounds a fear of sexuality and a repressive intent in this area, which are typical of the sixteenth-century Catholic reform movement. Moreover, he has had opportunities, before various courts in Artois, to drive home the ideas he puts forth. For in the France and Low Countries of his times, justice pursued deviation with regard to sexual norms with a new rigour. Were not polygamists hanged in France, whereas in the past it had been considered sufficient to have them lashed and sent home with bedposts hung from their girdles? The anonymous Artesian adds that he has seen the latter penalty still practised in Artois in 1608.[15] As for Desmasures, regarding adultery he distinguishes between people of 'condition honneste' in Artois, who must pay a fine and make honourable reparation, and 'personnes viles et abjectes', who are thrashed and banned from the county.[16] Similarly, he also draws our attention to the increased sexual repression, which, as in France, expressed itself in the growing severity of the judgements passed on infanticidal mothers, who in theory were liable for the death penalty, or in the condemnation to degrading penalties of married men who frequented prostitutes. Numerous other examples could be given. A remark of Desmasures suffices to exemplify the evolution. He recounts that before the Council of Trent a public brothel, controlled by a kind of municipal officer called King of the Debauched, was tolerated at Arras. Since then, it had officially been closed.[17]

The judges therefore played an important role in the application of Tridentine ideology to society and in particular to the masses. Proof of this might be brought with regard to the example of the poor and the vagabonds, who had no place in a world ruled by a work ethic more constraining than hitherto, and who had become fair game for police and justice.[18] In the same way, the battle against superstition and sorcery provides evidence of the scope of the acculturation of the masses in the sixteenth and seventeenth centuries.

Though invented and systematised by churchmen at the end of the Middle Ages, demonology was put to work by lay judges, from the most humble to the most prestigious, fuelling an intense witch hunt from the middle of the sixteenth century onwards. Civil authorities, supported by the courts, endeavoured for more than a century to extirpate the Devil and his accomplices. Hundreds were burned at the stake in France and the Low Countries. And as I have shown in detail elsewhere,[19] magistrates inculcated in the masses, and particularly in the peasants, a veritable pedagogy of fear, the better to separate them from their ancestral superstitions. In other words, lawyers, who were keenly conscious of the importance of their mission to defend Christianity, were seen by all contemporary witnesses of this confrontation as establishing the frontier between good and evil. Thus they transmitted the teaching of priests, and all the effort of the Counter-Reformation, directed at transforming the often polytheist and animist rural people into Tridentine Catholics. By defining precisely the diabolic figure, the elites were able much more efficiently to force those they governed to obey a terrible and vengeful God, who alone could help human beings triumph over the Devil.[20]

The battle against popular superstition occupied an important place among the preoccupations of the magistrates, and condemnations for witchcraft, which remained rare compared to the total number of crimes prosecuted, were its most spectacular form. However, lay judges frequently had occasion to deal severely with less flagrant but everyday offences among the people, such as belief in diviners and faith healers, abuse of relics or amulets, erroneous opinions, blasphemies, sacrileges, and heterodox pursuits, such as the flagellation of the statue of a saint who had not granted what was asked of him. In these seemingly trivial matters the magistrates patiently and painstakingly wove a new popular morality. The exemplary character of the penalties provides us with the main evidence in this respect. Once again, justice joined in pedagogy of the masses. Blasphemy, for example, was pursued more and more. In the Low Countries, a public notice of 5 October 1531 dealt with graduated punishments for relapses. The anonymous Artesian, a century later, notes that 'it seems that this penalty was remitted at the judge's discretion, who punished this offence more or less severely according to the circumstances'.[21] He then enumerates many examples and describes diverse punishments: making public reparation, being put in the pillory, carrying a cask, having the tongue cut out, being exposed with a notice defining the crime committed, being imprisoned with a diet of bread and water, being branded with a red-hot iron, banishment, and so on.

Blasphemy was included, like sacrilege and witchcraft, among crimes of *lèse-majesté* against God. In their rigorous persecution of it, the courts worked for a change in popular behaviour. Applying the rulings of political and religious authorities, they tried by coercion and by setting examples to impose on the masses new languages and attitudes. Desmasures expresses it well when he comments on a royal ruling of 1554 which was not directed at blasphemies, but only 'scandalous and very vulgar terms among the simple populace, like *bougre* ... *wuyot* [cuckold] or *conard, mort Dieu* ... scandalous and damaging to the honour of others, which should be banned in all properly-policed states', more especially since these words give a bad example to children.[22]

Lawyers of the sixteenth and seventeenth centuries bore within them the vision of an Ideal City which embodied the decrees of the Council of Trent. Like the ruling secular and ecclesiastical authorities of their time, they considered this City to be besieged by the Devil, heretics and deviants. They consciously participated in its defence. In addition, they felt themselves charged simultaneously with the elimination of perils, the extermination of witches and inveterate criminals, and the inculcation of their own ideals, or at least such of them as the masses could retain, in the superstitious and backward populace. The sword of justice therefore eliminated those beyond recovery. It was raised menacingly over deviants, to order them to get back into step, after a reparation, a penitence, a degrading penalty, or a fine had been imposed on them. In this second case, magistrates became cultural intermediaries between the elites and the masses, for they helped the former to dominate the latter.

The consolidation of the judicial pyramid was reinforced in the early modern period by an increase in the magistrates' prestige. The majesty of their offices was made apparent in various ways: by the robes in which they appeared, the position they occupied in processions or triumphal entries, the deference which they exacted from the populace. Indeed, members of the great courts of justice privately considered that they took part in sacred rites while partaking of power, since 'the office of magistrate is a gift of God', as the anonymous Artesian says, adding that 'power is granted only to magistrates to punish delinquents'.[23] The interminable list of sentences given by the same writer covering resistance, outrages, or insults against judges or officers shows that the whole profession wished to place itself above the ordinary run of mortals: any violence directed towards the person of a magistrate had to be more severely punished than that committed against an ordinary person. Consequently the humble sergeant of a prison, as well as the counsellor of a sovereign court, took part in this 'sacramentalising' of justice. The phenomenon is also to be explained, in a period when police forces were few, by the need to protect lawyers from the often brutal reactions of the population. Fear of a particularly rigorous punishment for attacking officers and judges dissuaded many individuals from taking the risk. But this deterrent was only partially successful, for legal commentators recited long litanies of more or less serious transgressions: a fruit-seller of Arras, who had slandered the municipal office of the *Petit Marché* simply by saying she 'would have nothing to do with Messieurs', was condemned by the *échevins*, on 3 August 1580, to make an honourable reparation and pay a fine. This was combined with the threat of banishment and the lash in case of relapse.[24]

The rift which opened up progressively in the sixteenth and seventeenth centuries between the magistrates and the population they administered recalls that which at the same time grew up between the *curé* and his flock. Indeed, the Council of Trent had made priests distinguish themselves from the faithful by wearing vestments, practising celibacy and following a certain mode of life. Fundamentally, though, this retreat away from the ordinary world in both cases allowed the institutions and individuals concerned to assume the role of cultural intermediaries, authoritarian messengers of the civilisation of the elites and the written word among the mostly illiterate rural and urban masses.

There were, however, in the sixteenth and seventeenth centuries *curés* as little educated as their faithful, and subordinate judges unable to write: at Bouvignies (Nord) in 1679, eight of the twenty feudal knights of the barony, that is, 40 per cent, made a cross to mark their names at the foot of procedural documents.[25] Among them figures the lieutenant of the village! Such men continued to belong to a popular and oral culture, especially since their mode of life was not always distinct from that of their fellow countrymen. They played an acculturising role none the less. In fact, priests were more and more controlled by the ecclesiastical hierarchy. As for subordinate judges, they assimilated the new values of the elites and the law they were charged with applying in diverse ways, for the general tendency – which was a little further advanced in the Low Countries than in France – was towards a tightening of the bonds between subordinate judges and superior courts. The Council of Artois, for example, created by Charles V, gradually came to control the jurisdictions of the entire county, including the powerful *échevinage* of the city of Arras. In short, the impulse towards organisation and hierarchy resulted in a weakening of ecclesiastical, municipal and seignorial power in face of the advancement of that of the king.[26] In these circumstances, royal officers controlled less educated village judges more and more effectively. This development was completed during the reign of Louis XIV. Henceforth, subordinate courts, in France as well as in recently conquered Flanders, had to ask the opinion of superior jurisdictions at each important stage of proceedings and were not permitted to use torture without authorisation.

The example of Bouvignies in 1679 illustrates the phenomenon and explains how the spirit of the elites was communicated to local judges. The six witchcraft trials which took place at that time were the occasion of constant to-ing and fro-ing between the village halls of justice and the jurists of Douai. The civic legal experts gradually explained to their ignorant rural colleagues the finer points of demonology. They clearly urged them to deal severely, while hitherto country magistrates had been content with seeking out evil practices and superstitions, which perhaps would not have led the accused to the stake. A painstaking study of these trials shows that a consensus finally evolved between the legal experts of Douai, who preached the greatest severity, the village judges, who eventually profited from the trials, and the inhabitants, who came to give evidence against witches so that they might be clearly distinguished from them.[27]

In summary, the feudal knights of Bouvignies took part in the work of purifying their community and, in the general sense of the term, educating their fellow countrymen. They enabled Tridentine morality and religion to triumph over rural superstition and the Devil. Like the purifying flames of the stakes, they served as links between the world of the elites and that of the masses. And it matters little that a certain number among them did not know how to read: did they not learn the law and their craft by presiding at their courts, listening to the opinions of the Douai jurists being read, discussing demonology or how to obtain confessions?

All magistrates, even the most humble, took part in the battle against the paganism of the masses. The judicial pyramid cast a shadow ever more vast and ever more menacing over the society of the time. The repression of crime turned towards a tight control of popular behaviour. Lay judges at all levels were on the look-out for religious and moral deviations, ranging from the most trivial, like blasphemy, to the most terrifying, like witchcraft. They thus worked for the establishment of new mechanisms of power based on the submission of souls and of the body.[28]

Who better than judges, in effect, to bring royal power down on the bodies of the tortured and condemned? The theses of Michel Foucault on the judicial-political function of torment, which enabled power to retemper itself and affirm its omnipotence, find an echo in the manuscript work of the anonymous Artesian. Concerning larceny, this seventeenth-century magistrate says that he has often seen ear-cropping practised. He gravely inquires why this penalty is imposed. Hippocrates gives him a reason: he claims that severing the veins behind the ear prevents reproduction. The anonymous writer comments: 'the ears of thieves are cut to prevent them breeding and to extinguish their progeny'. He adds other ideas to this: 'There is nothing more subject to disdain than a man who has lost one or both his ears and it is the greatest affront which could be made to him.' Besides, according to certain writers, 'to pull off an ear, is to have punished and maimed the entire body'.[29] Here are added to the notion of exemplary penalties those of shame and ignominy. In the final analysis, the culprit is denied legitimate possession of his body. Justice, and therefore the king who is its source, constrains and beats the body at its own whim. Proof is thus given that justice retains absolute control, and it even appears that this includes the possibility, if Hippocrates is right, of limiting crime by extinguishing progeny.

As bearers of the ideology of the Counter-Reformation and of absolutism, lay judges played a leading role in the acculturation of the rural and urban masses in the sixteenth and seventeenth centuries. Their discourses and their attitudes to criminals indicate a social ideal which recalls the monastic model and still more that offered by the Society of Jesus. Chastity, repression of sexual deviance, a sense of restraint and the refusal to be led astray by excessive passions, the necessity for everyone to keep his or her place in the divine plan of organisation of the universe, must, according to them, guide the steps of the 'honnête homme'. It is clear that magistrates thought of themselves as the privileged defenders of a besieged city. Reality taught them that the masses could not easily attain to the social, moral and religious ideal which they defended, but at least it was possible to encourage them to approximate to it. For that purpose it was necessary to constrain the body, put souls under submission, be vigilant in the defence of Christianity against the Devil and his henchmen – in a word, to supervise and tightly control the ordinary world.

The judges of the sixteenth and seventeenth centuries were laymen only in appearance. Their person, their ideology and their actions linked them with the missionaries of the Catholic Counter-Reformation. They belonged to the shock troops charged with inculcating a new definition of the sacred in the polytheist and animist masses, a new definition of authority and obedience. They took an active part in the vast offensive led by the elites against popular culture.

Notes: Chapter 4

1   R. Muchembled, *Culture populaire et culture des élites dans la France moderne (XVe– XVIIIe siècle). Essai* (Paris, 1978).
2   Among recent works: Ph. Sueur, *Le Conseil provincial d'Artois (1640–1790)*, Arras, Comm. Départmentale des Monuments Historiques, Vol. I (= only vol. publ.) (Arras, 1978).
3   Bibliothèque Municipale de Lille (hereafter: BML), MS 380, Receuil d'affaires criminelles, 336pp.
4   E. Fournier, 'La personne et l'oeuvre de Pierre Desmasures, jurisconsulte artésien du XVIIe siècle', *Bull. de la Soc. d'Etudes de la Province de Cambrai* (May–June 1934).
5   BML, MS 510, eighteenth-century copy of Desmasures, *Livre VI*: 'Remarques et observations ... sur la coutume generale d'Artois ...'
6   ibid., fol. 2318 r.
7   BML, MS 380, pp. 49–50.
8   ibid., p. 90.
9   BML, MS 510, fols 2318 r and 2527 v – 2528 r.
10 See, for example, Claude Le Brun de la Rochette, *Les Procès civiles et criminels, divisé en cinq livres* (Rouen, 1611), and the manuscripts cited above, nn. 3 and 5.
11 BML, MS 380, pp. 171–290 (qualified homicide, pp. 44–7, and larceny, pp. 48–73).
12 ibid., pp. 175–6, 178.
13 ibid., p. 185.
14 ibid., pp. 252–5.
15 ibid., pp. 241–2.
16 BML, MS 510, fol. 2452 v.
17 ibid., fols 2479 v – 2480 r – v.
18 See J.-P. Gutton, *La Société et les pauvres en Europe (XVIe–XVIIIe siècles)* (Paris, 1974).
19 R. Muchembled, *La Sorcière au village (XVe–XVIIIe siècle)* (Paris, 1979); and my contribution to M.-S. Bouchat, W. Frijhoff and R. Muchembled, *Prophètes et sorciers dans les Pay-Bas, XVIe–XVIIIe siècle* (Paris, 1978).
20 See J. Delumeau, *La Peur en occident, XIVe–XVIIIe siècles: Une cité assiégée* (Paris, 1978).
21 BML, MS 380, p. 312.
22 BML, MS 510, fols 2317 v – 2318 r.
23 BML, MS 380, pp. 90, 127.
24 ibid., p. 139.
25 R. Muchembled, *Les Derniers Bûchers: Un village de Flandre et ses sorcières sous Louis XIV* (Paris, 1981), table 8, pp. 270–1.
26 Y. Bongert, *Le Droit pénal français de la fin du XVe siècle à l'ordonnance criminelle de 1670*, Paris, Les cours de droit, 2 vols (Paris, 1972–3).
27 Muchembled, *Les Derniers Bûchers,* notably pp. 53–76.
28 Muchembled, *Culture populaire*, pp. 229 ff.
29 ibid., pp. 247 ff. and BML, MS 380, pp. 57–8.

5 Against the Acculturation Thesis

JEAN WIRTH, translated by John Burke

In 1910 the French sociologist Lucien Lévy-Bruhl published *Les Fonctions mentales dans les sociétés inférieures*, and in 1922 *La Mentalité primitive*. The concept of *mentalité* which these books introduced very swiftly came in for criticism, in particular from Marcel Mauss.[1] As early as 1913 Lévy-Bruhl regretted the use of this vague and equivocal expression, as also the equally unfortunate use of 'primitive'. His notebooks, published in 1949, show that eventually he himself recognised the identity of mental structures in all known societies. But the harm had been done; though anthropologists became more prudent, historians threw themselves at this fashionable word. Half a century later it remains characteristic of the so-called *Nouvelle Histoire*.

From 1965 onwards French historians borrowed, at first timidly, another long word from anthropologists, acculturation, and I fear it will have as brilliant and controversial a career as that enjoyed by *mentalité*. The term acculturation appears in American anthropological literature about 1880.[2] It indicates, in an imprecise manner, phenomena of cultural contact and exchange. If it is usual to make use of a neologism to indicate a still badly defined phenomenon, it is less usual for a word usage to develop without it being satisfactorily defined. In 1904 the *Century Dictionary and Encyclopaedia* defined acculturation as 'the process of adoption and assimilation of foreign cultural elements'. This definition would be acceptable if phenomena of well-delimited exchange were studied under the name of acculturation, such as the introduction of coffee or tobacco to Europe, but that is not what it concerns. The concept serves on the contrary to account for cultural changes in so-called primitive societies in contact with whites. A degree of blindness is required to describe the 'acculturation' of American Indians in terms of cultural exchange.

In 1936 Redfield, Linton and Herskovits drew up a memorandum to reactivate acculturation studies and proposed a new definition of the concept: 'Acculturation comprehends those phenomena which result when groups of individuals having different cultures come into continuous first-hand contact, with subsequent changes in the original cultural patterns of either or both groups.'[3] The expression 'groups of individuals' is a revealing one: it excludes all attempts at distinction between the changes which affect, for example, the personnel of an embassy, immigrant workers, or an ethnic group on the way to extermination. In the 1950s a reaction finally took place against this, in a Europe faced with very different realities made evident by the struggles of decolonisation. Gluckmann in England,

Balandier in France, but also a political figure like Franz Fanon, who fought in the FLN and became Algerian, were to bring to the forefront the economic, social and political situation in which changes, that is to say colonisation, occurred.[4] The discussion of the concept of acculturation thus reached a new stage. Certain individuals, such as Balandier, preferred not to use it any longer; others, for example, Bastide, used it cautiously. While this alteration was taking place, the word acculturation became known to the public and came to tickle the ears of historians. In 1965 the Committee of French Historians placed the theme in the programme of the Congrès International des Sciences Historiques in Vienna.[5] Alfonse Dupront introduced the series of talks by discussing the history of the word and its possible application for historians. Although his paper was more remarkable for its enthusiasm than its caution, it never occurred to him for a moment to style as acculturation the internal evolution of a society.

Today, the fact of an acculturation of the Western 'masses' by their 'elites' is on the way to becoming a commonplace, patronised by French historians of renown, particularly Pierre Chaunu, Jean Delumeau and Robert Muchembled. The acculturised masses would be first of all the peasants, then, up to a certain point, townsmen. The term 'elites' is to be understood to mean intellectuals and the upper classes. Speaking of the disappearance of an ecclesiastical 'magic' at the beginning of the modern period, Muchembled considers that 'this mutation stems evidently from the activity of intellectual and religious elites, which is to say, from the upper strata of society'.[6] For his part, Chaunu stresses the role of reformers and attributes more or less 'acculturising' enterprises to them.[7] Delumeau speaks of a 'new and growing willingness to "acculturise" which existed among the elites' at the beginning of the modern period. According to him, 'forceful attempts were made to introduce the religious and moral framework of an austere Christianity into populations — too often recalcitrant to this rigorous order'. He explains the 'general falling into step' in terms of a 'great cultural fear' and a 'lack of ontological security'.[8]

This approach does not seem to stem from a preoccupation with the notion of culture. Far from defining culture as a global manifestation of a society, these historians tend rather to see in it the comportment of a group of individuals, in as much as it distinguishes itself from another group of individuals. I speak of a 'group of individuals' because I do not know whether for these authors the elites in question constitute a social class. The elites act on the masses to acculturise them by means of education, which is to say, instruction and preaching, but also by repression, that is, the proscription of manifestations of popular culture, and punishment. In actuality, acculturation is carried out on sexual life, magic and religion, festivities and language.

Judgements on the phenomenon vary. It undoubtedly arouses more antipathy in Muchembled, who seems to argue for less damaging forms of cultural evolution, than in Chaunu. In *La Peur en occident*, Delumeau explicitly seeks to delimit the church's responsibilities. On the other hand, these researches set out from a common presupposition: the elites possessed a learned culture, perhaps inherited from the Middle Ages, and sought to impose it on the rest of society. According to Muchembled, 'two very different worlds, very separate mentally from one another, joined and interpenetrated, with all the traumatic effects which hence resulted'.[9] This point of view seems to me especially questionable, since it is concerned with explaining the disappearance of wholly trans-social phenomena, like ecclesiastical 'magic' and festivals. In fact, the existence of these phenomena presupposes the participation of disparate social groups. It is difficult to consider ecclesiastical benedictions or liturgical dances as manifestations of a popular culture separated from clerical culture. For them to disappear, it is necessary and sufficient that one group refuse contact, which is precisely the opposite of acculturation.

However, the acculturation thesis does not always assume an imaginary zero point where two separate cultures ignore each other in the middle of the same society. This thesis rather suggests that the elites escape ancestral traditions sooner, adopt a critical point of view vis-à-vis these traditions, then impose it. This view is not entirely without foundation, since those who react most quickly are thus designated elites, in the same way that the man who generally draws first is considered a crack shot. Sometimes, too, the elites overshoot the mark, wishing to acculturise too much at once, and must then confront resistance by popular mentalities and social tensions. Here the acculturising reformers of Chaunu come into view. The problem is then to discover whether there was such antagonism between an avant-garde elite of reformers and the traumatised masses. This leads us to examine more closely the conditions in which religious change unfolds. I have chosen for this purpose two examples, one taken from Muchembled, the other from Chaunu, for it is by these authors that the acculturation thesis is presented in the most elaborate and systematic manner.

In *Culture populaire et culture des élites*, Muchembled describes French popular culture at the end of the Middle Ages and studies its progressive disappearance.[10] What he terms popular culture could elsewhere simply be called culture, for the sexual, medical, magical, religious and festive practices which he describes concern the entire society, with, of course, differences of emphasis. The most important of these differences could well be that between rural and urban cultures. This distinction appears quite pertinent, notably in the matter of festivities. One could, if one wished, accept the expression 'popular culture' if by that were understood a culture in which dominated social classes participated.

Difficulties begin with the study of its disappearance. The elites progressively took from the people their festivities, magic and religion. The two principal agents of this acculturation were church and state. But it is difficult to see which social classes controlled these institutions, or rather, which social relations brought about changes. Here is an imprecision which could give rise to misunderstandings. I would like to give an example of this.

To illustrate the action of preachers against popular culture, Muchembled borrows from the chronicler Enguerrand de Monstrelet the story of the Carmelite Thomas Conecte who traversed Flanders in 1428–9.[11] Since few 'acculturising' preachers in fifteenth-century Flanders are known to us, the example deserves attention. At first sight the case is clear: Conecte attacks eccentric modes of dress, immorality and gaming. But let us take a closer look at Monstrelet's text.

When the Carmelite entered a town, his triumphal entry was organised by the authorities, which might in fact suggest the anti-popular character of his preaching. 'Nobles, bourgeois and other notable persons of towns where he was would make certain that a well-boarded, great wooden scaffold was erected for him in the most suitable place', says Monstrelet. However, he did not preach against the *menu peuple* – far from it. His first target was the eccentric appearance of high society women; he pursued with a fanatical hatred those high coiffures with a train then in fashion, the so-called *hennins*. Not content with slating them, he encouraged young children to pull on the trains. The drollery and the festive character of such a sermon can be imagined. Ridiculed by this unsympathetic treatment, but meanwhile wishing to participate in the festivity, these ladies adopted, for the occasion, the austere coiffes of the Beguines, 'imitating a snail, which, when one passes close to it, draws in its feelers', says Monstrelet. Of course, when Conecte left, the feelers began to emerge again. After the sermon, the Carmelite also burned games on a bonfire, which recalls the action of Savonarola at the end of the century. The comparison, as we shall see, is not far-fetched.

Directed as it was against the dominant classes, the preaching of Conecte was by no means unpopular. 'By the blasphemies which he would commonly pronounce, in particular against nobles and persons of the church, he acquired great love and renown from all people in all the countries he went in, and was by them most honoured and exalted', says Monstrelet. He acted rather as a tribune of the people who, again according to Monstrelet, 'made many speeches in praise of the common people'. The lay rulers did nothing against him, but received him sumptuously, perhaps to avoid a riot. On the other hand, churchmen detested him.

Muchembled omits the end of the story. In 1432 Conecte made his way to Rome. The pope invited him to preach before him and his refusal to do so led to his arrest. He was brought before the cardinals who declared him a heretic and sent him to the stake. If one wishes to present the cultural changes of the period entirely in terms of acculturation, then one must admit that the Carmelite, allied to the masses, sought to acculturise ecclesiastical and noble elites.

The example is significant, because it allows us to locate the themes of religious controversy. More precisely, the preaching of Conecte, as described by Monstrelet, presents the theme of polemic against sumptuary extravagance which is otherwise encountered only intermittently, together with a well-nigh universal theme, anticlerical polemic. It lacks one essential trait of contemporary heresy: attacks on ecclesiastical 'magic' or, if one prefers, on the pretensions of the church to supernatural power.

There is virtually no trace of the battle against the sumptuary practices of nobility and patriciate in what is known about heretical teaching in the fifteenth-century Low Countries.[12] Moreover, a glance at the paintings of the period shows that over the century costumes inspired by those of the court disappeared, especially the *hennins* which were replaced by white coiffes, elegant but chaste. Towards 1500, in the work of Quentin Matsys, for example, *hennins* have become an element of caricature in pictures like the *Ugly Countess* (in the National Gallery in London). Conecte doubtless did not run any great risk in preaching against *hennins*. The common people were for him; so also, very probably, were the bourgeoisie, while the ecclesiastical authorities remained outside the conflict.

The fight against games seems to me to be part of the same attack on the nobility. Games, like dances, were not, of course, the prerogative of nobles, but they were symbolically linked to the noble mode of life, as in the engravings of Israel van Meckenem at the end of the century. Other social classes, in an attempt to isolate and bring pressure on the nobility, were willing to undergo at least temporary conversion to a puritan attitude. This explains the autos-da-fe which were inspired, in a revolutionary context, by the piper of Niklashausen, and the success of Savonarola at Florence which was achieved with techniques identical to those of Conecte, including the use of children as police.

Anticlericalism is the second major theme of Thomas Conecte. By the exaltation of poverty and the imitation of Christ it is linked to the former theme. The Carmelite, accompanied by his disciples, made his entry into towns seated on an ass. He refused money as remuneration, which seems to have been an indirect reproof of simoniacal priests. Such criticism was also a result of his puritanism. The only explicitly anticlerical grievance in Monstrelet's account concerns the taking of concubines by priests. Like the condemnation of the noble way of life, condemnation of the immorality of priests constitutes a typical example of puritanism. Conecte placed a cordon between the men and women among his listeners to avoid all contact between the sexes during the sermon.

Even a brief perusal of the *Corpus Inquisitionis Neerlandicae* reveals that anticlericalism, represented by attacks against simony and clerical immorality, constitutes an essential theme.[13] From the *Corpus* I have extracted forty-one cases, for the period 1400–1520, in which the nature of the heresy appears clearly.[14] Twenty-one of these cases comprise attacks against priests, nearly always against the secular clergy. In fact, it is necessary to ask oneself whether practically all heretics were not primarily anticlericals, for unorthodox views on the sacraments, confession, indulgences, or relics strongly called into question the power and pretensions of priests.

The attacks on *curés* are common coin in the preaching of the Franciscans, Augustinians and Carmelites. These latter knew how seductive such attitudes were to the people and sought in this way to substitute themselves for the secular clergy in the distribution of the sacrament and confession. Here again, it would seem truly paradoxical to speak of an acculturising theme. On the other hand, this type of preaching could degenerate into an attack on ecclesiastical practices. In effect, three stages can be discerned which led from anticlericalism to the most grave doctrinal errors:

(1)   To attack simony and the taking of concubines by priests is not, strictly

speaking, heretical. It was considered 'injuriosus' or 'seditiosus' by inquisitors.

(2) To preach that the distribution of the sacrament by a priest in a state of mortal sin is without value. This time, one fell into doctrinal error.

(3) To deny completely the efficacy of sacraments, the intercession of saints, pilgrimages, or indulgences. It was this which constituted the attack on ecclesiastical 'magic'.

Of the forty-one cases, twenty-three can be placed in the third category. Ecclesiastics are implicated in seven of them. Lay persons, mostly artisans, are implicated in four cases in which details of profession are given. It can be inferred that the majority of heretics, whose status is not specified, were of the common people.

There are reasonable grounds, therefore, for assimilating the attack on ecclesiastical 'magic' to heresy. On the other hand, the religious authorities hardly ever pursued excess in so-called popular piety;[15] I have found only four cases where doctrinal error does not have a secularising effect. These concern a visionary to whom a soul from Purgatory appeared, a monk who claimed the transubstantiation of St John by Christ, a university scholar who attacked the authority of Aristotle on contingencies and a millenarian Franciscan.[16]

It thus seems that the so-called ecclesiastical elites, instead of 'acculturising' other people, defended themselves against those who questioned their functions and practices. Though not the monopoly of the common people this questioning is well represented in the *Corpus*. One may characterise the evolution leading to the religious crisis of the sixteenth century in any way one likes, but it would be difficult to find a less appropriate name for it than acculturation. To use this word would be tantamount to characterising thus all evolution taking place within a culture.

In *Le Temps des Réformes* Pierre Chaunu proposes a sociological interpretation of the implantation of Protestantism.[17] He distinguishes three factors favourable to the Reformation: distance from Rome, widespread literacy and the fragmentation of political power. This leads him to think that the Rhineland corridor, rather than the Saxony of Luther, brought together all the circumstances favourable to this change. Now the Reformation was carried out in almost every other territory. As Chaunu rightly says, it is not the tidal wave of reform which needs explaining, but the fact that it did not submerge everything. Therefore he examines the characteristics of the Lutheran and humanist reforms in order to judge their different ability to succeed.

In Saxony, where the cultural situation was far from being as favourable as it might have been, Luther implemented a moderate 'acculturising' reform, while where the situation was very favourable, humanist reformers appeared who were much more radical due simply to these favourable conditions. Their radicalism progressed through violent acculturation and revolutionary change. 'The humanist reform is elitist and only finds a limited popular response; it is essentially an acculturising reform', says Chaunu.[18] Its excesses led to its failure. As examples of 'acculturising' reformers Chaunu cites Karlstadt, on whom Luther laid hands when he returned from the Wartburg, and Müntzer who perished in the Battle of Frankenhausen, but above all Zwingli.

The most developed portrait of an acculturising reformer is indeed that of Zwingli. He would rely on the support of the dominant classes to impose a rigorous reform: 'Under his influence, the bourgeois authorities in Zürich imposed on the people, without having converted them to the cause, a form of ecclesiastical life which was at odds with their [the people's] traditions and sensibility.'[19] From 17 November 1523 he imposed his *Christian Instruction* by a 'massive recourse to the constraint of a state he controlled well'. Chaunu tries to specify the interaction of social classes: 'In fact, this humanist reform adopted by the "upper middle class" of those who could both read and write and the well-schooled drew the hatred of popular sensibility.'[20] Hence there was a 'counter-current in favour of traditional religion',[21] which Luther knew how to avoid in Saxony.

Chaunu's analysis is attractive, but it rests on three presuppositions, the validity of which must be examined:

(1) the assimilation of humanist to radical reform;
(2) the attribution to humanist reform of supposedly acculturising changes;
(3) the existence of a mass traumatised by these changes which would have accepted neither religious revolution nor political revolt.

Can humanist reform be assimilated to radicalism? The majority of reformers, radicals or not, came at first under the influence of Erasmus, but this influence tended to become muted, to the advantage of that of Luther. By radicals, Chaunu seems to indicate less conservative reforms than Luther. This forms a very large category in which it is necessary to distinguish supporters of orderly evolution, such as Zwingli in Zürich and Bucer in Strasbourg, and supporters of violent action, such as Müntzer, Hubmaier and, to a lesser extent, Karlstadt. To me it seems difficult to attribute their more or less radical positions to the influence of humanism, for that influence was often exercised on people whose religious and political behaviour was the most conservative possible. The Lutheran reform seemed too seditious to numerous humanists, such as Scheurl, Pirckheimer and Peutinger, not to mention the Cardinal Albrecht of Brandenburg.[22] Once the Reformation was under way, support for religious compromise was often drawn from humanist circles – that of Capito in Strasbourg and Melanchthon in Wittenberg, for example. The confusion between humanist and radical reform therefore runs the risk of diverting attention from political and social factors which determined the positions taken by reformers, regardless of their humanist background.

We must now consider whether the reformers, humanists or not, really implemented 'acculturising' changes, in the first place in the transformation of religious ceremony. For the sake of brevity, we will limit discussion to the problem of images, which are generally seen as an essential support of so-called popular piety, but a comparable discussion could as easily be furnished for a problem such as that of the Eucharist.

In Wittenberg, iconoclasm broke out while Luther was in refuge at the Wartburg, whence he returned in the spring of 1522 to calm people's minds. This iconoclasm cannot be blamed on Karlstadt, who disapproved of the tumult and would have liked an orderly evolution.[23] It is rather the Augustinian Gabriel Zwilling who really played the role of leader. The riots began in the autumn of 1521 and the first altar was demolished on 3/4 December. The first publication hostile to images was Karlstadt's pamphlet *Von Abtuhung der Bylder* which came out on 27 January 1522. Luther did not systematise his position until 1525, in *Wider die himmlischen Propheten*.

The situation in Zürich is still more interesting. In 1520 a person originally from the county of Toggenburg was condemned to decapitation for having lacerated a picture representing the crucifixion with the Virgin and St John, blaspheming the while, 'Idols serve for nothing and are no help'.[24] The influence of Zwingli on the iconoclastic movement does not become evident until September 1523.[25] He also preferred an orderly evolution, but was overwhelmed by the iconoclasts. In fact, his influence, like that of Leo Jud, was limited to the realm of theory. Their attacks on the cult of saints served as arguments for the iconoclasts, but they adopted no position on the images themselves. The first pamphlet on the subject was that by Ludwig Hätzer which was approximately contemporary with the troubles of September, so that it is difficult to say whether it helped to provoke them. Zwingli did not systematise his position until the beginning of 1525, in his response to Valentin Compar.

In Strasbourg, the first iconoclastic riots occurred in September 1524.[26] The council tried to check the violence and reach a compromise. On 31 October the parishioners of St Aurelia removed the images from their church, after a unanimous decision. St Aurelia was very much a parish of the common people. Its flock consisted chiefly of gardeners who were ministered to by the city's main reformer, Martin Bucer. It is tempting to attribute the iconoclasm of his parishioners to him. In fact, it was they who wanted Bucer as their preacher and they obtained him only irregularly. The first pamphlet directed against images dates from June 1524. It is the work of the radical lay theologian Clement Ziegler, a gardener by profession.

It is unnecessary to multiply examples; the above suffice to characterise the process. Iconoclasm did not stem from great reformers: none of them had taken up a position on images before 1525. Their leadership was hesitant before that date and they took refuge in legalism, as did Zwingli when consulted in December 1522 about a woman of Lucerne who was summoned to return to the Beguines the statue of St Apollinarius which religious scruples had prompted her to remove, although she had originally offered the statue as a vow.[27] It would also be quite incorrect to regard iconoclasm as a popular activity which might have imposed itself on the reformers, because it lacked a popular tradition. It did not accompany the uprisings preceding the Peasants' War, the ideology of which included the cult of saints.[28] Before 1520 there was practically no iconoclasm at all. In fact, these manifestations occurred when the popular anticlericalism came into contact with Lutheran attacks on the cult of saints. While the reformers placed the problem of intercession, which they regarded as idolatry, at the heart of the debate, their hearers took up the concept of idolatry in its most literal sense and attacked the images themselves. This new attitude was quickly rationalised by second-rate but radical reformers, basing themselves on a literal reading of Deuteronomy which was not very subtle but effective.

If, as I believe, iconoclasm occurred at the meeting-point of Reformation preaching and a more traditional anticlericalism, it is necessary to try to shed more light on the social origins of the iconoclasts. In Wittenberg, students seem to have played a considerable role. But what was the situation in non-university towns?

The unexpected events in Zürich in September 1523 were the act of a mostly artisan group, among which may be counted a weaver, a carpenter, a cordmaker and a tailor. They had support among the lower clergy and perhaps also in the council. But, most important, we know the context in which their opinions were formed. The bookseller Castelberger had been running a small biblical school since 1522 in order to facilitate the reading of holy writ by semi-literate people and to make it known to the illiterate. This was not an isolated phenomenon. Other schools of this type existed in Switzerland. In Alsace, public readings took place at the guildhalls. On the eve of the Peasants' War, Johannes Sapidus, director of the Latin school of Sélestat, practised this type of agitation among vine-growers.[29] In Strasbourg, the gardener Ziegler gave commentaries on the Bible to his colleagues.[30] These phenomena throw doubt on Chaunu's contrast between an 'upper middle class' of those who could both read and write and the rest of the population who were hostile to them. This antithesis proves even less adequate when we consider that the events of September 1523 in Zürich were immediately dwarfed by the iconoclasm in the surrounding villages. In Höngg and in Wipkingen, the removal of images was decided by an overwhelming majority in public discussion.

In Strasbourg, as we have seen, the gardeners played the decisive role. Having removed the idols from their parish church, they destroyed the tomb of the saint in spite of, or rather because of, her miraculous reputation. In December 1524 they relieved the church Saint-Pierre-le-Jeune of statues of the Virgin and St Anne. In March 1525 six burghers made a petition for the removal of idols from the cathedral. The council gave way very gradually between 1524 and 1530.

In Basle, iconoclasm was late but violent.[31] On 10 April 1528 the guilds of carpenters and masons attacked the idols at Saint-Martin. The imprisonment of those responsible led to a demonstration of solidarity by the guilds on 15 April. On 23 December the gardeners petitioned against the mass, supported by twelve guilds out of fifteen. On 4 January 1529 both an iconoclastic demonstration and a counter-demonstration by traditionalists took place. We have some figures: the iconoclasts brought together 3,000 armed townsmen, the traditionalists less than 400.

It is all the more difficult to describe these changes according to an acculturation model, because they were largely stimulated by the revolutionary pressure of 1525. Thomas A. Brady has shown that in Strasbourg the principal concession granted by the City Council to the dominated classes in order to save the régime was religious change. In his excellent book on the Peasants' War, Peter Blickle has demonstrated that the united pressure of peasants and common townsmen brought about religious change in towns in spite of the councils' resistance, while repression in many cases resulted in the re-establishment of Catholicism.[32]

In these circumstances, the claim that there were masses traumatised by such change appears to me to be wishful thinking. Matters are particularly clear in Zürich where this change only disturbed a minority and for reasons which were not essentially religious. A *dévôt* called Kleinbrötli protested against Jud's sermon of 1 September 1523. He considered that no one had the right to remove images which others had paid for and that those objecting to this could go to Strasbourg.[33] The democratic discussion which took place in Höngg enabled a certain Claus Buri to announce a comparable opinion: that images could not be removed without legal permission. The commander of the Knights of St John at Küsnacht, Conrad Schmid, was afraid that too hasty a removal of images would be injurious to popular devotion. However, eventually he let himself be entirely convinced by Zwingli, who agreed with Schmid only in theory, pointing out that in reality there was no popular opposition.[34] In fact, the only opposition came from canons of the cathedral, certain members of the Small Council and above all from the burgomaster Marx Roist. The abolition of images was decreed on 15 June 1524, the very day of Roist's death.

Elsewhere no popular resistance to the abolition of images is in evidence. More generally, neither religious change, nor the revolutionary pressure to which it was closely linked in Germany, provoked any popular counter-current. No masses rose up to defend the monks; and at this point we should recall that repression of the peasants would not have been possible but for the return of mercenaries to Germany after their victory in Pavia.

If there can be no question of an elite 'acculturising' the masses, it would be equally false to view such religious change as the product of a popular ideology shared only by the dominated social class. On the contrary, in the towns which have provided our examples, an important section of the bourgeoisie belonged to the movement and the theologians who approved of it; Zwingli and Bucer, for example, were not revolutionary leaders. It is not unusual to find spontaneous removal of images by their donors. I have already mentioned a case of it at Lucerne. The cord-makers of St Gall acted in the same way, while in Höngg, a donor reacted to the public discussion by taking down the image which he had offered not long before. The movement rebounded, therefore, upon the original donors themselves.

So as not to limit myself to the critique of a thesis, may I end by proposing an alternative explanation of iconoclasm? For the moment it is difficult to give figures which would illustrate the rise and fall of pious donations, but one can safely say that the later fifteenth and early sixteenth centuries saw an unprecedented increase in images. In less than two generations church furnishings reached a saturation point which, even from the aesthetic point of view, must have had an unpleasant effect. For patrician families, as also for the professions, the donation of works of art was the principal means of affirming social status. In his report on Germany, Machiavelli remarks on the absence of private sumptuary expenditure, and in particular the poverty of domestic furnishings.[35] However, we can assume that, towards 1520, the churches were saturated in this respect. Unless new ones were built or a programme to increase the numbers of the clergy was put into operation it was necessary to put a stop to this development. Now it is certain that no one wanted there to be more clergy, least of all the clerics who fought one another to defend their daily bread.

It was therefore necessary to stop, or at least considerably reduce, the production of sacred art. The artistic crisis which Germany experienced was not limited to the Reformed territories. Artists like Barthel Beham, who found work in a region which remained Catholic, were few and far between. The cessation or decline of donations had a grave political consequence; the unchanging decor of churches gave a fixed and rapidly inadequate image of the social hierarchy, newcomers being denied the means of affirming their status.

To destroy the most ancient donations and replace them with new ones would have removed from families the certainty that they were spending their money on durable articles, which in turn would have been prejudicial to the importance of donations. Wholesale removal was therefore the egalitarian solution to the problem. Iconoclasm occurred in the most democratic cities, while the feudal principalities preserved, as far as possible, the old ecclesiastical furnishings. Between these extreme solutions, all varieties of compromise can be distinguished, as, for example, in Wittenberg and Nuremberg.

If this theory is correct, it explains why iconoclasm was not limited to the common people. The cessation of sumptuary expenditure run riot was without doubt a matter of concern to many donating families and donors in power. They preferred to spend money on public assistance, to construct public buildings, decorate their dwellings, or to invest. This change affected only one part of the clergy, the most reactionary members of city councils and families who came to make exceptional donations. The austerity of the Reformed ceremony is better explained thus than by a wish for fanatical acculturation.

In conclusion, we must try to understand how as inappropriate a concept as acculturation came to pass into the domain of the history of Europe. There is, of course, the attraction which historians feel for concepts borrowed from more theoretical disciplines. However, as far as the borrowing of the concept of 'acculturation' is concerned, it is necessary to think carefully about three presuppositions which appear so natural that they are not easily put into question:

(1) The greater part of a population would be backward compared to an elite. This backwardness would be linked to a lack of initiative, a difficulty in adapting to novelty and, in particular, a whole reserve of ancestral practices which evolve very slowly and resist change.

(2) The different social groups would exist in different rhythms and

times. Above all in France this illusion could have been due to the orientation of historical research for half a century towards the study of social groups in isolation from a given context. Alain Guerreau has well pointed out the danger in a recent book, *Le Féodalisme*.[36] By viewing a society as a sum of social groups, the study of relations between these groups, which is to say, the dialectic of change, is entirely neglected. These restrictions, whose origin is of a methodological nature, lead to the illusion that different cultures can exist within the same culture. They thus make room for a thesis like that of acculturation.

(3) Finally there is the evolutionist presupposition, according to which populations live in a profound irrationality, in a magical world from which they little by little detach themselves, thanks to their elites, to arrive at rationality, which is more or less to be identified with the historian's ideology. This last point leads to considerations about rationality which go beyond the limits of this paper. But I do not see what gives anyone the right systematically to presuppose the existence, before the period studied, of a greater presence of religion, magic, the sacred and irrationality, from which it subsequently became possible to detach oneself. If the medieval chronicler began man's history with original sin, the historian tends to begin from a comparable myth. He or she places at the foundation of history primitive people who are terror-struck before the forces of nature which they neither dominate nor understand, adoring everything which moves, and even things which do not. According to recent research – I am thinking particularly of Jean Delumeau's *La Peur en occident* – such primitive beings survived until the Enlightenment. In the final analysis, the acculturation thesis is based on the hypothesis that these primitive beings actually existed, for it is they that the elites would be concerned to 'acculturise'. This hypothesis implies that the sacred is pre-existent and creates the necessity to explain how it came to be demolished. It has the great disadvantage of neglecting the human generation of the sacred. While the history of religion neglects the study of this generation, it remains a modest appendix to theodicy. Regardless of the varying opinions professed by historians, it thus loses sight of its object.

Notes: Chapter 5

1 M. Mauss, *Oeuvres* (Paris, 1968–9), Vol. II, pp. 125 ff. This text dates from 1923.
2 On the history of the word, consult: G. Gurvitch (ed.), *Traité de sociologie* (Paris, 1958–60), Vol. II, pp. 451 ff. (chapter edited by G. Balandier); R. Bastide, 'Acculturation', in *Encyclopaedia Universalis*, Vol. I, pp. 102 ff.; A. Dupront, 'De l'acculturation', *XIIe Congrès international des sciences historiques*, Vienna, 1965, *Rapports*, Vol. I, pp. 7–36; N. Wachtel, 'L'acculturation', in *Faire l'histoire*, ed. J. Le Goff and P. Nora (Paris, 1974), Vol. I, pp. 124–46; E. M'Bokolo, 'Acculturation', in J. Le Goff, R. Chartier and J. Revel (eds), *La Nouvelle Histoire* (Paris, 1978), pp. 21 ff.
3 R. Redfield, R. Linton and M. J. Herskovits, 'Memorandum for the study of acculturation', *American Anthropologist*, Vol. XXXVIII (1936), pp. 149–52. Equally the following may be consulted: M. J. Herskovits, *Acculturation: The Study of Culture Contact* (New York, 1938); R. Beals, 'Acculturation', in *Anthropology Today. An Encyclopedic Inventory* (Chicago and New York, 1965), pp. 621–41 (1st edn, 1953).

4 G. Balandier, *Sociologie actuelle de l'Afrique noire* (Paris, 1963) (1st edn, 1955); F. Fanon, *L'An V de la révolution algérienne* (Paris, 1959); id., *Les Damnés de la terre* (Paris, 1961). I have been unable to consult: M. Gluckmann, 'Analysis of a social situation in modern Zululand', *Bantu Studies*, Vol. XIV (1960).

5 Cf. n. 2 above.

6 M.-S. Dupont-Bouchat, W. Frijhoff and R. Muchembled, *Prophètes et sorciers dans les Pays-Bas, XVIe–XVIIIe siècles* (Paris, 1978), p. 29.

7 P. Chaunu, *Le Temps des Réformes. Histoire religieuse et système de civilisation* (Paris, 1975).

8 J. Delumeau, *La Peur en occident* (Paris, 1978), pp. 400, 414.

9 R. Muchembled, *La Sorcière au village (XVe–XVIIIe siècle)* (Paris, 1979), p. 220.

10 R. Muchembled, *Culture populaire et culture des élites dans la France moderne* (Paris, 1978).

11 E. de Monstrelet, *Chronique*, ed. L. Douet d'Arcq (Paris, 1857–62), Vol. IV, pp. 302–6; Vol. V, pp. 43–4 (Société de l'histoire de France, Publications, Vols CV and CVIII).

12 cf. P. Fredericq, *Corpus Inquisitionis Neerlandicae* (Ghent and The Hague, 1889–1906).

13 ibid. The first three volumes cover the period studied here.

14 The following numbers are the ones in question: Vol. I: 248, 249, 261–4, 266, 271, 272, 276, 279, 289, 292, 297, 299, 300, 304, 330, 332–5, 336–43, 345, 349, 350, 352, 353, 354, 356, 357–8, 359, 363, 366, 371, 396, 398, 400, 401, 408; Vol. II: 120, 122, 127, 132, 139–40, 181, 184–5; Vol. III: 45, 48–9, 106.

15 For reasons which I cannot develop here, it appears impossible to me to view witch-hunting as the result of a battle against popular religion or culture. Furthermore, out of 162 cases registered by Fredericq between 1400 and 1520, only fifteen trials are for sorcery.

16 These are the numbers 304, 336–43, 345 and 357–8 in Vol. I.

17 Chaunu, *Le Temps des Réformes*.

18 ibid., p. 489.

19 ibid., p. 497.

20 ibid., p. 489.

21 ibid., p. 492.

22 B. Moeller, *Villes d'empire et Réformation* (French trans., Geneva, 1966); id., 'Die deutschen Humanisten und die Anfänge der Reformation', *Zeitschrift für Kirchengeschichte*, Vol. XX (1959), pp. 46–61.

23 C. C. Christensen, *Art and the Reformation in Germany* (Athens, Ohio, and Detroit, Mich., 1979), pp. 35 ff.

24 E. Egli, *Aktensammlung zur Geschichte der Zürcher Reformation in den Jahren 1519–1533* (Zürich, 1879), no. 126.

25 On iconoclasm in Zürich, Ch. Garside, Jr, *Zwingli and the Arts* (New Haven, Conn., and London, 1966), contains all the useful information. Meanwhile the following may be consulted with profit: W. Köhler, *Zwingli und Luther. Ihr Streit über das Abendmahl nach seinen politischen und religiösen Beziehungen*, Vol. I (Leipzig, 1924).

26 On iconoclasm in Strasbourg: F. Rapp, *Réformes et réformation à Strasbourg. Église et société dans le diocèse de Strasbourg (1450–1525)* (Paris, 1974); T. A. Brady, *Ruling Class, Regime and Reformation at Strasbourg, 1520–1555* (Leiden, 1978); Christensen, *Art and the Reformation in Germany*.

27 Garside, *Zwingli and the Arts*, pp. 99 ff.

28 cf. J. Wirth, *Luther. Étude d'histoire religieuse* (Geneva, 1981), pp. 54 ff.

29 P. Adam, *L'Humanisme à Sélestat* (Sélestat, 1973), p. 23.

30 R. Peter, 'Le Maraîcher Clément Ziegler. L'homme et son oeuvre', *Revue d'histoire et de philosophie religieuses*, Vol. XXXIV (1954), pp. 255–82.

31 cf. Christensen, *Art and the Reformation in Germany*, pp. 93 ff.

32 P. Blickle, *Die Revolution von 1525* (Munich and Vienna, 1975), pp. 156 ff.

33 Garside, *Zwingli and the Arts*, pp. 104 ff.

34 ibid, p. 140.

35 Machiavelli, *Oeuvres complètes*, ed. E. Barincou (Paris, 1952), p. 129.

36 A. Guerreau, *Le Féodalisme. Un horizon théorique* (Paris, 1980).

6 Dechristianisation in Year II: Expression or Extinction of a Popular Culture

MICHEL VOVELLE, translated by John Burke

If my contribution to a reflection on religion, indeed, more generally, on popular culture at the end of the eighteenth century, concentrates on the traumatic episode of the dechristianisation of Year II, which from the winter of 1793 until the spring of 1794 shook revolutionary France, this does not stem from a desire for paradox. In taking this crisis as a moment of truth, I should like to look at the substance of this popular culture, taking into account the complex dialectic which at once associated and opposed it to impulses arising in dominant groups.

The Opposite of a Received Idea

To begin, we must reject the deeply rooted view that the violent conflagration of dechristianisation was accidental, an incongruous, superficial and superimposed episode which by no means mirrored the depths of collective mentalities, save only by the traumatic shock which it was able to precipitate, and in any case an event which in its origins as in its development remained foreign to the people. The force of this cliché is in part the result of a rather unexpected consensus which has been made of it: conservative historiography of religion viewed (and continues to view) the dechristianisation as a campaign launched by a small group of impassioned revolutionaries in the delirium of the moment, as a radicalised Jacobin revolution. But Jacobin tradition, relying on the very sources of Robespierrist tradition, has long been occupied in minimising this episode, perhaps as a result of the difficulty in accounting for it, but also in an attempt to whitewash the image of the Revolution. From Mathiez to Daniel Guérin, in differing terms, there has been an attempt to revitalise the Robespierrist idea that the dechristianisation was a Hébertist invention, and a diversion offered to the people, even if people did not go so far as to believe, like some of the Jacobins, that it was the Machiavellian fruit of a counter-revolutionary conspiracy to set the masses against the new regime. Some recent studies, even while wishing to renew the approach to the problem, have conformed to this image in their fashion: for Richard Cobb, who follows the dechristianisation offensive of the revolutionary armies with precision, the accent is still placed on the destructive and localised actions of commandos from outside, which had no local roots and produced little resonance. And J. Dautry, a prudent historian, could write, making a slightly unfair point against Cobb: 'The British historian R. C. Cobb has never convinced me that the dechristianisation had been a profoundly popular phenomenon, that defrockings and mascarades had shaken the Catholic faith in a great number of humble people.'

On the basis of these verdicts it is easy to reach the generalising conclusion that the dechristianisation of Year II was an exogenous and above all an urban movement, a scandalous epiphenomenon, in which actresses of the opera and prostitutes took the part of goddesses of Reason, and which, after the blaze had quickly died down, gave way to the sterile and academic festivities of the Directory. I have proposed a different interpretation in several works on dechristianisation concerned with a long period of time ('Baroque piety and dechristianisation'), with the event itself in the short term ('Religion and revolution: dechristianisation in Year II'), or with certain of its most characteristic expressions ('Metamorphoses of the fête in Provence'). There can be no question here of going over the whole argument, which will be familiar. Considering the theme of this volume, I wish to tackle more precisely the problem of what this traumatic event has to tell us about religion and popular culture, at the moment when the gigantic Tridentine offensive was running out of steam, being replaced in dominant groups by the bourgeois ideology of the Enlightenment. When the chips were down, did popular groups – as spectators or victims – remain dumb and passive? And this popular culture, did it then have enough vitality to participate, in its entirety, in a conflict which apparently took place on another level, even if ideological conditioning of the masses was at stake?

In apparently contradictory, but in fact complementary terms, two approaches present themselves.

Reactions to Dechristianisation, or the Revolt of the Rural Areas

The first approach is that which apparently gives satisfaction to those who claim that dechristianisation, an imposed movement, found no acceptance among the people. It rests on the, sometimes violent, reactions of rejection in the revolt of the rural areas.

This is an extraordinary field which I have begun to work without claiming in any way to have exhausted its riches, given the difficulties of documentation which it presents. But it is surprising that it should not have given rise to more historical investigations, allowing a confrontation between different theses. The fact is that the network of popular attitudes and behaviour which it reveals is far from being perfectly orthodox. This comes to light if we scratch below the surface of what has long remained the privileged, indeed unique, source by which these reactions to dechristianisation are known, in other words the monographs of a generally hagiographic tendency favouring the confessors of the faith. They were published in the last century – sometimes very soon after the event and therefore nourished by oral tradition – often by ecclesiastics, or if not, as fruits of local erudition. This limited hagiographic literature, which often turns into examples of 'De mortibus persecutorum', thus prolonging the tales of suffering and tribulation of good priests and of the punishment of their enemies, is not totally obsolete, and presents us with a structured, revealing discourse, even if the idealised image of a good, unanimously Christian people, risen (with the exception of a few black sheep) in defence of religion, demands more thoroughgoing examination. To do this I have had recourse to the evidence of the opposing side: representatives on mission, directories of Departments or districts, or national agents and popular societies.

For the south-east quarter of France, to which I have limited my inquiry, it is possible to reconstitute a whole geography of sites of trouble, a chronology and a sociology as well, approximate at least, of the actors and actresses involved in the movement. Without going into a detailed analysis, which would go beyond the limits of this essay, certain areas stand out, which came to life one after the other as the dechristianisation movement spread.

In the very broadly defined south-east quarter which I have studied – a quarter of France, or twenty-three Departments – resistance to dechristianisation was essentially localised and lasted from the winter of 1793 to the spring of 1794. There is no moment of origin for these movements for in the autumn of 1793, on the eve of the dechristianising conflagration, the sites of trouble on the religious question were already very numerous, from Lozère to Aveyron, indeed on the frontier of Gard and Ardèche. But in fact, to simplify, it could be said that two moments of culmination reveal themselves. The first lasted from Brumaire to Nivôse and above all Frimaire, notably in the Departments of the centre and Massif Central. The second was noticeably more southern, although it sometimes reactivated the trouble-spots of previous months; it continued from spring to summer, with violent peaks in Ventôse and Germinal, subsequently to disintegrate in a dust cloud of generally undisciplined acts in Messidor and Prairial, just when the feast of the Supreme Being was celebrated.

Traces of the geography of these troubles can be discerned in that of the responses of the clergy to the constitutional oath at the time of the Civil Constitution. This clearly singles out the zones which had exhibited recalcitrance from the beginning: thirty-two important sites on the right bank of the Rhône, from Beaujolais to Auvergne and Vivarais, compared with only a dozen from Savoie to Dauphiné and Provence. The contrast is obvious. Negative response was extremely marked from Forez and *Lyonnais* to Haute Loire and Ardèche, took in Cantal, Lozère and Aveyron, and affected Gard and Hérault as well. On the opposite side of the river, the trouble-spots were undeniably more localised, from Bresse to the Jura, at certain Alpine sites or in Provence. Without going into unnecessary detail, it is impossible not to recall the great stirrings in Forez at the beginning of Frimaire when men and women rose up between Roanne and 'Montbrisé' (formerly Montbrison), in a country where the letter, written in gold letters, of the hand of God circulated – an agitation which spilled over almost immediately into the Lyons area. But in Ventôse these trouble-spots blazed up again and extended to the north of the Haute Loire and Ardèche. The least that can be said about the regions between Aveyron and Lozère, but also about Auvergne, between Cantal and Puy de Dôme, was that the mountain areas were in a turmoil at that time. In Languedoc a lively agitation came to light in Frimaire, quite as marked around Montpellier or Lodève as in the north of Gard; it rose again in the spring, when the entire region from Montpellier to Nîmes was inundated with the wares of the rosary merchant, who was denounced by the anxious authorities. And this was also the region where the Calvinists of St Jean du Gard strongly resisted the dechristianisation measures. But in the spring of 1794 it was the whole of Languedoc which awakened anew, from Aveyron to Haute Loire, passing through Ardèche.

More silently, the alpine world from Tarentaise to Maurienne generally relied on passive resistance; but in Drôme it was the canton of Chabeuil, in a region of confessional contact, which saw an explosion in Pluviôse, and in the spring all the frontier region of Bas Dauphiné and Haut Comtat, from Buis to Malaucène or to Orange, was in opposition, while the Representative Dherbez Latour encountered open resistance between Manosque and Sisteron, and hardly dared venture into the mountains around Castellane, 'the true cesspool of priests', nor even in his own country, in Barcelonnette, where a visionary who prophesied was denounced.

When one attempts to go beyond this simple overview, one finds in its original characteristics a whole subsidiary and hidden stratum of a popular and partly self-servicing religion. 'Chrétiens sans église' ('Christians without a church')? The older studies at our disposal have tended to place emphasis on the parallel hierarchies of the recalcitrant church at work in rural areas. And there is no question of denying its presence and activities which were particularly evident in the mountains of the central plateau where there was a large number of hidden priests (from Auvergne to Rouergue or in Vivarais). But elsewhere, in places where massive emigration had taken place, facilitated in the Alps and Midi by the proximity of the frontier, one surprisingly finds reactions among the rather self-enclosed people of these regions.

These 'people' – who are they? Both favourable and hostile sources, for once in agreement, emphasise the role of women. They formed the massive village groups (in Forez), they were the 'béates' of Haute Loire, they were members of the old confraternities, dissolved but clandestinely reconstituted in Manosque or Puy, and there were even such isolated cases as the visionary denounced in Messidor in the Barcelonnette district, or the prophetess reported the following month in Aveyron. At the same time, outside our field of observation, at Vic Dessos in Ariège, it was an old woman who posed 'as a prophetess for payment'. Finally, among the Calvinists of St Jean du Gard, one of the most violent spokesmen was a woman, even at the tribune of the *Société Populaire*.

Did men conceal themselves? It is not unlikely that they may have preferred to push women forward (as in Forez), but also that the

Representatives on mission may have tried to belittle the movement by feminising it in disdainful terms. It remains true that men's participation was limited, and in spite of the support by bands of recalcitrant conscripts from the mountain areas, there was not the 'Nouvelle Vendée' one might have feared. Where men were arrested, they were depicted as simpletons, that is, as labourers and peasants, and as hostile to urban initiatives. Such descriptions may not have been of an innocent nature, but the rare statistics available on the accused confirm this popular, if not exclusively peasant, character (in St Jean du Gard, for example, three stocking-makers, two masons, one agricultural worker and one butcher).

The forms of expression spontaneously invented by these groups of 'Christians without a church' reveal a return to gestures and practices of which the prelates of former times, even before the Jacobins, had disapproved: 'fanatisme' was pushed (thus in Drôme, in the district of Buis) to the point of ringing the bell at the least excuse – even in the case of thunderstorms, following all the popular traditions. And in this world where defence of the occasionally concealed village bell assumed a particular importance, all these groups were assembled on the summons of the tocsin. An underground circuit of diffusion of information and of contacts was thus created. This can be judged from the success met with in the whole of Languedoc by the makers of rosaries. The most characteristic, even if not a new form, was that letter written in gold characters by the hand of God which mobilised the peasants of Forez. The object, the written text and the spoken word thus became associated in an ambiguous and ephemeral return of the most repressed and ancient forms of popular religion. Likewise, the visionary women who had previously been reported in their mountain sanctuaries were evidence of a resurgence of an ancient millenarianism, even if attempts were made to belittle their influence: it was alleged that the prophetess at Vic Dessos operated 'for payment', and it was claimed that the visionary woman of Aveyron pretended to heal successfully 'all illnesses ... a new Cathérine Théot ... a marvel come out of the old furnaces of priests and kings. She draws crowds in many communities. The prophet Daniel brings them certain plasters from heaven ...' However, at Barcelonnette there clearly was 'a fanatic who claims to be inspired, who inflames these spirits'. Such persons, born of the troubles of the moment, gave rise to true panic pilgrimages which frightened the authorities.

Exceptional behaviour? Curiosities? It was in the interest of the revolutionary authorities to minimise the importance of such events and, conversely, of pious hagiographers in the following century to pass over in silence these hardly orthodox manifestations. But I am convinced that such episodes could be found as late as the end of the revolutionary period, and not only during the dechristianising blaze. Let us take a random example, one known to us only through an erudite *Drômois* journal. It is that of Louise de Venterol, a village shepherdess from the Buis region (whence her surname came) who died at the age of 17 in a retreat under a staircase where she hid her sanctity. Her case resembles those told by medieval hagiographies. At the time of the Consolat her remains attracted hasty bands of pilgrims from the whole region, until the Prefect sent his gendarmes to take away the mummy, and store it in the granaries of the Prefecture, where she was found by the journal's author much later. Shortlived panic pilgrimages of a difficult time.

Besides these paroxysms, the day-to-day clashes between the people and the authorities in the dechristianisation period are revealed by a whole range of reactions. In some places there were gatherings of mobs at the sound of the tocsin, followed occasionally by counter-revolutionary vandalism, uprooting the pole, or destroying the statue of Liberty in response to revolutionary vandalism. Elsewhere there were non-violent demonstrations: attention has been drawn to the women of Aveyron, for instance, who united in the deserted churches where they burned wax candles, or better still to the White Masses celebrated by laymen, of which there is frankly little trace. But in following these chronicles, one sometimes stumbles across the unexpected and I know of few more suggestive documents in this area than the record left by a peasant of Maurienne, published long ago by F. Vermale, which illustrates the defensive struggle seen *from the peasants' point of view*. It highlights the desperate defence of the bell and church silver, but testifies at the same time to the very strong polarisation of opinions regarding the value of this patrimony for the village community. Occasionally there appear extreme forms of reappropriation, when one discovers, for example, in the ranks of persecutors smitten by divine justice, some who had hidden the monstrance or the church's ciborium in order to preserve them from the Jacobins of the city – but who had not subsequently replaced them.

To conclude with a word on the theme of the struggle in defence of popular Christianity against dechristianisation, I would say that the episode must be seen as an important, indeed essential, turning-point. Under all its aspects, even the most unexpected, it announced the compromises which were to take place during the following century (and until the episode of church inventories in 1905) between peasant communities and priests who had been repressive enough agents a short time previously of Tridentine pastoral thought, but temporarily associated with the common defence against the expropriations of the state and against the new ideology it tried to impose. Never let it be said, however, that these compromises were made in all innocence.

The Other Camp: Dechristianisation Accepted

To reduce popular reactions to dechristianisation to uncertain struggles and a mixture of bad feelings and localised explosions in mistreated rural areas, would be to see only one aspect of the whole evidence. It seems clear that such a movement was only able to assume a corresponding amplitude because it had been accepted. It has long been obvious that the epicentre of this movement was situated in the heart of rural France, in Nièvre, and not in Paris; and it is known that far from being encouraged, dechristianisation was condemned severely by the revolutionary government, and particularly by the Robespierrist group, beginning above all with the decree of Frimaire on freedom of worship. Was dechristianisation therefore a spontaneous movement? Certainly not, but neither was it imposed from on high; it was carried by a highly politicised current of opinion, of which it is one of the key themes. It remains to define the contours of this current of opinion, the forms and limits of its penetration and the response it was able to provoke among the people. I will linger no longer than necessary over a demonstration, which I have developed elsewhere, of the weaknesses inherent in the interpretation of the dechristianisation of Year II as exogenous, or imposed. In classic historiography, the individual action of Representatives on mission is successively, or sometimes simultaneously, condemned, like the actions of the revolutionary armies, as an 'instrument of the Terror in the Departments', or more sweepingly as the work of little groups of activists, Hébertist or Jacobin 'extremists', who are generally seen as outside intruders come from elsewhere.

A detailed reconstruction of the propagation of dechristianisation, such as that which I have undertaken for a quarter of a century, shows that the initiative of Representatives on mission was highly relative. Although there can be no question of denying that the activism of an Albitte, a Fouché, or a Javogues weighed heavily, the list of results at ground level shows that there were a number of regions where this activism was broken up by the resistance of the people, while conversely highly affected provinces did not receive any active Representatives. In the same manner, the undeniable activity of the revolutionary army in the Lyons region came to a close in Frimaire when it was disbanded, so that it had no effect in the following spring; nevertheless, that is when the entire Midi was in a state of upheaval.

Even taking account of the most modest agents – districts, national agents, or *sociétés populaires* – it is really within the communities themselves that local exponents responsible for the dechristianisation campaign should be sought. This is an arduous task, for it is not at all easy to establish such a sociology. The continuous fabric of testimonies only reveals a rather thin collection of activists. Let us recognise, to begin with, that the militants are for the most part bourgeois: two-thirds in our statistics are men of law, 'bourgeois' ex-priests, or members of liberal professions (physicians or teachers), a fifth are artisans or retailers. This leaves little room for peasants and wage-earners. Nevertheless, they may be glimpsed by the wayside. There is the father of Riquelle, peasant and mayor of Maillane in Year II. Mistral speaks of him evoking the old *Provençale* woman who in 1848, asking when 'the time of the red apples' would return, remembered having been the goddess of Reason of her village when she was 17 years old. But not far away, near Apt, oral tradition still remembers 'Lou Cagaire', an audacious sansculotte who had lowered his own *culottes* on the village altar! Elsewhere, in Haute Savoie, another oral tradition sketches the scene of the burning faggots of the auto-da-fé in the village square and the dance into which the *curé* found himself drawn by force by a local sansculotte called 'the dragon' on leave from the army (but all the ambiguity of the nickname can be felt). In this comic procession one also encounters the sansculotte of Brignoles, who narrowly escaped the clutches of the devout for trying to burn down confessional boxes.

These instances represent 'types' (*espèces*), in the sense understood by Diderot, or individual cases, even if occasionally a more recognisable group cuts across our path, such as the sansculottes of the village of Fontvieille near Arles, who were enamoured of equality and hence harboured reservations about the Davidian scenario of the feast of the Supreme Being proposed to them. They decided instead to file off – in alphabetical order. Altogether, the highly colourful individuals which we have evoked here are no more atypical, in their own manner, than the prophets or visionaries whom we have discovered in the other camp.

However, in order to understand the undeniable success, in a whole province of the rural world, of a dechristianisation which was not merely received, but actually lived in incontestably popular terms, we must go beyond these individual cases. Rather than become bogged down in an impossible sociology, we must analyse the actions themselves, beginning with the characteristic expressions which are represented by the feast and the procession; and we shall also find a return of the carnivalesque.

In the global history of the revolutionary feast, the dechristianisation episode occupies a singular position. It defines a specific point of emphasis, even if we can detect beforehand (sometimes from 1791 onwards in certain areas of fermentation such as Avignon) the original figurations of what was to become the great liberation lasting from the winter of 1793 until the spring of 1794. An unbridgeable gulf arose between the great liturgies of the early Revolution, still framed in traditional forms, and the Thermidorian or Directorial feasts, with their painstaking regard for a new elaborated model, from which flowed resurgences and new creations of popular invention. Here is perhaps one of the nuances – rather than a reservation – which I would apply to the description proposed by Mona Ozouf, because she has partially misunderstood the originality of this moment (even if in other respects she allows a place of merit to certain festivities which approximate to it, such as the planting of maypoles, which sprang from a spontaneous and provincial initiative).

This period of dechristianisation was a giant carnivalesque blaze beginning in the winter of 1793 and prolonged until the spring of 1794. The statistical count which it is possible to provide, as exhaustive as possible within the limits of Provence, confirms the fact while permitting quantification. The masquerade of dechristianisation manifested itself in a whole network of celebrations – the death of the tyrant, the celebration of Lepeletier and the martyrs of Liberty – which proliferated in the winter and early spring of 1794, and which, moreover, materialised without concern for mixture of genres. And it seems that there was nothing fortuitous in a sequence of events which ran in the tradition of carnival, considering that it took place during the traditional carnival season (even if it was a prolonged carnival, ignoring Lent), to which the Corpus Christi (*Fête Dieu*) celebration of the Supreme Being finally put a stop.

Recurrence of 'folklore' or return of village culture – isn't this to force the issue too much?

In returning to the various aspects of the dechristianisation masquerade, while remaining vigilant not to apply models of popular culture (well on the way to folklorisation) in a mechanical fashion, it is not difficult to find a whole series of acts or traits which were adapted from a heritage of very long standing.

To begin with, it was the internal order of the procession which mirrored this heritage. While the feasts of the Constituent Revolution often ran in the structures of official ancien régime liturgies, and while from the feast of the Supreme Being of Prairial (Year II) to the cycle of Directorial fêtes precise and composed scenarios were elaborated on a national scale, the dechristianisation feast was characterised by a mixture of genres and a prolixity and profusion of composite groups. Certainly there were precedents, and since April 1792 the Jacobins of Avignon, returning to their city from which they had been expelled temporarily, had provided the example of such a procession, in which Bacchus, astride his barrel, was pulled by twenty-two asses, one among other elements in a pageant mixing derision and proclamations. But in the winter of 1793 this trait became systematically employed, even in proper Carnival time, when Entrevaux celebrated the capture of Toulon in a march-past where Liberty, Reason, Mars and Victory led a civic *branle* which ended with an auto-da-fé. In Fréjus, a little while later, on 30 Nivôse, for the Martyrs of Liberty celebration, twenty-seven extraordinarily mixed groups associated the exaltation of the heroes' memory with dechristianisation proclamations ('death is nought but eternal sleep') and the exaltation of Reason, in the midst of a great gathering in which corporate groups, such as the army and the 'useful citizens', were mixed up with a float containing great men's works and the administrators of charity! But as much could be said of the fraternal fête in Marseilles which, on 1 Germinal, brought together thirty-three groups which extended from the chariot of Hercules to the agricultural plough, to a representation of the Montagne or to the delegation of the revolutionary workshops.

But these feasts, which, in their naive pedagogical method, retained a concern for solemnity, were no more than a first stage. The true masquerade went further and became a procession of true derision. There as well, there were local precedents. Since 1791, in the Midi, grotesque effigies of notorious counter-revolutionaries had been hanged on street-lamps in Marseilles, then in Aix. In the spring of 1792, in the same region, a procession held at Avignon in April was echoed at Arles where, it is said, a bust of the Eternal Father was promenaded, women and young girls being forced to spit on it.

From August to December 1792 the fires of joy for the fall of the royalty were quite naturally transformed into autos-da-fé and masquerades. At Aix as in Nice (and as in Paris), coffins or catafalques laden with royal attributes were burned, while in January 1793, after the execution of the king, the imitation of the burning of Caramentran became evident during this carnival period in the Midi: effigies of the king and queen in Avignon, of the counter-revolutionary mayor Loys in Arles.

It was from September 1793 to March 1794 (Ventôse, Year II) that the wave of masquerades and autos-da-fé, often indissociable, culminated, the masquerade ending in an auto-da-fé. The most elementary scenarios were confined to a promenade of 'dépouilles', the cast-off items of fanaticism and superstition, followed by their combustion in the public square. This was the procedure in the *Provençal* Midi, in cities and towns such as Marseilles, Arles, Avignon, Toulon, Brignoles, Draguignan, Nice, Grasse, Antibes and Manosque, but also in modest villages. Sometimes (at Arles, Entrevaux, Grasse and Monaco in Provence) the procession adapted charivari rituals. In Arles, a sansculotte tied up on an ass agreed to take the thankless role of a 'chiffoniste' counter-revolutionary showered with jibes. At Grasse, as in Monaco (in Pluviôse and Ventôse), posthumous judgement was passed on the tyrant Capet (Grasse) or on a pope (Monaco), before the mock execution took place, by fire at Grasse, by drowning in Monaco ... poor old Caramentran!

The form which in the context of the dechristianisation campaign was most directly adapted from the charivari is undeniably the procession of the mitred ass. Once I believed it possible, in the course of a very wide spatial survey, to follow its diffusion by contamination from the epicentre of the Nièvre region outwards. However, the earliest examples I have found since then in the Midi, which date from the end of 1791 (Avignon), effectively prove that it is actually a case of simultaneous manifestations, reactivating an old Carnival heritage. It remains true that during the dechristianisation offensive, the first example reaches us from Nièvre, which puts Fouché on the stage, in the well-known debate on whether an ass should be crowned. The answer is equally well known: that would be too degrading for the animal. One month later, in Pluviôse, the mitred ass turned up again in Lyons at the time of the apotheosis of Chalier, then in Nivôse at Armes (St Etienne) during the festivities for the recapture of Toulon (a cart drawn by asses carried the royal effigies while the city of Toulon admitted 'I am the whore of kings'). In the same period, in Montbrisé (Montbrison), at the time of the feast of Reason, chasubles and albs served as accessories to their humble mounts. But the scenario was repeated in a number of modest burghs or small towns in *Lyonnais*, and extended by the burning of effigies of Capet and representatives of fanaticism. By contact, in Ain and Isère, detachments of the revolutionary army caught the habit of promenading the *curé* as a prisoner, in the company of an ass festooned with sacerdotal ornaments.

It is undeniably in the centre of France, but also more precisely in the Lyons region, where these manifestations are met with in greatest number. In the south-east quarter examples remain scarce (St Enimie in Lozère), with the exception of the *Provençal* Midi where we have encountered its different forms, which ranged from the simple promenade of the cast-offs of the ancien régime and superstition (Nice, Toulon), to an adaptation of the charivari or the trial of Caramentran (Arles, Entrevaux, Grasse, Monaco). It is at Entrevaux, a strong frontier post, that the procession of the mitred ass ended, four months after its invention in Nièvre.

The fraternal banquet appeared as a natural complement to the masquerade and carnivalesque blazes of the dechristianisation festivities. From January to March 1794 the banquets, a common practice since the beginning of the Revolution, underwent a change of character. In Marseilles, for example, on the occasion of the tyrant's death in January 1793, tables were set up, by the city's wards and indeed professions, and sheep were roasted, while casks of wine were brought out. This characteristic became accentuated at Carnival time. In Nice, in Nivôse of Year II, after the promenade of the goddess of Liberty, each citizen brought out a table before his house and everyone could serve himself. In Fréjus, ten days later, the idea of a frugal banquet was born spontaneously at the exit of the Temple of Reason; and each one brought out tables. But it is necessary to go to Arles to find, stemming from the horrified pen of an ecclesiastic chronicler, the record of a banquet by which were celebrated for three days the marriages of nine local priests; a reflection, says our author, of the 'impure orgies of pagan saturnalia'. And it is in Arles once more that on 20 Messidor the memorial celebration of the young Bara resembled a sort of picnic where, it is reported, each participant contributed some of the following: bread, a bottle, turnips, onions, garlic, pears, artichokes, a bit of cheese, lard, salami, 'anchovy of herring', indeed 'some venison'. Even if the banquet seems to have become generally institutionalised at the end of the spring of 1794, although the Representatives in the Midi were less hostile there than in Paris, it is right at the heart of the dechristianisation offensive that it blossomed.

Does the fraternal banquet complement the masquerade and was it a southern curiosity? It would be tempting to think so and to conclude that the practice is found where eighteenth-century descriptions relate that the custom was 'to bring out tables', particularly in eastern Provence from Fréjus to Nice. But examining the matter more closely, on the scale of the south-east quarter in its entirety, it is evident that the fraternal banquet blossomed most between Frimaire and Nivôse within an area which encompassed Haute Loire, Rhône, Mont Blanc, Ain and Drôme, thus highlighting, rather than the Midi, a region which could be called *Lyonnais*. Honesty compels us to point out that there existed, as a counterpoint to this carnivalesque theme, an antagonistic call for civic or republican Lenten observance, which was tied at the same time to restrictions (lack of meat) and a moral option. 'The true republican must favour privations', it was written in Moustiers (Basses Alpes; perhaps Moutiers, Mont Blanc), one of the two places where this demand is encountered, on the event of the feast of the Supreme Being, and one circumstance undoubtedly explains the other.

The promenade of the charivari, the incineration of Caramentran, the carnivalesque banquet, the fancy-dress ball, derision and mixture of genres: we really have the impression from these examples of taking part in a revenge of popular culture on the constraints of the discipline imposed by the Tridentine reconquest. This revenge can also be encountered in less obvious forms in similar acts which were less significant in appearance, but charged with meaning: the world turned upside-down. There is a priest who is forced to dance at the civic *branle* in front of the bonfire in the church square, and there is the reappropriation of the church by the community in the form of the Temple of Reason, of the bell, occasionally of church furnishings. The exploit encountered more than once (in the manner of the Lyons region) is that of the sansculotte who drinks from the chalice, asking the Eternal Father – if he exists – to strike him down. This would be the extreme point of this 'heated liberation on the boil'.

This poses the problem of appreciating the real bearing of this behaviour. Was it simply concerned with a redeployment of the ancient formal structures of popular protest and its wandering, still living forms, which later, as they had reached their death-throes, were inventorised by the folklorists of the late nineteenth century: the bonfire, the effigy, the procession of the charivari? One could hardly be at a loss to extend the list, for although we have concentrated on expressions proper to the carnivalesque sequence of the winter of 1793–4, there would be much to say on the Mayday celebrations of Liberty, likewise re-employed since 1792, and which were born out of rural France – out of a 'folkloric' practice. But to limit ourselves to this interpretation would leave in the dark a whole part of the problem of the dechristianisation's popular content.

At this point the question of the amplitude and significance of revolutionary forms of popular religiosity confronts us. This is an immense topic and I do not aspire to do more than touch lightly on it. Formerly it was treated with contempt or derision, but the pioneering contribution in this field of the articles by Albert Soboul, written as much on the martyrs of the Liberty cult – Marat, Chalier, Lepeletier – as on patriotic saints, deserves due recognition here. In my own work (*Religion and Revolution*) I have endeavoured to investigate one aspect of these themes more thoroughly, concerning the diffusion of the martyrs' cult, or even of the goddess Reason.

For it is precisely from there that it is necessary to start, once the diffusion of this vivid personification of the cult of Reason, not only in the towns, but occasionally also in the villages of the Midi, has become evident. Whatever might have been said subsequently, it was never fallen women or any 'opera girls' (where would these have been found?) who played these roles. Riquelle, whom Mistral evoked long after the event, in the bloom of her seventeen years, her breasts offered and her thighs unveiled in the church of Maillane, was the mayor's daughter. She represents a figure, daughter or spouse, which turned up elsewhere, even if, in great cities like Marseilles, it was rather militants and 'amazons' who assumed this role, such as 'Cavale' or 'Fassy', for instance, who were to pay the price of having been goddesses for a day by a terrible death under the blows of cut-throat royalists in Year III. Only later (a fact which itself deserves attention) did a process of infantilisation of the goddess take place at the time of the neo-Jacobin restoration in Year IV, as shown by the parade of a young girl in a burgh near Toulon (La Garde) – a development mirrored in Provence by the evolution over a very long period of time of the role of the 'belle de Mai', far-off reflection of the cult of Maya, who would also become infantilised. However, the parallel is not without significance.

These goddesses of Reason, were they seen as an object of scandal, as one tradition reports? I am not sure; there are shortcomings in such an understanding. The very wide diffusion of the practice shows that it was accepted, at least in certain regions. And such isolated, but revealing, evidence perhaps helps us to understand the phenomenon. 'Today the living mother of the father land was given a procession', noted the Avignon weaver Coulet without any negative comment in his *livre de raison*. From 'Good Mother' to 'mayre de la Patrie vivante', who was, moreover, vivacious and good-looking, the passage had been truly traumatic. The much more concealed problem of this massive feminisation on the level of the creations of collective imagination must remain open; by putting the father to death – God or the king – it crystallised the fixations of the new religiosity on maternal images.

In order to continue, or form a counterpoint to, the preceding, I will do no more than recall the problem of the trinity or of the revolutionary triad of the martyrs of Liberty, Marat, Lepeletier and Chalier, if only for the sake of recapitulating that these devotions, indeed, these cults (an Arlesian orator cries out 'we must have no cult but Marat's') it seems to me were accepted to a greater extent than credited in the literature. Doubtless they were accepted unequally. The map, on the scale of the whole of France, which I proposed at the beginning of this essay from indications furnished by the revolutionary toponymy, very precisely overlaps the map of the sites of actual and accepted dechristianisation. Locally, the intensity with which *manes* were celebrated, that of Lepeletier in the Midi, for example, in the framework of a series of unquestionably spontaneous feasts, attests to the impact of this new Pantheon of intercessors, rather than to that of a new trinity, for the positioning of the theme within a trinitarian structure is undoubtedly an addition: Marat and Lepeletier, heroes and martyrs (the litanies 'O cor Jesu', 'O cor Marat' must be recalled), were accepted in diverse regions. The cult of Chalier, however, remained a curiosity of the Lyons region. It is therefore rather as new martyrs, close by virtue of their sufferings, and hence even intercessors, that these heroes became popular and they had a very ambiguous relation of official impulses, the authorities having been led once again to take up and accept creations which originated on a popular level.

This was even more so where local creations of female patriotic saints, the existence of which was pointed out by A. Soboul, were concerned: wives or daughters, martyrs, in the republican west, in the struggle against Breton royalism, the saint who rises to the sky on tricoloured wings, or again St Pataude, the humble heroine of the 'tomb of the Young Girl', still visited in Teillay, in Ille et Vilaine, near Redon. She was massacred – shot or hanged – by the Chouans near a tree of the forest. A very recent newspaper report (*Ouest-France*, 28 August 1979) described the oak which surmounts the tomb, and the heterogeneous accumulation of objects: children's clothes, shoes (St Pataude intervenes for unsteady toddlers), statuettes of the Virgin, a plastic doll, and so on. 'Merci', says a marble ex-voto. There is a trace, transfer, reappropriation, or refabrication of marginal saints of forest or *terroir*, those very same whom Tridentine religion had chased away and proscribed. Are they to be dismissed because of their marginality, even if the example cited above is a good demonstration that we are concerned with much more than an ephemeral creation of the moment?

A last examination, before we conclude this essay, must be made of the forms of messianism themselves, indeed forms of revolutionary millenarianism. The double heritage of conservative and Jacobin approaches, which take literally the at once disdainful and uneasy condemnation formulated in the spring of Year II, could lead to a dismissal of the episodes which occurred around Catherine Théot, 'Mother of God', of Dom Gerle and their circle; the view, in a word, of those mystics for whom the millennium had already begun and who found its most positive expression in the most radical revolution. But other examples can be brought to mind – are they the only ones? – such as that of the Bonjour family of Fareins near Lyons who were *curés*, devout men and women and opinionated Jansenists who expected the coming of the prophet Elias in his fiery chariot, and experienced the Revolution as the Great Event. It was Georges Lefebvre who was first to insist on the clear nature of the way in which the French Revolution was received as 'good news' by the masses. Is it astonishing that in the context of popular sensibility this expression, with its religious connotations, should have been taken literally?

Let us conclude this essay. At times, the differences between the two popular groups we have followed in parallel, radical as they can appear, seem to blur. The offensive in defence of the opinionated was ambiguous on more than one occasion, and was not to be accounted for in the martyrology established in the succeeding century, but, on the contrary, carefully concealed. On the other hand, more than one Representative on mission or bourgeois Jacobin in Year II fully participated in the rejection reflex and radical incomprehension of the Committee on Public Health, regarding dechristianisation as incongruous and scandalous.

In this double movement and its background of well-kept silences lies the difficulty in appreciating the dechristianisation of Year II in its truly popular dimension, as one of the last expressions (and the last in violent form) of a subordinate culture which still refused to disappear.

Bibliography

(a)   General Works on the Religious History of the Revolution
A. Aulard, *Le Christianisme et la Révolution française* (Paris, 1925).
V. Bindel, *Histoire religieuse de la France au XIXe siècle: Histoire religieuse de Napoléon ... les évêques de Bonaparte* (Paris, 1940).
A. Latreille, *L'Église catholique et la Révolution française,* 2 vols (Paris, 1946–50).
J. Leflon, *La Crise révolutionnaire 1789–1846*, Vol. XX of *Histoire de l'Église*.
A. Mathiez, *Contribution à l'histoire religieuse de la Révolution française* (Paris, 1907).
A. Mathiez, *La Révolution et l'église* (Paris, 1910),
A. Mathiez, *Robespierre et le culte de l'Être suprême* (Le Puy, 1910).
A. Mathiez, *La Question religieuse sous la Révolution française* (Paris, 1929).
B. Plongeron, *Conscience religieuse en Révolution* (Paris, 1969).

(b)   Dechristianisation: General Works, Exemplary Monographs
C. Cler, 'La déchristianisation de l'an II dans le quart Sud-Est de la France: l'idéologie dans les libellés, pétitions et adresses à la Convention nationale', unpubl. *Mémoire de Maîtrise* (Aix-en-Provence, 1971).

R. Cobb, 'Les débuts de la déchristianisation à Dieppe', *Annales historiques de la Révolution française* (cited hereafter as *AHRF*) (1956).

M. Dommanget, *La Déchristianisation à Beauvais et dans l'Oise* (Paris, 1918).

B. Plongeron, 'Autopsie d'une église constitutionelle: Tours de 1794 à 1802', in *Actes du 93e congrès national des Sociétés savantes*, Tours, 1968 (Paris, 1971).

R. Rémond, 'La déchristianisation: état présent de la question et des travaux en langue française', *Concilium*, no. 7 (1965).

L. P. Sardella, 'La déchristianisation de l'an II dans le quart Sud-Est de la France: essai de cartographie historique', unpubl. *Mémoire de Maîtrise* (Aix-en-Provence, 1971).

M. Vovelle, 'Essai de cartographie de la déchristianisation sous la Révolution française', *Annales du Midi* (1964).

M. Vovelle, 'Déchristianisation spontanée et déchristianisation provoquée dans le Sud-Est', *Bulletin de la Société d'Histoire moderne*, 4 October, 1964.

M. Vovelle, *Religion et Révolution: la déchristianisation de l'an II* (Paris, 1976).

(c) Married and Renounced Priests

J. Chardon-Bordas, *Inventaire des archives de la légation en France du cardinal Caprara* (Paris, 1975).

M. Reinhard (ed.), *Les Prêtres abdicataires pendant la Révolution française*, Commission d'histoire économique et sociale de la Révolution française (Paris, 1965).

D. Ligou, 'Sur le protestantisme révolutionnaire', *Revue d'Histoire du Protestantisme française* (1958).

A. Mathiez, 'Les prêtres révolutionnaires devant le cardinal Caprara', *AHRF* (1926).

(d) The Forms of Dechristianisation: Toponymy, Silverware

A. Aulard, 'Les noms révolutionnaires des communes de France', *Revue de Paris* (1926).

L. de Cardenal, 'Les noms révolutionnaires dans l'Aude et l'Hérault', *Folklore* (1939).

R. de Figuères, *Les Noms révolutionnaires des communes de France* (Paris, 1901).

A. Mathiez, 'L'argenterie des églises en l'an II', *AHRF* (1925).

(e) Revolutionary Cults

A. Aulard, *Le Culte de la Raison et le culte de l'Être suprême* (Paris, 1892).

A. Mathiez, *La Théophilanthropie et le culte décadaire* (Paris, 1904).

A. Mathiez, *Les Origines des cultes révolutionnaires* (Paris, 1904).

Abbé Sicard, *A la recherche d'une religion civile* (Paris, 1895).

A. Soboul, 'Observations sur le culte de Marat', note in *AHRF* (1958).

A. Soboul, 'Sentiment religieux et cultes populaires pendant la Révolution: saintes patriotes et martyrs de la Liberté', *AHRF* (1957).

(f) The Agents of Dechristianisation: Representatives on Mission

J. Borie, 'Le Conventionnel Jean Borie', *Bulletin de la Société Hist. et Arch. de la Corrèze* (1930).

A. Boudier, 'Le Conventionnel A.L. Albitte', *Bulletin de la Société d'Etudes locales ... de la Seine inférieure* ([Rouen], 1931).

J. Combet, 'Les arrêtés de Robespierre jeune dans les Alpes-Maritimes', *AHRF* (1917).

P. Gaffarel, 'La Mission de Maignet dans les Bouches-du-Rhône et en Vaucluse', *Annales de la Faculté des Lettres d'Aix* (1912).

Fr. Gonon, *Un Forézien célèbre: Claude Javogues* (Saint Étienne, 1938).

P. Vaillandet, 'La mission de Maignet en Vaucluse', *AHRF* (1926).

(g)   The Agents of Dechristianisation: Revolutionary Armies

R. Cobb, 'La commission temporaire de Commune Affranchie', *Cahiers d'Histoire de Lyon* (I/1957).

R. Cobb, 'Les armées révolutionnaires des départements du Midi', *Cahiers de l'association Marc Bloch de Toulouse*, no. 1 ([Toulouse], 1955).

R. Cobb, 'L'armée révolutionnaire à Lyon et dans la région lyonnaise', in *Albums du crocodile* (Lyons, 1952).

R. Cobb, *Les Armées révolutionnaires, instrument de la Terreur dans les départements*, 2 vols (Paris, 1963).

G. Dumont, *Les Bataillons de volontaires nationaux, cadres et historique* (Paris, 1914).

M. Reinhard, 'Les armées révolutionnaires étudiées par R. Cobb', *AHRF* (1964).

7 The Anabaptists and the State Churches

KLAUS DEPPERMANN, translated by Ian Waite

Even to those who had witnessed its birth, the essence of Anabaptism always seemed protean and difficult to grasp. The various feuding groups were united only in their acknowledgement of adult baptism and even the meaning of this symbol of faith was subject to differing interpretations. At one end of the spectrum there were the Swiss Brethren, a biblicist group who shared the idea of *sola scriptura* with the reformers, and who considered the Sermon on the Mount a binding law. At the other, there were the spiritualist groups from Appenzell and St Gallen, who disregarded all Christian norms in respect of marriage and the use of force in the name of the 'freedom of the Spirit'. While, in the 'Schleitheim Confession', Michael Sattler and his fellow believers pledged themselves to strict pacifism, Melchior Hoffman and the Münster Anabaptists, who were his intellectual descendants, proclaimed the extirpation of the godless, which in this case meant all officially consecrated clergymen, Catholic as well as Protestant. Menno Simons and Balthasar Hubmaier believed in the possibility of a Christian government. The southern German and Swiss Anabaptists, however, considered this an impossibility after the experiences of the Peasants' War. Anabaptist christology revealed further differences. Denck, Kautz and Hätzer, for example, came close to adopting anti-Trinitarian points of view, whilst Sattler remained orthodox and Hoffman's concept of the Trinity was thoroughly monophysite. Differing points of view on the questions of private property or the validity of a rigorous anti-modernist system of ethics led to even more splits within the movement.

In the light of this, the problem of the original goals or indeed of the real nature of this movement of protest, against the Roman Catholic Church as much as against the official Reformation, becomes relevant. Different observers reached different conclusions. The Strasbourg reformers Bucer and Capito were prepared to distinguish between a biblicist peaceful form of Anabaptism, as practised by the Swiss Brethren, and a spiritualist tendency which was more or less inclined to use force. The more peaceful Anabaptists they considered to be children of the Reformation who had been led astray, and were prepared to recognise them as brothers in Christ.[1] But Luther, Melanchthon, Zwingli and Bullinger dismissed all Anabaptists as anarchists and social revolutionaries. They considered the more peaceful kind to be mere wolves in sheep's clothing who were only waiting for the right moment to strike. As for the others, they were nothing more than professed disciples and successors of the detested Thomas Müntzer.[2] The view of the Anabaptists in established historiography has been coloured by

95

the Melanchthon and Bullinger versions over the centuries. The different assessments of Sebastian Franck and Gottfried Arnold were never allowed to carry as much influence.[3] Only in the twentieth century has this judgement been reversed. This is due to the efforts of Ernst Troeltsch and his admirer and disciple Walther Köhler. In Troeltsch's eyes the Swiss Brethren, a sect founded by Grebel and Sattler, embodied the very type of a Christian sect whose professed goal it was to restore primitive Christianity and re-establish the absolute rule of natural law by avoiding any form of compromise with Christianity as it had developed since its earliest days. As champions of the freedom of conscience and the separation of church and state, the Swiss Brethren could be considered pioneers of the modern age, more modern to be sure than the official reformers, who clung to the medieval *corpus christianum* and used it to preserve the theologically doubtful instruments of infant baptism and the persecution of heretics.[4] In the quarrels between Zwingli and the Swiss Brethren, Walther Köhler saw a struggle between Christianity and established culture, the national churches and the free churches, between the moral values of society and Christian ethics. In contrast to Troeltsch, he also attributed a strong enthusiastic element to the early Swiss Anabaptists: 'Whoever looks for a balance between society and Christianity, and who finds its sociological expression in the national church, will find himself on Zwingli's side. However, he will not be able to disguise the fact that this is a compromise.'[5] Like Fritz Blanke,[6] his Zürich successor, Köhler sympathised secretly with the more peaceful Anabaptists who had had the courage to break with a 1,500-year-old ecclesiastical tradition which had become corrupted by compromise with the world, especially with respect to the alliance of throne and altar. American research into Anabaptism, particularly by those historians who are close to the Mennonites, has adopted the ideas of Troeltsch, Köhler and Blanke with enthusiasm and developed them considerably. In the studies of Bender, Littell, Yoder, Bauman, Peachey and Davis the biblicist, independent and pacifist groups – those groups, in other words, who drew their inspiration from Michael Sattler, Konrad Grebel and Menno Simons – are extolled as the 'real', 'essential' and 'evangelical' representatives of Anabaptism. The militant groups and the spiritualist Anabaptists who diverged from this mainstream kind are dismissed as marginal.[7]

By the 1920s Karl Holl had developed an opposing point of view.[8] His objections were renewed in the 1970s by James Stayer whose findings rested on more solid evidence and did not suffer from Lutheran preconceptions. In *The Anabaptists and the Sword* (1972) Stayer proves that the ideal of the peaceful, separatist free church was, until 1535 at least, by no means shared by the majority of Anabaptists. This only became the case after they had suffered two catastrophes. The Peasants' War afflicted the Anabaptists of south Germany and Switzerland, whilst in north-west Germany and Holland the collapse of the Anabaptist kingdom of Münster led to a reassessment of their position. The question of the nature and identity of the Anabaptist protest movement thus calls for a reassessment. Following James Stayer and using this author's own research, this contribution sets out to compare the original aims, the development and final state of two fully separate groups of Anabaptists. Both groups, the Swiss Anabaptists and the Strasbourg or Lower German Melchiorites, later the Mennonites, were originally popular movements which eventually narrowed down into small, exclusive communities. The investigation poses the following questions: How was it possible that these movements attracted considerable numbers of people in their early stages? How did the authorities and the official reformers react to this radical protest movement? Finally, how did the Anabaptist movement itself respond to persecution by the established authorities?

The ecclesiological question of adult baptism is absent from the beginnings of both the Swiss and the Lower German Anabaptist movements. The question arose relatively late, only after violent arguments with the official reformers had occurred. One can conclude from this that neither Konrad Grebel, the founder of the Swiss Anabaptist movement, nor Melchior Hoffman, the patriarch of the Strasbourg movement, the Lower German and Dutch Anabaptists, conceived from the outset of convening a 'holy remnant', a 'church without stains or wrinkles', separated from the masses of the damned by applying the baptism of faith. The alienation between Zwingli and his radical friends, who went on to found the Swiss Anabaptist movement, developed in the course of a dispute about the justification for tithes and the levying of interest. The Zürich proto-Anabaptists considered tithes 'the cornerstone of a corrupt religious structure', which permitted the exploitation of the poor, and parasitical lazy-bones such as monks, nuns, abbots and canons to live in prosperity, as well as the usurpation of the rights of the community; with the result that the Christian church's principal tasks, such as proper care of parish preachers, the poor, widows and orphans were neglected.[9] They therefore demanded the immediate abolition of tithes and their reintroduction as a local matter administered by the parishioners. In addition, the proto-Anabaptists attacked the practice of levying interest on capital loans. The reason, according to them, was that interest stood in contradiction to the New Testament commandment to love one's neighbour. Zwingli, on the other hand, was in favour of continuing the payment of tithes as long as the secular authorities willed it so. However, he did concede that current practices were not in accord with God's justice and should be reformed. He was equally in favour of the levying of interest, as this represented an obligation which had been freely entered into, while no one had a legal right to another person's capital.[10]

In the areas administered by Zürich – Höngg, Grüningen, the communities of Marthalen, Benken, Wildisbühl and Truttikon – as well as in the peasant communities governed by the city of Schaffhausen, especially in and around Hallau, agitation by the proto-Anabaptists led to widespread refusal to pay tithes. To those peasants who listened to the voices of the religious radicals, the monks, nuns, the higher clergy and, to a certain extent, the common priests were parasitical, self-interested, sinful and gluttonous – not pastors but ravening wolves. The first spokesman of the anti-tithe movement, Simon Stumpf, the pastor of Höngg, considered it necessary to slay the 'priestly brood', presumably thinking of the Abbot of Wettingen to whom his peasant flock paid their tithes.[11]

Then in 1523–4 the idea of the free communal choice of a minister came to the fore, together with the demand for the abolition of tithes. Wilhelm Reublin, who played a leading role in the southern German Anabaptist movement, was elected preacher of the village parish of Witikon. This election was carried out in defiance of the right of patronage held by the chapter of Zürich's Great Minster. Initially, the Zürich authorities tolerated this breach of the law on condition that the tithes continued to be paid by the parish. Just as Reublin had done in Witikon, so did Johannes Brötli become preacher in Zollikon at the request of the community. The chaplain who had been appointed by the Great Minster chapter was simply pushed aside and the city council of Zürich was not even asked to confirm the election. After he had been expelled from Zollikon, Brötli was elected in the same revolutionary way in Hallau, later the centre of the Peasants' War in eastern Switzerland. Hans Krüsi also owed his incumbency in Tablat, near St Gallen, to a decision of the local parish. Following the example of St Paul, and indeed of Andreas Karlstadt in Orlamünde, Brötli and Krüsi did not want to be supported by tithes, benefices, or fees, but by voluntary communal donations and their own labour. Krüsi, formerly an assistant teacher, even went so far as to learn the weaver's trade in order to appear in the eyes of the radical peasants as a preacher conforming to Scripture. The Anabaptist movement sought 'lay apostles' who could practise a second, worldly profession alongside their spiritual duties. Theologically, the demand that priests should be elected by their parish was grounded in the general conviction to be found amongst all reformers of the 'priesthood of all believers'; psychologically, it was rooted in the newly awakened self-consciousness of the peasants and artisans. In Zwingli's own words, written in 1524, 'Christians no longer seek out their anointed priests, and even cow-herds and goose-herds are more learned than their theologians. And every peasant's house is a school, wherein one can read the New and the Old Testaments, the highest arts of all.'[12]

Peter Blickle has drawn attention to the fact that the Revolution of 1525 depended upon two principles: elections were to be the criterion for the distribution of offices; and the *Gemeinde* (community) was to be the basis for the formation of political decisions.[13] Both of these principles were held by Anabaptists of the Zürich territory in 1523–4, and in the villages belonging to St Gallen and Schaffhausen in east Switzerland in 1525. Zwingli, however, wanted to preserve the authority of Zürich's city council over the rural communities of its subject territories, just as the council of Schaffhausen did over its surrounding dependent villages. According to Zwingli, the urban authorities, which were committed to the truth of the Gospel, should carry out the Reformation in the territories subject to them. The tension which had existed since the later Middle Ages between the city and its rural communities was one of the principal causes of the origin and spread of Anabaptism.

In the autumn of 1523 the conflict between Zwingli and his radical friends, Grebel, Mantz and Stumpf, intensified over the issue of the abolition of images and the introduction of an evangelical communion service. The two sides agreed with each other over fundamentals: the adoration of images was considered to be idolatry, and both considered the Catholic celebration of the mass a blasphemy. But Zwingli wished the decision about the precise timing of the abolition of images and the introduction of an evangelical communion service to be left to the city council. Simon Stumpf maintained that a community, even without the council's approval, had the right to enact a religious reform which was required by the Holy Ghost. In contrast, Zwingli declared that the civil authority should determine both the time and the method of the introduction of the communion service and the abolition of images.[14] True to this principle, he obeyed the civil authority when it expressly forbade him to celebrate an evangelical communion at Christmas 1523.[15] From this moment he was nothing more than a cowardly scribe in the eyes of his former protagonists.[16] The final breach between the official Zürich reformers and the proto-Anabaptists occurred as a result of the quarrel over adult baptism. In the country parishes of Zollikon, Hallau, Witikon, Tablat and in the town of Waldshut the baptism of believers did *not yet* represent the association of a small and exclusive community of visible saints. On the contrary, baptism was administered to almost the entire population of these villages.

In spite of the precepts of the Sermon on the Mount, the inhabitants of the town of Waldshut, and the communities of eastern Switzerland favouring adult baptism, were determined to use force if necessary to defend their autonomy. That autonomy was usurped in 1525 and they defended their elected ministers against their erstwhile authorities. In Waldshut the Anabaptists expelled anyone who refused to take up arms. Thus in 1524/5 the rebellious peasant movement and Anabaptism coalesced in the region of Schaffhausen, St Gallen and Waldshut. The ringleaders of the rebellion were local ministers committed to the Anabaptists, or leaders of the community such as Balthasar Hubmaier, Wilhelm Reublin, Hans Krüsi, and earlier, in Höngg, Simon Stumpf. James Stayer correctly asserts, when referring to the majority of the Swiss Anabaptists who lived in these rural communities, that 'the first stage of Anabaptism was congregational and not separatist, and placed its faith in self-defence rather than pacifism'.[17] This militant, congregationalist Swiss Anabaptism became entangled with, and disappeared in, the catastrophe of the Peasants' War. The urban Anabaptists of Zürich, led by Grebel, Mantz, Blaurock and Castelberger, did not follow this course to the bitter end. Nevertheless, they also desired, as did Stumpf, Reublin and Hubmaier, a radical root-and-branch reform of church, state and society. Accordingly they approached Zwingli with the demand that the old Zürich council be overthrown and replaced by a newly elected Christian council. Such a council should carry out a radical programme of reform regardless of the external situation and in spite of 'the weak in spirit'.[18] The demand was rejected firmly by the socially conservative-minded Zwingli. In his opinion the concept was both politically unrealistic and theologically unsupportable. By the summer of

1524 the urban Anabaptists of Zürich had recognised that Zwingli's refusal to head the revolutionary party, coupled with the distribution of power in the city, meant that a radical, scriptural Reformation was out of the question. The powerful opposition to any rapid and complete attempts at reform soon led the proto-Anabaptists of the city to place more emphasis upon the individual imitation of Christ, the attempt to lead a life in accordance with the rules of the Sermon on the Mount. Zwingli, who was a keen observer, did not overlook the way in which this movement oscillated between two goals: between the desire to institute a radical reform, using force when necessary, and on the other hand, a desire to lead a life in imitation of Christ and in accordance with the Sermon on the Mount. In his treatise of 1524 entitled 'Whosoever gives occasion to violence', he describes the conduct of the urban proto-Anabaptists as follows: 'At first they are not prepared to recognise any authority and then they are; but then no one is a Christian who belongs to an established authority. One minute they want a church of their own and the next they declare that no authority should protect the preaching of the Gospel by force. First, they tell us to slay the clergy who lead people astray, and then we are expected to let them preach without hindrance.'[19] As the situation in Zürich became more and more hopeless for the radicals, they tended increasingly to turn to the Sermon on the Mount with its injunction to turn the other cheek. In a famous letter to Thomas Müntzer dated 5 September 1524 (that is, at the beginning of the uprisings in the landgraviate of Stühlingen, but a full six months before the beginning of the general peasant uprising), the urban Anabaptists of Zürich, led by Konrad Grebel, stated their rejection of violence.[20] At the same time they also wrote that there was no likelihood of a radical and thorough-going reform ever taking place. True Christians, in their eyes, were henceforth a small flock of defenceless sheep condemned to be the prey of wolves. This world was not something which could be transformed into the kingdom of God, but a seductive labyrinth in which what mattered was to keep one's soul pure by rejecting force and violence. Thus even before the defeat of the peasants, one can perceive the development of a mentality in which pacifism, separatism and the advocacy of a free church were elements. Hanspeter Jecker has pointed out that the bearers of such thoughts were generally free-thinking intellectuals who did not possess offices or preside over communities.[21] Personal dissatisfaction, or the refusal of academic chairs at Zürich's *Grossmünster* might have played a role in their adopting such resigned attitudes.[22]

After the terrible defeat of the peasants, Michael Sattler called the remaining confused and scattered Swiss Anabaptists together and established them in the tradition of Grebel and Mantz in the 'Schleitheim Confession' of 1527.[23] The 'Schleitheim Articles' draw a sharp line between the Anabaptists and all those who attempt to establish territorial or urban reforms which depended on the unity between state and church. They no longer express any confidence in the civil authority to institute a Christian reform. They assert the irreconcilability of Christianity and secular government because, as the articles put it, the essence of the state lies in the application of force and the exercise of authority. At the same time they reject armed popular uprisings as a means of achieving reform and the kind of spiritualism which in the name of the freedom of the spirit disregards the commandments of the New Testament. Instead they advocate the complete separation of Christians from the corrupt state churches and civic communities. This was to be achieved by three means: by refusing all oaths and loyalties, by refusing all civic offices and by refusing to take up arms. In addition, alehouses and popular festivals were to be avoided, and those neighbours who were godless or hopelessly compromised were to be shunned.

Thus, it was only after the peasants' defeat and the failure of the militant congregationalist Anabaptists that the idea of a separatist, free church movement began to gain ground among the Anabaptists of Switzerland. Baptism of believers became a means of identifying and gathering the small group of elect sheep which were not of this world. To the Swiss Brethren the 'world' seemed nothing but a kingdom of shadows and darkness alien to the true Christian. Amongst themselves they tried to achieve the same goals which they had originally tried to see through in the official church. They wanted to establish a community of equals, whose leader, elected by them all, carried out his duties in the interests of the whole community. In order to create a pure eucharistic community, a strict church discipline was introduced and offenders suffered the penalty of exclusion. Those aggressions which had previously been directed outwards were henceforth directed at the members of their own community in the form of a rigorous control of morals and thought. This, however, led to frequent 'purges' and splits amongst Anabaptist communities and even to the repeated removal of their leaders, a feature early deplored by Pilgram Marbeck.

Zwingli's response to the 'Schleitheim Confession' was the Latin tract 'In Catabaptistarum strophas elenchus', written in July 1527. In this tract it becomes evident that the peaceful, pacifist and separatist Anabaptists were just as unacceptable to him as the militant ones who had thrown in their lot with the rebellious peasants.[24] He mistrusted their peacefulness and strict moral code, and insisted on associating them with their violent and profligate stepbrothers, from whom in fact they sought to distance themselves. Quite apart from that, Zwingli also maintained that the Swiss Brethren, that is to say, the followers of Michael Sattler, endangered the Reformation and contributed to the undermining of the body politic. He argued that they were guilty of believing that good works were necessary for salvation, because they believed in free will, considered that adults must decide to be baptised in order to achieve a state of grace, and believed in the possibility of leading a life free from sin and in the possibility of a pure church. The strict avoidance of the allegedly ungodly and withdrawal from the world was, in Zwingli's eyes, nothing other than the spiritual arrogance of pseudo-heavenly beings. The true Christian, in Zwingli's opinion, should not seek to separate himself from his sinful neighbour, but try to overcome his own self-seeking. For Zwingli, the church is the community of imperfect brothers and sisters who, trusting in God's good grace, attempt to improve their lives by following Christ. This church would be a *corpus mixtum* until the end of time. Whoever sets himself up as judge and attempts to separate the wheat from the chaff before the day of the great harvest will only destroy the whole crop.

Zwingli was also convinced that the Anabaptists presented as much danger to the state as they did to the church. The precept of the Sermon on the Mount which commands people to 'turn the other cheek' does not apply to those in authority; neither does the injunction, from Matthew 20:25–6, not to differentiate between servant and master in the church. The secular power was obliged to protect those who suffered injustice, just as it was obliged to proceed with all its authority against those who committed injustice. The nature of secular authority was in no way purely a function 'of the world and of the flesh'. On the contrary, as Zwingli asserted, the pious and godly judges were the best judges, for the godly judge is possessed by the spirit of justice and, thanks to his strength of spirit, his *constantia*, is immune from the temptations of passion, anger and greed. Whosoever attempted to keep good Christians away from secular offices was responsible for endangering the just world order. Finally, it was necessary to administer oaths for the maintenance of the civic community. Such oaths were not, as the Anabaptists believed, a commitment to a particular form of behaviour in the future, but rather an appeal to God to witness the truth of the declaration being made. That is, the oath is the explicit act of placing oneself under the authority of God's judgement, in the event that one commits perjury. The government had for these reasons the duty to act against even the so-called 'peaceful' Anabaptists as much as against the militant ones.

As a consequence, the introduction of the Reformation into the Swiss cities led to the brutal expulsion of the Anabaptists by the new religious authorities. Basle undertook radical expulsions only after 1529. At first the exiles found refuge in the villages of the Aargau, but a more secure refuge was offered by the isolated homesteads of the alpine region. Among their new neighbours there were few informers. Frequently neighbours refrained from taking over the confiscated property of Anabaptists – anyone who did so risked being ostracised by the village community.[25] However, the Swiss Anabaptists contributed little to Swiss peasant uprisings after 1527. They lost their mass following when it became evident that they neither could nor wanted to succeed in the establishment of the free election of ministers, the abolition of tithes and the complete autonomy of the village community. Their habit of separating themselves from others and their development of an alternative ascetic and archaic culture contributed to the growing gap between them and the rest of the population. During the seventeenth and eighteenth centuries, persecution and contempt pushed them further into a theology of martyrdom in which suffering was evidence for the possession of the truth.

If one compares the Swiss Anabaptists with the Melchiorites, the future Mennonites, who formed the second large group of Anabaptists, several important differences immediately become apparent.[26]

(1) There were no peasants amongst the Melchiorites. Like the urban Anabaptists of Basle and Zürich, they were recruited mainly from among the artisans of the lower guilds and from members of the middle class who

were not fully integrated, such as printers and apprentice merchants. Refugees who did not possess citizenship were also frequent recruits.

(2) The Melchiorites were dominated by urgent apocalyptic expectations to a far greater extent than were the Swiss Anabaptists. Right at the beginning of his public career Melchior Hoffman was prophesying the end of the world and Second Coming for 1533, seven years after the beginning of the eschatological *furioso*. He did not believe that the Reformation would succeed until 1530, but expected instead that the Antichrist would temporarily dominate the true church.

(3) In the imminent persecution preceding the end of time, even the letter of Holy Scripture would suffer. The godly would have to trust in the 'inner word' which unfolds in the heart; they would have to rely on dreams, visions and an inspired, allegorical interpretation of the Scriptures by the 'Witness of the All Highest'. In contrast to the Swiss Brethren, the Melchiorites originally were extreme spiritualists.

(4) The impression made by the defeat of the peasants led Hoffman to reject any form of rebellion against the secular authorities. Instead he proposed that evangelical princes and magistrates should play a leading role in the introduction of the Reformation, thus acting as protectors of the true church. This was the reason why he did not seriously contest the appointment of evangelical ministers by the secular authorities, although he did point out that in Livonia there was not one preacher who had been appointed to his office by free communal election as was laid down in the New Testament. He was a bitter opponent only of the appropriation of secularised church property by members of city councils in Livonia and Schleswig-Holstein. Over a long period of time he strove for an official recognition of his missionary activities – not without success. He owed his position as preacher in Kiel to the Danish king, Frederic I. To the end of his life, Hoffman placed his faith in the pious civil authorities instituting a Reformation from above. He therefore resolutely rejected the appeal of the Swiss Brethren to refuse all worldly offices. Hoffman shared Luther's opinion that a Christian could even carry out his duties as jailer and hangman with a good conscience as long as he was acting in an official capacity.

However, Hoffman was at one with the Swiss Brethren in their anti-clericalism. The 'slick smatterers' ('geschmierte Nasengeister'), as he sometimes called the Protestant preachers and established Catholic priests, were for him nothing more than avaricious servants of the dead letter who had not the slightest idea of the living spirit. He did attempt for quite some time to maintain good relations with Luther and Bucer – he considered himself their equal – but from the very beginning he demanded that a pastor should be the servant and not the lord of his flock. He called for the reintroduction of the constitution of the earliest Christian communities, where, according to 1 Corinthians 14, all the members of the community had the right to expound the Bible during the service and to reveal their own spiritual experiences. He insisted on the need to break up the church's monopoly on the exposition of the Bible and combined this with a rejection of auricular confession, which he considered the church's most important means of controlling the life-styles of individuals. Like Brötli, Krüsi and Karlstadt before him, he too practised a lay profession, in his case that of the furrier, in order not to be a financial burden to his parish. He also called for the abolition of religious orders and the removal and destruction of images in the churches. In this he was no different from the Swiss proto-Anabaptists. Even his belief in the symbolic function of the Eucharist and his rejection of Luther's eucharistic doctrine were products of his anti-clericalism. He was afraid that if the evangelical ministers' pronouncement of the sacramental words were believed to bring about Christ's real presence in the communion bread and wine, then the evangelical ministers could reassume a mediatory function, coming between God and the members of their flock. Just like the majority of the Swiss Anabaptists, the Melchiorites originally wanted a reform of the church as a whole and not the separation of a select group as a free church. However, like Hubmaier in Waldshut, Reublin, Brötli and Krüsi in Switzerland, Hoffman also arrogated for himself the right of self-defence. So when the steward Stackelberg, acting under the orders of the Archbishop of Riga, attempted to arrest him in January 1525 he was prevented by a violent and angry crowd. The incident led to the deaths of four villagers and twenty more suffered severe injuries.

In 1529 Hoffman's doctrine of the eucharist led to his exclusion from the Lutheran church and his expulsion from Schleswig-Holstein. Moreover, the Strasbourg reformers Bucer and Capito, who had originally greeted him as an ally in their eucharistic controversy with Luther, now rejected him because of his allegorical exposition of the Scriptures and his monophysite christology.

Hoffman reacted to this double disappointment by going over to the Strasbourg Anabaptists, but without accepting the Schleitheim principles of separation, pacifism and the rejection of public offices. Unlike the Swiss Brethren, the Melchiorites had a blueprint for a new hierarchical community structure which provided for the superiority of 'apostolic messengers' and 'prophets' over the ordinary members of the congregation. Swiss Brethren and Melchiorites were, however, at one in their criticism of the reformations of Wittenberg and Zürich, for these had sown no 'fruits of the faith' amongst the ordinary people. In Hoffman's opinion the fault for this lay with the reformers' doctrines of justification and predestination. These caused faith to become an empty figment of imagination, and made God responsible for evil. In contrast to his previous views he now preached his belief in free will, whose co-operation was needed in the process of achieving salvation, and in the omnipresence of grace, which was available to all people for their salvation, if only they desired it. He considered the world to be fundamentally capable of conversion to goodness through a revolution initiated by men. After 1529 he came under the influence of the Strasbourg prophets Lienhard and Ursula Jost. Under their influence he conceived of an interim, theocratic kingdom which had the task of rooting out godless clerics, thus preparing for the Second Coming. Right to the end of his life he remained convinced that only 'pious authorities', that is to say, the governing councils of the imperial free cities, particularly Strasbourg, were capable of conducting the final struggle against the 'diabolical trinity', the pope, the emperor and the priestly horde misleading the people. But since no evangelical magistrature appeared to be taking the task in hand, Jan van Leiden and Jan Mathijs attempted to institute God's kingdom at Münster through a revolution from *below*, quite against the declared wishes of Hoffman. The Strasbourg wing of the Melchiorites, however, distanced itself from the Münster Anabaptists, just as the Grebel–Mantz circle and Michael Sattler had previously distanced themselves from Hubmaier and the militant eastern Swiss Anabaptists. After the bloody suppression of the Münster experiment in June 1535 the majority of the Melchiorites came under the influence of Menno Simons. Gradually they became transformed into the peaceful Mennonites. Hoffman's influence could be seen in Menno Simons's position with respect to secular government, but in general it is fair to say that the Mennonites adopted the position of the Swiss Brethren in matters of ecclesiology and ethics. The Mennonites also placed the charismatics firmly under the authority of the Bible and of the community. After the failure of the uprising of 1535 the conception of a peaceful, separatist and biblicist Free Church gradually gained acceptance in north Germany as well. The use of force and a spiritualism which had no connection with the Bible were scorned.

In summary, a comparison between the two largest groups of Anabaptists which developed independently of each other, the Swiss Anabaptists and the Melchiorites (later the Mennonites), shows clear parallels in their general evolution. Both groups began with the idea of a radical reformation of all spheres of life, particularly of the church, which should lead to a restoration of the constitution of the early Christian communities according to 1 Corinthians 14. When it became clear that, since the secular authorities were opposed, the only means to achieve this was force, both movements split into militant and pacifist wings. Only after military defeat did the idea of a separatist, pacifist Free Church gain general acceptance in both groups. This withdrawal from the world led in both cases to a loss of support amongst the common people. The erstwhile radical revolutionaries became 'die Stillen im Lande' – the quiet country folk.

Notes: Chapter 7

1 Compare in this respect the cautionary epistle of the preachers of Strasbourg directed against Kautz and Denck, of 2 July 1527 in *Quellen zur Geschichte der Täufer*, Vol. VII (*Elsass*, pt I), ed. M. Krebs and H. G. Rott (Gütersloh, 1959), pp. 110, 114, (henceforth cited as *QGTE*). See also the letter of consolation by Capito to the captured adherents of Michael Sattler in Horb, *QGTE*, pt I, no. 84. See also the intercession of Capito for the imprisoned Anabaptists with the mayor of Horb, *QGTE*, pt I, no. 83. Calvin also distinguished between a spiritualist and a biblicistic Anabaptism. See: R. Stauffer, 'Zwingli et Calvin, critique de la confession de Schleitheim', in M. Lienhard (ed.), *The Origins and Characteristics of Anabaptism* (The Hague, 1977), p. 130.
2 See J. S. Oyer, *Lutheran Reformers against Anabaptism* (The Hague, 1965); H. Fast, *Heinrich Bullinger und die Täufer* (Neustadt an der Aisch, 1959).
3 S. Franck, *Chronica, Zeitbuch und Geschichtbibel* (n.p., 1551), pp. clxxviii–clxxxvi ('Von Widerteuffern oder Teuffern'). G. Arnold, *Unparteyische Kirchen- und Ketzerhistorie*, 3rd edn (Schaffhausen, 1740–2), Vol. I, pt 2, bk 16, ch. xxi, pp. 856–99 ('Von denen Wiedertäuffern').

4 E. Troeltsch, *Die Soziallehren der christlichen Kirchen und Gruppen* (Tübingen, 1912), pp. 794–815.

5 See W. Köhler's introduction to Zwingli's testimony in the trial of the Anabaptists, in: Huldreich Zwingli, *Sämtliche Werke*, Vol. IV (Leipzig, 1927), p. 161 (= *Corpus Reformatorum*, Vol. XCI, henceforth *CR*). Henceforth cited as *ZwW*.

6 F. Blanke, *Brüder in Christo* (Zürich, 1955).

7 cf. H. S. Bender, *Conrad Grebel (c.1498–1526): The Founder of the Swiss Brethren* (Goshen, Ind., 1950); F. H. Littell, *The Anabaptist View of the Church*, 2nd edn (Boston, Mass., 1958); J. H. Yoder, *Täufertum und Reformation in der Schweiz*, Vol. I: *Die Gespräche zwischen Täufern und Reformatoren, 1523–1528* (Karlsruhe, 1962), and Vol. II: *Täufertum und Reformation im Gespräch: Dogmengeschichtliche Untersuchung* . . . (Zürich, 1968); C. Bauman, *Gewaltlosigkeit im Täufertum*, Studies in the History of Christian Thought, Vol. III (Leiden, 1968); P. Peachey, *Die soziale Herkunft der Schweizer Täufer in der Reformationszeit* (Karlsruhe, 1954); K. Davis, *Anabaptism and Asceticism: A Study in Intellectual Origins* (Scottdale, Pa, 1974).

8 K. Holl, 'Luther und die Schwärmer', in id., *Gesammelte Aufsätze zur Kirchengeschichte*, Vol. I: *Luther* (Tübingen, 1932), pp. 420–67. This article is a lecture held in 1922.

9 cf. J. Stayer, 'Die Anfänge des Schweizerischen Täufertums im reformierten Kongregationalismus', in *Umstrittenes Täufertum*, ed. H. J. Goertz (Göttingen, 1975), p. 30. The early Anabaptists' anticlericalism is emphasised in H. J. Goertz, *Die Täufer: Geschichte und Deutung* (Munich, 1980), pp. 40–76.

10 *ZwW*, Vol. II, pp. 458–525 (= *CR*, Vol. LXXXIX); also in the tract, *Wer Ursache gebe zu Aufruhr*, in *ZwW*, Vol. III, pp. 399–400 (= *CR*, Vol. XC); *ZwW*, Vol. III, pp. 388–9 (on the obligation to pay interest which was due).

11 *ZwW*, Vol. IV, p. 170 (= *CR*, Vol. XCI).

12 *ZwW*, Vol. III, pp. 360–1 (= *CR*, Vol. XC).

13 P. Blickle, *Deutsche Untertanen: Ein Widerspruch* (Munich, 1981), p. 117.

14 *ZwW*, Vol. II, p. 784 (= *CR*, Vol. LXXXIX).

15 E. Egli (ed.), *Aktensammlung zur Geschichte der Zürcher Reformation in den Jahren 1519–1533* (Nieuwkoop, 1973), no. 436 and no. 464 (reprint of the 1879 edition).

16 *Quellen zur Geschichte der Täufer in der Schweiz*, Vol. I, ed. L. von Muralt and W. Schmid (Zürich, 1952), p. 8. Henceforth cited as *QGTS/Z*.

17 Stayer, 'Die Anfänge des Schweizerischen Täufertums', p. 48.

18 *QGTS/Z*, pp. 120–2, 127; *ZwW*, Vol. IV, pp. 206–7, 590–1 (= *CR*, Vol. XCI); *ZwW*, Vol. VI/1, pp. 32, 37 (= *CR*, Vol. XCIII).

19 *ZwW*, Vol. III, p. 404 (= *CR*, Vol. CX).

20 *QGTS/Z*, pp. 13–21.

21 H. Jecker, 'Die Basler Täufer', *Basler Zeitschrift für Geschichte und Altertumskunde* (1980), p. 63.

22 H. Bullinger, *Der Wiedertöufferen ursprung, fürgang, secten, wäsen, fürneme und gemeine jrer leer Artickel* (Zürich, 1561), bk 1, p. 9.

23 *Quellen zur Geschichte der Täufer in der Schweiz*, Vol. II: *Ostschweiz*, ed. H. Fast (Zürich, 1973), pp. 26–36.

24 *ZwW*, Vol. VI/1, pp. 21–196.

25 cf. E. H. Correll, *Das schweizerische Täufermennonitentum: Ein soziologischer Bericht* (Tübingen, 1925), p. 67.

26 For detailed evidence see K. Deppermann, *Melchior Hoffman: Soziale Unruhen und apokalyptische Visionen im Zeitalter der Reformation* (Göttingen, 1979).

Part Three

Religion and Social Control

8 Lutheranism and Literacy: A Reassessment

GERALD STRAUSS

About a dozen years ago Professor Lawrence Stone published an influential article in *Past and Present* on the factors affecting the condition of education and literacy in early modern Europe. He gave a prominent place among these factors to religion, especially to Protestant religion, because, as a religion of the book, Protestantism encourages reading, and therefore tends to promote literacy in society. He writes:

> In the early sixteenth century the Catholics were fearful of heresy because of Bible study, whereas the reformers were fearful of superstition because of lack of Bible study ... At this critical turning point in history [that is, the first large-scale social repercussions of mass production printing] the Protestants seized on the new invention but the Catholic world, after initial encouragement, soon realized its subversive potential and turned against it.[1]

Professor Stone develops this argument primarily in relation to English Puritanism. But he advances his explicit association of Protestantism with Bible-reading, and hence with reading itself, as a generalisation on the whole age of the Reformation.

This argument will be recognised as a commonplace in the vast literature on the Reformation, as well as in the much smaller, and mostly recent, body of writing on early modern European literacy. Most scholars seem to have concluded, or seem to assume, that the Protestant Reformation greatly advanced literacy because Protestantism was, much more than Catholicism, the religion of the word, and therefore of reading, and because it insisted on every individual's right – indeed his duty – to experience the word for himself. Reading was promoted–so the argument goes–to allow people to exercise this right and fulfil this duty. Schools were established and vernacular Bibles made available. And all this happened first in Germany, where Martin Luther turned the New, and then the Old, Testaments into plain German, and where he and his fellow reformers encouraged men and women to discover the truth for themselves by encountering it at first hand in Scripture; where a flood of Bibles issued from the presses, and where schools were established or improved so that a condition of general literacy might be created and perpetuated in the population.

This, or something very like it, is the common view of things.[2] The emblem for it is the title page illustration in John Foxe's *Actes and Monuments* where a group of devout Protestant men and women holding their Bibles is contrasted with a circle of suspicious-looking Catholics fingering their beads.[3] The task I have set myself is to find out whether this picture is in fact true as far as Luther and the German Reformation are concerned. Did Luther's Reformation promote Bible-reading? Did it advance common education? Did it therefore and thereby extend literacy in the population? At issue is not so much the general question of education and literacy itself. It is a fact that schools of all levels, including popular German language schools, increased in number and quality in the age of the Reformation;[4] it is also true, though not so readily demonstrable and quantifiable, that literacy spread through the German population in the course of the sixteenth century.[5] These questions, I say, are not at issue here. What *is* at issue is the link between these phenomena in German social history and Martin Luther's Reformation as their efficient cause. *Was* Luther, was the Lutheran Reformation with its dedication to *sola scriptura*, really responsible for the expansion of schooling and literacy in the sixteenth century?

First a few words about this expansion. It may not be generally known that Germany experienced in the sixteenth century a large-scale growth of educational institutions. I am not now referring to such intellectual forcing houses as the classical Gymnasia, the elite boarding schools for the super-bright, or the universities. The expansion I refer to is of common, elementary local schools where rudimentary teaching was given to the children of ordinary people. Most of the facts concerning this development lie buried in regional histories and specialised monographs, most of all in huge piles of documents in local archives. They show that in region after region in the Holy Roman Empire, in princely states and ecclesiastical domains and cities and towns, networks of schools were organised in the course of the sixteenth century, often building on older foundations, but in every case extending, strengthening what already existed, if not starting anew. The goal was a centralised system of general education controlled from the chancellery or the consistory, locally financed though supplemented, where needed, by government aid. Needless to say, this ambitious, modern-seeming aim was not always achieved. But as an objective it emerges clearly from the documents. Its purpose appears to have been twofold: to guarantee the production in the future of trained professionals for service in state and church; secondly, to equip the populace at large with enough reading and writing to enable them to function in their various stations in life. By and large these goals seem to have been met. Towns and cities had fine Latin schools, of course, many of them institutions of great distinction. But village schools, too, were common, though many of them seem to have led a shaky existence, frequently shut down for harvest work, or bad weather, or impassable roads or a bridge down, or owing to a great dying among the children, or because parents were too poor or tight-fisted to pay the trifling sum it took to keep the schoolroom heated and the teacher in bread and beer. Nearly always, however, they started up again to teach at least two of the conventional three Rs along with a little religion. As a result of all this, basic functional literacy does seem to have spread through the population.[6] I cannot prove it statistically, and I do not want to estimate percentages. But my work with the sources has left me with a definite impression that a considerable portion of the populace in towns and countryside was being trained to read and to write. For precisely what purpose, however, and with exactly what consequences, is not at all clear. The documents from which I take the evidence for the existence of schools and the relative prevalence of literacy tell me very little about the objectives to which these conditions related.

In the absence of a good answer to the question of purpose – why so much schooling for the populace, why literacy for the many? – it has been generally supposed that Lutheranism was the critical factor in the promotion of schools and the advance of public literacy in early modern Germany. This is the supposition I want to question. Let me begin to do so at the source: Luther himself. What does Luther say about the objectives of schooling, about reading, and especially about reading the Bible?

This question is easily answered. Luther said a great deal, and most of what he said favoured the school as a specialised institution for preparing a professional cadre, one that was capable of assuming positions of leadership in church and state: pastors and preachers, theologians and church administrators, lawyers and bureaucrats, teachers, doctors. This is the argument of his two most important pieces of writing on the subject: *An Admonition to the Councillors of All German Cities to Establish and Maintain Christian Schools* of 1524, and the sermon *Children Should Be Sent to School* of 1530.[7] Both are vigorous, indeed passionate, polemics for his conviction that academic learning – especially the languages and arts of the liberal curriculum – are indispensable in a Christian society. Luther aimed his fire at two quarters from which this conviction was just then under attack: spiritualists, *Schwärmer*, and others of that ilk, men who claimed for their ideas the authority of immediate divine inspiration, and to whom the study of Greek and Hebrew was therefore nothing but idle pedantry; secondly, a kind of vulgar bourgeois utilitarianism which – so Luther feared–was starving out the academic schools. Luther's own aims for schooling were both sharply focused and broad. He is for general education. He even favours obligatory school attendance.[8] All youngsters – girls along with boys, poor as well as rich – should learn to read and write. But these objectives have little to do with the benefits of a general education or with any attempt to raise the level of public virtue. Their chief purpose is to identify and select able pupils, to skim off the best and move them – only the boys, of course – rapidly through the better schools and Gymnasia to the university and on to their careers.[9] In this way no boy of talent would be lost to society, and church and state would never need to worry about their *Nachwuchs*, the steady supply of qualified young men to help manage state and church.[10] There is no doubt that this is what Luther had chiefly in mind when he wrote about education in 1524, in 1530 and to the end of his life. When the opportunity arose to put the principle into practice, he made it the foundation of public education in his own state of Saxony. In *The Visitors' Instruction to the Pastors in Saxony* of 1528, a comprehensive blueprint for the new state church, written by Melanchthon and with a preface by Luther, it was stated at the very beginning of the section on education that children must attend school 'so that men may be trained who are qualified to teach in the church and govern in the world'.[11] Nothing is said in this document, a model school and curriculum plan as it became, about general or popular education, secular or religious. Provision is made for 'Christian instruction',[12] but this, as everything else, is given only in Latin. Latin as a language and as a culture is the heart of the whole programme. Lessons and books were those of the traditional arts programme. The overriding aim of the procedure was to separate the able from among the many and complete the quality education of the former.

But this cannot be the whole story. If Luther and Melanchthon, and their colleagues in the movement, believed it to be the chief aim of schools to produce qualified public servants, they did not see this as their only aim. They acknowledged the existence below the network of Latin schools of a host of German vernacular schools where the rudiments of reading, writing and religion were given to a large, scattered, intellectually undifferentiated, urban and rural juvenile population. What should be taught in these schools? In view of the reformers' mostly disparaging remarks about the common crowd,[13] what kind of education, especially what sort of religious education, did they think the masses should receive? Ought *Herr Omnes* to be a fluent reader? Should the *Pöbel* read the Bible? Can one trust the *Haufen* to read it with the right understanding? Let us see what Luther has to say on the subject of common Bible-reading, a subject that would seem to go to the heart of the Reformation as a social and cultural event, as opposed to an event merely in the history of ideas.

A survey of Luther's words on this point shows him favouring the principle of 'Every man his own Bible-reader' until about 1525 – a year that was in many respects the great divide in the history of the Reformation – then falling mostly silent on the subject and, at the same time, taking actions that effectively discouraged, or at least failed effectively to encourage, a direct encounter between Scripture and the untrained lay mind. In 1520, in the *Appeal to the Christian Nobility of the German Nation* – a sweeping reform plan for church and society – he put it to his public that

> Above all other things, Holy Scripture must be the foremost and common subject in universities and secondary schools, and the Gospel in elementary schools. And would God that every town had a girls' school in which young girls were taught a daily lesson in the New Testament, either in German or in Latin, so that by the time a young Christian person had reached the ninth or tenth year, he would be familiar with the entire Holy Gospel.[14]

Even more explicitly revealing of Luther's intentions in these early years of the Reformation are the short prefaces he supplied for his 1522 German translation of the New Testament. It is my purpose in these introductory remarks, Luther says, to make sure that the common man 'will not be looking for commandment and law where he should instead look for Gospel and promise' – in other words, mistake the whole meaning of the Gospel.[15] There is so much confusion abroad now on religious matters, Luther says, unhappily, that the simple person needs a guide to the right understanding of Scripture. Clearly he meant his new translation of the Bible to be placed in the hands of the public at large. Of the Gospel According to John, and of Paul's Epistle to the Romans, he says that they are 'the true kernel and marrow of these books, and every Christian should read these first and foremost and' – he goes on – 'by means of daily reading make them as common and ordinary to himself as his daily bread'.[16]

But in later years Luther seems to have grown increasingly doubtful of people's ability to understand these essential distinctions. It is significant – it is certainly interesting – that most of the references to 'reading' the Gospel by ordinary people are dropped from the otherwise unchanged prefaces to the 1546 edition of his New Testament.[17] From the preface to the New Testament as a whole they were omitted altogether; only two indirect references to common reading remain, one in the preface to Acts, the other in the introduction to Romans.[18] Luther did not entirely abandon his view that the Bible is simple for the simple, difficult only for the subtle and devious – 'the smart alecs and wheeler-dealers in the world', as he put it in an after-dinner remark.[19] Nor did he let go of his basic conviction that all reform must be accomplished within the individual conscience, where the Gospel has to take root and produce an internal change, before external constraints – laws, regulations, and such – can work. But by the second half of the 1520s he no longer thought that this internal change could be effected by means of private Bible study. On the contrary; he seems to have anticipated chaos and confusion as the results of such ungovernable personal relations with the Bible, and he could point to enough recent events to give substance to his fears. Expert guidance was needed now: above all, preaching by authoritative interpreters. He had hinted at this as early as 1524, in his appeal to city councilmen, where he asked rhetorically: Why bother with Latin, Greek and Hebrew when we have the Bible in German now? and answered: Because no one can know what the Scripture really says without first having studied it in the original tongues. Even among the church fathers, he goes on, those who didn't know Greek and Hebrew 'weren't sure of what it all meant'.[20] Later he grew adamant on the need for expertise. 'Nowadays everyone thinks he is a master of Scripture', he said, 'and every Tom, Dick and Harry imagines he understands the Bible and knows it inside out.' 'But', he went on, 'all the other arts and skills have their preceptors and masters from whom one must learn, and they have rules and laws to be obeyed and adhered to. Only Holy Scripture and the Word of God seems to be open to everybody's vanity, pride, whim and arrogance, and is twisted and warped according to everybody's own head. That is why we have so much trouble now with factions and sects.'[21] To counteract this trend he began to publish works of popular indoctrination, above all the two catechisms of 1529. As everyone knows, the catechism caught on marvellously, and before long catechism-teaching became everywhere the approved and authorised method of religious instruction. It carried Luther's own imprimatur – 'The catechism is the layman's Bible', he said; 'it contains the whole of what every Christian must know of Christian doctrine';[22] even more important, it served the interests of church and political authorities who came to depend on catechisation as by far the most effective, efficient and, above all, the safest means of instilling in the multitude a reliable knowledge of religion – that is to say, of the officially formulated and established creeds of the Lutheran state churches then in process of building.

The proof of this can be found in the school ordinances issued by every Lutheran state (and also by most Catholic states) from about 1530.[23] These ordinances are impressive documents. They are authoritative, being published as integral parts of comprehensive ecclesiastical constitutions which established the legal framework for the operation of church and religion in a given state. They set down explicitly, in detail and with the power of the state to back it up, what was to be taught, to whom, when, how, from what books, in what manner, to what purpose. Few of them say very much about the Bible as a text for religious study in class, or anything about individual Bible-reading as a practice to be developed in the populace or a habit to be instilled in the young. The overwhelming majority of school ordinances assign only the catechism as an instrument of religious instruction for the school population at large.

Take the *Schulordnung* of the Duchy of Württemberg of 1559 as an example: a good example, because this more than any other curriculum plan became the model of school organisation in German territories and cities in the second half of the sixteenth century.[24] The New Testament turns up among the assigned books only in the fifth and sixth forms of the Latin school curriculum, and then it is the Latin and Greek New Testament, taken up in conjunction with the *Aeneid*, with Isocrates and with the *Cyropaedia* of Xenophon.[25] The Bible is studied also in so-called *Klosterschulen*, boarding schools where future ministers were trained, but that goes without saying.[26] In other words: only where the ablest students had already been segregated does the Gospel make its appearance as a study text, and then only in the learned languages. As for German-language schools, where – as the ordinance puts it – 'the children of working parents ... learn to pray and do the catechism, and in addition are taught to write and read and sing psalms',[27] – in these popular schools no Bible is listed among the books, no New Testament.

Similar provisions are found in the school ordinances of Mecklenburg, 1552;[28] Pomerania, 1563;[29] Saxony, 1580;[30] and so on. When the Bible makes its appearance in the curriculum, as it usually does in the fourth or fifth form, always in Latin and/or Greek, its reception has been prepared by several years of catechism drill. In the lower forms, beyond which most children never advanced, and in the common German schools, Bibles were scarcely to be found, only the catechism.[31] There are some exceptions to this pattern.[32] I could not be wrong, however, in concluding from my reading of most of the published and many of the vast number of unpublished school programmes that the great preponderance of these plans neither included Bible-reading among the subjects taken up in school, nor seems to have regarded training in this as an obligation to the young. Stories from the Old Testament, yes; selected passages from the evangelists, yes; Psalms and Proverbs, yes. But consecutive Bible study, or efforts to develop in the young a habit of turning to the Bible, no.[33]

The reason for this shift in the official Lutheran attitude is not difficult to grasp. Relying on the catechism instead of the Bible was a way of playing it safe. Catechisms spelled out the approved text and meaning of all the essentials of the creed. Catechisms came in many forms and levels, for all ages, varieties of intelligence and stages of preparation. They were suitable for memorisation: Luther's own Shorter Catechism of 1529 established this as one of their chief purposes. Incessantly repeated, they rooted basic religious precepts in the memory and thus ensured habits of correct thought – at least this is what contemporary learning theory taught.[34] In their explicit application of divine commands to the obligations of civic life, catechisms shored up the pillars of society.[35] No catechism explanation of the fourth commandment therefore failed to underline, often heavily, the God-imposed duty to obey not only father and mother but, as well, all one's superiors in the ranked order of society. Luther himself recommended this use of the catechism as an instrument of socialisation. He said – in the preface to the Shorter Catechism of 1529, addressed to his fellow pastors – that, although no one can be forced to learn against his will, 'one must drive the common crowd until they know what counts as right and what counts as wrong in the land where they live and earn their bread'.[36] In other words, one must teach respect for, and loyalty to, prevailing social and political conventions. This goal could never be achieved by Scripture alone with its many ambiguities requiring informed explanation. The catechism, on the other hand, was safe, certain and – it was believed – effective. 'One single schoolboy can bring the catechism to a whole household', it was said. To its proponents, therefore, the catechism seemed a wonderful, self-proliferating device for effecting reform in religious and civic life, both in attitudes and in behaviour. Lutheran theologians and pedagogues really believed this.

Now, catechism teaching and catechism recitation were predominantly oral activities. They had to be if they were to have any chance of succeeding with a population still largely illiterate or at best minimally literate. Memorising and repeating the catechism was every child's duty; saying it back when required to do so was the adult's obligation at visitation time and occasionally in church. Fluent reading was not necessary to these tasks, nor, indeed, reading of any kind. Catechisation had a long oral tradition to fall back on and could flourish in a culture of non-readers. This is not a judgement about literacy itself, only about the linkage usually made between learning to read on the one hand and, on the other, Lutheran reliance on the Bible as a spur or incentive to reading. There was plenty of interest in the former. Governments fostered literacy in many ways,[37] and from below, too, demands were often raised for schools and effective teaching, especially teaching of reading and writing. The documentation for this is large.[38] But this documentation bears witness, above all, to the practical, utilitarian aims of a citizenry more and more alert to the importance of literacy as a precondition of keeping or raising one's place in a changing world,[39] and of governments apparently beginning to associate literacy with political loyalty. We do not yet know exactly what went on at these two levels. One *can* say, however, and I think we should say, that the evidence for claiming that Lutheran authorities wished to turn a whole population into a nation of Bible-readers, and for this reason promoted general literacy – that the evidence for this claim is exceedingly thin.

But what about all those Bibles that poured throughout the century from the publishing houses of Wittenberg, Augsburg, Basle, Zürich, Hagenau, Grimma, Leipzig, Nuremberg, Strasbourg, Erfurt?[40] Where did they go? Who read them? This question is not difficult to answer. Most of them went to parish churches and pastors' libraries, purchased by governments or bought out of church revenues, as directed by church authorities. Prices of Bibles were on the steep side in the sixteenth century: 2 gulden, 8 groschen for the first complete German Bible of 1534 – equivalent to more than a month's wages of an ordinary labourer at that time. The 1522 New Testament fetched from a half to one-and-a-half gulden. Half a gulden is what a mason's or carpenter's journeyman earned for four days' work. These were all folios. The quartos and octavos came later, but they were not cheap.[41] Not very many people could afford to buy them – and there were in sixteenth-century Germany no Bible-distributing agencies, as they did come into existence two centuries later among the Lutheran Pietists of Halle. In fact, most German Bibles printed in the sixteenth century were bought by parish churches out of public funds to be used by impecunious ministers, and by pastors and ministerial candidates, who were obliged, by law, to own them.[42] One example: the princes of Anhalt in Saxony purchased a quantity of the 1541 Wittenberg Bible, fearing, as they wrote,[43] that with Luther said to be ill and preoccupied now, this edition might well turn out to be the last authoritative text to appear in print. Similar action was taken by governments in every territory and city.[44] There were enough parishes in Lutheran realms, and enough young men preparing for the ministry, to account for most of the Bibles produced in Germany in the sixteenth century. The archives hold thousands of book lists submitted by Lutheran pastors to their superiors, most of them with two or more Bibles.[45] Of course I do not claim that no layman ever owned a Bible. We know of many who did, and many of these no doubt read it, although it has also been pointed out that household Bibles could serve several purposes other than reading.[46] Nor am I denying that men and women were apt to be moved by an eloquent preacher or by the touching words and affecting melodies of Lutheran hymns to turn to the Bible. One can imagine this happening, probably often. But if it did, this was not in consequence of, or because it reflected the intention of, Lutheran authorities. They favoured the catechism, at least for the great mass of their subjects.

To summarise: the facts as we can establish them do not substantiate the generally accepted supposition – which no one has ever felt obliged to prove – of a causal link between the Lutheran Reformation and popular Bible-reading. If one wishes to argue that Lutheran authorities promoted direct contact between people and Bible, one must first ask: what people, in what circumstances? I think it highly likely that Lutheran churchmen and magistrates distinguished between well set-up burghers expounding God's word at home to their wives, children, relations, apprentices, domestic servants and, on the other hand, the day labourer, the village tradesman, the farm hand and the lonely widow in her cottage at the edge of the hamlet.

Clearly the Bible was safer with the former than with the latter, not only because they were apt to be better educated, but also, perhaps mainly, because their social position shielded them from the host of hazardous ideas that a less established, less contented person might draw from his or her personal occupation with the sacred text. Lutherans never forgot the traumatic experiences of the 1520s when even trained minds had – so Luther thought – fatally misread the Bible. The acrimonious theological controversies of the second half of the century did nothing to lessen the overriding concern with orthodoxy. Confronting an increasingly pluralistic and unstable religious situation, Lutheran authorities were far too scared of heterodoxy to urge, or encourage, people to meet the Bible on their own terms. For a senior schoolboy to study the New Testament in the orderly sequence of a closely supervised school programme was one thing. To read it as a lay person, without guide or control, was quite another. This point is strengthened if we turn for the sake of comparison to one of the better-known advocates of unrestricted Bible-reading in the early sixteenth century, Valentin Ickelsamer, a distinguished grammarian and teacher in Rothenburg, Augsburg and various other places. In introducing his *Right Method for Learning to Read in a Short Time*, a teach-yourself manual printed in 1527, Ickelsamer declares that never has the ability to read been so precious as it is at the present time. Every person, he says, can now read the word of God for himself, not only read it but – he goes on – 'be a judge of it, all by himself' (*desto bass darin urteilen möge*).[47] Now, this is exactly what Lutheran authorities were afraid of: judging for themselves, by the unqualified. Why did Ickelsamer favour it? Because he was a partisan of Andreas Karlstadt; he was a *Schwärmer*, a spiritualist. He believed in direct inspiration. He attacked Luther for having broken with Karlstadt over this issue. He said that 'the Gospel gives us the freedom to believe and the power to judge',[48] and he meant it.

There, I think, is the crux of the matter. Sixteenth-century Lutherans never managed to dissociate Bible-reading from the spiritualist heresy, and in a world predominantly peopled by non-Christian worldlings (in Luther's two-realms terminology), the possibility for false inferences from ignorant or wrong-headed or deluded reading were legion, and their consequences terrifying. Hence the turn away from Scripture and towards the catechism, where there was nothing to judge, only to memorise and repeat.[49]

But this leaves us with the question: why, then, did governments support popular literacy? If the evangelical impulse was absent, or had been suppressed by fears of causing trouble, and if basic religion could be most effectively taught orally by means of the catechism, why bother to promote reading and writing in the population?

I do not claim to have a satisfactory answer to this question, but some hunches about it may be of interest to students of the Reformation and society in early modern Europe. Undoubtedly the primary motive was the principle of selection, which has been described. The expanding state and the aggressive church needed a large recruiting pool for their proliferating bureaucracies, at least the top echelons of which required specialised training in law, theology, letters, pedagogy, and so on. A strong elitist impulse was, therefore, at work from the base to the peak of the educational system.

But this does not mean that the great mass of ordinary people was seen only as so much dross to be discarded when the nuggets had been picked from among them. I think sixteenth-century rulers took their duties as Christian princes seriously. They never forgot that they would in time be called upon to justify their conduct to their maker. Their intentions towards their subjects – all their subjects – tended to be benevolent, however misguided some of their actions may appear to us now. They were not likely therefore to turn a deaf ear to the many requests for schooling reaching them from towns and villages across their realms. They knew of course that these pleas reflected entirely practical needs. People wanted to read and write so as to be able to hold their own or advance in the world. Petitions for school support make this quite clear, and there are thousands of such pleas in the archives.[50] This kind of pressure from below has been called the 'pull factor' in the growth of literacy.[51] Favourable governmental response, the 'push factor', was occasioned by sympathy with such popular requests, but also by independent calculations, and not only for the purpose of selecting the ablest to staff government bureaucracy. Rulers were told by their theologians that reading is a godly activity, a divine command; and as Christian magistrates they were not inclined to disobey it. This is why the preambles of so many school ordinances quote Paul, 1 Timothy 13: 'Continue with reading, admonishing, teaching,' (in Luther's version), and go on to comment that 'not for nothing is reading mentioned first in this passage'.[52] There was also the notion – to which Luther alluded in his 1524 tract to city councillors – that readers make good citizens.[53] Bucer pointed this out to the magistrates of Strasbourg. 'Practice in reading will make the common people more polite, peaceful, and disposed to the civic life', he said. The alternative was ignorance of law resulting in social chaos.[54] I think governments accepted this argument and for this reason, too, did what they could to broaden the base of literacy. There is a puzzle in this. We today would think that literacy makes people more independent-minded, but this could not possibly have been the objective of sixteenth-century governments. How, then, did rulers reconcile their benign accommodation to public desire for literacy with their conservative aims as heads of the Reformation state and the Reformation church? I think the replacement of the Bible by the catechism makes it possible for us to understand what happened. Once public education had been firmly set in the track of catechisation, with the catechism the single source of religious knowledge, authorities no longer needed to fear the spread of false ideas. In an approved Lutheran catechism one could not find a false idea. This was certainly not true of the Bible, and it was always from the Bible that deluded spirits in recent experience had drawn their destructive ideas. Thus, given the central position – virtually the monopoly – of the catechism in school and in parish education, there was no further need for anxiety about unpredictable consequences of common reading.

But I suspect that even in this indirect way via the catechism Lutheranism did not have much to do with the rise of literacy. We know, to be sure, of one famous instance in early modern Europe where the Lutheran Reformation appears to have achieved nearly total literacy in a population. This happened in Sweden where, beginning in the late seventeenth century and culminating in the eighteenth, the established church undertook to make all men and women in the country read the catechism and give proof of this accomplishment by passing annual examinations. Excellent parish records were kept of these examinations, and they tell the story which, on the level of literacy at least, appears to be a success story.[55] Swedish authorities were quite free in the use of techniques of negative reinforcement designed to make everyone conform and perform. They withheld communion and refused permission to marry to those who flunked the test. This method seems to have worked. Egil Johansson's tables drawn from Swedish parish records give impressive evidence of success. By the middle of the eighteenth century virtually 100 per cent of men and women in Sweden could read. But what sort of literacy was this? People couldn't write a line – they were obliged only to learn to read. And whether they understood what they read is a question to which statistics cannot supply an answer. I am inclined to doubt that they did.

In any case no comparable effort was made in Germany. German authorities did not use Swedish strong-arm methods for compelling people to learn their catechism. And without effective force there was no way in which catechism study could have led to a steady increase in literacy in Germany, for there was nothing about the catechism that made people wish to read it. If they read it at all, or even if they merely memorised it by rote, they learned words, not sense. This we know from what I take to be a highly reliable source: the record of parish visitations carried on annually in all German states from the middle of the sixteenth century on. The verbatim protocols of these visitations, which were conducted jointly by church and state officials who used printed questionnaires for gathering their information, reveal abysmal ignorance in the population on nearly every point of the creed.[56] I find it difficult to imagine, after going through most of these visitation protocols for the sixteenth and early seventeenth centuries, that ordinary people, even after a century of formal religious instruction by means of the catechism, had much of a sense of themselves as Lutherans or Catholics or, indeed, as Christians. They knew much too little religion. Many knew none at all. At best they could parrot a phrase or two from the catechism. Of what it meant, few could give an intelligent account. This being the result of catechisation, it is not possible to imagine that catechisms were much of an inducement to reading. Nobody learned them without being coerced.

Which brings me back to my earlier conclusion: For our explanation of how literacy came to grow in the sixteenth century we must look to mundane, pragmatic causes, not to the Lutheran Reformation. To suggest otherwise is to mark out a false trail. I imagine that people in the sixteenth century, as in other times, had a rather good idea of what mattered to them in life, and a doctrinaire orthodoxy imposed on them by an authoritarian church by means of a rigid catechism was no part of it. Protestant pastors and politicians could not understand this. They were truly mystified that people should wish to resist the saving message. I have no doubt that these men were high-minded and selfless. That they failed in their evangelical endeavour is no reflection on the merit of what they tried to do, though it is, I think, a sign of the instinct people seem to have for protecting themselves from uplifting ideas forced on them from above. Whether we read this sign as a sad or a hopeful comment on human nature depends on how we feel about the idea.

Notes: Chapter 8

1 L. Stone, 'Literacy and education in England 1640–1900', *Past and Present*, Vol. XLII (February 1969), pp. 77–8.

2 cf. H. G. Haile, 'Luther and literacy', *Proceedings of the Modern Language Association*, Vol. XCI (1976), pp. 816–28: 'From a secular viewpoint, surely the most far-reaching effect of Luther's activity was the radical increase in literacy from the early 1520's on through the rest of the century' (p. 817). Haile's article actually offers no evidence for an increase in literacy. It deals mainly with Luther's ability to stimulate the imagination and thus heighten the *quality* of literacy.

3 The Foxe illustration is cited by E. Eisenstein, *The Printing Press as an Agent of Change* (Cambridge, 1979), Vol. I, p. 415.

4 I summarise the evidence for this in my *Luther's House of Learning. Indoctrination of the Young in the German Reformation* (Baltimore, Md., 1978), ch. 1.

5 For arguments for this expansion of literacy, see ibid., pp. 193–202; also R. Engelsing, *Analphabetentum und Lektüre: Zur Sozialgeschichte des Lesens in Deutschland* (Stuttgart, 1973), chs 5–7; B. Könneker, *Die deutsche Literatur der Reformationszeit. Kommentar zu einer Epoche* (Munich, 1975), Introduction.

6 This paragraph is a summary of findings I describe in *Luther's House of Learning*, chs 1 and 9.

7 *An die Ratsherren aller Städte deutschen Lands, dass sie christliche Schulen aufrichten und halten sollen* (1524), Weimar edition of Luther's works (hereafter cited as *WA*), 15, pp. 27–53; *Eine Predigt, dass man Kinder zur Schule halten solle* (1530), *WA* 30^{II}, pp. 517–88.

8 *WA* 30^{II}, p. 545; ibid., p. 586: 'Ich halt aber, das auch die oberkeit hie schuldig sey, die unterthanen zu zwingen, ihre kinder zur schule zu halten.'

9 Luther to Margrave Georg of Brandenburg, 18 July 1529, *WA Briefe* (hereafter cited as *WA Br*), 5, no. 1452.

10 *WA* 30^{II}, pp. 520, 545–6, 557–67, 586. See also Luther's preface to Justus Menius's *Oeconomia Christiana* (1529), *WA* 30^{II}, pp. 60–3. Also *WA Tischreden* (hereafter cited as *WA Tr*), nos 4033, 5557, 7032 and many others.

11 *Unterricht der Visitatoren an die Pfarrherrn im Kurfürstentum Sachsen* (1528), *WA* 26, p. 236.

12 ibid., p. 238.

13 For example, Melanchthon, *Unterricht der Visitatoren* in *Werke in Auswahl*, ed. R. Stupperich, Vol. I (Gütersloh, 1951), pp. 228, 234, 246, 268; Luther, *Deutsch Katechismus*, *WA* 30^{I}, p. 126. On the use of the term *Pöbel* in the sixteenth century, see R. H. Lutz, *Wer war der gemeine Mann? Der dritte Stand in der Krise des Spätmittelalters* (Munich and Vienna, 1979), pp. 82–3.

14 *An den christlichen Adel deutscher Nation* (1520), *WA* 6, p. 461.

15 *WA Bibel* 6, p. 2.

16 ibid., p. 10.

17 ibid., pp. 3, 5, 7, 9, 11.

18 ibid., pp. 414–15 (Acts); Vol. 7, pp. 2–3 (Romans).

19 *WA Tr*, no. 5468 (1542).

20 *An die Ratsherren aller Städte* (1524), *WA* 15, p. 39.

21 *WA Tr*, no. 6008.

22 ibid., no. 6288.

23 The Protestant ordinances are collected in R. Vormbaum (ed.), *Die evangelischen Schulordnungen des sechzehnten Jahrhunderts*, Vol. I (Gütersloh, 1860). For examples of Catholic ordinances, see G. Lurz (ed.), *Mittelschulgeschichtliche Dokumente Altbayerns*, Vol. I, Monumenta Germaniae paedagogica, Vol. XLI (Berlin, 1907).

24 The Württemberg *Schulordnung* of 1559 is printed in Vormbaum, *Die evangelischen Schulordnungen*, pp. 68 ff.

25 ibid., p. 73.

26 ibid., pp. 102–27.

27 ibid., p. 71.

28 ibid., p. 64.

29 ibid., pp. 172–3, 177–8.

30 ibid., pp. 293–4.

31 For another example see the Lutheran theologian Johann Marbach's *Bedencken von den Schulen, wie die im Furstenthumb Zwaienbrucken antzurichten seien* of 1558 (printed in K. Reissinger, *Dokumente zur Geschichte der humanistischen Schulen im Gebiet der bayerischen Pfalz*, Monumenta Germaniae paedagogica [MGP], Vol. XLIX, Berlin, 1911, pp. 14–38). Marbach confines the Bible to the upper classes, where it is read in the learned languages. Lower classes study only the catechism.

32 For example, Hamburg, *Schulordnung* 1529: Vormbaum, *Die evangelischen Schulordnungen*, p. 21; Hessen, *Schulordnung* 1594: W. Diehl (ed.), *Die Schulordnungen des Grossherzogtums Hessen*, MGP, Vol. XXXIII (Berlin, 1905), pp. 206, 208.

33 L. C. Green, 'The Bible in sixteenth-century humanist education', *Studies in the Renaissance*, Vol. XIX (1972), pp. 112–34, agrees that 'there was much less direct teaching of the Bible in Protestant schools of central Europe than is commonly supposed by those who have not had access to the original sources' (p. 113), but seems also to accept at face value what he calls the 'Protestant principle that every baptized person, as a priest before God, must be able to read his own Bible ...' (p. 118).

34 On the uses of catechism and catechisation in Lutheran education, see my *Luther's House of Learning*, cited n. 4 above, ch. 8.

35 For a demonstration of this argument, see ibid., pp. 140–50, 169, 239–46.

36 'soll man doch den Hauffen dahin halten und treiben, dass sie wissen was recht und unrecht ist bei denen, bey welchen sie wohnen, sich neren und leben wollen': *WA* 30^I, p. 272.

37 I present the evidence for this in *Luther's House of Learning*, pp. 10–28.

38 ibid., pp. 195–6.

39 I base this assertion on my reading of local school documents in a number of German archives, particularly correspondence between village communities and territorial governments, mostly on financial matters. An especially rich source is Württembergisches Hauptstaatsarchiv Stuttgart, Series A 284.

40 On the printing history of Luther's Old and New Testaments, see the introduction by P. Pietsch to 'Bibliographie der deutschen Bibel Martin Luthers 1522–1546', *WA Bibel* 2, pp. xx–xxviii; J. Luther, 'Der Wittenberger Buchdruck in seinem Übergang zur Reformationspresse', *Lutherstudien zur 4. Jahrhundertfeier der Reformation* (Weimar, 1917), pp. 261–82; W. Walther, *Luthers deutsche Bibel* (Berlin, 1917); O. Clemen, *Die Lutherische Reformation und der Buchdruck* (Leipzig, 1939); H. Volz, *Hundert Jahre Wittenberger Bibeldruck 1522–1626* (Göttingen, 1954), pp. 17–93; id., *Martin Luthers deutsche Bibel. Entstehung und Geschichte der Lutherbibel* (Wittig, 1978); id., in *Cambridge History of the Bible*, Vol. III (Cambridge, 1963), pp. 94–102; L. Febvre and H.-J. Martin, *L'Apparition du livre* (Paris, 1958), pp. 442–3.

41 On the prices of the various editions of Luther's Bible, see H. Volz, *Hundert Jahre Wittenberger Bibeldruck*, pp. 19, 79–80; Clemen, *Die Lutherische Reformation*, p. 25.

42 This assertion rests on my reading of two kinds of sources: (1) Church constitutions (*Kirchenordnungen*) which mandated Bibles in churches and in the private libraries of pastors (these are published in E. Sehling, ed., *Die evangelischen Kirchenordnungen des XVI. Jahrhunderts*, Leipzig, 1902–11, continued by the Institut für evangelisches Kirchenrecht der evangelischen Kirche in Deutschland, Tübingen, 1963 ff.; (2) the protocols of Lutheran visitations throughout the sixteenth century, which, among other

concerns, investigated the contents of pastors' libraries. For a general discussion of visitation records, see my *Luther's House of Learning*, ch. 12.

43   Sehling, *Die evangelischen Kirchenordnungen*, Vol. II, pp. 547–8.
44   Some additional examples: *Gemeine Verordnung und Artikel der Visitation in Meissen und Voitland* (1533): Saxon officials are to see to it 'dass von einer jeden kircheneinkommen den eingepfarrten selbs zum besten und zu irer sel heil … folgende pücher erkauft, eingepunden und in jede pfar verordnet sol werden…'; eleven titles are mentioned, including Luther's Latin and German Bibles (Sehling, *Die evangelischen Kirchenordnungen*, Vol. I, pp. 194–5; see also ibid., pp. 244–5, 314, 349; *Kapitelordnung* issued by Friedrich Margrave of Brandenburg for Brandenburg-Ansbach, 1565 (Sehling, op. cit., Vol. XI, p. 351: every pastor must own a German Bible; *Visitationsordnung* for Pfalz-Neuburg, 1558 (Sehling, op. cit., Vol. XIII, p. 123); also *Generalartikel* 1576 (ibid., p. 175); *Visitationsordnung* for Hessen 1537 (Sehling, op. cit., Vol. VIII, p. 98): all towns and villages 'nach des gemeinen Kastens Vermögen' must buy for one gulden every year 'rechte gute nutzlichen biblische und andere dergleichen pücher'; again, 1566 (ibid., pp. 223–4): every parish church to spend part of its income on buying for its pastors books, especially the Bible in several languages; also Sehling, Vol. XV, p. 81 for County Hohenlohe 1553; Sehling, Vol. III, p. 448: Liegnitz und Brieg in Silesia; Sehling, Vol. II, p. 194: County Mansfeld, 1554; Sehling, Vol. I, p. 620: Oelnitz, 1582.
45   On the contents and implications of one such book list, see my article 'The mental world of a Saxon pastor', in P. N. Brooks (ed.), *Reformation Principle and Practice: Essays in Honour of Arthur Geoffrey Dickens* (London, 1980), pp. 159–70. See also the rich information on pastors' libraries in B. Vogler, *Vie religieuse en pays rhenan dans la seconde moitié du 16e siècle, 1556–1619* (Service de reproduction des thèses, Université de Lille III, 1974), Vol. I, pp. 468–71.
46   D. Cressy, *Literacy and the Social Order. Reading and Writing in Tudor and Stuart England* (Cambridge, 1980), pp. 48–9.
47   V. Ickelsamer, *Die rechte weis, auffs kürtzist lesen zu lernen, wie das zum ersten erfunden unnd auss der rede vermerckt worden ist … sampt dem text des kleinen Catechismi* (n.p., 1527; 2nd edn, Marburg, 1534), p. 53. Ickelsamer's treatise is reprinted in facsimile in H. Fechtner (ed.), *Vier seltene Schriften des sechzehnten Jahrhunderts* (Berlin, 1882).
48   'weil uns das Evangelium freyheit zu glauben, und gewalt zu urteyln gibt': *Clag etlicher Brüder an alle Christen*, 1525, reprinted in L. Enders (ed.), *Aus dem Kampf der Schwärmer gegen Luther*, Flugschriften aus der Reformationszeit X: Neudrucke deutscher Literaturwerke des XVI. und XVII. Jahrhunderts, no. 118 (Halle, 1893), p. 44. On Ickelsamer, see H. Noll, *Der Typus des religiösen Grammatikers im 16. Jahrhundert, dargestellt an Valentin Ickelsamer* (Marburg, 1935).
49   For a description of the methods of catechism teaching, see my *Luther's House of Learning*, pp. 165–75.
50   For example, Staatsarchiv Neuburg, Grassegger-Sammlung no. 1535[III], fol. 108 r (1584): 'So ist auch der nutz, so aus den schulen folgt, unaussprechlich, in dem oftmals eines armen Mannes kind durch Mittel eines so geringen anfangs zu hohen dignitet und ehren kombt.' In 1614 the Bavarian *Landtag* deputies resisted Maximilian I's attempt to abolish German schools with the argument that 'nicht alle Bauernkinder mögen bauern werden … aber einer, der seine Muttersprache weder schreiben noch lesen kann, gleichsam schier wie ein todter mensch ist', quoted by A. Kluckhohn, 'Die Jesuiten in Baiern …', *Historische Zeitschrift*, Vol. XXXI (1874), pp. 405–6.
51   Cressy, *Literacy and the Social Order*, p. 184.
52   For example, Mecklenburg *Kirchenordnung* 1522 in Vormbaum, *Die evangelischen Schulordnungern*, pp. 59–60; 'Und ist vom lesen ausdrücklich geboten 1 Tim 4, "Du solt anhalten mit lesen, trösten und lehren". In welchem spruch das lesen nit vergeblich am ersten genannt ist.'
53   *WA* 15, p. 45.
54   'Das volck wurdt zu burgerlicher beywonung uss erfarung und ubung des buchstabens dester geschlachter, freuntlicher und geneigter, so sonst uss unwissenheit, der groben natur nach, wütet mit unwurss färheit und kein achtung des rechtens und der billichkeyt geben mag': R. Stupperich (ed.), *Martin Bucers deutsche Schriften*, Vol. II (Gütersloh, 1962), p. 400.

55 E. Johansson, 'The history of literacy in Sweden in comparison with some other countries', *Educational Reports Umea*, Vol. XII (1977).
56 See my discussion of the evidence concerning mass understanding of religion in my *Luther's House of Learning*, chs 13 and 14.

9 The Limits of Godly Discipline in the Early Modern Period with Particular Reference to England and Scotland

BRUCE LENMAN

Historians have been too ready to ascribe to Protestantism attitudes shared by the Roman Catholicism of the Counter-Reformation, or indeed by most of pre-Reformation Latin Christendom. Of no topic is this truer than the commitment of the Reformed kirk in Scotland to impose Godly Discipline on Scottish society. Of that commitment, there can be no serious doubt. The Scots Confession of 1560, drawn up by six Fathers of the Scottish Reformation headed by John Knox himself, and officially adopted by the Reformation Parliament in August of that year, laid down in article XVIII 'the notis, be the quhilk the trewe kirk is decernit fra the false'. There were three 'notes, signes, and assured takens': the true preaching of the Word; the right administration of the sacraments; and 'Last, Ecclesiastical discipline uprightlie ministered, as Goddis Worde prescribes, whereby vice is repressed, and vertew nurished'.[1] The significantly named *First Book of Discipline* also drawn up in 1560, though not similarly endorsed by Parliament, devoted its Seventh Head to the theme 'Of Ecclesiastical Discipline' which it saw as 'reproving and correcting of the faults, which the civill sword either doth neglect or not punish', and argued that such discipline was essential to the upholding of the kirk of God.[2]

The *Second Book of Discipline*, produced in 1578 by the Presbyterian party in the General Assembly of the Kirk, under the leadership of Andrew Melville, showed no weakening on this point. It laid responsibility for Godly Discipline on the shoulders of the elders of the kirk and gave presbyteries 'power to excommunicat the obstinat'.[3] The Reformed kirk had an elaborate typology of sins. First came those which were capital and deserved excommunication and death. These ranged from wilful murder through adultery and sorcery to abortion and open blasphemy. Second came those not under the civil sword yet meriting public repentance, such as fornication, drunkenness, swearing, brawling, sabbath-breaking, and so on. Third came those which were less heinous but which deserved admonition, like vain words, uncomely gestures, negligence in hearing the Word or abstention from the Lord's Table. The kirk hoped that the state would deal with the first category of offences, though in practice secular authority was never prepared to implement the full severities of Mosaic law. The second class of sins were appropriate for the public procedures of the ecclesiastical courts, while those guilty of the third category were to be admonished privately 'by one or two of those that did first espy the offence; which, if the persons suspected hear, and give declaration of amendment, there need be no further process'. However, if this modest and winning admonition was to be spurned, it was to be repeated in the presence of two or three witnesses, and if this more formal rebuke was rejected, the offender was to be cited before the minister and elders for the crime and sin of contempt of brotherly admonition.[4]

Only when it is realised that the procedure detailed for the admonition of the third category of sins is virtually a verbatim transcript of the Gospel According to Saint Matthew, chapter 18, verses 15 to 17, does it become clear that the underlying assumptions of Godly Discipline are an aspect of historic Christianity and not an eccentricity of particular churches. When Francis Junius (François Du Jon), a Calvinist minister in Amsterdam, said, in an open letter to Philip II of Spain in 1565, 'for, as the nature of man is such that he desires to ease his conscience and to cast off the Yoke of God, it is necessary that he should be bridled and kept under discipline, otherwise he will become as a horse that has bolted, indulging in uncurbed licentiousness and rejecting the fear of both God and men',[5] he was not being contentious, but reciting a universally accepted platitude current among contemporary ruling elites. Godly Discipline was always a matter of correcting sins and vices. The distinction between the two categories was simple and is conveniently summed up in a mid eighteenth-century compendium written by Louis Habert, doctor of theology of Paris and teacher at the Sorbonne: 'peccatum est actus moraliter malus; vitium vero est habitus seu dispositio per se inclinans ad actum moraliter malum'.[6] So sin was a conscious defiance of the moral order willed by God, and vice more by way of a bad habit. The relationship between crime and sin has never been straightforward and indeed, arguably, no very clear distinction can be drawn between the two concepts since an element of moral turpitude is very often regarded as implicit in those offences which secular courts categorise as crimes and penalise. The parameters of the concept of sin itself have always been debatable. To the moral theologian sin is in practice primarily a matter of interpersonal relationships, including of course that most important of all such relationships – the relationship between God and Man. However, there was room for a great deal of argument about the precise nature of the Divine Law which the Christian was obliged to respect. A good example is the extensive debate in the medieval Western church in the thirteenth and fourteenth centuries about the status of the provisions in the Book of Leviticus against marriage within prohibited degrees, and other moral lapses. At first Levitical Law was regarded as part of Divine Law, but then Duns Scotus, the late thirteenth-century Scottish Franciscan philosopher, argued it possessed no inherent sanction under the New Covenant unless endorsed by the church.[7] This unsettled debate continued through the Reformation. In Scotland after 1560 John Knox wanted the full rigour of Levitical punishments, but found that there was too much opposition in kirk and state.[8] However, the medieval clergy knew that there were clearly defined sins and means of disciplining the natural propensity of humankind to indulge in them.

Penitentials lovingly categorised original, mortal and venial sins but two factors severely limited the impact of this system of intimate moral discipline on the great bulk of medieval populations. One was the relative scarcity and frequently low spiritual calibre of priests, particularly in the countryside where most people lived. It tended to be the upper classes, and especially upper-class women, who could afford the clerical attention necessary for an extensive use of the sacrament of penance. Countess, later Saint Elizabeth of Thuringia, could retain as confessor to herself and her maids the austerely fanatical priest Conrad of Marburg, whose penances often included severe floggings whose scars were borne by the countess and her ladies for weeks. The weals were status symbols, as was the ferocious Conrad, later Germany's first official inquisitor until someone assassinated him.[9] Until Innocent III (under pressure from growing urban forces) approved bodies committed to active evangelisation amongst town populations, such as the new mendicant orders, the medieval mind tended to regard the full penitential system as normally operative only in monasteries and nunneries. *Vita religiosa*, the religious life, meant a monastery.[10] On top of all this, a second factor ensured that there was no sustained yearning from the more religiously inclined sections of the laity for access to a highly personal religious discipline. This was the ingrained tendency of medieval people to think in terms of communal self-purification rather than individual penance. As late as the late sixteenth-century religious wars in France, this form of medieval mass breast-beating was one of the strands in the activities of the Catholic Holy League in cities like Rouen, where penitential processions sought to avert the wrath of God in the shape of the threat of a heretic king.[11]

A great deal of popular piety in the medieval and indeed in the early modern period was clearly syncretist in nature. It combined attitudes appropriate to pagan magic-making with Christian forms. The ecclesiastical authorities were notoriously ambiguous in their response to this phenomenon. In theory they deplored superstition. In practice, as long as superstitious practices did not inconvenience them, and enhanced reverence for the clergy, they condoned what they could hardly have suppressed. Criticism of superstition as an obstacle to true piety, and demands for a far more personal concept of the Christian Life to be widely propagated amongst the laity, first assumed irresistible momentum with the rise of Christian Humanism in the late fifteenth and early sixteenth centuries. Humanist writers reacted against the Pelagian implications of much fifteenth-century devotion, which sought by repeated devotional acts such as the Stations of the Cross, Angelus, or Rosary, to win that divine grace which it was thought God could hardly refuse 'to those who do what lies within them'. Instead they preached a return to Scripture, focusing on the precepts of the Sermon on the Mount and St Paul's stress that the grace won uniquely by Christ must inevitably transform the behaviour of the true believer. This was the central tendency of the thought of that remarkable circle of friends, John Colet, William Grocyn, Thomas Linacre, William Latimer and above all Thomas More, whom Erasmus first met in and around Oxford in 1499. In the sparkling satire *Praise of Folly* which he published in 1511 Erasmus went so far as to say that the eucharistic ritual could be positively harmful if the observer did not realise the need for an inward spiritual experience matching the outward symbols.[12]

Christian Humanism, with its emphasis on the mind and spirituality, tended to the ascetic. Personal religion implied personal responsibility and the need for submission to that Godly Discipline which enabled the believer to lay desire as it were in the tomb, so as to help himself to rise to a new life in Christ. It is perhaps not without significance that in More's *Utopia* premarital intercourse was severely punished and the penalty for a second act of adultery was death.[13] Christian Humanism was not the only source of moves towards a more evangelical and personal piety, and its relationship with the Reformation is a subject over which historians will presumably bicker for ever, but what is clear is that after the great divisions marked by the successive waves of the Reformation and the Catholic reaction embodied in the Council of Trent, pressure for a more austere and personal religious discipline effectively enforced at parochial level was in no way the monopoly of one camp.

Hugh Latimer, briefly Bishop of Worcester in the late 1530s, and a notable Protestant preacher burned at the stake outside Oxford on 16 October 1555 by the Catholic regime of Queen Mary Tudor, provides a good example of contemporary Protestant emphasis on the problem of personal sin. In one of the 'Sermons on the Lord's Prayer' which he preached in 1552 before Katherine Duchess of Suffolk, he came to the petition 'lead us not into temptation' and remarked, 'And this is a necessary prayer; for what is it that we can do? Nothing at all but sin'.[14] However, Tridentine Catholicism could produce figures like St Carlo Borromeo (d. 1584), the nephew of Pope Pius IV and after 1565 the first resident Archbishop of Milan for over a century, who drove rather than urged his people into a new era, exhorting and disciplining them with the same austere determination which ravaged his own frame with fasting and devotion. Borromeo ordered men and women to worship in separate buildings to keep their minds from carnal worldliness. It is ironic that his uncle Pius IV, who carried through the Council of Trent to its successful conclusion, was a Renaissance pope of the relaxed and worldly school, but his successor, the grimly devout Pius V (d. 1572), who owed his election in large measure to the efforts of Borromeo, came up to the relentless standards of the Archbishop of Milan, and put the fear of God into the Romans as Borromeo had into the Milanese.[15] It is significant that Borromeo at one stage was demanding the right to raise an armed episcopal police force to impose the new Tridentine discipline on his people, a request which the Spanish government of Milan understandably rejected.[16]

Thus, in concentrating on two adjacent Protestant countries like England and Scotland for the purpose of analysing the scope and limits there of Godly Discipline in the early modern period, this study is essentially probing specific regional variations on a theme common to all Western

Christendom. Godly Discipline was a universally respected ideal, but one which invariably faced positive and passive opposition, and whose degree of translation into fact therefore varied greatly from society to society. One great advantage in studying the two British realms is that though the pattern of Godly Discipline developed quite differently in them, radical Protestant opinion on both sides of the Border maintained a steady stream of comment based on the assumption that a far greater degree of parallelism ought to have been achieved than in fact proved possible. The English radical Christopher Goodman left Geneva for Scotland at the height of the Scottish Reformation, to help establish a Calvinist discipline in Ayr and indeed in St Andrews itself, the ecclesiastical capital of Scotland. John Knox was at an early stage in his career a leading puritan clergyman in the Church of England. When, as in 1572, English Puritans pressed for reconstruction of the Anglican Church according to the example of 'the best reformed churches', they clearly had in mind Scotland and Geneva as well as the Netherlands and the Huguenot Churches.[17]

Though good Protestants in both England and Scotland stood for a religion of personal responsibility and for a direct unmediated relationship between the believer and his or her God, it would be quite wrong to think that they turned their backs on the medieval tradition of corporate responsibility towards the Almighty. Rather did they, in an age of rapidly maturing nationalisms, tend, at one level at any rate, to think of the destiny of nations as showing forth the purposes of Divine Providence. Both the Elizabethan bishop Thomas Cooper and John Knox resoundingly denied the possibility of mere chance or accident in this mortal world. Knox declared that 'Fortune and adventure are the words of Paynims, the signification whereof ought in no wise to enter into the heart of the faithful'. Providence might at times be inscrutable, but Oliver Cromwell was not the only seventeenth-century Englishman who was convinced that many specific providences could be read and interpreted aright by godly men. The believer stricken by disease or an adverse turn of circumstance was actively encouraged to look within himself for the moral turpitude which had aroused God's anger. At both the official level of the leadership of church and state, and at the humbler level of popular emotions, it was usual to ascribe national disasters to the Wrath of God provoked by the sins of the people.[18]

If the Scots shared the English obsession with Providence, they went one decisive step forward from it by embracing in the seventeenth century a covenant theology which found its supreme expression in the National Covenant of 1638, drawn up when the crisis between Charles I and his Scottish subjects was approaching the point of no return. Covenant theology was not without continental roots and Archbishop Laud was disappointed in his hopes that the Reformed church in general would denounce the rebel Scots,[19] but Scotland was unusual in having a provisional government actually prepared to implement the ideal of a formal written bond between the nation and God. At the first crisis of the English Civil War in 1643, when it looked as if King Charles might well win in his largest realm and thereby acquire the power to crush his northern one, the

Scots came to terms with the English Parliament in the form of a Solemn League and Covenant taken by the Convention of Estates in Edinburgh in August 1643 and by the English Parliament in September. It contains the following statement, made on behalf of the godly inhabitants of England, Scotland and Ireland:

> And because these kingdoms are guilty of many sins and provocations against God and his son Jesus Christ, as is too manifest by our present distress and dangers, the fruits thereof, we profess and declare before God and the world our unfeigned desire to be humbled for our sins and for the sins of these kingdoms, – which are the causes of other sins and transgressions so much abounding amongst us . . . [20]

In short, a providential or covenanting theology brought a corporate sense of guilt to reinforce that very necessary concern for the suppression of individual sins which was enjoined by all orthodox theologies, on sound Scriptural warrant. What is intriguing is the very different practical consequences which flowed from a common, indeed a commonplace, theological position adopted by the rulers of both British kingdoms before, after and during the Great Civil War. Though a good deal of detailed research remains to be done, it does seem fairly clear that what a great authority has called 'the ambivalent English Reformation'[21] never succeeded in erecting a Godly Discipline which in scope, depth and endurance over time was truly comparable to that achieved in the Northern Zion of Lowland Scotland, which is not to say, of course, that godly Englishmen did not try.

One of the central problems of the study of sixteenth-century ecclesiastical discipline is as resistant to analysis in England as in Scotland. This is the question of the precise impact of the Reformation on the processing of moral cases in courts ecclesiastic. The trouble is that source survival in the post-Reformation era is so vastly greater than it is in the pre-Reformation period that the sources are hopelessly out of balance and allow of only broad conclusions. Two points are clear. First, that all the procedures of denunciation of moral backsliders before the congregation and humiliating public penance existed in the pre-Reformation period. A splendid suit in the Court of Chancery gives us a glimpse of the misfortunes of William Waring, cordwainer of Pembroke in the county of Hereford, who alleged that in 1529, for no good reason save ill-will, the parish priest of Pembroke and the clerk to the Commissary Court of Hereford compelled him to process, wet-through, in his shirt, 'bare-foot, bare-leg and bare-head, – with a candle in his hand' as a penitent, and then made him kneel so long on cold stones in church while they sang a service that he acquired a cold in the head which led to expensive and embarrassing complications like medical bills and all his hair falling out. Alas, further evidence showed that the plaintiff shot at marks for wagers on holy days, kept a mistress and had abandoned his wife. His suit was dismissed with costs.[22]

Secondly, it is clear that the Reformation caused the English government to underline the legitimacy of the new regime by stressing, often in parliamentary statutes, a commitment to a moral purge of society. Such purges tend to characterise legitimacy-seeking rulers.[23] A Jacobean commentator also complained that statutory mention of moral offences encouraged English secular judges, anticlerical in bias since the late medieval era, to cast doubt on all ecclesiastical jurisdictions – something Henry VIII never envisaged.[24] On 13 April 1546 that monarch addressed a proclamation to the Lord Mayor and Sheriffs of the City of London in which he announced his determination to suppress the notorious but ancient and licensed brothels in Southwark on the south side of the Thames known as the 'Bankside Stewes' on the grounds that toleration of such depravity '– in open places called the Stewes and there, without punishment or correction', was to tempt the wrath of Almighty God. Brothel-keepers and whores were therefore to go before Easter 'to their natural countries'. By 1547 Henry VIII had been succeeded by Edward VI and by 1549 Bishop Latimer was complaining, in a sermon to the young monarch, that putting down the Stewes had proved notably ineffective, for unlicensed whorehouses were spreading apace, not only 'on the Bancke', but in London proper in such areas as the Liberties of the Clink and Old Paris Garden.[25]

Nevertheless, it is important that the Henrician Reformation was followed by such gestures. Its early stages had seen very real threats to the moral authority of an incipiently schismatic government. The Venetian ambassador reported that in October 1531 a mob of 7,000–8,000 women (including many men in disguise) had left London intending to lynch the king's paramour Anne Boleyn, who was staying at a villa on the Thames. Anne escaped by boat, and the government chose to hush the whole business up.[26] Puritanical rigour as a means of validating new regimes seems to be a cross-cultural phenomenon, as valid a concept in the Iran of Ayatollah Khomeini as in sixteenth-century Europe. Its practical impact inevitably varies with the degree of sincerity in the commitment of the ruling elite and the efficiency of the means, be they co-operative or coercive, available to them for moulding the society below them. Henry VIII was an inherently less puritanical character than the Ayatollah Khomeini, and Carlo Borromeo's proposed episcopal gendarmerie would probably have proved less effective than the self-appointed vigilante 'Groups for the Segregation of the Sexes' who in Iran in 1980 were arresting and handing over to local revolutionary councils women who had indulged in mixed bathing, an offence which earned them twenty-five lashes apiece.[27] Intriguingly, Lord Ellesmere, James VI's Lord Chancellor of England between 1603 and 1617, seems to be an early example of a man conscious of the fact that moral discipline was a transcultural phenomenon. Complaining to his colleagues on the bench of Star Chamber in 1605 about the inadequate punishment for slander, he suggested English law might usefully borrow from the Aztecs of Mexico the practice of laceration by inserting thorn spikes in the tongue or ears. The use of maguey spikes, both penitential and punitive, was illustrated in such works as the Aztec *Codex Mendoza*, prepared for the first Viceroy of New Spain, captured by a French ship at sea, and eventually sold to Richard Hakluyt, the Elizabethan geographer.[28]

However, there is one other important variable in the process of imposing a validating moral discipline on a society. This is the extent to which the power-wielders within that society can actually agree on the precise nature and scope of the discipline, and on the means whereby it is to be imposed. Arguably it was inability to sustain a consensus as to how and, more importantly, by whom Christian moral discipline should be enforced which in the long run undermined the effectiveness of courts Christian in England. The subject is a complex one and under-researched, but it does seem possible to offer a working model which makes sense of the known general trends.

First, it must be stressed that, in the opinion of a distinguished student of the records of English ecclesiastical courts, 'the church courts were never busier, nor ecclesiastical discipline more intense, than in the post-Reformation decades'.[29] Medieval legal machinery was taken over by Tudor and Stuart lawyers who worked it with an unprecedented vigour and, indeed, in the late sixteenth and early seventeenth centuries with a sense of sharp urgency born of real fear of social disorder. Of course, a great deal of the business of church courts was to do with cases about tithes, legacies, or matrimonial contracts, but the disciplinary dimension in cases of inter-personal morality was a real one ranging from defamation through sabbath-breaking to the sin of fornication. A careful student of ecclesiastical discipline in the diocese of York between 1560 and 1640 has concluded that, while local variations in contumacy could be substantial, it is possible to risk the generalisation that only 40–50 per cent of the population were amenable to ecclesiastical discipline.[30] The figure is not in fact unimpress-ive, the more so in that church courts were only part of a much wider mechanism for the enforcement of moral discipline. All justices of the peace, for example, had to take cognisance of sexual immorality because it was their duty to secure affiliation orders against the fathers of bastard children, or in the event of failure to decide which parish had to maintain an unacknowledged child. York was in any case relatively remote from the centres of power. Essex, infinitely more under the eye of central authority, had very active lower ecclesiastical courts indeed. Between 1600 and 1642 the archdeacon's court, whose business was weighted towards sexual offences and failure to attend church, dealt with 756 presentments from the village of Kelvedon with its 400–600 souls, while only seventy-one people from Kelvedon were dealt with by quarter sessions.[31]

If there was obviously a consensus among the ruling classes of pre-Civil War England about the need for Godly Discipline there were equally obviously endemic tensions within the ruling elites as to the means of enforcing it. One tension of great importance was that between central government and the local elites who as justices of the peace had to operate national policies and who in the period between 1577 and 1631 can be shown to have become increasingly resentful at the attempts of conciliar government at the centre to harry, spy on and punish them for insufficiently zealous execution of such instructions as Books of Orders.[32] National policies on social issues were regarded as necessary, but a substantial degree of local discretion and initiative for the ruling class was fundamental.

Another source of tension and difficulty in operating a system of Godly Discipline was ideological conflict. In Lancashire, for example, in the late sixteenth century, so many of the justices of the peace had pronounced Roman Catholic sympathies that central government policy with respect to religious uniformity was bound to be obstructed. More damaging in the long run for the vitality of the moral discipline of the Anglican Establishment was the progressive alienation of Puritan opinion. There was absolutely no difference in theory between Puritans and their bitterest foes in the Anglican hierarchy over the question of moral discipline. Archbishop John Whitgift whose appointment to Canterbury in 1583 marked the start of a violent anti-Puritan offensive in the Church of England laid down as query 17 in his Visitation Articles for Bath and Wells Diocese in 1583: 'How many adulteries, incests and fornications are notoriously known to have been committed in your parish since Easter 1580; how many offenders in any such faults have been put to open penance and openly corrected; and how many have been winked at and borne withal, or have fined or paid money – to escape open punishment and correction; and what their names and surnames be?'[33] Nor was this purely propaganda, for after consulting the bishops and securing the support of Queen Elizabeth Whitgift issued on 19 October 1583 Articles which, as well as attacking both Papists and Puritans, endeavoured to reform glaring ecclesiastical abuse and which laid down, among other points, that ecclesiastical penances were not to be commuted for money payments except in a few rare cases, and then for good reason.[34]

Nevertheless, it is clear that the vigorous enforcement of Godly Discipline became increasingly identified with Puritans, and R. C. Richardson insists that 'a study of patronage reminds us that puritanism and its attendant godly discipline took firmest root not when they were in opposition to influential laymen but when they had their support'.[35] Puritan preachers increasingly saw themselves as the inspirers and exhorters of a new race of lay saints – gentlemen in office who would embody the true vocation of a godly magistracy by imposing on society without fear or favour that Godly Discipline which corresponded with the divine will.[36] It was therefore an appalling shock to this particular group when the church and secular courts which they, above all others, had been prepared to operate with rigour, were turned against them in the third decade of the seventeenth century by the rising Arminian faction in the church led first by Richard Neile, Bishop of Durham and Winchester, and from 1632 Archbishop of York,[37] and then by his protégé William Laud, Charles I's last Archbishop of Canterbury. In the parish of Terling in Essex, for example, a tight-knit group of devout, puritanical farmers mainly of yeoman rather than husbandman status had emerged between 1615 and 1629 to dominate every key post in parish government. They co-operated with Puritan incumbents to discipline the moral and religious behaviour of their less godly and poorer fellow parishioners.[38] The godly were genuinely deeply concerned about what they saw as the contempt for God's laws and ordinances displayed by the bulk of the population. A great Puritan preacher, John Angier, minister of Denton Chapel, devoted a whole chapter of a book to the problem of those who slept through church services, either in part, or 'from the beginning to the end, as if they come for no other purpose'.[39] He went on to discuss such knotty problems as what to do when a neighbour of superior social standing dozed off. The answer was to find a social equal of the sleeper and ask him to do the nudging!

Obviously there was extensive resistance, ranging from inertia to positive hostility, to the moral offensive of the rigorists. There was nothing uniquely Protestant or peculiarily English about the problem. Jansenist clergy faced it in early modern France when they tried to impose more rigorous standards on their flocks.[40] What was striking in England was the heights to which the campaign for moral reformation were carried through the dual offensive of Sword and Word which culminated in the execution of Charles I and the setting up of the Commonwealth regime. All that could reasonably be done by pouring in able preachers and funds was, by and large, done by the Commonwealth church, so it is highly significant that the outstanding authority on this campaign for reformation of manners has concluded that it ultimately failed in the face of resistance at local level. What was left behind was the nonconformist conscience, not a transformed godly society. Even the apparent triumph represented by the fact that the lowest recorded illegitimacy figures in early modern English history correspond with the era of the Commonwealth is almost certainly illusionary, a function of under-registration, not fact. Edmund Hopwood, most ferocious of Lancashire justices in the drive for godliness in the 1650s, sent many bastard-bearers to the house of correction. He also probably drove many out of parishes within his jurisdiction, as part of a general tendency amongst the bastardy-prone section of the population to keep away from his attention.[41]

It is known that there were periods when the efficacy of sixteenth-century English ecclesiastical discipline was temporarily limited by adverse circumstances. Such periods seem to have occurred intermittently during the changes of religion under Henry VIII and Edward VI, and Elizabeth certainly refused to allow her bishops to act firmly against recusants in the first years after her accession, in the shrewd belief that many survivalist Catholics would eventually conform to Anglicanism if not provoked by ecclesiastical censure.[42] However, England never experienced the extraordinary set of circumstances obtaining in Scotland in the first decades after the Reformation-Revolution of 1560. The English Reformation was inspired by the Crown and the structure of church courts was substantially available almost immediately after the break with Rome, for use by the new regime. The Scottish Reformation was carried through in spite of the Crown, which only recognised it at the end of a period described by a great authority as 'An Unstable Situation, 1560–7'. John Knox inserted the *First Book of Discipline* into his *History of the Scottish Reformation* to show 'what the worldlings rejected'. The medieval church was suspended rather than abolished and there was a long struggle before a Protestant alternative with effective jurisdiction was widely accepted.[43]

Gathered congregations of Protestants (the so-called 'Privy Kirks') had certainly existed even before the Reformation. In September 1559 John

Knox told a correspondent that such congregations were established in St Andrews, Dundee, 'Sanct Johnstoun' (Perth), Brechin, Montrose, Stirling and Ayr. He added, more in wonder than praise, that 'Christ Jesus is preached even in Edinburgh'. The basic unit, which was also a unit of jurisdiction, was the kirk session composed of the minister and the elders and deacons. The latter were originally elected annually, with no bar on continuity of service. Like other minority religions in history, this dissenting faction tried to impose strict moral discipline on its own followers. The very first entry in the St Andrews Kirk Session Register is dated 27 October 1559 and records the public penitence of 'Robert Roger, schipwrycht, cittiner of Sanctandrois' who after sermon expressed his penitence before the congregation for the sin of adultery 'to the exemple of utheris to commit nocht the lyke'.[44] On 22 November 1559 William Rentoun went through a similar public penance for admitted adultery with Margaret Aidnam. It is interesting that already on the 2nd of that month 'James Reky, tailyeour' had been delated to the minister and elders of the congregation for having entertained Rentoun and his paramour in the Reky family house. Duly 'penitent and obedient', Reky was ordered to expel Margaret from his house and do public penance before the congregation.[45]

Many Protestant clergy were caught unawares by the sudden triumph of Reformation in 1560. They had no real programme for the implementation of their ideas on a national scale. Church and society were seen as ideally moving in concert. Though it is clear that in pre-Reformation Scotland it was quite normal for a baron court to add secular punishment, such as loss of tenancy, to the ecclesiastical censures incurred by moral offences as grave as adultery,[46] the failure of the medieval kirk to effectively implement Godly Discipline was a Protestant platitude. Protestants were anxious to replace the real or alleged indifference of the pre-Reformation kirk by a new and intense interest in the personal lives of all parishioners. Elders and deacons furnished an unprecedented scale of lay participation in the campaign to revitalise the parish unit. Yet in 1560 militant Protestants were everywhere a quite small minority. Even in the burghs there seems to have been only limited popular enthusiasm for the new creed. Pressure from nearby lairds appears to have been decisive in tipping the balance on certain town councils in favour of the Reformation. When a local laird was both Protestant in sympathy and provost of the burgh, as in St Andrews and Montrose, his voice could be difficult to ignore. Lord Ruthven, a local noble who was also Provost of Perth, undoubtedly seized the initiative in committing both himself and the burgh to the Reformation. By comparison, a great regional prince like the Earl of Huntly, working in close association with strongly Catholic lairds (many of them from his own Gordon kin), could block the advance of the Reformation for a decade after 1560 in Aberdeenshire. In 1570 the Reformed Kirk's Commissioner in Aberdeen asked to be relieved of his job because 'there was no obedience in these parts and the ministers were not answered'.[47] In Edinburgh, Mary Queen of Scots soon after her return to Scotland in 1561 started to manipulate municipal elections, co-operating with a group of ultra-conservative 'moderate' Protestants, to resist any radical Protestant regime in the burgh, and especially to block the establishment of effective Godly Discipline.[48]

However, the ruling classes of early modern Scotland were not like the elites who led and manipulated the Dutch revolt against Spain. The town regents and gentry who dominated the United Provinces which eventually established their republican independence did not really change their basic early opposition to 'salvation by coercion', whether at the hands of the Inquisition or at the hands of the Dutch Reformed Kirk. They were determined that the discipline of the new establishment should not become a 'new monkery', and they effectively clipped the wings of the Reformed *predikanten* by allowing them to discipline only their own full members in a society which insisted on free choice in religion. Indeed the ruling elites usually were careful to stop short of full church membership for themselves.[49] In Scotland the medieval tradition of close co-operation between secular and ecclesiastical authorities was much more deeply rooted. Gradually, as the baillies (that is, magistrates) in the burghs became Protestant, it was possible to secure overlapping personnel between the kirk session and town council. In St Andrews in 1569 the session, exasperated by the obduracy of two relapsed fornicators, 'referrit the punition of them to the magestratis', while on another occasion an offender was summarily handed over to the baillies already present on the session 'to be civile correckit and punist'. In December 1585 James Douglas, Provost of Elgin and an elder on the kirk session, was himself convicted of fornication before it, but it is significant that he was spared public penance in exchange for glazing a church window.[50]

Such tactical concessions strengthened rather than weakened the system of Godly Discipline by making it more palatable to the ruling class, though there were always tensions when the kirk tried to extend Godly Discipline to the nobles. It did not try to do so very often, a fact not unconnected with the survival and indeed expansion of lay patronage at the Reformation. A very high percentage of parish incumbents, especially after the extensive secularisation of ecclesiastical property rights, were nominated by the nobility or the Crown. A kirk session in a parish which might be wholly owned by a great lord was hardly likely to beard him for minor or indeed major peccadilloes. The next level of Reformed court ecclesiastic, presiding over a group of kirk sessions, was the presbytery, and it had just about enough status to grapple with the great of the land, but presbyteries were the last major ecclesiastical court in Scotland to develop after the Reformation. Only in 1581 did the General Assembly of the Kirk call for their erection, ordering that thirteen be established at once. By 1593 there may have been as many as forty-seven, but it has been argued that even where they existed by 1600 their existence 'was sometimes insecure and their ability to maintain effective discipline limited'. In 1602 the presbytery of Ellon summoned George Gordon and Lady Haddo before them to answer charges of adultery. In the conservative north-east this was bold indeed, for Lady Haddo was a great Gordon noblewoman. The couple turned up with their own minister, who abused the presbytery, and a mob of violent and noisy supporters. The couple were admonished, but the verdict was that marvellous Scottish one, 'not proven'. The revival of episcopacy under James VI, especially after 1610, meant some reduction in the autonomy of presbyteries, but they increased in number and effectiveness, playing an important role in pastoral and disciplinary work.[51]

After a major contretemps over attempts by the presbytery of Aberdeen to excommunicate Huntly in 1604–5, King James VI through his Privy Council laid it down that no presbytery or synod (the next highest church court) might commence a process of excommunication against an aristocrat without prior notification to the commissioners of the General Assembly of the Kirk, who in turn were to notify the Crown.[52] Although the clash between Godly Discipline and social hierarchy was never quite resolved, such procedures, and the domination of ecclesiastical courts by the propertied and powerful, ensured that in the long run holders of private jurisdictions were prepared to allow their authority to be used to reinforce and underpin that of the kirk. This was quite vital, for Scotland was pre-eminently a land of heritable jurisdictions. A very large part of the kingdom was held *in regalitatem* in units which varied from quite compact burghs like Dunfermline to huge principalities like the domains of the Earls of Argyll in the south-west Highlands and Islands. In their most developed forms Scottish regalities were literally mini-kingdoms which excluded the King's Writ for every crime except high treason. This is, of course, one reason why the Crown in the early seventeenth century was so anxious to assert its control over the kirk, whose 900 or so parishes covered all of the kingdom, and which, under the rule of Crown-appointed bishops, provided the sovereign with a sort of shadow civil service everywhere. Charles I made such prominent use of bishops in his government that by 1638 the bulk of the nobility and gentry were prepared to countenance the abolition of prelacy. When it was restored after 1660, Scottish bishops were specifically warned against offending the nobility.[53]

Again, it must be emphasised that such tactical concessions strengthened rather than weakened the ability of the Restoration kirk to enforce Godly Discipline. The series of ascending ecclesiastical courts from kirk session to presbytery and synod survived, as they had in other periods when an episcopal order existed in the Church of Scotland and the bishop could in effect bring royal power to bear on the situation. The result could be awesome for all but the very highest persons in the land. On 6 June 1667, for example, the presbytery of Orkney, sitting in Kirkwall with My Lord Bishop presiding, ruled 'that when any incestuous persons come before them' the presbytery clerk should 'notify the samen to the sheriefe'.[54] Thus the combined power of church and state could catch the defaulter between them, for incest, like adultery, was a civil as well as a religious crime.

Regardless of the precise regime operative in the Church of Scotland (and between 1560 and 1690 there was continuous change), Godly Discipline could only be enforced at parish or burghal level if the powers and personnel of secular courts ultimately supported their ecclesiastical counterparts. For example, in rural areas kirk sessions simply had to be able to count on the support of the baron courts which were the courts of first instance all over Scotland, even in areas fully subject to the King's Writ.

Ultimately such support was usually forthcoming. Sheriff courts also recognised the need to support and sustain the jurisdiction of the kirk. In 1615 the sheriff court of Orkney sitting in Kirkwall provided a succinct statement of the ideology behind this impressive solidarity:

> Forsameikle as sinne and iniquitie is and hes bein the caus of Godis heavie plaigues and judgmentis, and the caus of great desolatioun in kirk and politie within this cuntrey for laik of discipline and putting of the actis of the kirk, quhilk hes been meikle compleimit in times past, to dew executioun – it is statuit and ordanit for punishment of sinne and vyce that the actis of the kirk, maid and to be maid be the ministerie and thair sessioun of kirk agenes transgressouris and sinneris, be put to dew executioun with all rigour in example of utheris to do the lyk; and to this effect that the bailie of ilk parochin and his officer concur and assist thair ministeris, elderis and thair officeris in putting of all sik actis and statutes maid or to be maid in thair sessioun of kirk to dew executioun.[55]

Obviously one of the recurring problems of enforcing moral discipline was the person who simply refused to turn up before the appropriate ecclesiastical tribunal, when duly cited. The kirk session of Anstruther Wester, a small trading burgh on the coast of Fife just across the Firth of Forth from Edinburgh and the Lothians, addressed itself to precisely this problem in February 1576 and minuted as follows: 'Because dyvers personnes being warned to compeir befoir the assemblie disobeyes, therefor ordane that the disobeyers be pundit [that is, fined] for the first falt 2s., the second falt 5s., the third 13s. 4d. This act was maid with consent of the baillies that it may have the mair strength.'[56] The same kirk session later made it clear that it was prepared to reciprocate the support it enjoyed from the municipal authorities, for it ruled that 'Whasaever sall be convict in deforcing or stubborn rebelling or disobeying the magistrate, baillie or officer, sall be debarred from all benefit of the Kirk'.[57] This interchanging of cases and mutual interlocking of authority between the secular and the eccesiastical was absolutely standard in the burghs. In Kirkintilloch, which was erected a burgh of barony under Lord Fleming in the sixteenth century,[58] the municipal authorities regularly referred appropriate cases to the kirk session, either after dealing with what they saw as the civil side of the matter, or simply because they thought matters such as the scandalous raising of an unsubstantiated charge of adultery were more appropriately handled by the kirk.[59]

Behind such transfers there lay, of course, the ultimate sanction of secular authority. When, for example, a couple were remitted to the kirk session 'for thaire scandallous language', they were offered the presumably unacceptable alternative 'or else to remove the woman out of the Toune'.[60] This interlocking of authority can be confusing, especially if set alongside the Presbyterian emphasis on the separation of civil and ecclesiastical jurisdictions. After the Cromwellian conquest of Scotland in 1651 the English occupying forces set out systematically to break the power of the nobles, who were deprived of their hereditary jurisdictions, and of the Kirk of the Covenant, much of whose authority over morals was transferred to secular justices of the peace. As commander-in-chief of Scotland after 1654 General Monck received an indignant petition from the ministers of Edinburgh and sundry other brethren in the ministry in which the petitioners insisted 'that we are traduced as medlers with civill affaires, whereas, as we have renounced by covenant all civill power, se wee nor midle – nor intend ever to medle with civill business, but are resolved, by the Lord's grace, to keep ourselves closse to such matters as are merely ecclesiastick, pertinently belonging to ecclesiastick courts'.[61] What the brethren of the ministry took for granted was mutual support between the two swords and overlapping personnel. Without such interpenetration both swords lost much of their edge.

In practice, before the traumas of the civil war period, the two swords in Scotland usually worked very closely together indeed. A good example at the level of baron court and parish comes from the parish of Menmuir in 1633 when arrangements were being made, at the very end of the year, for the future collection of fines imposed by the kirk session:

> Convenit the Lairds of Balnamone and Balyordie, the gudeman of Balrownie, [and] Balhal with the rest of the gentilmen and elders of parische, quha for ingathering of the penalties appointed Patrick Collace beddell kirk officer to the office and gaf him pouar till pund [that is, fine] in any of thr bounds and promesit gif heid be till cause thair officer concur wt him, quha accepted of the office and promest fidelitie and diligence under the paan of depositione fra al ofices.'[62]

What is very intriguing about this particular record is the way in which a substantial farmer-proprietor ('the gudeman') was associated with the local lairds as a member of the gentry. Such farmers were certainly members of the ruling strata, if scarcely technically of gentry status. The point is underlined by another minute of the same session in 1630, when they had to tackle an offender whose membership of the Christian flock was clearly dubious:

> The sesione understanding that Cristal Ballache bes suspect of witchcraft and that he wes banishit befor for using of charmes and that he repares till nae Kirk on the Sabath and that he is put out of the paryche of Stracathro as a pratizer of charmes and ane suspect of witchcraft ordeins that he be removit at Whitsunday out of this paryche – and to that effect will deall with the gudeman of Findowry in whose bounds he presenthe – dwells.[63]

Defiance of ecclesiastical censure was in fact quite common, usually in the shape of refusal to accept a penalty, either by silent default or, less frequently, in hot-blooded abuse and denial of jurisdiction. It was the ability of the system to contain such challenges which was the measure of its very real power. Thus, the elders and deacons of Crail, another small Fife trading burgh, had on 31 December 1566 found Andrew Few, senior, guilty of a foul and unsubstantiated slander against Janet Pearson. He had alleged 'that the said Janit haid ane of hir barnis whilk was nocht hir husbandis but ane uthir man callit James Keigis albeit in werity all the bernis that ewer the said Janit haid wos in the tym of hir mariage with hir husband Andro Balcomy'. Few was ordered to seek his victim's forgiveness on his knees before the whole congregation. He did not, and she came before the session asking that their decision 'be registrat in the townis bouikis with executionis to pas thairupon'. The magistrates present upon the session then 'interponis thair decryt iudiciall that the said Andro Few sall fowfull all the pointis of the decryt above wrettin this next Sunday quhilk is the XII of Januar instant under the payne of warding of him within the thouboitht [tolbooth, that is, jail] of this burcht and all uthir payne and charge that eftir may follow of the law'.[64] Thus a challenged, but just and reasonable judgement was made to stick.

By no means all the business before a kirk session concerned moral discipline. Administrative, charitable and purely religious matters were also important on its agenda. Higher church courts were less interested in the minutiae of parish morals. Presbytery tended to be used to overawe the odd recalcitrant sinner, but the bulk of its work was organisational and professional, in the sense that it represented the brethren of the ministry conjoined for purposes ranging from ordination to ruling that 'the act made by the last Synod against wagabond beggars should be intimated out of pulpite to the severall congregationes of this presbyterie'.[65] Synod operated on an even more general level, without quite approaching the alpine heights of politics and theology normally reserved for General Assemblies. However, the synod of Argyll in 1659, when concerned with the inadequacy of the ministry in Ardnamurchan, Moidart and Arisaig, was down-to-earth enough to write 'to the Laird of Lochiell for his interest in these places to rectifie the said abuses'. Cameron of Lochiel, High Chief of his clan, was a power in the land. Even he paled in significance before 'my Lord Marquesse of Argyll', High Chief of the great Clan Campbell and a devout ruling elder from the session of Inverary. When Argyll was charged to compose differences between a minister and his congregation, those differences vanished, at least in the presence of so great a regional prince.[66]

At its most effective, the Scots kirk's discipline rested on close co-operation in its courts between the clergy and the lay eldership which, though itself stratified in social status and practical function, represented the dominant lay elements in contemporary society. In England it is arguable that so close an intermeshing of the ruling classes with the machinery of moral regulation was never achieved. The Crown kept a much tighter control over courts ecclesiastic under the Anglican settlement. Those gentlemen represented in the House of Commons, and many nobles in the Lords, were always in practice reluctant in the Elizabethan and early Stuart period to approve predominantly government-inspired proposals about tighter regulation of personal conduct in such fields as drunkenness, dress, bastardy, swearing and the observance of the Sabbath. Widespread support for any such measures was usually only apparent outside minorities like government officials or committed radical Protestants when it could be argued that purely secular considerations of order and good government required them. Most such bills failed.[67] The more radically inclined Protestants of a Puritan persuasion had survived the reign of Elizabeth and the campaigns against them after the strengthening of ecclesiastical discipline by Archbishop Bancroft mainly because archdeacons' courts were not strong enough. In the early seventeenth century groups of Puritans at local level clearly began to move forward into the attack, using the ecclesiastical courts as part of their campaign to impose Godly Discipline on others, but after 1625 these very Puritans were shocked to find that the small minority of Arminian divines who had captured control of the Church of England by winning the ear of Charles I were in a position to use the courts ecclesiastic with unprecedented rigour to harry Puritans for their refusal to conform to Arminian liturgical standards.[68]

By 1640 allegations that an Arminian episcopate was too lenient towards moral offenders had become a standard theme in English Puritan attacks on the bishops of Charles I. It was alleged that they were so obsessed with cultivating the concept of hierarchical sacramental authority in church and state that they pursued adultery and fornication with insufficient rigour. The triumph of the Commonwealth regime in England is often seen as involving draconian moral regulation epitomised by the Act of 10 May 1650 'for suppressing the detestable sins of incest, adultery and fornication', an Act which carried on a well-established tradition of giving secular authorities power to punish moral offences such as bastard-bearing and brothel-keeping, but which very radically stiffened the penalties. Closer examination shows that the act was almost purely symbolic, and never an effective part of the criminal code. It was strongly opposed within parliament and only passed in a form which made successful prosecution virtually impossible.[69] Nor was this unrepresentative of the views of the bulk of the parliamentary leadership, as the Scots discovered when they sent representatives to the Westminster Assembly of Divines in 1643, with a view to securing an agreed pattern of liturgy, discipline and government for the established churches of both kingdoms.

One major problem was the presence on the English side of Independents fundamentally opposed to any concept of a national church. However, all the English representatives were hostile to the Scots concept of a system of church courts autonomous from civil authority. As Robert Baillie, a 'moderate' in Scots terms, complained, the English would tolerate only 'a lame Erastian presbytery'.[70] The cynical parliamentary lawyer Selden was well aware that effective Godly Discipline required the co-operation of the secular authorities. As he said, 'Men do not care for excommunication because they are shut out of the church, or delivered up to Satan, but because the law of the kingdom takes hold of them. After so many days a man cannot sue, no, not for his wife, if you take her from him.'[71] In the last analysis Selden simply was not prepared to grant any church court any claim to independent authority or jurisdiction whatsoever. His erastianism was unusually extreme, but it was an erastian dislike of a jurisdiction beyond their control, a dislike rooted in the socially and ideologically fractured nature of the English body politic, which made the English parliamentarians ensure that the demise of the Westminster Assembly was 'mute and inglorious'. After September 1648 it was reduced to serving as a body to examine the suitability of ministers of religion. In October 1649 that final power was taken from it.[72]

Though there was to be at least a partial revival of Godly Discipline in parts of England under the Anglicanism of the Restoration, the lack of consensus revealed in the mid seventeenth-century crisis was ultimately fatal to its survival, especially after the traumas of the Glorious Revolution of 1688 and the need to grant formal toleration to at least Protestant dissenters. The Scots had the advantage of starting with a far smaller and less complex society and the opening stages of their revolt against Charles I reinforced rather than seriously strained the vital working alliance between laymen and clergy based on commitment to further reformation in kirk and state. With the split in the English ruling class and the outbreak of civil war in England, with resulting pressures for Scottish intervention, the Covenanting movement in Scotland came under appalling stress. In particular the use of ecclesiastical discipline against the many nobles who chose to participate in the Engagement signed with Charles I in December 1647 and in the invasion of England on his behalf in 1648 which was defeated at Preston, effectively snapped the all-important working alliance between the secular and clerical leadership.[73] It was the achievement of the Restoration bishops in Scotland to re-establish this alliance, though it has been argued that religious conflict during the Restoration, coupled with the traumas of revolution in 1688–90, 'fatally weakened the authority of the church courts'.[74]

Certainly a very high proportion of the Scots nobles and lairds remained Episcopal in sentiment and rejected the purely Presbyterian settlement of 1690. Where a highland laird was a sympathetic Presbyterian Whig like Grant of Grant, kirk sessions could still after 1700 seek his concurrence in the suppression of scandal, but when on top of upper-class defections hard-core Presbyterian support was after 1730 rent by schism, due to the restoration of lay patronage in Scotland by parliament in 1712, the classic pattern of a national Godly Discipline began to disintegrate. It survived patchily for a long time, indeed aspects of it were so ingrained in the national psyche that they survived well into the nineteenth century, but the percentage of immorality cases, always the most sensitive, gradually declined in kirk session after kirk session; the truly recalcitrant became an insoluble problem. Nostalgic Scotch Presbyterians were by the late nineteenth century reduced to the position nostalgic and puritanical Englishmen who joined the Societies for the Reformation of Manners in the late eighteenth century had been reduced to – that of trying to revive the spirit of Godly Discipline when the ruling class consensus on which alone such discipline could be effectively built was a mere memory.[75]

Broadly speaking there were thus two basic requirements for an effectively enforced Godly Discipline. One was the will on the part of church and state to enforce it. The very definition of Godly Discipline was a measure of that will. For example, before 1573–4 the Spanish Inquisition concerned itself hardly at all with fornication cases, but after circular letters from the

Inquisitor-General dated 20 November 1573 and 20 November 1574, the Inquisition prosecuted many cases of fornication until the 1590s.[76] Will alone, however, was not enough. Some societies were more difficult to discipline than others. The northern Netherlands proved resistant to Habsburg coercion and eventually set up a republican regime which lacked both the means and the will to strive for a uniform Godly Discipline. England proved too complex, divided and recalcitrant a society for its seventeenth-century governments to forge any coherent moral ascendancy over it.

It was above all in relatively simple and homogenous societies where local communities internalised the spiritual and moral values of a national church that Godly Discipline was most effective. Such were Scotland and Sweden, and it is no accident that both laid heavy emphasis on education as a means of access to God's Word.[77] In both countries it was the parish, at least in the countryside where the vast bulk of people lived, which was the basic unit of the political and moral order. Historians of the Swedish church have tended to lay insufficient emphasis on the life of the farming community as expressed through its parish institutions. Indeed, what has been for generations the only big book by an English-speaking historian on the Swedish national church, Bishop John Wordsworth's *The National Church of Sweden*, mentions parish life hardly at all.[78] Rather have ecclesiastical historians concentrated on the great bishops of the early reformed period, and on church-state relations.

The standard Swedish church history is not much better. It does mention parish discipline, but obviously finds it amusing that this could range from discouraging smoking of tobacco in church yards to the lesser and greater excommunication.[79] Only very recently has an attempt been made to see parish justice as an important mechanism whereby peasant society in Sweden governed itself, controlled dissent from social norms and tried whenever possible to heal rifts in the local community by Christian reconciliation.[80] Obviously a serious religious dissent and division would have paralysed such a system. Johannes Loccenius, the great Swedish jurist, laid down that unity in religion was a fundamental rule of the realm.[81] It was certainly a prerequisite for a workable parish society. Both in Scotland and in Sweden the rise of large-scale Evangelical dissenting bodies sealed the final doom of the parish as the agent of a national Godly Discipline.

Notes: Chapter 9

1 G. D. Henderson (ed.), *The Scots Confession 1560* (Edinburgh, 1960), p. 44.
2 J. K. Cameron (ed.), *The First Book of Discipline* (Edinburgh, 1972), p. 165.
3 J. Kirk (ed.), *The Second Book of Discipline* (Edinburgh, 1980), p. 200.
4 D. Hay Fleming, 'The discipline of the Reformation part II', *The Original Secession Magazine* (May 1878), pp. 603–4.
5 The letter is printed in translation in E. H. Kossman and A. F. Mellink (eds), *Texts Concerning the Revolt of the Netherlands* (London, 1974), pp. 56–9.
6 *Compendium Theologiae Dogmaticae, Et Moralis Ad Usum Seminariorum Auctore D. Ludovico Habert* (Editio Novissima, Placentiae, 1775), p. 103.
7 D. S. Bailey, *The Man-Woman Relation in Christian Thought* (London, 1959), p. 143.

8 J. K. Cameron, 'Scottish Calvinism and the Principle of Intolerance', in B. Gerish (ed.), *Reformatio Perennis* (Pittsburgh, Pa, 1981), pp. 113–28.

9 N. Cohn, *Europe's Inner Demons* (London, 1975), pp. 24–31.

10 L. Rothkrug, 'Popular religion and holy shrines: their influence on the origins of the German Reformation and their role in German cultural development', in J. Obelkevitch (ed.), *Religion and the People 800–1700* (Chapel Hill, NC, 1979), p. 77.

11 P. Benedict, 'The Catholic response to Protestantism: church activity and popular piety in Rouen, 1560–1600', ibid., pp. 168–90.

12 Erasmus of Rotterdam, *Praise of Folly and Letter to Martin Dorp*, trans. Betty Radice with introduction and notes by A. H. T. Levi, Penguin Classics edn (Harmondsworth, 1971).

13 Thomas More, *Utopia*, trans. P. Turner (Folio Society edn, London, 1972), pp. 103–5.

14 *Sermons by Hugh Latimer Sometime Bishop of Worcester*, Everyman edn, (London, n.d.), p. 364. For Latimer's career and death see D. M. Loades, *The Oxford Martyrs* (London, 1970).

15 M. R. O'Connell, *The Counter Reformation 1559–1610*, Harper Torchbook edn (New York, Evanston, Ill., and London, 1974), ch. 3.

16 C. D. Riley, 'The state of Milan in the reign of Philip II of Spain' (unpublished Oxford D.Phil. thesis, 1977), p. 245.

17 J. Kirk, ' "The Polities of the Best Reformed Kirks": Scottish achievements and English aspirations in church government after the Reformation', *Scottish Historical Review*, Vol. LIX/1 (no. 167, April 1980), pp. 22–53.

18 K. Thomas, *Religion and the Decline of Magic* (London, 1971), ch. 4.

19 J. K. Cameron, 'The Swiss and the Covenant', in G. Barrow (ed.), *The Scottish Tradition* (Edinburgh, 1974), pp. 155–63.

20 J. P. Kenyon (ed.), *The Stuart Constitution* (Cambridge, 1966), p. 265.

21 A. G. Dickens, 'The ambivalent English Reformation', in A. G. Dickens *et al.*, *Background to the English Renaissance* (London, 1974), pp. 43–56.

22 There is a transcript of some of the evidence of the 1532 suit in Chancery printed under 'Ecclesiastical discipline (1529)', in J. V. Cunningham (ed.), *The Renaissance in England* (New York, 1966), pp. [5]–[7].

23 A point made most cogently by Christina Larner in V. A. C. Gatrell, B. Lenman and G. Parker (eds), *Crime and the Law* (London, 1980), pp. 72–3.

24 See comments on fols 202–3 of an early seventeenth-century treatise on ecclesiastical jurisdictions, Lambeth Palace Library, MS. 2026.

25 E. J. Burford, *Bawds and Lodgings: A History of the London Bankside Brothels c.100–1675* (London, 1976), pp. 129–31.

26 Item 701, 24 November 1531, *Cal. S. P. Venetian*, Vol. IV, ed. R. Brown (London, 1871), p. 304. I am indebted to Dr Susan Brigden for drawing my attention to this reference.

27 *Daily Telegraph*, Wednesday, 25 June 1980, carried a report of such an incident at Nowshahr, a city on the Caspian Sea. The regime proposed to build walls reaching several hundred yards out to sea to allow simultaneous but separate bathing.

28 L. A. Knafla, *Law and Politics in Jacobean England* (Cambridge, 1977), p. 63. There is a convenient introduction to this great Aztec source, with commentaries by Kurt Ross, in *Codex Mendoza Aztec Manuscript* (Fribourg, 1978). For a fascinating discussion of the profoundly repressive nature of Aztec social psychology and religion see C. A. Burland, *The Gods of Mexico* (London, 1967).

29 R. A. Marchant, *The Church under the Law: Justice, Administration and Discipline in the Diocese of York 1560–1640* (Cambridge, 1969), p. 1.

30 ibid., p. 217.

31 J. A. Sharpe, 'Crime and delinquency in an Essex parish 1600–1640', in J. S. Cockburn (ed.), *Crime in England 1550–1800* (London, 1977), Appendix, p. 109. We await the first large-scale study of ecclesiastical discipline in early modern England, currently being prepared by Dr M. J. Ingram of the Queen's University, Belfast. His thesis, 'Ecclesiastical justice in Wiltshire, 1600–1640, with special reference to cases concerning sex and marriage' (Oxford D.Phil., 1976–7), provides a foretaste.

32 P. Slack, 'Books of Orders: the making of English social policy, 1577–1631', *Transactions of the Royal Historical Society*, 5th Series, Vol. XXX (1980), pp. 1–22; and J. Walter and

K. Wrightson, 'Dearth and the social order in early modern England', *Past and Present*, Vol. LXXI (1976), pp. 32–42.

33 'Archbishop Whitgift's Articles for Bath and Wells Diocese 1583', printed as item XXVIII in W. P. M. Kennedy, *Elizabethan Episcopal Administration*, Vol. III, Alcuin Club Collections, XXVII (London and Milwaukee, Wis., 1924), p. 157.

34 P. McGrath, *Papists and Puritans under Elizabeth I* (London, 1967), pp. 213–14.

35 'The godly discipline: the alliance between patrons and preachers', in R. C. Richardson, *Puritanism in North-West England* (Manchester, 1972), pp. 144–9.

36 M. Walzer, *The Revolution of the Saints* (Cambridge, Mass., 1965), ch. 7.

37 R. A. Marchant, *The Puritans and the Church Courts in the Diocese of York 1560–1642* (London, 1960).

38 K. Wrightson and D. Levine, *Poverty and Piety in an English Village: Terling, 1525–1700* (New York and London, 1979), chs 6 and 7.

39 John Angier, *An Helpe to Better Hearts for Better Times* (London, 1647), ch. VI, 'Sleeping'. I am indebted to Dr Keith Wrightson for this reference.

40 R. Briggs, 'The Catholic Puritans: Jansenists and Rigorists in France', in D. Pennington and K. Thomas (eds), *Puritans and Revolutionaries* (Oxford, 1978), pp. 333–54.

41 K. Wrightson, 'The nadir of English illegitimacy in the seventeenth century', in P. Laslett, K. Oostereveen and R. M. Smith (eds), *Bastardy and its Comparative History* (London, 1980), pp. 176–91. I am deeply indebted to my colleague Dr Keith Wrightson for helpful discussion on several of these points, as well as the stimulus of his scholarship over many years, and am particularly grateful that he made available to me his thesis, 'The Puritan Reformation of Manners with special reference to the counties of Lancashire and Essex 1640–60' (Cambridge PhD, 1973), and the typescript of his book, *English Society 1580–1680* (London, 1982).

42 R. B. Manning, *Religion and Society in Elizabethan Sussex* (Leicester, 1969), ch. 7.

43 G. Donaldson, *The Scottish Reformation* (Cambridge, 1960), ch. 3.

44 D. Hay Fleming (ed.), *St. Andrews Kirk Session Register, 1559–1582*, Scottish History Society, Vol. IV (Edinburgh, 1889), p. 5.

45 ibid., pp. 5–6.

46 M. H. B. Sanderson, *Scottish Rural Society in the Sixteenth Century* (Edinburgh, 1981), discusses in chapter 2 the complex issues of the impact of the baron court on the personal lives of the rural population.

47 I. B. Cowan, *Regional Aspects of the Scottish Reformation*, Historical Association, General Series no. 92 (London, 1978), pp. 28–34.

48 M. Lynch, *Edinburgh and the Reformation* (Edinburgh, 1981).

49 A. Duke, 'Salvation by coercion: the controversy surrounding the 'Inquisition' in the Low Countries on the eve of the Revolt', in P. N. Brooks (ed.), *Reformation Principle and Practice: Essays in Honour of Arthur Geoffrey Dickens* (London, 1980), ch. 8, pp. 135–56.

50 I. B. Cowan, 'Church and society in post-Reformation Scotland', in *Records of the Scottish Church History Society*, Vol. XVII (1971), pp. 185–201.

51 W. R. Foster, *The Church before the Covenants: The Church of Scotland 1596–1638* (Edinburgh and London, 1975), ch. 5.

52 M. Lee, *Government by Pen: Scotland under James VI and I* (Urbana, Ill., Chicago and London, 1980), p. 43.

53 G. Donaldson, *Scotland James V to James VII* (Edinburgh, 1965) is the best general introduction to these problems in seventeenth-century Scotland. For a general discussion of the structure of Scottish courts see *An Introduction to Scottish Legal History*, Stair Society, Vol. XX (Edinburgh, 1958).

54 *Presbytery of Orkney*, entry for afternoon of 6 June 1667, Orkney Island Archives ref. 4/3.

55 R. S. Barclay (ed.), *The Court Books of Orkney and Shetland 1614–1615,* Scottish History Society, 4th Series, Vol. IV (Edinburgh, 1967), pp. 25–6.

56 Kirk Session Minutes, Anstruther Wester, 7 February 1576, Scottish Record Office (hereafter SRO) CH2/624/2.

57 ibid., 9 March 1590/1.

58 G. S. Pryde, *The Burghs of Scotland* (London, 1965), p. 57.

59 G. S. Pryde (ed.), *The Court Book of the Burgh of Kirkintilloch 1658–1694,* Scottish History Society, 3rd Series, Vol. LIII (Edinburgh, 1963), p. 109 – entry for 24 July 1680.
60 ibid., pp. 107–8 – entry for 22 June 1680.
61 'Greevances concerning the affairs of the Kirk of Scotland with the Remedies thereof', article 7, printed in Rev. W. Stephen (ed.), *Register of the Consultations of the Ministers of Edinburgh and Some Other Brethren of the Ministry Volume I, 1652–1657* Scottish History Society, 3rd Series, Vol. I (Edinburgh, 1921), pp. 80–7.
62 Menmuir Kirk Session Minutes, 29 December 1633, SRO, CH2/264/1, fol. 10^v.
63 ibid., 2 May 1630, fol. 6.
64 Burgh Court Book of Crail, Vol. for 'Apr. 30 1566 to Feb 10 1569', entry for 7 January 1566/7, Crail Burgh Records B10, in custody of University Archives, University of St Andrews.
65 W. MacKay (ed.), *Records of the Presbyteries of Inverness and Dingwall 1643–1688*, Scottish History Society, Vol. XXIV (Edinburgh, 1896), p. 332, entry for 25 November 1673, Presbytery of Dingwall.
66 D. C. Mactavish, *Minutes of the Synod of Argyll 1652–1661*, Scottish History Society, 3rd Series, Vol. XXXVIII (Edinburgh, 1944), p. 202 – minute of 'Provincial Assembly of Argyle at Innveraray the second Wednesday of October 1659'.
67 Joan R. Kent, 'Attitudes of Members of the House of Commons to the regulation of 'personal conduct' in late Elizabethan and early Stuart England', *Bulletin of the Institute of Historical Research*, Vol. XLVI (1973), pp. 41–71.
68 Manning, *Religion and Society in Elizabethan Sussex*, ch. 10; Wrightson and Levine, *Poverty and Piety*, chs 6 and 7.
69 K. Thomas, 'The Puritans and adultery: the Act of 1650 reconsidered', in Pennington and Thomas, *Puritans and Revolutionaries,* pp. 257–82.
70 F. N. McCoy, *Robert Baillie and the Second Scots Reformation* (Berkeley, Calif., 1974), ch. 5.
71 S. H. Reynolds (ed.), *The Table Talk of John Selden* (Oxford, 1892), pp. 66–7.
72 S. W. Carruthers, *The Everyday Work of the Westminster Assembly* (Philadelphia, Pa, 1943), p. 3.
73 The best survey of the disintegration of the Covenanting movement is D. Stevenson, *Revolution and Counter-Revolution in Scotland 1644–1651* (London, 1977).
74 S. Davies, 'The courts and the Scottish legal system 1600–1747: the case of Stirlingshire', in V. A. C. Gatrell, B. Lenman and G. Parker (eds), *Crime and the Law: The Social History of Crime in Western Europe since 1500* (London, 1980), p. 153.
75 For a survey of some of these problems see the introduction to section 10 – 'Church courts' – in P. Rayner, B. Lenman and G. Parker, *Handlist of Records for the Study of Crime in Early Modern Scotland* (List and Index Society, forthcoming). The best introduction to the Societies for the Reformation of Manners is T. C. Curtis and W. A. Speck, 'The Societies for the Reformation of Manners: a case study in the theory and practice of moral reform', *Literature and History*, Vol. III (1976), pp. 45–64. For the use of membership of the kirk session in the nineteenth century as a test of business respectability see A. A. MacLaren, *Religion and Social Class: The Disruptive Years in Aberdeen* (London, 1974).
76 B. Bennassar (ed.), *L'Inquisition espagnole, XV–XIXe siècle* (Paris, 1979), pp. 313–26. I owe this reference to my friend and colleague Dr Geoffrey Parker.
77 This phenomenon is well known in a Scottish context where it is part of the national mythology, though its effectiveness is difficult to measure. For the remarkable achievements in reading literacy in early modern Sweden, see E. Johansson, *The History of Literacy in Sweden* (Umea Educational Reports, no. 12, 1977).
78 J. Wordsworth (Bishop of Salisbury), *The National Church of Sweden* (London, 1911).
79 H. Pleijel, *Swenska Kyrkans Historia, Femte Bandet 1680–1772* (Stockholm, 1935), pp. 92–9.
80 J. Sundin, 'Kontroll-Straff och Forsöning: Kyrklig rättvisa på sockennivå före 1850', in id. (ed.), *Kontroll och Kontrollerade: Formell och informell kontroll i et historiskt perspektiv* (Umeå, 1982), pp. 39–85.
81 M. Roberts (ed.), *Sweden's Age of Greatness* (London, 1973), p. 132.

10 Legitimation Crises and the Early Modern State: the Politics of Religious Toleration

MARY FULBROOK

Edwin Sandys asserted in a sermon delivered in sixteenth-century England that

> This liberty, that men may openly profess diversity of religion, must needs be dangerous to the Commonwealth. What stirs diversity of religion hath raised in nations and kingdoms, the histories are so many and so plain, and our times in such sort have told you, that with further proof I need not trouble your ears. One God, one king, one faith, one profession, is fit for one monarchy and commonwealth ... Let conformity and unity in religion be provided for; and it shall be as a wall of defence unto this realm.[1]

Similar political justifications of religious uniformity were enunciated by individuals of otherwise widely differing persuasions in early seventeenth-century England. Sir John Eliot, later imprisoned in the Tower of London for parliamentary opposition, claimed that 'Religion it is that keeps the subject in obedience'; and William Laud, who as Archbishop of Canterbury played a central role in attempted Stuart absolutism, maintained 'it is impossible in any Christian commonwealth that the church should melt, and the State stand firm. For there can be no firmness without law; and no laws can be binding, if there be no conscience to obey them: penalty alone could never, never, do it. And no school can teach conscience but the church of Christ.'[2] Such quotations could be multiplied indefinitely in pre-revolutionary England: it was taken as axiomatic that religious unity was a prerequisite for political stability.

This assumption is echoed, if in a more generalised form, in the writings of certain modern social theorists. Notions of legitimacy and legitimation have been developed as central to understanding the modes of maintenance and transformation of the social order. In this chapter I want to examine, first, the specific problem of the conditions under which a state in early modern Europe was or was not likely to pursue policies of religious uniformity. I shall do this with reference to three cases of early modern European states which, in their respective periods of attempted absolutism, developed rather different policies with regard to toleration in church and state. Secondly, I want to examine the theoretical problem of the role of legitimation in political stability and change. For this, I shall focus specifically on the consequences of attempts to impose religious uniformity in England immediately before the outbreak of the Civil War. Bishop Edwin Sandys may have felt that 'with further proof' he need not trouble his listeners' ears. In the present context, however, I can hardly adopt such a cavalier approach; and I hope, in fact, to be able to show that in his main proposition, Edwin Sandys was wrong.

The Politics of Religious Toleration

Theories of religious toleration have, very broadly, fallen into two main areas. The most pervasive are those which treat toleration as a problem in the history of ideas. Gradually, with periodic checks and reversals, the idea of religious toleration was developed and extended, receiving a great boost with the Enlightenment, and eventually becoming accepted, to a greater or lesser extent, in a large number of modern states. The other type of approach tries to relate the rise of toleration to socio-economic or political changes. According to this approach, religion played a fundamental and intrinsic role in feudal relations of production; but with the emergence of formally free wage labour under capitalism, and the depersonalisation of contractual relationships in the market, it ceased to play a central role. Alternatively, religion played a crucial role in the emergence and consolidation of separate, centralised nation states in early modern Europe; once the system of national states was established, national and international politics no longer needed to be carried out in terms of religious profession. Evolutionary theories go further, and postulate the emergence of a more differentiated stage of societal evolution, in which religion becomes progressively separated from the political and economic arenas.[3]

There are resonances of truth in each of these approaches, but none is entirely satisfactory, for both empirical and theoretical reasons. The history of ideas approach fails to explain why ideas which are generally available are successfully acted upon and become historically effective only in certain circumstances and not others. The type of approach focusing on differences in interpersonal relationships in feudal or capitalist societies, like the sort of approach focusing on the formation of nation states, tends to fall into a supra-historical societal functionalism, and fails to explain particular historical variations among different societies and states at comparable levels of political or economic development. The evolutionary theories require acceptance of metatheoretical assumptions which have similar shortcomings, and evolutionists tend ultimately merely to redescribe, rather than explain, patterns of historical change.

Here, I want to propose a somewhat more differentiated theory which is based on analysis of politics and religion in three particular early modern states: England, Württemberg and Brandenburg-Prussia. My basic postulate is an anti-evolutionary one: that there is no essential and necessary 'rise' of religious toleration, and that, in any particular place and period, one must analyse the particular combinations of circumstances which help to determine the degree to which policies of religious uniformity or of toleration are possible. The periods on which my analysis is based are those of attempted absolutist rule in each case. In England, I would argue that this period comes at a chronologically earlier time than in Württemberg or Prussia: thus I shall be dealing with England from the mid sixteenth to the mid seventeenth centuries, whereas the comparable periods in the political development of Württemberg and Prussia are from the late seventeenth to the late eighteenth centuries.

We find some interesting variations in the relations between politics and religion, and in degrees of policies of religious uniformity or toleration, among these three states. In England, as the quotations at the beginning of this chapter illustrate, there was a widespread belief that religious uniformity was necessary to political stability; yet there were disagreements over what that uniformity should consist in, and for considerable periods of time a relatively wide diversity of orientations were in practice tolerated within a more or less latitudinarian church. But at other times, strenuous efforts were made to impose a more rigorous, narrowly defined uniformity of religion. This was particularly so during the period of Charles I's attempted personal rule. In Prussia, at the time of attempted absolutism, the opposite policy was pursued by the state: the Hohenzollerns were in favour of active policies of religious toleration. But simultaneously, the established state churches in the various provinces – which the Hohenzollerns were attempting to co-opt and bring under the central control of the state – were narrowly concerned to enforce a strict uniformity of doctrine and practice against any latitudinarian tendencies. The situation in the contemporaneous state of Württemberg was different again. Here the rulers were, to some extent as in Prussia, at least partly in favour of religious toleration, although religious policies were not as actively pursued by the Württemberg dukes in comparison with the rulers of Prussia. But the Lutheran state church, in contrast to Prussian Lutherans, was much more latitudinarian with respect to differences of opinion within its midst, while at the same time being concerned to defend its monopoly status against the external threat of Catholicism. Lutheranism in eighteenth-century Württemberg was conceived within much broader limits than Lutheranism in early eighteenth-century Prussia.

These variations cannot be accounted for, I would contend, in terms either of the availability of ideas of religious toleration, or of levels of economic or political development. Capitalist relations of production had perhaps developed further in seventeenth-century England than in eighteenth-century Prussia; Enlightenment ideas were equally available to Lutherans in eighteenth-century Prussia and Württemberg, yet they responded differently to their stimulus, ranging from retrenchment to receptivity. And in each of the three states at the relevant times there were attempts by rulers – more or less successful depending on a variety of circumstances – to introduce the apparatus of absolutist rule.

The key may be sought by examining the internal structural relationships among church, state and crucial political groups, in particular conditions and with reference to particular religious minorities. The structural inter-relationships help to explain the limits and possibilities of certain types of action; the particular circumstances and particular movements reveal how these structural potentialities operate at any given time. By analysing the cases at these two levels, one may first develop certain generalisations about likely tendencies or patterns of development; then by feeding in the histori-cally unique particularities one may develop specific historical explanations of particular individual outcomes.

The initial set of elements and relationships which is important is com-prised of the following: the nature of the church; the nature of the state; the nature of crucial social-political groups; and the relationships among them. The church may be economically strong, and independent; or it may be economically weak, and dependent on the patronage and support of external groups or individuals. The social status of the church's personnel, the clergy, may be high or low. The cultural orientations and social impli-cations of the church as an institution will depend to a considerable extent on these variables, and in particular on the degree to which it is constrained or affected by the interests of certain social groups among the laity, as we shall see in a moment. The state may be unitary, having a relatively long tradition of national cultural unification, or it may be an emerging com-posite state, made up of a variety of territories with different cultural and political traditions and social profiles. Rulers attempting to introduce absolutism may have to deal with a single Diet or Parliament; or with several separate Estates, divided both on constituency of representation and on territorial lines. The politically important social groups may consist in a feudal, territorial nobility, relating to an enserfed peasantry; or a domes-ticated, court-oriented nobility, along with a freeholding peasantry and strong burgher classes; or it may be that the society is comprised of status groups in which there is no strong indigenous nobility. Policies of religious toleration or religious uniformity, as developed in practice, depend not only on positions on each of these variables, but also on the relationships among variables. Thus the church, whether strong or weak, may be closely allied politically with the state; but conversely, it may have closer links with the Estates, and thus find itself in some tension with, or opposition to, the policies of a centralising state. The interests of the social groups among the laity who can affect the church's policies may also differ, complicating the relationships among elements.

Let us be more specific, and apply this abstract schema to the three cases of England, Württemberg and Prussia, at the relevant periods. (It may be noted that all three were Protestant states: I have not attempted to consider the extension of my theory to Catholic states, for which a number of adaptations would be required.) We can summarise the profiles of these three cases according to the relevant variables, as in Table 10.1. In the interest of brevity, these characterisations of church, state and society in the three cases will not be further substantiated here.[4] What then were the consequences of these structural configurations in given circumstances, and

Table 10.1   *Structural Variables and Relationships*

	England 1560–1640	Württemberg 1680–1780	Prussia 1690–1740
Church	Economically weak: patronage of Crown and laity. Reduced but rising social status.	Economically strong: independent wealth; no local benefices, centrally salaried pastorate. High social status.	Economically weak: patronage of Crown and laity. Very low social status.
State	Unitary nation state. Parliament. Decentralised local government.	Unitary nation state. Single Diet. Decentralised local government.	Composite state. Regional Estates. Centralised state bureaucracy.
Society	Domesticated aristocracy; increasing commercialisation.	No indigenous aristocracy; small peasant and burgher property-ownership.	Feudal aristocracy; enserfed peasantry, declining towns.
Interrelations	Church linked with ruler; but lay interventions and ambiguities.	Church independent, but allied with Estates and upper social ranks.	Church dependent on regional Estates and local nobles; but ruler seeking to gain control.

with reference to particular religious minorities?

What we are concerned with is religious toleration in the weakest sense: freedom for particular minorities to differ from what is represented as orthodoxy by the state church. This does not imply a general freedom for difference of worship and belief, associated with formal equality of professions, in the abstract; all I am concerned with in this chapter is a specific freedom in practice (whatever the formal legal position) for particular groups in particular circumstances. Let us take, for these purposes, the attitudes of the three Protestant states and state churches to the inherently similar Puritan and Pietist movements, which were inner-churchly movements for religious reform based on a Biblicist, individualist, experiential Christianity. The Puritan and Pietist movements originated as attempts to achieve completion of what they perceived as an essentially unfinished Reformation. Yet they received very different receptions in each case. In England, while individuals in the state church might be sympathetic towards Puritan aims and concerns, the church was constrained, by virtue of its dependence on the state, to view Puritanism with some ambivalence and at times active opposition. This was particularly the case when the other religious extreme in pre-revolutionary England, Catholicism, was perceived as politically less of a problem – as, for example, after the defeat of the Spanish Armada. Conversely, where Catholicism was powerful and constituted a political threat, as in north-western England, Puritanism might be tolerated, even encouraged, in aid of the government's fight against the 'old religion'. As the Privy Council suggested, Puritan preachers in north-west England would 'instruct the people the better to know their duty towards God and Her Majesty's laws and to reduce them to such conformity as we desire'.[5] In Württemberg, where the church was strong and independent, inner-churchly Pietism posed no serious political threat, and could gradually become incorporated as a legitimate element in a broad, latitudinarian church. In Prussia, where the church was weak and dependent on the local Estates and nobles, both internal and external aspects of the Pietist movement represented a serious threat to the professional status of the church; thus the Prussian church, in contrast to its counterpart in Württemberg, responded to Pietism with active hostility and opposition. But the links of the dependent church in Prussia were with the Estates, who helped to determine the church's response, and not with the state, as in the case of the dependent church in England. And unlike in England, the state in Prussia actively supported Pietism as a junior partner in its fight against the entrenched interests of the Estates in the localities. These responses may be summarised as in Table 10.2.

Table 10.2   *Responses to a Religious Minority: the Cases of Puritanism and Pietism*

	England 1560–1640	Württemberg 1680–1780	Prussia 1690–1740
Church	Ambivalent	Toleration	Hostile
State	Ambivalent	Toleration	Active support
Outcome	Some opposition, depending on circumstances	Development of toleration in latitudinarian church	State support of toleration against narrow uniformity of church

Returning to the wider issue, the particular intersections of the sets of variables outlined above, in the context of certain general circumstances and in relation to particular religious minorities, help to determine the historical outcomes concerning religious toleration. A unitary nation state such as England, with an economically weak, politically dependent state church, would naturally attempt to co-opt the church into the maintenance of social order; that it might ultimately fail in this attempt arose from the considerable powers of the wider laity in the affairs of the church. A composite state such as Prussia, developing a specialised secular state bureaucracy, might attempt to infiltrate and gain control of the state church through sponsorship of a heterodox religious movement such as Pietism, while the church itself, allied with threatened provincial interests, would be opposed to policies of latitudinarianism and toleration. A unitary state such as Württemberg, which faced a politically strong, economically independent state church, would be able to affect religious policies only marginally and under favourable circumstances, and in general the church would, from a position of relative strength, be able to be relatively tolerant of differences of opinion within its midst. Other cases could also be analysed in terms of the variables and relationships suggested here. Thus, for example, one could examine the fates of the Pietist movements in other early modern German states: an obvious first additional case would be that of the Electorate of Saxony, where the church was (as in England, but unlike in Prussia) closely allied with the state, and where Pietism was perceived as a social and political threat. August Hermann Francke was accordingly forced to leave Leipzig, geographically so close to, yet socially and politically so different from, the town of Halle where he eventually settled.

Legitimation Crises and the Early Modern State

Let me now turn to the other half of this chapter's title: legitimation crises and the early modern state. How far can this sort of analysis of religion and politics in early modern states throw light on theories concerning legitimation and power?

It will be necessary first to outline very briefly the theories relevant to this discussion. In one way or another, the main nineteenth- and twentieth-century traditions of social thought have given religious ideologies a large role in the maintenance of social order. For Marx, this was implied through such notions as 'false consciousness'; for Durkheim (whose theories of religion were ultimately just as subversive of its ontological status as were Marx's), the role of religion was conceptualised in terms of collective representations; for Weber a more differentiated approach allowed for the autonomy of religious experience as refracted differently for different social groups, while even so religious beliefs played an important role in certain modes of political legitimation. Parsonsian theorists took up the notion of a value consensus as informing the maintenance of social order;. and neo-Marxist theorists of various persuasions have also discussed the contribution of cultural legitimations to political power, ranging from Althusser and the structuralists to Habermas and the Frankfurt school, as well as theorists in the recently revived Gramscian tradition.

There are many distinctions and differences among this galaxy of approaches. But cross-cutting the more obvious differences is one particular distinction which is of importance here. This distinction has to do with the presumed location of legitimation. Is legitimation an aspect of the system of rule itself, claimed by ruling elites to characterise and justify their domination? Or is it conceived rather as 'legitimacy': that is, the actual acceptance of the political system by those who are ruled? The explanatory implications of the two terms – legitimation, and legitimacy – are rather different. The first, unlike the second, does not necessarily imply the active assent of the governed to the cultural rationalisations of domination by those who govern. This may be illustrated with reference to the approaches of Weber and Habermas, for example. In Weber's concept of modes of legitimation of authority, the reference is to the claims and self-interpretation of the rulers; contrary to common misconceptions, Weber's political sociology does not necessarily imply the actual consent of the governed in particular systems of power relationships – this latter is for Weber a question for empirical investigation, not a metatheoretical presupposition. Thus Weber's conception of legitimation is rather a classificatory tool, and not an explanatory device providing the key to the ways in which modes of domination are sustained or transformed. By contrast, other theorists do claim that legitimacy, or the acceptance of a regime by those who are governed, is central to political stability or change. Habermas, for example, suggests that in late capitalist societies, as the state increasingly intervenes to control and steer economic crises, administrative crises will become displaced and reappear as crises of legitimation and motivation. For Habermas, structural, systemic crises become translated into experiential, societal crises; and late capitalist societies may well avoid economic crises only to find that they are faced instead by cultural crises of legitimation, or loss of legitimation on the part of the governed.[6]

Returning to the historical material discussed above, my analysis would suggest the following: the active consent of the governed – that is, 'legitimacy' – does *not* play a major role in political stability. The consensus (within certain limits of variation) of the governors, on the other hand – that is, agreement over 'legitimation' – *is* central. This is not to suggest an elite theory of politics. Rather, it is to imply that it is only when the relative consensus of elites breaks down that the incoherent potential opposition of the governed to an unequal social and political order may be transformed into an active, alternative political force. This process takes place in two ways: first, the formation of a coherent, oppositional political consciousness; and secondly, the development of political alliances and of practical opportunities for organised political action. Let me illustrate these assertions.

In pre-revolutionary England, as we have seen, prevailing assumptions about political legitimation were conceived in religious terms. At the same time, it can be argued, the mass of the population may not have been actively impelled by any sense of religious motivation: religion may, contrary to the assertions of secularisation theorists such as Bryan Wilson, have been relevant to most people's lives mainly in relation to mundane matters of social belonging and local administration. Active Catholics, or active Puritans, or even committed middle-of-the-road members of the church, were numerically probably a minority of the population, although assertions such as this are hard to substantiate. From what specialist research has been done, it seems that a large proportion of the population was prepared pragmatically to accept, with variations in degree of understanding and approval, whatever religious settlement was in force. The relatively large number of people – as much as one-sixth or one-fifth of the population in some places – who were prepared to remain excommunicate indicates the disregard of many for the spiritual sanctions of the church. The existence of religious indifference (though probably not active atheism at this time), along with the continued activities of a variety of religious minorities of the left and the right (if anachronistic labels can be used), is simple and ready evidence of a lack of general consensus on religion. Such a point hardly needs labouring.[7]

For much of the time, and particularly under conditions of some tolerance, when a diversity of views (within certain limits) could flourish in the country and be represented at court, this lack of general unity or active popular consensus did not matter very much. But the situation became rather different in the late 1620s and 1630s. The period which saw the breakdown of parliamentary government and the attempt at prerogative, absolutist rule, constituted a period of structural crisis. The facts of English social and political structure, including the socio-economic and political strength of the governing classes, the decentralisation of local government, the lack of a separate central state bureaucracy and standing army, militated against the successful introduction of absolutist rule in England. Most crucially, the monarchy failed to achieve sufficient financial and administrative autonomy to conduct an independent foreign policy. We can also say that this period of structural crisis saw a crisis in the broad consensus over legitimation *among the political elites*. For this was the period of the rise of the Laudian faction in the church, the so-called Arminians; a rise which was bitterly resented by a wide variety of members of the English governing classes for a wide variety of reasons, partly theological, partly social, political and economic. This breakdown of an elite consensus, with Laud's attempt to impose a stringent and narrow religious uniformity as an integral aspect of the new monarchical pro-gramme of absolutism, had two important consequences. First, it served to form and develop a set of alliances in a conscious, coherent, opposition. Laud succeeded, where sixteenth-century Puritans had failed, in uniting people of diverse persuasions ranging from the 'moderate centre' of the episcopal church through to the most ardent independents and presby-terians, against the new uniformity of the Arminian High Church. Simultaneously, the practical policies of Charles I's prerogative government succeeded in creating a remarkable unity of political opposition on the part of the local governing classes, immediately evident when Parliament was called (from financial necessity) in 1640. At this time, the second consequence of the breakdown in broad elite consensus became important. For the formation of two opposing parties in the period 1640–2 was partly conditioned by the active emergence of the masses into national politics, as parliamentary leaders, on the one hand, fostered and worked with popular movements, while on the other hand others were drawn back to support of the king through increased fears of the consequences of popular social and political unrest.[8]

This sketch would indicate that the structural crisis of the English state, experienced in the 1620s and 1630s, was accompanied by a crisis of legiti-mation among the ruling elites. The consequence of the latter was first, the formation of a conscious, active opposition, and secondly, through the breakdown of elite consensus, the active emergence of popular movements as vital to the course of national politics at the beginning of the 1640s. Such an interpretation implies that theories of legitimacy must be turned on their heads. What needs explaining is *not* how particular political systems create active consent among the governed – in other words, legitimacy. Rather, what must be explained is how governmental crises are precipitated which produce breakdowns in dominant modes of legitimation among the governors, producing active dissensus, or coherent opposition, instead of pragmatic passivity, among the general population.

Conclusion

Let me briefly summarise the argument and implications of this chapter. In the first half, I attempted to show that the problem of religious toleration cannot be treated purely as a question in the history of ideas; nor can it be treated in evolutionary terms, whether couched in the Marxist terminology of modes of production, or in non-Marxist characterisations of stages of state formation or societal development. Policies of religious uniformity or toleration depend to a considerable extent on the historically contingent constellations of relationships among state, church and social groups as they developed in different areas in post-Reformation Europe. One implication of this is that, while general European cultural movements may be mapped (as Peter Burke has done in his analysis of the dissociation of elite culture from popular culture in the early modern period), yet to understand for any particular area the ways in which elites may or may not have tried to use the church as an instrument of social control, we must enter into the unique configurations of specific structural interrelationships of institutions and social interests in particular forms of state.

In the second part of this chapter, I have suggested that rulers are better advised to avoid creating active and coherent dissensus than to attempt to ensure the general legitimacy of their regimes. This is not to deny that at a variety of levels religion can play a useful role in transforming the focus of legitimation. As *Oberkonsistorialrat* Süssmilch reported in 1756, for example, on the beneficial consequences of Pietist educational activities in the East Prussian provinces: 'Der alte eigensinnige Litauer ist durch den Unterricht fast ein ganz anderer Mensch in der bürgerlichen Gesellschaft geworden und übt jetzt auch die Pflichten gegen die Obrigkeit ... Welch schöne Belohnung der darauf gewandten Kosten und Mühen.'[9] But at the level of the regime as a whole, it is – from the point of view of rulers interested in maintaining their domination – better to avoid the structural overlap of political and religious conflict implied by strenuous policies of uniformity. The comparison between the political passivity of the anti-absolutist Pietists of Württemberg and the political activity of their spiritual brethren, the revolutionary Puritans in England, is an illustration of this; and the toleration by the state of the Pietists in Prussia, combined with the hostility of the church, ensured the collaboration of the Prussian Pietists in the project of building, rather than opposing, the Prussian absolutist state. There are many other implications and questions raised by my theme, which I have not had the time to touch on here. But at the most general level, I would conclude that in their assertions on religious uniformity in particular, and legitimacy in general, Edwin Sandys, Archbishop Laud and Habermas were all mistaken.

Notes: Chapter 10

1   Quoted in P. McGrath, *Papists and Puritans under Elizabeth I* (London, 1967), p. 1.
2   Sir John Eliot quoted in H. R. Trevor-Roper, *Archbishop Laud 1573–1645*, originally publ. 1940, 2nd edn (London, 1962), p. 5; Archbishop Laud quoted in C. Russell, 'Arguments for religious unity in England, 1530–1650', *Journal of Ecclesiastical History*, Vol. XVIII, no. 2 (October 1967), pp. 201–26, here 213–14.
3   A full bibliography of approaches cannot be given here. See for some examples: W. K. Jordan, *The Development of Religious Toleration in England*, 4 vols (London, 1932, 1936, 1938, 1940); H. Kamen, *The Rise of Toleration* (London 1967); some suggestive remarks in H. Lehmann, *Das Zeitalter des Absolutismus* (Stuttgart, 1980); and the articles on societal and religious evolution by Parsons, Bellah and Eisenstadt in the *American Sociological Review*, Vol. XXIX (1964).
4   Full substantiation of my characterisations of these cases, and of the Puritan and Pietist movements, can be found in my book, *Piety and Politics: Religion and the Rise of Absolutism in England, Württemberg and Prussia* (Cambridge, 1983), on which the first part of this paper draws.
5   Quoted in R. C. Richardson, *Puritanism in Northwest England* (Manchester, 1972), p. 146.
6   My argument on Weber is derived from a juxtaposition of his substantive writings with his methodological and conceptual work. For Habermas's theories, see particularly J. Habermas, *Legitimation Crisis* (Boston, Mass., 1975); see also in connection with the following discussion, M. Mann, 'The social cohesion of liberal democracy', *American Sociological Review*, Vol. XXXV, no. 3 (1970), pp. 423–39; and P. Converse, 'The nature of belief systems in mass publics', in D. Apter (ed.), *Ideology and Discontent* (New York, 1964).
7   An attempt at a numerical estimate for the end of the Elizabethan period is made in M. M. Knappen, *Tudor Puritanism* (Chicago, 1939), pp. 333–4, n. 24. On the numbers remaining excommunicate, see R. Marchant, *The Church under the Law* (Cambridge, 1969), p. 227, and R. Houlbrooke, 'The decline of ecclesiastical jurisdiction under the Tudors', in R. O'Day and F. Heal (eds), *Continuity and Change: Personnel and Administration of the Church in England, 1500–1642* (Leicester, 1976), p. 245. On atheism, see, for example, G. E. Aylmer, 'Unbelief in seventeenth-century England', in D. Pennington and K. Thomas (eds), *Puritans and Revolutionaries* (Oxford, 1978); and on popular religion in general, see K. Thomas, *Religion and the Decline of Magic* (New York, 1971).
8   Again, of course, a complete bibliography of relevant material cannot be given here. For a few references, see: W. Lamont, *Godly Rule* (London, 1969); Trevor-Roper, *Archbishop Laud*; N. Tyacke, 'Puritanism, Arminianism, and counter-revolution', in C. Russell (ed.), *The Origins of the English Civil War* (London, 1973); V. Pearl, *London and the Outbreak of the Puritan Revolution* (London, 1961); B. Manning, *The English People and the English Revolution* (Harmondsworth, 1978).
9   Quoted in A. Nietzki, *D. Johann Jakob Quandt. Generalsuperintendent in Preussen und Oberhofprediger in Königsberg 1686–1772* (Königsberg, 1905), p. 60.

11 The Distances between the Lower Classes and Official Religion: Examples from Eighteenth-Century Württemberg Protestantism

MARTIN SCHARFE, translated by
Deborah Monroe

Depicting the Problem

We should emphasise two points about our theme. First, we must employ the plural: 'the *distances* between the lower classes and religion'; and secondly, we must refine the theme by using a double plural: 'the distances of the lower classes from religion *and the distances between themselves*'. To do otherwise would not do justice to the complexity of the relationships and developments involved. I will demonstrate this by example.

Dusslingen is an old Württemberg Protestant village situated a few miles south of Tübingen. Nothing in the archival material indicates that the Dusslingers – primarily small farmers and craftsmen – would always have conformed to the behavioural mandates of the official church. There is the widespread negligence usual for the time in fulfilling religious obligations: poor attendance at services; absence from school; breaking the Sabbath by work, play, idleness, mischief; dissidence about the Lord's Supper; and, in addition, so-called superstition. These constitute *one* of the kinds of distance which, according to contemporary definition and penal law practices, were a low form of criminality; they are therefore not to be downgraded by us today as simply laziness, but must be understood as constituting more or less justified differences to official religion – or ones left to us to justify. The other kind of distance gets more headline attention, which means it has left its own reams of case proceedings behind. It is not idle, and, irrespective of its causes, not indifferent or possibly apathetic normal absence from church; rather it is conscious, resolute, even aggressive recusant separatism in the literal sense: Anabaptism which embedded itself in a minority, involving the well-known appeal to the Gospel, common sense and the evangelical freedom of Christians. It is therefore obviously advantageous to speak not of 'the' distance of the lower classes to official religion but of *different gradations and forms of distance*.

To be sure, conflicts are predetermined by the existence of differing degrees and forms of distance. These relate not only to the well-known conflicts between dissidents and those pious and loyal to the church who

157

allied themselves with the official representatives of the state church in so far as they issued denunciations. There were also conflicts between like-minded separatists and – as we might very tentatively term them – the 'idleness-separatists' (who, on occasion, could also form a coalition with the church loyalists).

In the above-mentioned village of Dusslingen in 1850 (the date is incidental to the use of the case as an introductory example) an Anabaptist was buried while the minister was out of town. A layman from elsewhere delivered the funeral address. The minister wrote in his report to the local deanery in Tübingen:

> During the burial, which attracted a large group of curiosity-seekers, Mr Schauffler from Stuttgart proceeded to deliver a sermon [that is, despite the fact that the head of the Dusslinger separatists had given assurances that this would not occur] in which he not only took the liberty of attacking the evangelical church, but explained that the sight of these numerous graves was a sorry one, because in contemplating those who sleep there one could have no hope; except when one, like the deceased who has been re-baptised, comes into the grave, then one can be reassured, and the like.

The minister wrote that this incident precipitated 'great indignation in the community and almost led to an unfortunate scene in the cemetery, where people favoured throwing Mr Schauffler down the cemetery steps'.[1] The Dusslingen incident is not only an example of how coalitions and conflicts were formed; implicitly it indicates the strength of the factions as well.

Certainly the norm far into the nineteenth century was loyalty to the church and the honest fulfilment of 'religious obligations' (*Glaubensp-flichten*, to use, at least in the Reformed sense, a self-contradictory term). We know this from the reports systematically prepared and transmitted by Württemberg ministers;[2] and it applies more than ever to the eighteenth century. The possibility and potential for alternative interpretations, world-views and patterns of conduct should not be overestimated, especially not in a territory that succeeded as early as in the first half of the century in domesticating its irritatingly obstinate Pietism by integrating it into the Lutheran state church.[3]

Defining the Historical Terrain

Let me try briefly to characterise the eighteenth-century Duchy of Württemberg: it was the only large Lutheran Protestant state in the German south-west, with about 9,500 square kilometres and 650,000 inhabitants around 1800;[4] there was no landed nobility, no Curia of Knights[5] – instead the estates were represented in the provincial diet. Though this system was occasionally precarious in the eighteenth century, the absolutist state was never able to assume fully its characteristic form; in essence it was always a 'dualism of prince and bourgeois-peasant estates'.[6] This in no way means that state affairs were poorly or loosely organised – on the contrary: the almost perfect 'unity of Church and civic community'[7] produced colossal all-encompassing control and regulation of both church and everyday life for every Württemberger. Since the mid-seventeenth century the most important control mechanism in each community was the morals court presided over by the local clergy, the *Kirchenkonvent*. The theological basis for overall supervision of the subjects was provided by Lutheranism, as defined in the *Confessio Augustana*, the *Confessio Virtembergica*[8] and various ecclesiastical ordinances.[9] Lutheran Protestantism was enshrined by law,[10] and this remained unchallenged even between 1737 and 1797 when the dukes were Catholic.[11] As late as the eighteenth century secular officials of the duchy still had to subscribe to the Formula of Concord.[12]

Besides this, general compulsory schooling had been introduced at an early date.[13] This really was compulsory – that is, it was supervised and punishable by the *Kirchenkonvent* in cases of delinquency. From the end of the seventeenth century there was also Sunday religious instruction for school-leavers, and from 1722 obligatory confirmation.[14] All of these were means of social, cultural, moral-ethical and ideological formation of the individual, means of civilising the Württemberger.

The Civilised Württemberger

All of this had its effect in structuring mentalities. I cannot resist citing a 'classical dictum' from a farmer about the value of church-going: 'Besser wurscht jo nit, aber hosch ällbott dei Riereng ond kommscht nit ganz vom Zigs aweg!'[15] – 'You won't be any morally better for it, but you always get the feeling that it does something for the heart, spirit and soul, and you never really get out of touch with the thing'. *Zuigs, Zeug, Ding, Sache* (the thing) means primarily 'possession' and also has a cognitive component – this is, one does not unlearn or forget the Christian content of the lesson. Alternatively, *Zeug* also has a habitual component – that is, one remains in the habit and practice of Christian behaviour. Finally, *Zeug* is also – in the words of that knowledgeable and sensitive observer, Dieter Narr – a 'universal – an all-encompassing word which includes everything to do with an ordered and reputable life'.[16]

You won't be any better for going to church, but you always have your feelings and you never get completely away from the thing – I consider this slightly distanced but none the less reasoned and conformist view to be the result of the Württemberg style of mentality-moulding, as achieved in the eighteenth century; and we should regard it as a fundamental trait of Württemberg popular culture of that time.

If this is the norm, let us now turn to my actual theme, the deviations. Even if they are difficult to assess quantitatively, and may prove to be quantitatively insignificant, deviations may be qualitatively meaningful. They are cultural alternatives, or to put it carefully – attempts to create or re-create an adequate and 'fitting life-style and culture' out of a given situation. They are attempts to take, adopt and develop in the face of opposition those elements from the 'cultural heritage' which belong to a 'Second Culture' and even constitute it. They represent wilfulness, defined by its distance from official and dominant culture.

In the main section of my contribution, I would like to deal with four problems: (I) that of the different degrees of distance; (II) distances from official religion which manifest themselves likewise as moral, and (III) as political-cultural aggression; and (IV) the question of the causes of the attempted distancing.

I   Defensive and Offensive Distance

I would like to approach the problem of the degree of distance by using the categories of defensive and offensive distance. I shall illustrate this with examples of attendance at school, communion and services, and the breaking of the Sabbath. I will contrast the 'defensive' to 'offensive' distance as ideal-types.

The German school (*Volksschule*) was the basic pillar of ecclesiastical indoctrination. That is why school absences and the excuses made for them are exceptionally well documented in the protocols of the *Kirchenkonvente*. I can illustrate this with a few random cases. In June 1793 the following was recorded about two normally virtuous and pious vine-dressers from Tübingen (the vine-dressers belonged to the poorest inhabitants of this university town):[17]

> Young Abraham Waiblinger, vine-dresser, asked to have his 11-year-old daughter's school absence excused because his wife had died a few months ago and he had to spend the whole day, from early morning onwards, on his plot. And since he also had a one-and-a-half-year-old child to care for, his eldest daughter had to take care of this child. And therefore, as sorry as he was about it, she must miss school, since he claimed that as a poor man he cannot afford to hire a maid to care for the baby, and it cannot be otherwise . . .

> Johannes Kost, vine-dresser, brought forward the same excuse for the absence of his son, Johannes Andreas, namely, that he must mind his younger sibling because both he and his wife have to spend almost the whole day in the field and the baby is only a month old and cannot be left alone. He cannot afford to hire a person for that.[18]

Only ten years later, in November 1803, a separatist in Rottenacker, a Württemberg diaspora-exclave on the Danube (I will return to this later), was questioned about the same offence:

> 'How is it that he hasn't sent a child to school for fifteen weeks and did not send one yesterday for the school visit?' – 'He does not send any child to school anymore.' – 'But why not!' – 'Because the principles of the parsons are completely false; it has taken long enough to get rid of all that was dinned into him at school . . .' – 'Doesn't he know that it is a government regulation that he send his children to school?' – 'Even if it is a government regulation that children are sent to school, he won't send

them because they would be led astray there, because things are taught wrong there. He now supplicates against the school.'[19]

There is little to add to these examples. The Tübingers *would like to*, but *cannot* get out of their situation; they agree they are being negligent, but do not know what to do. The Rottenacker man, however, *could* but does not *want* to; he sees *no* offence, he justifies his behaviour with subcultural theology.

Very similar ideas are evident in the reasons given for not attending *communion*. One must bear in mind that public confession and absolution on Sunday were preceded by private confession, and this, in turn, was preceded by personal application which involved the precise registration of the communicants on confession tickets.[20] This explains why, for example, marriage troubles could be a reason to stay away from confession.

Tübingen, 1776:

> Matthäus Sauter and his wife are cited because they have failed to attend Holy Communion for quite a while ... His wife came forward and excused herself by stating that the secular authorities are repugnant to her and that she could not go because of this ... The wigmaker Hippert is reminded that he has not been to Holy Communion in four years. He excused himself with his marriage difficulties ... Margareta Eckenpergerin, an unmarried daughter of a potter, is cited and reprimanded for leading an immoral life and for not attending Holy Communion as a result ...[21]

In contrast, the deposition of a 30-year-old man interrogated in 1725 from the deanery of Herrenberg is completely different in tone and content: self-confident, defiant, no trace of a guilty conscience or apologies:

> 'Isn't today's Last Supper, the Holy Communion, instituted by Christ?' – 'No, it is a man-made law.' – 'Whether in today's Communion we do not administer Christ's body and blood to the flock.' – 'Certainly not. We only pretend that it is Christ's body and blood.'[22]

The degree of originality in the theological explanation and its traditions will not be discussed here. For the moment we are only interested in the differing behavioural patterns of people who distance themselves from the official 'grace-dispensing' ('Gnadenanstalt') church. There are also serious differences, of course, regarding the question of attendance at church.

While the separatists of the eighteenth century simply refused to attend church services, citing biblical quotations and referring to false instruction (examples will follow), the other Christians went dutifully to church – and slept,[23] or chatted, or bashed their heads in bloody fighting about their precedence in taking a pew;[24] these were their answers to the Gospel being preached from the pulpit.

The category of defensive distance from the law about observing the Sabbath includes the Tübingen butchers, who picked up animals from the surrounding villages on Sunday during the church service. Any admonition or punishment was to no avail against the economic interests of the butchers, who none the less did not dare to use those interests as their excuse. They used evasion: they apparently did not hear the clock, or the cattle were lame and too slow, and so on.[25] A separatist butcher from the Herrenberg region, by comparison, stated in an interrogation in 1725, in answer to the question why, while 'wanting to uphold the rule of Christ', he 'is out riding to pasture on Sunday with his livestock during the church service and when one goes to church': 'bringing the livestock to pasture has to take place, the estate of shepherds is ancient, he does not find in the Holy Scripture that one has to observe the Sabbath by going to church, Sunday can be made sacred in any number of ways'.[26] The question is, why did the Herrenberg butcher develop a butchers' and shepherds' theology, at least *in nuce*, and why did the Tübingen butchers not do the same? Why was one defiant and why did the others try to talk their way out of it?

These were a few examples of defensive and offensive distance among those subject to official religion in a territory and at a time in which – as suggested in the introduction – the domination of religion in daily life was very strong. There is certainly room for disagreement about such attempts to characterise and differentiate 'distance'. However, pairs of opposites, such as 'apathetic-creative' or 'conservative-progressive', would not do justice to this issue either. This has been demonstrated by Hartmut Lehmann in a new interpretation of the various disturbances which followed an attempt to introduce an 'enlightened' hymn-book in Württemberg in 1791. He does not find mindless conservatism at work (as the incident had previously been interpreted – perhaps with the help of Pietist ideology), but rather discerns a response to new provocations, a protest against the joint action of spiritual and secular authorities.[27]

II   Bed Separatism as a Moral-Cultural Protest

The private sphere, as we define it, was not always so sharply distinguished from the public.[28] There are lengthy protocols of hearings held in 1771/2 about separatists of Gochsen am Kocher, in the deanery of Neuenstadt, which lies in the northern corner of the Duchy of Württemberg, because they had converted the innkeeper of the 'Oxen' inn. The accusations were as usual: absence from church and communion. What is interesting is that quite a different, an intimate refusal occasioned very considerable administrative and public disturbance: separatist men and women refused the so-called 'conjugal obligation' ('amicitiam conjugalem') to their respective spouses, so taking separatism quite literally. They moved into beds of their own. Separatist women firmly denied what they were apparently accused of: that they considered marriage a form of prostitution and the work of the midwife as sinful employment,[29] that they drove men to masturbation[30] and 'that they fast away the womanly flower'.[31] The weaver Simon Winter said of his wife: 'she refused him his conjugal duty once or twice, for which he boxed her ears a couple of times, that is all'. And the wife added 'that she complained sometimes because she considers the *Officium Conjugale* sinful, and that she appealed to her husband's conscience because she felt it should end some time since they are both so old (the woman is 44). Since that time she considered the obligation her cross and did not fight it anymore.'[32]

The blacksmith Friedrich Pfeiffer, also a bed separatist, provided a theological justification for his abstinence, 'from Matthew 19, 12 . . . Those who have castrated themselves in order to enter the Kingdom of Heaven, God has made free. He who has the Son, has Life, etc. That they abstained was not an attempt to rid themselves of sinful semen. Crucifixion of the flesh means not doing as the flesh wills. They do not say that living together in marriage is prostitution. Other people can do as they please.'[33]

Finally, the above-mentioned innkeeper Bernhard Schreiber whose bed linen played a role in the investigation (whether the pollution happened 'energetically' or during his sleep),[34] states that his life's goal is 'to mortify the sins'[35] and to achieve 'the true bridal purity' through crucifixion and death of the flesh.[36] In contrast to other separatists in town – at least according to his father-in-law – he insists 'stubbornly that conjugal cohabitation is harlotry'.[37] In fact, the Gochsen inn-keeper answered the question about the origins of his separatist views thus: 'None gave him instructions to lie separated from his wife. He looked to the Holy Scripture for a reason and found that none would see the Lord without sanctification.'[38] Nevertheless, one must certainly ask whence came the specification of what constitutes 'sanctification'. Bernhard Schreiber's accusers mention a meeting with a merchant from Allgäu and a business trip to Frankfurt in the autumn of 1771[39] – one should not, indeed, overlook the significance of outside contacts.

The history of the cultural tradition of sexually ascetic Protestantism is so complicated that it is advisable to refer to a few striking intermediate stations to what I would call, paradoxically, the emancipation of the flesh. It is certainly emancipation if one finds: (1) reflection about human sexuality; (2) definition of the role of human sexuality; and (3), taken together, the preservation of, and constant referral to or even practice of, liberality and flexibility in which diverse shades of sexual impulses or an acquired constancy regarding them can be observed. All three points can be observed in our example: tendencies towards graded sexual asceticism, not just in the negative sense of restriction, but in the sense of a concentration of the individual's energies on the one hand, and of differentiation of individual human possibilities and needs on the other.

This is quite clear in the position of Ernst Christoph Hochmann von Hochenau (1670–1721), who worked primarily in the small territories of Hessen – and it is unthinkable that it should have had no preliminary stages. His position should be understood as clearly differentiated from libertine-Pietist currents which were developing at the same time.[40] It seems to me that this had more effect in Württemberg than the position of the younger Count Zinzendorf (1700–60) towards marriage and sexuality.[41] Hochmann did not establish a community in the true sense of the word,[42] but he had a large number of contacts. His 'Detmolder Glaubensbekenntnis'

(Detmold confession) of 1702 seems to have had a particular impact. The greater part is devoted to 'the estate of matrimony' and distinguishes five levels of marriage.[43] In Württemberg itself the respected lawyer Johann Jacob Moser (1701–85), drawing upon Spener's *Pia Desideria*, published his own treatise on 'theological thoughts about marital cohabitation'. He introduced three qualitatively different kinds of marriage, those of the unconverted, the awakened and the reborn.[44]

We must assume that these sorts of reflection were common and were continually infused with new impulses through the oral dissemination of relevant theological literature – the case of the Gochsen separatists seems to be a clear example of such a transmission of culture and separatist ideas.[45] However, imported ideas *alone* certainly did not make the Gochsen separatists unruly – we do find references to familial and social strains. Bernhard Schreiber, the innkeeper, stated that his wife 'was so vexed during her pregnancies and cried at night, and so he thought he would try lying alone ... also because of the children, so that it would be quieter. Therefore two children now lie with him and one with the mother' – we have reason to assume that this means in each parent's bed, and not in their own. And then he admitted 'that he once said to his wife, as the children were crying so: one had enough children and enough debts as well'.[46]

One should not, therefore, overlook the poverty motive which arises from time to time. None the less, this motive of social strain cannot be seen in isolation and made into an absolute explanation. Poverty by itself certainly did not bring about the religious rebellion which here is simultaneously a very subtle rebellion in intimate life against societal expectations. It would be more relevant to proceed along the lines of an insistence on self-determination, whatever its origin: 'I don't go to public church services', says the innkeeper from Gochsen, 'I refuse godparenthood, I do not recognise conjugal duty' and, he adds, in diffidence as well as defiantly: 'I simply have no urge to go to Holy Communion.'[47]

III 'Confusion of Ideas and Conscience' and 'Misconstrued Feelings of Political Freedom': Political-Cultural Protest

'Muddled notions' is a favourite expression of the authorities; subordinate folk tend to fall for them easily, as they say. Recently, Rainer Wirtz, in analysing the views and activities of the Odenwald farmers in 1848, tried to interpret such 'muddled notions' as being the result of a restructuring of ideas, definitely systematic in nature which was based on daily (and through the generations, internalised) experience. He saw this as a necessary 'muddling of ideas'.[48] This interpretation also applies to 'misconstrued feelings of freedom'[49] (if not to all of their manifestations). The cheerful, happy 'Pregizerianer'[50] who feel totally free and self-justified and who sing 'songs from the old Esslingen songbook to the melody of the little sailor' can also rise to defiance: the law, according to one of them in Altbach near Esslingen in 1813, 'for which he is being reprimanded, is only a law of the secular, not of the ecclesiastical authority'. People breach the instructions on how to conduct assemblies. The constabulary is treated with impudence and so rendered ineffective. The place of assembly, a house across from the mayor's and parson's houses, had been specifically chosen (as the parson suspected) 'to show that the authorities are no longer respected'.[51] The incident suggests that the idea of spiritual freedom itself rests in the routine experience of subjugation.

A series of interrogation protocols from the early eighteenth century regarding separatists from the Gäu and Schönbuch-Herrenberg, Hildrizhausen, Mötzingen, Remmingsheim, south-west of Stuttgart, shows how closely this experience is connected to the entanglement of secular and ecclesiastical rule, and to what explosively disfunctional perceptions the endurance of the overpowering disciplinary methods of the unity of throne and altar could lead. The clergy do not have the Word of God, 'but merely chat about it', 'preach for the pay and are people's servants', serve 'only for the sake of their salary and stomach'. They let all their incidental fees be paid, although they are salaried by the authorities, 'and the people have to earn this by drudgery'. The clergy were thieves and murderers because they got a position 'by buttering up patronage'. Correspondingly, the official functions of the pastors were harshly criticised (and one has to remember that all of these remarks were not made with one hand over the mouth, half-drunk at an inn, but expressed to the dean in the interrogation): communion is a man-made law; Christ left the decision whether to go to church or not to the individual; baptism is nothing more than casting a spell, that is, ceremonial magic; presence at baptisms and burials of one's own child 'in honour of the child . . . is just a custom', after all, one 'is not master' here; baptism does not accomplish rebirth, 'if the rod cannot achieve the same'. And the acrimony of a butcher's analysis is astonishing: 'What did he consider the preachers to be? – They are necessary for keeping the people in fear.'[52]

The early date of these collective opinions and modes of behaviour indicates that long before the late bourgeois revolutions, firmly rooted plebeian, proto-bourgeois ideas about democracy were widespread, fed by daily social experience and legitimised by a wilfully unorthodox interpretation of the Gospel. We must also take into account that the petty bourgeoisie, the small craftsmen and farmers of the second half of the eighteenth century, were constantly and acutely threatened both politically and economically – and the separatists recruited from this circle and not from the very poor. They were threatened by the hard grip of state and church (threats, orders, punishments); by manufacture, the putting-out system and the beginning of factory industry; by conscription, which, of course, could disrupt the agrarian base of the family; threatened, too, by the alarming news they heard of world politics.

With reference to these relationships and developments, the fact must be explained that towards the end, and at the turn, of the century 'all sorts of serious cases of muddled conscience' were registered by the authorities.[53] For example, in Fellbach, a parish near Stuttgart, in the year 1794, nine Pietists refused to serve in the local militia.[54] They explained 'that they would rather die than submit to drill'. 'Instead of paying attention to the commander or looking at the platoon leader, they either look up to the sky or down at the ground añd stand there like statues and do not pay attention to anything.' They were imprisoned overnight and afterwards asked 'if they would fulfil their duties as all loyal subjects of this land ought to do and like all other citizens' sons', and submit to the drill or not. The answer was: 'They do not intend to', and the grounds were: 'It is written in Matthew 5: "Blessed are the peacemakers, for they shall be called the children of God"; further, "Thou shalt not kill", some paragraphs later, "love your enemies, bless them that curse you, do good to them that hate you, and pray for them who despitefully use you and persecute you".'[55]

The Gospel here is firmly against secular order. But what gives the event additional emphasis is the fact that the other members of the militia – who certainly could not readily cite biblical texts – rebelled as well! They used 'the coarsest expressions against the official at Fellbach, insisted that the provisors and scribes drill along with them or else they would not go, beat the drum to bits, went into the woods and pulled up an oak that supposedly belonged to the steward Merz and carried it home ... Now having something to set fire to, and not in the mood to drill, they are said to have announced that they would not go to the exercise-grounds until the separatists showed up.'[56]

The Fellbach example reminds us again of the different possibilities – sketched out in the introduction – of relationships to authority. There is additional evidence here – although the emphasis lies in the confrontation with the political rather than the ecclesiastical authorities (if one can distinguish hypothetically between these forms of authority) – of the explosive political potential of radical Christian ideas and forms of behaviour. Here we can see the explosive power of plebeian theology, which does not really explode in Fellbach, but which does in Rottenacker. Rottenacker is a Württemberg village on the Danube, an enclave in a surrounding Catholic region. In 1804 it was taken over by troops because of its separatists.[57] The accusations were: continual refusal to send children to school, uttering slander, gross impudence, abuse of the government, resistance and insubordination to the secular authorities and, not least, refusal to accept conscription (that is, conscientious objection) – this, in any case, is how it was summarily listed in the memorandum on separatists of 1816.[58]

What did, in fact, lie behind such insubordination, which produced so massive a reaction from the state? In the Württemberg legislation the threat of expulsion from the territory for conscientious objection appears in 1794, 'now that their religious beliefs influence their civic attitudes ...'[59] In 1806 the penalty was changed from expulsion to forced labour in imprisonment within a fortress.[60] The same year, it was stipulated that separatists who appeared before a magistrate were to have their hats forcibly removed by the beadle and their cockades, stars and other insignia torn off.[61] In 1808 it was decreed that the recalcitrant who refused to send their sons and daughters to school were to have their children forcibly removed at once and sent to the Stuttgart orphanage; after the children had been confirmed, however, an apprenticeship or servant's position should be found which was far away from their home and parents.[62] All of these orders were repeated in 1809, 'because their political principles disrupt the state'; 'such perverse people' were to be removed 'from civil society immediately'.[63]

So what was dangerous about the Rottenacker separatists? A report from 1803 has Georg Adam Strübel, a weaver, saying: 'he does not go to church anymore, and he knows one thing for sure, he shits (*salva venia*) on the church, the old whore, and the rest of the parishioners follow the Devil's teaching. "Schüle" [Stephan Huber] and Schulhanns [two other separatists] know more than ten clerics put together ... He does not raise his hat to the pastor and steward anymore; he wouldn't even think of it.' The carpenter Michael Feilen got drunk at an inn and reviled 'spiritual and secular authorities too loudly', and said, 'we don't need any authority'. While he was chopping wood, the shoemaker Daniel Huber said: 'We don't need a schoolmaster, a magistrate or a cleric.' And the weaver Friedrich Gemmi thought: 'the number one in the consistory, that *Herr Spezial*, is a knave of Babylon and therefore they cannot do anything to us [the separatists]. If they should, however, do anything to us – we shall see what happens. They don't need the senior magistrate, the pastor and the steward; the church is an old whore and a pigsty and must be destroyed.' One Sunday almost all of them skipped church services, went to the nearby town of Munderkingen, caroused in four inns and then went home to the inn at Rottenacker – it was the day of official celebrations for the elevation of the Duke of Württemberg to the Prince-Electorship (30 April 1803).[64]

IV   'Religious Enthusiasts' as 'Political Offenders'

The history of the Rottenacker protest reads like a thriller: brawls, flight, hiding prisoners, foul insults. All of this is political enough, but in addition there are obvious links with revolutionary France.[65] A 'liberation song' is found in the possession of the shoemaker Stephan Huber; he and the weaver Johann Georg Braumgardt apparently speak French, certainly a carry-over from their soldier days. In the evening they yell at the entrance of the parson's house: 'Leschmukel [as written by the parson first in German and then in Latin] le predicateur, lèche mon cul', that is, 'kiss my ass, cleric'! And then there is the 'uniform' of blue-white-red, and the Jacobin-like caps: 'Lately they wear dark blue jackets and white cotton caps with red bands.'[66]

Individual instances of the new political 'language' were thus in use before 1848, such as in the Württemberg lowlands. But the authorities were watchful. In 1806 in Horrheim, in the district of Vaihingen, as separatists began to refuse manorial and communal labour service, taxes and contributions, six offenders were immediately escorted to imprisonment in the Asperg fortress by a nineteen-man military troop. The Royal High Court remarked 'that these people no longer behave as mere religious enthusiasts but as political offenders whose aim, apparently, is to overthrow civic order by combining their energies'.[67] Christoph Greulich, from Nordheim near Heilbronn, served as spiritual head of this movement. Among his partisans was the separatist tailor Andreas Albig of Kochendorf, who 'officially retracted all allegiance to the authorities and expressly declared that he no longer wanted to do labour service, pay tax, or other contributions'. 'According to the official report', the state minister informed the king, 'this Albig was caught as a ringleader in the revolt of the tailor-apprentices a few years ago in Berlin and sentenced to one-year's confinement in the fortress. Two years ago, the same induced his fellow masters to draft a written law that fixed a higher wage for tailors than the one established by the authorities and which stipulated that cheaper labour was punishable.'[68]

Whereas Christoph Greulich renounced his Württemberg 'civil rights and subject status with the declaration that he was moving to the new Jerusalem',[69] one recognises a new conceptual and behavioural model in the attempt of Andreas Albig and his tailor colleagues to defend themselves collectively against exploitation (not least of all under the pressure of new modes of production, especially noticeable in the textile industry), and to create different hiring conditions. It is the repudiation of traditional feudal allegiance. What is new about this, and sets a course for the future, is its social-political perspective. The New Jerusalem is more than ever situated in the concrete and imminent hereafter.

Traditions, Experiences, Developments

There remains the general task of exploring the causes of these attempts to gain distance, of these movements of withdrawal on the part of the subjects.

To be sure, the daily experiences of class position forms the foundation upon which protests, manifestations of distance, and resistance can emerge. But the existence of this foundation is not enough. There must also have been a latent distance in the collective consciousness which was fed by the ambivalence, or by the different functions, of religion. To express it in the language of Max Weber,[70] there was legitimatory religion 'for those down below' – to use a historically and empirically intelligible picture of society. However, this ambivalence is structurally and personally embodied in the clergy, the very reason why it is called 'spiritual authority'. These daily experiences were supported by either an ancient epistemological tradition[71] or by attempts to interpret the Gospel in a progressively more subversive way. Much more thinking, discussing and communicating was going on and stored in the 'collective memory', to quote Halbwachs,[72] than is generally assumed. The postulate of the unreflected stance of the 'common man' is time-honoured, but elitist and false. Sometimes it needed only a push from outside – for example, the French Revolution, or the Berlin tailors' revolt – for a language already well thought out and subjectively conveyed to become a common cultural language. Recent theories of culture rightly consider this to be the creative role played by the subordinate classes in the making of history.

It must be re-emphasised that those who actively distanced themselves from the official church were in the minority. This would be true even if I had included Pietism, so important in Württemberg, and which certainly also stood consciously apart from the territorial church. And it should be reiterated that occasionally a coalition was formed, between those loyal to the church and those who distanced themselves defensively, a coalition directed against the offensive rebels. The 'Separatist Club' in Rottenacker[73] showed solidarity in all sorts of subversive acts: when they could, they would appear before the authorities in groups (they claimed they had 'no master'), they would harbour and hide refugees, they would jointly defend houses (windows and doors were barricaded at the approach of the beadle), and they shared the cost of court-martial procedures. At the same time the minority character of the movement is clear: around 1800 there were seventy separatists in Rottenacker. The provost (Schultheiss), burgomaster, court and magistrates turned to the Elector (!) for help in 1805: 'for three years we have witnessed unprecedented scenes'; the community had 'already lost all credit'. The provost single-handedly interfered with the livelihood of the unpopular citizens. He ordered a violent search of their houses – citizens armed with sticks bashed the doors in – a 'lively scuffle ensued in which even a few aged women separatists had to endure abuse'. The provost reinstated thrashing for the separatists – a punishment which had been abolished some years before.[74]

We do not yet know what fed such confrontations – although there are plenty of theories about it. They will have to be explored in the archives. In any case, it is clear from the conflicts (or, actually, distances) between the parties that the new conceptual and behavioural patterns of the separatists, who were simultaneously an avant-garde and tied to tradition, did not yield to a consensus or coalition within a larger framework, by which I mean: deliberate and conscious absenteeism from church, ideological pluralism (at least de facto, if unintended), the separation of church and state, the creation of systems giving meaning and sensibility to one's world, and of new behavioural models such as free churches, associations, political parties, trade unions, and the like. All this developed more strongly than ever before in the late eighteenth century, but remained embryonic, a stuttering and not yet intelligible language; and, above all, almost everything was closely bound up with the ecclesiastical and religious context: revolutionary political-social demands without a biblical justification are evident in Württemberg only about the time of the Revolution of 1848. These ideas unfolded culturally for the first time in the nineteenth century – because they now had a social function – after the economic and social situation had changed fundamentally. That, however, was not the theme of this sketch.

Notes: Chapter 11

1   Letter from the pastor Hildebrand of 14 October 1850: Evang. Dekanatamt Tübingen, ungebundene Akten, Archive no. 57 (Dusslingen, 1650–1872), fasc. 57c: Anabaptist sects [in Dusslingen], 1847–63. Regarding these animosities we should keep in mind that the Dusslingen 'Sect of the Saved' had been active for several decades, and attracted a considerable outside public. On 10 May 1830 even the Württemberg Minister of Home Affairs reported to the king that the 'sect of Pietists' which had asked 'for a most

benevolent ordinance allowing them to hold private services without being disturbed' was engaged in the healing of allegedly possessed people (as in Würtingen and Belsen in 1828). A case in Belsen had caused a sensation, because the patient had died during the exorcism. Hauptstaatsarchiv Stuttgart, Bestand E 14, fasc. 1445 (= Kabinettsakten IV).

2   cf. M. Scharfe, 'Protestantismus und Industrialisierung im Königreich Württemberg', in P. Assion and I. Hampp (eds), *Forschungen und Berichte zur Volkskunde in Baden-Württemberg 1974–1977* (Stuttgart, 1977), pp. 149–62.

3   cf. H. Lehmann, *Pietismus und weltliche Ordnung in Württemberg vom 17. bis zum 20. Jahrhundert* (Stuttgart, Berlin, Cologne and Mainz, 1969); J. Trautwein, *Religiosität und Sozialstruktur: Untersucht anhand der Entwicklung des württembergischen Pietismus* (Stuttgart, 1972); M. Scharfe, *Die Religion des Volkes: Kleine Kultur- und Sozialgeschichte des Pietismus* (Gütersloh, 1980).

4   See, for example, W. Grube, 'Grafschaft und Herzogtum Württemberg', in *Das Land Baden-Württemberg: Amtliche Beschreibung nach Kreisen und Gemeinden*, Vol. I: *Allgemeiner Teil* (Stuttgart, 1974), pp. 187–96, esp. p. 234.

5   cf. A. Rapp, *Die Bedeutung der Konfession in der Geschichte Württembergs* (Tübingen, 1926), p. 8.

6   Grube, 'Grafschaft', cited n. 4 above, p. 193.

7   M. Brecht, 'Die Kirchengemeinde Derendingen im 17. und 18. Jahrhundert', in id., *Kirchenordnung und Kirchenzucht in Württemberg vom 16. bis zum 18. Jahrhundert* (Stuttgart, 1967), pp. 83–104, esp. p. 87.

8   1551. Included in Duke Christoph's great church ordinance of 1559. See Th. Eisenlohr (ed.), *Sammlung der württembergischen Kirchen-Geseze*, pt 1 (= A. L. Reyscher, ed., *Sammlung der württembergischen Geseze*, Vol. VIII) (Tübingen, 1834), pp. 106–284. For an edition in modern orthography, see E. Bizer, *Confessio Virtembergica: Das württembergische Bekenntnis von 1551* (Stuttgart, 1952).

9   See especially 'Cynosura Oeconomiae Ecclesiasticae Wirtembergicae; oder: Summarischer Extract deren in dem Hertzogthum Würtemberg zu Erhaltung Evangelischer Kirchen-Zucht und Ordnungen nach und nach ausgeschriebener Hoch-Fürstl. Rescripten, Decreten und Resolutionen' (1687), in Eisenlohr, *Sammlung*, pp. 392–465.

10   Rapp, *Die Bedeutung*, p. 7.

11   cf. Grube, 'Grafschaft', cited n. 4 above, p. 196.

12   cf. Rapp, *Die Bedeutung*, p. 7.

13   cf. E. Schmid, *Geschichte des Volksschulwesens in Altwürttemberg* (Stuttgart, 1927).

14   cf. Grube, 'Grafschaft', cited n. 4 above, p. 194.

15   Cited by D. Narr, 'Zum Charakterbild protestantischer Volksfrömmigkeit [1967]', *Hessische Blätter für Volkskunde*, Vol. LX (1969), pp. 63–76, esp. p. 67.

16   ibid. Now also in D. Narr, *Studien zur Spätaufklärung im deutschen Südwesten* (Stuttgart, 1979), pp. 129–41; the passage cited is on pp. 133 ff.

17   Cf. K. Braun et al., *Das andere Tübingen: Kultur und Lebensweise der Unteren Stadt im 19. Jahrhundert* (Tübingen, 1978).

18   Kirchen Convents Protocoll angefangen d. 14 Oct. 1773: Evangelisches Dekanatamt Tübingen, Gebundene Akten no. 23, 27 June 1793, p. 165. It is clear from ibid., p. 169, that the two children did still not go to school by the end of November. This source is hereafter cited as KKP.

19   KKP Rottenacker, 16 November 1803. The archival material from Rottenacker has been made available to me by Werner Dukek.

20   The most important legal documents in which this was laid down are: Duke Ulrich's small church ordinance of 1535, in Eisenlohr, *Sammlung*, pp. 42–59, esp. pp. 46–8; Duke Christoph's great church ordinance of 1559, ibid., pp. 106–284, esp. pp. 193 ff.; 'Fürstliche Ordnung, wegen Conformität der Kichen-Ceremonien, im Herzogthumb Würtemberg' (1668), ibid., pp. 347–77, esp. pp. 372 ff.; 'Cynosura Oeconomiae Ecclesiasticae Wirtembergicae' (1687), ibid., pp. 392–465, esp. pp. 430–3; 'Christliche Erinnerung an die Gemeinde Gottes die vorgängige Privatanmeldung der Communicanten bey ihrem Beicht-Vater betreffend' (1701), ibid., pp. 518–22; 'Gen. Rescript: Die Bekanntmachung der vorhergegangenen Erinnerung wegen der Privat-Anmeldung zur Communion betreffend' (23 December 1701), ibid., pp. 522 ff.; 'Erleuterung über die ausgeschriebene Beicht-Ordnung betr. die Privatanmeldung der Communikanten' (1705),

ibid., pp. 532–5; 'Gen. Rescript, betr, verschiedene Kirchen-Sachen – mit Postscript' (13 January 1739), ibid., pp. 602–11, esp. p. 604; and, finally, the basis for the pastors' reports of the nineteenth century: 'Synod. Erlass, betr. einen neuen Entwurf zu Verfertigung der Pfarr- und der Visitations-Relationen' (4 April 1811), ibid., pt 2 (= A. L. Reyscher, ed., *Sammlung der württembergischen Geseze*, Vol. IX) (Tübingen, 1835), pp. 215–43, esp. p. 226.

21 KKP Tübingen, 4 January 1776, pp. 29 ff.

22 Protocol of the interrogation of Jacob Werner Beck from Remmingsheim: Landes-kirchliches Archiv Stuttgart, A 26, fasc. 470. This source is hereafter cited as LKA Stgt.

23 A few examples from the neighbouring territory controlled by the imperial city of Ulm must suffice. Oellingen 1725: 'They [the church inspectors] also pay close attention to those sleeping in church. However, the pastor in the pulpit noticed them right away, harangued them, and they were punished.' Gingen 1746: 'if people sleep during the service, he [the pastor] wakes them, but without mentioning their names.' Merklingen 1742: 'The church inspectors praise the pastor, for he lets nobody sleep in church, but insists that they be waked by their neighbours.' See J. Endriss, *Die Ulmer Kirchenvisitationen des 17. und 18. Jahrhunderts* (Ulm, 1938), pp. 52, 57, 70.

24 See, for example, KKP Tübingen, 23 June 1791, pp. 143 ff.: On Ascension, during early morning service, two youngsters fight each other on the gallery of the *Stiftskirche* (one chokes his opponent, the other bites the former's fingers). The culprit is not fined, because of the poverty of his parents, but imprisoned in the 'tower' for twenty-four hours. For a whole series of rural examples from the eighteenth century, see M. Scharfe, 'Soziale Repräsentation im Kirchenraum: Sitzstreitigkeiten in der Martinskirche in Zell u.A.', *Alt-Württemberg: Heimatgeschichtliche Blätter der IWZ (Göppingen)*, Vol. X, nos 5 and 6 (1964).

25 For similar cases, see KKP Tübingen, for example: 25 April 1776 (p. 35), 11 May 1780 (p. 65), 16 August 1781 (p. 77), 14 September 1786 (p. 106), 30 October 1788 (p. 122), 30 July 1789 (p. 128), 27 August 1789 (p. 129), 24 March 1791 (p. 140), 14 April 1791 (p. 141), 19 May 1791 (p. 142).

26 Interrogation of Ulrich Dörtenbach: LKA Stgt, A 26, fasc. 470.

27 cf. H. Lehmann, 'Der politische Widerstand gegen die Einführung des neuen Gesangbuchs von 1791 in Württemberg: Ein Beitrag zum Verhältnis von Kirchen- und Sozialgeschichte', *Blätter für württembergische Kirchengeschichte*, Vol. LXVI/LXVII (1966/7), pp. 247–63.

28 The examples referred to in this section have been published, although in a slightly different context, in M. Scharfe, 'Fromme Rebellen: Religiös begründeter Widerstand gegen Institutionen', in B. Gladigow (ed.), *Staat und Religion* (Düsseldorf, 1981), pp. 159–79.

29 As late as 1816 a report from Altbach near Esslingen states that 'the wives of these separatists refuse the assistance of midwives during delivery'. The Württemberg state ministery recommends (and the king decrees) the forcible transfer to the Tübingen Clinicum in cases of refusal: Hauptstaatsarchiv Stuttgart (hereafter cited as HStA Stgt), Bestand E 31, fasc. 1228, 3/14 August 1816 (= Geheimer Rat I. Separatisten 1803–16). The Privy Council ('Geheimer Rat'), temporarily also the 'state ministry' (*Staats-ministerium*), were the authorities placed above the individual ministries and *collegia*, which prepared government decrees with immediate access to Württemberg's ruler. In the proceedings of the Privy Council, compared to those of the church, the separatists appear less as religious enthusiasts; attention was primarily drawn to their social and political significance.

30 'They do not even understand what we mean by this.' cf. the protocol drafted by *Spezial* Faber, Neuenstadt, 16 January 1772: LKA Stgt, A 26, fasc. 471.

31 ibid.: 'Dass sie die weibliche Blume abfasten.' 'Es sey eine freye Gnade, dass sie frey seyen.'

32 Protocol drafted by *Spezial* Faber, Neuenstadt, 9 January 1772, ibid.

33 As in n. 30.

34 His wife states: 'She had found his bed stained when they still lay together, as well as at the beginning of his lying alone. She could not say whether this took place with intent or during his sleep. Her father [Johann Adam Hilker] added to this that the latter could be possible. However, for some time now she had not found anything.' Schreiber himself

adds: 'The stains on the bed were not caused by intent, but during his sleep. Moreover, this had only occurred at the beginning and did not happen any more.' Source as in n. 32. Shortly before this, Schreiber's father-in-law, Hilker, had declared that the innkeeper of the *Ochsen* inn 'has abstained from marital cohabitation already for the last three years'. Although the innkeeper claimed to have 'simple *pollutiones nocturnae*', this was 'clearly untrue', according to Hilker, 'partially because he has been doing this for a very long time, partially also because he observes the strict fast imposed on him. Among themselves the separatists call such fasting, including the removal of sinful semen, a crucifixion and mortification of the flesh, and they claim that the flesh has to be overcome entirely before one is to achieve the pure bridal purity. Once the sinful flesh has been overcome, they eat and drink again that which is good, including coffee, etc.' Appendix drafted by Gochsen's local pastor, Winter, dated 20 November 1771 and added to his report of 18 November 1771: LKA Stgt, A 26, fasc. 471. All this should be looked at particularly within the context of the eighteenth-century discussion of onanism. Karl Braun, Tübingen, is currently preparing a doctoral thesis on this discussion.

35 As in n. 32.

36 cf. n. 34.

37 Appendix dated 20 November 1771, as in n. 34.

38 As in n. 32.

39 As in n. 32.

40 See the instructive article by R. Mack, 'Libertinärer Pietismus: Die Wanderungen der Pfarrerswitwe Wetzel', *Jahrbuch der hessischen kirchengeschichtlichen Vereinigung*, Vol. XXIX (1978), pp. 81–107.

41 See G. Reichel, *Zinzendorfs Frömmigkeit im Licht der Psychoanalyse: Eine kritische Prüfung des Buchs von Dr. Oskar Pfister: 'Die Frömmigkeit des Grafen Ludwig von Zinzendorf', und ein Beitrag zum Verständnis der extravaganten Lehrweise Zinzendorfs* (Tübingen, 1911), esp. ch. 6; 'Zinzendorfs Stellung zur Ehe' (pp. 171–92). On Zinzendorf's influence see also R. Geiges, *Zweihundert Jahre Herrnhut und Württemberg* (Gnadau, [1922]).

42 cf. H. Renkewitz, *Hochmann von Hochenau (1670–1721): Quellenstudien zur Geschichte des Pietismus* (first publ. 1935; Witten, 1969). I owe the reference to Hochmann's importance to Klaus Deppermann, Freiburg.

43 ibid., pp. 401–12; the 'Confession' soon became familiar knowledge in North America, cf. ibid., pp. 401 ff.

44 *Johann Jakob Moser's Theologische Gedanken von der ehelichen Beiwohnung unbekehrter, erweckter und wiedergeborener Personen: Nach der – einzigen – Ausgabe vom Jahre 1743 aufs neue herausgegeben* (Leipzig, 1900).

45 As, for example, the so-called Ephrata-monasteries; the first Ephrata-settlement based on celibacy was established in 1732 in Pennsylvania. See H. Schempp, *Gemeinschafts-siedlungen auf religiöser und weltanschaulicher Grundlage* (Tübingen, 1969), pp. 30–2.

46 As in n. 32.

47 ibid.

48 R. Wirtz, 'Die Begriffsverwirrung der Bauern im Odenwald 1848: Odenwälder "Excesse" und die Sinsheimer "republikanische Schilderhebung"', in *Wahrnehmungsformen und Protestverhalten: Studien zur Lage der Unterschichten im 18. und 19. Jahrhundert* (Frankfurt/M. 1979), pp. 81–104.

49 Pastor Kirchberger attributed such a feeling to the 'Yellow' or 'Bückleaner' (also 'Bickleaner'), the followers of the weaver Georg Bückle of Nellingen in the Blaubeuren part of the Schwäbische Alb. In 1854 Bückle was taken to the lunatic asylum of Zwiefalten, where he died in 1885. cf. Kirchberger, 'Die Sekte der Gelben', *Besondere Beilage des Staatsanzeigers für Württemberg*, no. 21/22 (16 October 1902), pp. 344–52; the cited passage is on p. 352. This is covered by specially voluminous archival records: LKA Stgt, A 26, fasc. 490.

50 A group of Pietists who considered themselves the disciples of pastor Pregizer of Haiterbach in Württemberg's Black Forest. cf. G. Müller, *Christian Gottlob Pregizer (1751–1824): Sein Leben und seine Schriften* (Stuttgart, 1961).

51 Pfarrer Wunderlich, 'Geschichte und Grundsäze der in Zell und Altbach im Mai 1813 entstandenen schwärmerischen Secte'. MS. in LKA Stgt, A 26, fasc. 487.

52 Herrenberg interrogations of 1718 and 1725: LKA Stgt, A 26, fasc. 470.
53 Letter written by the official Ditting addressed to the *Spezial* at Cannstatt of 3 May 1766, concerning a Fellbach Pietist: Dekanatsarchiv Cannstatt, no. 106c; cited after H.-V. Findeisen, 'Religiöser Separatismus als Herausforderung kirchlicher Organisationen (dargestellt am Beispiel des volkstümlichen württembergischen Pietismus im Dorf Fellbach bei Stuttgart von der Mitte des 18. bis zum Beginn des 19. Jahrhunderts)', unpubl. MS. (Tübingen, 1980); the cited passage is on p. 50. I wish to thank Hans-Volkmar Findeisen very much for allowing me to quote from his study. The following examples are cited from this work.
54 cf. ibid., p. 20.
55 Letters and protocols in HStA Stgt, A 213, fasc. 3096, of 27 May, 20 July and 21 July 1794, cited by H.-V. Findeisen, 'Religiöser Separatismus', as in n. 53, pp. 44 ff.
56 HStA Stgt, A 213, fasc. 3096, protocol written by the *Amtmann* on 20 July 1794. Cited ibid., p. 45.
57 A report from the Rottenacker *Kirchenkonvent* of 16 May 1803 states that this 'association' consisted of eleven married men (including, in six cases, the wives and, in one case, even the respective children), seven unmarried men and two women: LKA Stgt, A 26, fasc. 476.
58 LKA Stgt, A 26, fasc. 479.
59 General regulation concerning the relations between separatists and the territorial militia of 20 August 1794, printed in Kapff (ed.), *Sammlung der württembergischen Kriegs-Geseze*, pt 1 (= A. L. Reyscher, ed., *Sammlung der württembergischen Geseze*, Vol. XIX) (Tübingen, 1849), pp. 743–5, esp. p. 744. Note that the Fellbach cases of objection against militia service occurred shortly beforehand, in July 1794! cf. above, n. 55.
60 'Normal-Verordnung des Kön. Staats-Ministeriums, betr. die Bestrafung der Separatisten' of 5 November 1806, in Eisenlohr, *Sammlung*, cited n. 8 above, p. 72 ff.
61 'Cirk. Rescript der Ob. Land. Regierung, betr. die Behandlung unehrerbietiger Separatisten und das Verbot des Tragens von Abzeichen von Seiten derselben', of 3 July 1806, ibid., p. 59.
62 'Staats-Min. Erlass, betr. die Behandlung der Kinder widerspenstiger Separatisten', of 4 February 1808, ibid., p. 129.
63 'Erlass der Ob. Regier, an die Kreis-Aemter, betr. die Art der Behandlung der Separatisten', of 16 September 1809, ibid., pp. 175 ff.
64 See the proclamation of Friedrich II concerning his promotion to the Electorship of 30 April 1803, in A. L. Reyscher (ed.), *Sammlung der Staats-Grund-Gesetze*, Vol. II (= A. L. Reyscher, ed., *Sammlung der württembergischen Geseze*, Vol. II) (Stuttgart and Tübingen, 1829), pp. 643 ff.
65 Evidence indicating the sympathy of many separatists for the French Revolution has also been found earlier by F. Fritz, 'Die Wiedertäufer und der württembergische Pietismus', *Blätter für württembergische Kirchengeschichte*, Vol. XLIII (1939), pp. 102 ff.
66 KKP Rottenacker, 16 May 1803; LKA Stgt, A 26, fasc. 476.
67 HStA Stgt, E 31, fasc. 1228, 29/31 July 1806, 12 August 1806.
68 ibid., 12 August 1806. The 'rebellion' referred to in the cited passage probably was the Berlin strike of 1801, which was joined by approximately 200 tailor-journeymen. See J. Streisand, *Deutschland von 1789 bis 1815*, Lehrbuch der deutschen Geschichte, Beiträge Vol. V, 3rd edn (Berlin, 1973), p. 102.
69 HStA Stgt, E 31, fasc. 1228, 26 March/5 April 1804.
70 cf. M. Weber, *Wirtschaft und Gesellschaft: Grundriss der verstehenden Soziologie* (Tübingen, 1956), esp. ch. 5, pt 2: Religionssoziologie (Typen religiöser Vergemeins-chaftung), pp. 317–488.
71 cf. W. Brückner, 'Erneuerung als selektive Tradition: Kontinuitätsfragen im 16. und 17. Jahrhundert aus dem Bereich der konfessionellen Kultur', in *Der Übergang zur Neuzeit und die Wirkung von Traditionen: Vorträge gehalten auf der Joachim Jungius-Gesellschaft der Wissenschaften Hamburg am 13. und 14. Oktober 1977* (Göttingen, 1978), pp. 55–78; id., 'Zum Wandel der religiösen Kultur im 18. Jahrhundert: Einkreis-ungsversuche des "Barockfrommen" zwischen Mittelalter und Massenmissionierung', in E. Hinrichs and G. Wiegelmann (eds), *Sozialer und kultureller Wandel in der ländlichen Welt des 18. Jahrhunderts*, Wolfenbütteler Forschungen, Vol. XIX (Wolfenbüttel, 1982),

pp. 65–83. Brückner analyses in detail and with considerable knowledge the puzzle of the new formation of culture out of surviving sets of tradition. However, he neglects the fact that the social-historical process can transform tradition into something new.

72 cf. M. Halbwachs, *Das Gedächtnis und seine sozialen Bedingungen* (1925; Berlin and Neuwied, 1966).

73 This is what it was called by the Privy Council on 6 April 1805: HStA Stgt, E 31, fasc. 1228.

74 The king subsequently dismissed the provost from his function for his disciplinary offence: HStA Stgt, E 31, fasc. 1228, 19/22 May 1804, 13 July 1805, 27 July 1805, 13/27 June 1809.

Part Four

Religion and the Community

12 Religion, Communities and Moral Discipline in Late Sixteenth- and Early Seventeenth-Century England: Case Studies

MARTIN INGRAM

Most of the chapters in this book are regional, national, or even continental in scope. The horizons of this contribution, by contrast, are largely limited to the muddy streets of a few obscure villages in late sixteenth- and early seventeenth-century England. The reader may well feel some sense of anticlimax. Yet the local study undoubtedly has its uses. Most of the inhabitants of early modern Europe experienced religion in the context of small rural social systems. The microscopic study of these miniature environments can help to illuminate the role of religion in the everyday life of the community, and make it possible to chart in some detail the relationships between religious developments, changing cultural horizons, variations in moral attitudes and demographic, economic and social structural shifts. The results may serve to give substance to, and also to qualify, some of the general concepts – 'the reformation of popular culture', 'godly discipline', and so on – explored by the contributors to this volume and by other historians of early modern Europe.

The sources available for reconstructing the rural communities of early modern England, to which attention in this paper is confined, are manifold. They include tax lists; parish registers of baptisms, marriages and burials; manorial and estate records; wills and related testamentary and probate documents; parish records concerned with the upkeep of the church, poor relief and other aspects of local administration; and the records of secular and ecclesiastical courts.[1] Inevitably, these sources have their limits. Despite some flashes of light shed by vivid depositions or particularly forthright wills, much of the innerness of thought, feeling and belief within the community remains tantalisingly obscure. Nevertheless, it is striking just how much *can* be learned about the lives of villagers in the remote past. A succession of researchers, notably W. G. Hoskins, Victor Skipp, Margaret Spufford, David Hey, Alan Macfarlane, and Keith Wrightson and David Levine, have gradually extended the range of topics open to investigation at the local level, and have shown how parish studies, far from being 'parochial' in the negative sense of that word, can contribute to an understanding of national or even supra-national developments.[2]

This chapter reviews some recent English local histories of particular relevance to the themes of this volume, and presents the initial findings of a study now in progress. Of published works, Wrightson and Levine's study of the parish of Terling in Essex (south-east England) is especially pertinent.[3] The authors argue that certain changes in this community, occurring mainly in the late sixteenth and early seventeenth centuries, may be largely understood in terms of two powerful factors: first, a complex of demographic and economic shifts; and secondly, the introduction, via the more substantial inhabitants, of new standards of religious behaviour and personal conduct fostered by contact with literate, elite culture. While economic changes polarised the community in material terms, these new standards tended to drive a cultural wedge between the poorer sections of society and the 'better sort', and shaped and legitimated the attempts of the latter – motivated partly by economic considerations – to moralise the community. Terling thus emerges as a case study in the reformation of popular culture and the exercise of godly discipline, illustrating with a wealth of vivid detail a variation on these themes within a specific and carefully drawn economic and social context.

Both on account of their intrinsic interest and in order to facilitate comparison, Wrightson and Levine's findings will be reviewed in some detail. Terling was a medium-sized rural parish with perhaps 500–600 inhabitants in the early seventeenth century. Its economy was overwhelmingly agricultural, conducted on an individualistic basis with little manorial supervision. By the beginning of the seventeenth century much of the land in the parish was exploited in large units by wealthy yeoman and gentleman farmers specialising in the bulk supply of grain to local and distant markets, including London. However, smaller farmers and craftsmen, disposing of modest wealth, remained reasonably prominent in the social structure at this period. The chief manifestation of social structural change in the late sixteenth and early seventeenth centuries was an increase in the proportion of poor cottagers and landless labourers. The parish experienced a marked increase in population in the period from about 1540 to 1620. But the numbers of rich or substantial yeoman, husbandman and craftsman households remained fairly steady; it was the bottom levels of the social pyramid which expanded most.[4]

There were other changes in the village in the late sixteenth and early seventeenth centuries: together they reveal a remarkable convergence of economic, social structural, cultural, moral and religious shifts. One of the most striking, the original starting-point of Wrightson and Levine's researches, was variation in the incidence of bastard births. Bastardy shot up around the turn of the sixteenth century, the illegitimacy ratio[5] reaching a high point of over 9 per cent in the decade 1601–10. In succeeding decades, however, illegitimacy declined markedly, to a figure of under 2 per cent in the decade 1631–40. Wrightson and Levine suggest that the bastardy boom of the years around 1600 was the result of economic dislocations caused by the exceptionally bad harvests of the later 1590s. The fall in the bastardy ratio after 1610 was, in part, simply a return to normality; but it cannot wholly be explained in this way. There were subsequent periods of economic crisis in the early seventeenth century, admittedly less catastrophic than the late 1590s but none the less severe. Yet they did not produce marked rises in the illegitimacy ratio. Moreover, by the 1630s the incidence of bastardy was well below the level prevailing *before* the turn-of-the-century peak. In addition, there was over the period a decline in the incidence of bridal pregnancy (that is, the proportion of brides pregnant at marriage, as computed from information in the parish registers). These facts seem to indicate that in the years from around 1600 to 1640 attitudes to illicit sexuality were becoming increasingly strict.

Wrightson and Levine argue that the change was, in part, a spontaneous adjustment at all levels of village society to the economic conditions of the early seventeenth century, and represented one aspect of a broader pattern of increased restraint on fertility observable in the demographic history of the parish. But an adjustment of attitudes on the part of the more substantial inhabitants was particularly important. This adjustment was evident less in the matter of bastardy, which throughout the period was regarded as reprehensible in terms both of Christian morality and of its economic and social effects, than with regard to bridal pregnancy. Traditionally this had been tolerantly regarded, and before about 1620 cases in which a woman was pregnant at marriage rarely led to court action. Thereafter the situation changed: guilty couples were increasingly reported to the church courts by parish officers.[6]

Local officials also became increasingly intolerant towards unlicensed ale-selling, drunkenness, tippling, playing games and dancing, which could be regarded as wasteful of resources and likely to lead to promiscuity and disorder. By means of prosecutions in the quarter sessions and the church courts, and by pressure exercised locally, these forms of behaviour were subjected to a major attack in the early seventeenth century. Initially this onslaught met resistance from certain elements among the better-off inhabitants who were themselves susceptible to the delights of alehouse society and other forms of personal indulgence. This resistance was, however, largely overcome; and during the course of the early seventeenth century, drunkenness and other forms of 'disorderly' behaviour were increasingly confined to the poorer ranks of society. Even at this social level such behaviour became less common. Repression of the poor was aided by the very fact of their economic dependence: thus the parish charity established in 1626 furthered the programme of moral reform by making ineligible for relief 'those that are guilty of excessive drinkinge, profane swearing, pilfering, or other scandalous crimes . . .'.[7]

Wrightson and Levine indicate that these developments were intimately related to cultural and religious changes. They argue that the new policy of moral discipline involved a reorientation of values among the more substantial inhabitants of the village who largely dominated local offices, a growing willingness to prosecute offences rigorously instead of regarding them, as hitherto, with neighbourly tolerance. This change was facilitated by an increase in literacy among the more substantial groups in village society, which made them receptive to ideas generated outside the village, in the culturally elite world of the county justices and other gentry and of

Protestant religious writers urging the enforcement of order and moral reform. Such ideas were powerfully represented among the magistrates and ministers of Essex, including the ministers of Terling itself. Thus the yeomen and substantial husbandmen and craftsmen of the parish came to ally themselves with the standards of gentry and clerical elites, against their poorer neighbours who remained overwhelmingly illiterate.[8] The appeal of strongly committed Protestant, not to say Puritan, ideals consolidated this process of cultural stratification. From the 1580s there was a marked increase in the range and volume of prosecutions relating to religious observance, directed for the most part against the poorer inhabitants and designed to inculcate better standards of church attendance and participation in the sacraments. By the 1620s and 1630s, moreover, the 'better sort' of the villagers of Terling were dominated by men of strong Protestant piety. On the basis of evidence from wills, Wrightson and Levine establish the existence in these decades of a coherent group of about ten 'godly' laymen, deeply pious and closely linked by ties of personal friendship and religious fellowship with each other and with their ministers. Of these 'godly' laymen, all were rich or substantial, most were literate and most occupied key positions in the structure of village government and were in the forefront of the battle against sexual immorality, irreligion, drunkenness and festivities.[9]

By the 1630s, therefore, the nature of the community in Terling had been profoundly changed through the overlapping effects of a variety of forms of polarisation – economic, moral, cultural and religious. The 'better sort' perceived themselves to be superior in numerous ways: they were richer, better educated and more godly than the mass of the inhabitants.

A number of points for discussion, of particular relevance to the themes of this volume, may be singled out from this analysis. The first is the fact that, while the study proposes two main engines of change, economic and cultural-religious, their relative importance in influencing the various strands of development remains unclear. This is particularly so with regard to the diverse elements of the campaign for moral reformation. Did the assault on alehouses and drunkenness, for example, arise primarily from a concern to minimise idleness and waste in a period of economic difficulties, or were intrinsically moral and religious ideas of equal or even greater importance? Clearly, economic concerns and religious ideas could reinforce one another, and it would appear that, in Terling, they did so. In tracing the experience of this single community, it is not feasible to assess the relative importance of the two factors; nor, in a sense, is it desirable to try to do so, since the essence of Terling's development was the subtle interaction of a number of forces, and it would be artificial if not downright crass to insist on clumsy distinctions. Yet in wider perspective, in considering Terling as an element in the broader history of England and Europe, it would be valuable to isolate the relative importance of various forces of social change; and in terms of the concerns of this collection of essays it is of particular interest to assess the contribution of specifically religious ideas.

A second point of interest is the highly polarised picture of religious behaviour which emerges from the study. On the one hand we are shown the 'godly'; on the other, the 'multitude' of mainly poor folk who appear to be, if not entirely irreligious, at least more susceptible to the attractions of the alehouse and dancing green than of church and sermon and liable to prosecution for neglect of religious observances. Little attention is paid to individuals who did not readily fit either of these stereotypes, though by reading between the lines it may be inferred that such people did exist in Terling. This concentration on extremes of religious belief and behaviour (which partly reflects various forms of bias in the available evidence) is characteristic of much recent writing on religion in early modern England.[10] The danger is that it may obscure the importance, if not in Terling, then perhaps elsewhere, of unspectacular orthodoxy.

This point is related to the next. Of major interest is the very close relationship between Wrightson and Levine's findings and generalisations made by historians working on a broader English or even European canvas. As noted earlier, Terling can be seen as a case study in the reformation of popular culture and the exercise of godly discipline. It also illustrates the linkage which many historians have argued to exist between committed Protestantism and literacy, and the association postulated by Christopher Hill and others between Puritanism and prospering middling groups in society.[11] Whatever the merit of such generalisations as aids to understanding broad changes at a national or supra-national level, it might be expected that they would require extensive modification and qualification in a particular local context. To find so many major themes emerging with startling clarity within a short space of time in one small village, apparently selected for study virtually at random,[12] is indeed arresting. Of course, the clarity of the findings appears greater in the summary offered here, and indeed in Wrightson and Levine's own summary passages, than in the main body of their text where numerous complications and interpretative caveats are carefully recorded. Even so, the convergence of themes in Terling remains impressive. It is therefore not surprising that a number of historians, notably Christopher Hill, have drawn attention to Terling as a possible exemplar of key changes in late sixteenth- and early seventeenth-century English society as a whole.[13] It is hence of great importance to try to determine how far the experience of this parish *was* reproduced in other English rural communities. This question will be pursued in the following pages; it will eventually lead back to the other points of interest raised earlier.

Wrightson and Levine do not discuss in detail the representativeness of Terling, but they do suggest that the community 'provides one example, one variant, of a social process that was active elsewhere, though subject to considerable local variation in chronology and consequences'.[14] The basis for this opinion is that the general influences which shaped Terling's development were at work on a much wider scale. Certainly, the demographic and economic changes visible in Terling fit readily into what is known of trends in many of the fielden, mixed farming communities of lowland England.[15] In addition, the incidence of bastardy and bridal pregnancy in Terling conforms broadly to the patterns which Peter Laslett and others have established for England as a whole.[16] An increase in literacy, especially among the wealthier groups in society, also seems to have been widespread in late sixteenth- and seventeenth-century England, though there were considerable regional and local variations in degree and timing.[17] In many dioceses, at least, there was in the late Elizabethan and early Stuart period an increase in church court prosecutions relating to religious observance and personal morality; while in many counties there was an expansion of regulatory activity in quarter sessions and petty sessions, especially with regard to the sale and consumption of ale.[18] There is also a growing body of evidence relating to the spread of committed Protestant or even Puritan beliefs among the laity in rural areas.[19] But the precise impact of these developments at the parochial level, the way in which the various changes interacted and the effect on social relations within communities remain for the most part uncertain.

On general grounds, it is possible to hazard some guesses at the likely effects in different types of community. For example, in his most recent work Wrightson has pointed out that in parishes characterised by large populations, scattered settlement and egalitarian social structure, regulatory experiments were unlikely to succeed or even to be tried.[20] But the only really satisfactory way of testing how far the developments which occurred in Terling were replicated elsewhere is to make a series of detailed comparisons with other communities.

A considerable number of local studies already exist and might seem, at first sight, to provide the necessary basis for comparison. Unfortunately, none of them examines as wide a range of social phenomena as Wrightson and Levine or is as alert to the way in which the mutual influence of diverse forces may affect the nature of the community. David Hey's study of the forest-pastoral parish of Myddle in Shropshire over the period 1524–1701 tries to examine all facets of the life of the community, but the available sources prove inadequate for this task and many of the conclusions are too impressionistic to bear detailed comparison with Terling.[21] The economic and social structural changes revealed in Victor Skipp's study of five parishes in the Forest of Arden (Midland England) show some marked similarities with the situation in the Essex village, and the author's conclusion that 'by Stuart times gentlemen and substantial yeomen had come to dominate local society more strongly than ever before: not only economically, but socially and culturally' is suggestive.[22] Unfortunately, this idea of cultural domination is little developed.

Margaret Spufford's study of a number of communities in Cambridgeshire (eastern England) investigates literacy and religious belief alongside demographic, economic and social structural changes, and to that extent offers some basis for comparison with Wrightson and Levine's findings. Points of similarity emerge, but also apparent differences. For example, there is evidence of the spread of literacy and of an increase in committed Protestantism among the laity. But the available information does not clearly indicate, except perhaps in the fen village of Willingham, the emergence before 1640 of coherent 'godly' groups among the more substantial inhabitants. Rather it suggests the existence of a minority of particularly pious *individuals*, some of whom were from the lower strata of village society.[23] In the last resort, however, detailed comparison breaks down both because Dr Spufford's concerns are so different from those of Wrightson and Levine – her treatment of religion, for example, is oriented heavily towards tracing the antecedents and growth of nonconformist congregations – and because she omits discussion of bastardy, bridal pregnancy, the use of the secular and ecclesiastical courts to prosecute crime and disorder, the pattern of local office-holding and other phenomena which form so important a part of the analysis of social dynamics in Terling.

James Sharpe's brief study of the parish of Kelvedon Easterford (Essex) in the period 1600–42 does cover the prosecution of delinquency, and is of particular interest because of the village's close proximity to Terling: from it emerge some interesting points of similarity and contrast with the situation in the latter parish. Much like Wrightson and Levine, Sharpe emphasises the importance in village society of a loose oligarchy of prosperous yeomen and substantial traders who largely dominated the important parochial offices to the exclusion of the mass of the poorer inhabitants. However, Sharpe stresses that throughout his period of study a proportion of the members of this oligarchy continued to be involved in disorderly activities. This suggests that the moralisation of the upper ranks of village society which was so prominent a feature of Terling's history either did not occur at all in Kelvedon or happened in a much modified form or at a later date. Unfortunately, comparisons cannot be pressed much further because Sharpe's study – which was intended only as a preliminary report – does not provide enough information on the demography, economy, or social structure of the village, or on the cultural horizons or religious opinions of its inhabitants.[24]

Religion is, on the other hand, the main focus of attention in Patrick Collinson's short but subtle study of Cranbrook in Kent (south-east England). Sometimes regarded as a Puritan stronghold, Cranbrook certainly witnessed in the later sixteenth century a campaign against sexual immorality, drunkenness, festivities and lax religious observance. This campaign was probably spearheaded by the clergy (especially by Richard Fletcher, vicar from 1561 to 1587), but was apparently supported by a group of 'godly' laymen. There are, therefore, obvious parallels with Terling. On the other hand, Professor Collinson stresses that the attempts to moralise the parish met with only partial success; the 'godly' group seems to have remained relatively small in size (its social composition is uncertain: Collinson suggests that its members were neither very rich nor very poor); and the situation was complicated by conflict between successive vicars, who were by and large inclined to conform to the practices of the established church, and members of the godly laity who were attracted to presbyterian church views. But whatever the similarities and contrasts with Terling, the case of Cranbrook can make only a limited contribution to our knowledge of developments in *rural* communities, our main concern here. It is true that this huge parish, which covered nearly 50 square miles and was said to have at least 2,000 communicants in 1597, included extensive rural areas within its boundaries. But the main settlement of Cranbrook was itself a market town.[25] It thus invites comparison with other urban centres, such as Rye, Canterbury, Northampton and Salisbury,[26] rather than with country parishes like Terling.

Attempts to gauge the typicality of Terling by reference to other published studies thus founder. But at least a limited basis for comparison is offered in the following pages, which report the preliminary findings of a parish study now in progress. The community in question is Keevil in Wiltshire (south-west England).[27] To facilitate comparison, all the variables identified by Wrightson and Levine as of key importance in the development of Terling have, as far as possible, been investigated in Keevil. However, it must be stressed that some aspects of the history of this parish have not yet been investigated to the depth achieved by Wrightson and Levine. Moreover, the time-span is narrower: at present the study extends only from *c.*1560 to *c.*1640. But within these chronological limits – which correspond with the period of decisive change in Terling – the main lines of development seem clear, though further research may amplify or modify in detail the conclusions presented here. These conclusions are of considerable interest, revealing some striking similarities between Keevil and Terling but also a number of intriguing contrasts.

Though roughly comparable in size,[28] there were some basic differences between the two communities. A higher proportion of the land in Keevil was still exploited in small units and wealth was somewhat more evenly distributed. Many of the smaller landholdings were occupied by people who combined agriculture with weaving for the commercial market. Cloth production was, in fact, an important source of income within the parish, which was located on the edge of the broadcloth production area which covered much of western Wiltshire in this period. Though complicating the comparison with the almost wholly agricultural village of Terling, this fact has the advantage of providing a limited test of Christopher Hill's suggestion that the 'puritan' code of moral and social discipline had a particular appeal in clothing areas.[29] Keevil also differed from Terling in the structure of its local administration. Manorial institutions were much stronger in this Wiltshire parish and still supervised a communal agricultural regime, while an active court leet continued to regulate local affairs in the larger of the two tithings into which the parish was divided.

But Keevil was similar to Terling in that it suffered population pressure and economic stress in the late sixteenth and early seventeenth centuries. As in Terling, the effect of demographic expansion was to enlarge the poorer echelons of the social structure while leaving the numbers of the more substantial households relatively unchanged. The problem of poverty worsened in the second and third decades of the seventeenth century, partly because a long-term decline in the market for broadcloths, punctuated by severe short-term dislocations, tended to impoverish those families which were heavily dependent on industrial wages.[30] Bad harvests also caused periodic distress. The dearth years of the later 1590s were marked by a violent upsurge of mortality in the parish; and there were subsequent crises (though less catastrophic in terms of mortality) in the early seventeenth century, especially in the early to mid 1620s when bad harvests coincided with trade depression. Inferential evidence from a variety of local sources, and explicit contemporary comment, indicate that by this time the problem of poverty in the parish was a sizeable one, and the community faced difficulties with regard to the housing, employment and relief of the poor.[31] Yet by no means the whole of the parish was impoverished. At the upper end of the village social scale, families with medium-sized tenements were at least holding their own, while certain rich yeoman and clothier families – the latter tending over time to reduce their involvement in industry and concentrate more on farming – were doing extremely well in the economic conditions of the late sixteenth and early seventeenth centuries, consolidating and extending their landed wealth, and growing in status to the extent that one or two of the most prosperous aspired to the title of 'gentleman'.

Clearly there was wealth potentially available for redistribution within the parish, and to an extent the more substantial inhabitants responded to the problem of poverty by providing positive relief. Over the period 1550–1640 more than a third of wills included charitable bequests to the poor. The sums involved were generally quite small, mostly ranging from a few pence to a few pounds and usually representing only a small proportion of the total wealth of the testator; though there were a few more generous bequests.[32] Although detailed poor relief documents are lacking for this period, it is clear from incidental references that the statutory poor relief system, funded by compulsory rates, was also in operation, though its enforcement may have been sporadic. In 1625, at a time when the problem of poverty was probably at its most acute and there were said to be 'a great company of poor impotent people' enforced to dwell in barns and outhouses, the parish obtained leave to erect an almshouse – but the scheme was apparently not put into effect.[33] In any event, these positive responses to poverty have to be seen in context. In many respects the parish officers – drawn mainly from the upper ranks of village society – adopted a hardheaded approach to the problem, clamping down on the building of cottages without adequate land, restricting immigration and encouraging the unemployed to seek work elsewhere.[34]

This picture of worsening poverty and of economic polarisation between the wealthier inhabitants and the poor has strong similarities with the situation in Terling. To what extent did Keevil experience a corresponding reorientation of cultural, religious and moral values? Certainly there was a similar shift with regard to the incidence of, and attitudes towards, bastardy and bridal pregnancy. The illegitimacy ratio varied in roughly the same fashion in the two parishes, though the absolute incidence of bastardy was lower in Keevil throughout the period, and in the Wiltshire village there was no marked upsurge of bastard births in the wake of the bad harvests of the later 1590s.[35] The Keevil illegitimacy ratio, as computed solely on the basis of information from the parish registers, stood at 4 per cent in the 1590s; it fell markedly in succeeding decades to below 1 per cent in the 1630s. This picture of a decline in the incidence of bastardy is to some extent modified if we take account of cases which are known from church court and other records but which were not mentioned in the parish registers, since the proportion of unregistered bastards increased over the decades. Nevertheless, a definite decline in illegitimacy remains apparent. The growth in the numbers of bastardy cases omitted from the registers is itself of interest. It seems to have been symptomatic not of increasingly careless registration but of stricter attitudes to bastardy. The parents of bastards were increasingly harshly punished in the parish; in these circumstances, it may be inferred, unmarried mothers tended to make themselves scarce and became more reluctant to present their bastards for baptism in the village. Attitudes to bridal pregnancy also seem to have grown more strict. Cases of antenuptial fornication were increasingly reported to the church courts by parish officers; the incidence of bridal pregnancy declined in the course of the early seventeenth century to the remarkably low figure of 10 per cent; and by the 1620s the phenomenon appears to have been largely confined to poorer couples.[36]

The similarities between Keevil and Terling have so far been striking. Examination of the religious history of Keevil, and of the pattern of prosecution of various offences other than sexual transgressions, indicates certain differences. It should first be noted that the county of Wiltshire, though sharing to some extent in the 'increase in governance'[37] which has been postulated for England as a whole, was much less noted for a zealous, reforming magistracy and ministry than Essex. In Keevil itself, in the absence of a resident justice of the peace, the main official representatives of order were successive incumbents. Not much is known about the early Elizabethan vicars, but it is clear that Francis and Stephen Greatrakes, who served the cure, father and son, over the period 1588–1641, were both constantly resident, diligent, learned, preaching ministers. What of the laity? The evidence of wills offers one possible approach to the religious opinions of at least the middling to upper ranks of village society (few of the poor made wills).[38] One of the Marian martyrs came from Keevil,[39] and a few wills of the 1550s include staunchly Protestant professions of faith. Most of the religious preambles in wills of that date, however, suggest acceptance of Catholic beliefs. Catholic formulae disappeared after 1560 and Protestant preambles became more common. But the majority of Elizabethan and early Jacobean wills, especially in the period *c*.1590–*c*.1615, employed the neutral formula 'I bequeath my soul to Almighty God'. Thereafter, there was a marked change: elaborately worded Protestant preambles rapidly became much commoner and by the 1630s heavily predominated. But it would be a mistake to assume from this that by then Keevil was pulsating with godliness and that there had been a marked change in religious feelings since the beginning of the century. As is now commonly recognised, religious preambles are a very uncertain guide to the beliefs and attitudes of individual testators.[40] On close examination it seems clear that much of the variation can be explained in terms of the forms preferred by Francis and Stephen Greatrakes (and, probably, earlier ministers), who actually wrote most of the wills. Nevertheless, there may have been some shift in the attitudes of testators. By the 1620s and 1630s, elaborate professions of faith, by no means entirely stereotyped, seem to have been generally accepted as the most desirable form and were likely to appear even in wills not written by Stephen Greatrakes. This may conceivably represent the growth of a more informed and self-conscious Protestant piety in the will-making echelons of Keevil society, though it cannot be accepted as a strong indicator of such a development.

Potential access to the fundamental text of Protestantism, the Bible, was certainly growing. In Keevil, as in Terling, literacy increased in this period. The available evidence, drawn mainly from probate records, does not easily lend itself to quantitative treatment, but the main outlines of development are plain. In the reign of Elizabeth lay literacy in Keevil was rare, confined mainly to a few gentlemen or near-gentlemen living in the parish. By the 1630s perhaps half the substantial yeomen of the village were literate to the extent of being able to write a reasonable signature, and so also were a fair sprinkling of husbandmen and weavers. Ownership of Bibles increased, mainly among the richer yeomen. In the period 1590–1629 only about 4 per cent of sets of probate documents mentioned Bibles; by the decades 1630–49 the proportion had risen to about 18 per cent. These are, of course, likely to be minimum figures for the ownership of Bibles among testators, since books were by no means always separately itemised in probate documents.[41] On the other hand, it is by no means certain that these texts were actually read. As David Cressy has argued, Bibles could serve a variety of other functions including that of status object:[42] in Keevil it may be significant that in inventories of goods, where most of the references are found, Bibles often appear almost as part of the furniture, located in or on ornamental cupboards. It is conceivable that well-thumbed copies of cheaper editions of the Bible, too small in value to warrant a mention in probate records, existed in Keevil;[43] but positive evidence is lacking.

The evidence of Bible ownership, like that of testamentary professions of faith, is thus consistent with some growth of informed Protestant piety but does not amount to a compelling case. However, throughout the period from the late sixteenth to the mid seventeenth century a few wills do seem to indicate an exceptional degree of piety. Such wills are marked by a strikingly original or exceedingly elaborate religious preamble, and/or indications in the main body of the text, such as references to 'my well beloved Frinds in Christ',[44] that the testator's religious sentiments extended to an unusual degree to social relations and everyday activities. But few, if any, even of these testators can be safely labelled Puritan. Committed Protestant piety seems the aptest characterisation of their beliefs. These pious villagers were quite widely scattered in the social scale, and as a group were not particularly literate. But 'group' is a misleading term to use of them: they were scattered over time, they do not seem to have formed a close-knit nexus in the village and they certainly did not have a stranglehold on parish offices.

To what extent did Keevil experience a drive against alehouses, drunkenness, dancing and popular festivities, or determined efforts to inculcate more rigorous standards of religious observance? There was a slow increase in prosecutions for such offences as sleeping during service, other forms of misbehaviour in church or churchyard, and Sunday work. But the numbers of cases were small and hardly amounted to a crusade. There were prosecutions in the church courts, the quarter sessions and the local court leet for drunkenness and unlicensed ale-selling. But action was very sporadic, save for a certain bunching of cases in the early to mid 1620s (a time of acute economic distress), especially in the years 1624–5 when about fifteen men, mainly cottagers, poor undertenants and menservants, were prosecuted for alehouse-haunting and drunkenness.[45] It should be noted that the terms in which prosecutions were made were secular in tone: there was no suggestion, as there was in Terling, that drunkenness dishonoured the name of God. As regards the regulation of pastimes, numerous prosecutions for bowling were brought in the local court leet. The culprits were in many cases recurrent offenders and included some of the wealthiest and most influential men in the village: even the minister, Stephen Greatrakes, was prosecuted on one occasion.[46] The tiny fines levied for this offence were doubtless of no deterrent value; the prosecutions were probably significant chiefly as a minor source of seigneurial profit and not seriously intended to reform behaviour. Dancing and summer festivities seem to have flourished in the village and only came under attack twice. In the first incident, in 1611, the manor court ordered the destruction of the 'Kynge howse' set up as a bower for dancing and revels. It would appear from the sequel that the minister, or members of his family, were at least partly responsible for the order, and that their intervention aroused considerable resentment: some of the inhabitants responded with an obscene lampoon directed against Francis Greatrakes and his family.[47] The libel was written by the literate son of one of the wealthier inhabitants of the village, and the case serves as a reminder that learning did not necessarily lead to godliness. Festivities came under attack again in 1624, when five men were prosecuted in the church courts for a number of offences including dancing on Sunday. They asserted boldly in court that 'there is usually dauncing in Keevill upon the Sabaoth dayes aft[e]r ... evening prayer, w[hi]ch ... is noe otherwise then is allowed ...'.[48] This case suggests that festivities were still thriving at this time, despite the earlier attack; and the fact that one of the individuals prosecuted was the son of one of the most powerful men in the parish indicates that participation in these sports was by no means confined to the poor.

It is not entirely clear who initiated the prosecutions of 1624 and for what reasons. They may have been related to the severe economic conditions of the early 1620s, but other evidence suggests that they should at least partly be seen in the context of a feud among some of the richest and most influential men in the village. Religious and moral issues were raised in such feuds on other occasions. In a dispute between Roger Blagden and John Ford, both of them wealthy and prominent in parish government, Blagden caused Ford and his associates to be prosecuted in the church courts for adultery, open quarrelling at the Communion table and other matters.[49] On another occasion, in a suit in the Court of Star Chamber in 1619, Roger's brother Robert Blagden had accused one of his opponents of rudely disturbing the minister during divine service and of defrauding the poor, another of reviling the churchwardens and minister as asses, knaves and fools; while his enemies, in their turn, had charged Robert Blagden with setting a tapster on a stool to preach a mock sermon in an inn, and with doubting whether the writings of the apostles and prophets were true.[50] Whether these accusations were justified is doubtful (though, whatever his religious beliefs, Blagden was certainly not morally blameless; by his own confession he had committed adultery with a married woman and there was some doubt about the validity of his marriage).[51] But the point to emphasise is that in so far as religious and moral issues in Keevil were socially divisive, the splits were as much vertical as horizontal.

Compared to Terling, the religious life of Keevil appears less polarised in terms not only of horizontal social divisions but also of the general quality of religious observance and commitment, and less change is visible over time. The village had its pious members and its profligates, but the majority of people appear to have been neither; and, apart from the inconclusive evidence of will preambles and Bible ownership noted earlier, there are few signs of any major reorientation of religious sentiments in the period from the late sixteenth century to 1640. At least in the will-making echelons of society, virtually everyone was prepared to make a more or less elaborate profession of faith on his deathbed. Thus Robert Blagden, after a life of turbulent feuding with some of his neighbours in which his very belief in Christianity had been called in question, and with the memory of an adulterous past, prefaced his will with an elaborate profession of faith and left 13*s* 4*d* to 'Greatrax preacher of God[es] word in Kevell'.[52] Smaller or larger legacies to the minister of the parish were quite common – more than a third of wills in the period 1590–1640 include them – and may indicate a reasonable level of attachment to the clergy. Many testators also made some small bequest towards the upkeep of the parish church or of Salisbury Cathedral.[53] In their lifetime few parishioners appear to have made much demur about the payment of tithes or church dues; such disputes as occurred were mainly of a technical nature, involving allegations of unfair assessment and the like. Church attendance and other forms of religious observance were certainly not enthusiastically performed by everyone, and the general standard may not have been very high, but there is no solid evidence of widespread abstention or even reluctance to participate. There appear to have been few excommunicates in the parish at any one time. To be sure, excommunications were periodically decreed for contumacy in not attending to answer charges in the church courts. But most of the contumacious – many of them servants or other transients involved in bastardy cases – can be shown to have left the parish. With a few notable exceptions, established residents who incurred the penalty of excommunication were eventually reconciled to the church.[54] Of course, in assessing this picture of compliance it has to be borne in mind that the level of intensity of prosecutions concerned with religious observance was relatively low; greater zeal on the part of the parish officers who made presentments might have 'created' more reprobates.[55] In fine, the religious complexion of Keevil appears to have been orthodox but, in general, not enthusiastic.

This state of affairs provides an interesting contrast to the apparently more polarised and dynamic religious situation in Terling; and the divergence may provide a clue to the relative importance of economic as against cultural and religious factors in conditioning various aspects of social change and the exercise of moral discipline in English rural communities in this period. Comparison between the two villages suggests that in the case of attitudes to bastardy and bridal pregnancy, economic factors were of greater importance. In the absence of a strong Puritan religious drive in Keevil, a harsher attitude to these offences none the less developed. We cannot rule out the possibility that religious factors were to some extent involved. But it should be noted that the stricter attitude towards illegitimacy and antenuptial pregnancy did not necessarily entail any great reorientation of religious values. Although in the 1590s the bastardy rate was high relative to later decades, sexual morality was to all appearances already moderately strict, operating in the context of recognisably Christian principles. Only modest adjustments of attitudes and behaviour were necessary to effect the changes of the period 1590–1640, and it seems most plausible to find the stimulus for these adjustments in the severe economic conditions of the early seventeenth century. Yet these economic pressures did not effect a decisive reorientation of attitudes to games, festivities, or even drunkenness, nor did they stimulate a major campaign to enforce better standards of religious observance. In the light of this evidence, it seems reasonable to infer that specifically religious ideas were of crucial importance in producing the different pattern of events in Terling.

Assuming this to be correct, it must be asked why 'godliness' had less appeal in Keevil. There are many factors of possible relevance and no certain answer can be given. *Pace* Christopher Hill, it is obvious that involvement in the cloth industry was not a compelling stimulus to Puritanism. The somewhat more even distribution of wealth in Keevil and the strength of local institutions of self-government may have made for a rather more ideologically conservative atmosphere. Superficial analysis – the point needs to be confirmed by further research – suggests that the rate of turnover of families may have been less than in Terling, and this may also have made the community relatively impervious to new ideas. Other factors of possible relevance include the character and beliefs of the ministers of Keevil as against those of Terling; the fact that the county and diocesan authorities were apparently less aggressive and zealous in promoting new ideas of order than were their counterparts in Essex; the characters of individual villagers (in these tiny worlds, the influence for or against change of a few powerful individuals could probably be decisive); and the fact that the ruling families in Keevil were divided by bitter personal feuds.

We may conclude with an overall assessment of the comparison between Keevil and Terling and a brief discussion of its implications. There are enough points of similarity between the experience of the two villages to support Wrightson and Levine's suggestion that the history of Terling represented one variant on social processes of wider relevance but subject to considerable local variation. Yet the differences are also notable. Whereas Terling emerges as a striking exemplar of the reformation of popular culture and the exercise of godly discipline, in Keevil (at least up to 1640) the themes are visible in a much more confused and fragmented way. Was Keevil in this respect more representative than Terling? To judge by a detailed examination of the relevant church court records and a rather more superficial search of the quarter sessions files, the lack of any sustained campaign against alehouses, drunkenness, popular festivities and the like was typical of the great majority of rural parishes in Wiltshire in the period before the Civil War; and the same may have been true in other regions.[56] But the need for further research is patent, above all for more detailed studies of individual parishes which can alone reveal the complexities of events and show how the major currents of cultural and religious change operating in early modern England and Europe worked themselves out at the local level.

Notes: Chapter 12

1 These materials are discussed in A. Macfarlane, S. Harrison and C. Jardine, *Reconstructing Historical Communities* (Cambridge, 1977).

2 W. G. Hoskins, *The Midland Peasant: The Economic and Social History of a Leicestershire Village* (London, 1957); V. Skipp, *Crisis and Development: An Ecological Case Study of the Forest of Arden 1570–1674* (Cambridge, 1978); M. Spufford, *Contrasting Communities: English Villagers in the Sixteenth and Seventeenth Centuries* (Cambridge, 1974); David G. Hey, *An English Rural Community: Myddle under the Tudors and Stuarts* (Leicester, 1974); A. Macfarlane, *Witchcraft in Tudor and Stuart England: A Regional and Comparative Study* (London, 1970) (which makes extensive use of village study material); Macfarlane *et al.*, *Reconstructing Historical Communities*; K. Wrightson and D. Levine, *Poverty and Piety in an English Village: Terling, 1525–1700* (London, 1979).

3 Wrightson and Levine, *Poverty and Piety*; see also D. Levine and K. Wrightson, 'The social context of illegitimacy in early modern England', in P. Laslett, K. Oosterveen and R. M. Smith (eds), *Bastardy and its Comparative History* (London, 1980), pp. 158–75.

4 Wrightson and Levine, *Poverty and Piety*, chs 2–3.

5 That is, the ratio of illegitimate births to total births. This is, of course, a rather crude measure of illegitimacy: for some of the problems involved in its use, see P. Laslett, 'Introduction: comparing illegitimacy over time and between cultures', in Laslett *et al.*, *Bastardy and its Comparative History*, pp. 13–16.

6 Wrightson and Levine, *Poverty and Piety*, pp. 125–33; Levine and Wrightson, 'The social context of illegitimacy'.

7 Wrightson and Levine, *Poverty and Piety*, pp. 134–41, 177–9.

8 ibid., pp. 142–53; cf. K. Wrightson, 'Two concepts of order: justices, constables and jurymen in seventeenth-century England', in J. Brewer and J. Styles (eds), *An Ungovernable People: The English and their Law in the Seventeenth and Eighteenth Centuries* (London, 1980), pp. 21–46.

9 Wrightson and Levine, *Poverty and Piety*, pp. 154–9, 179–81.

10 For example, P. Clark, *English Provincial Society from the Reformation to the Revolution: Religion, Politics and Society in Kent 1500–1640* (Hassocks, 1977), esp. pp. 149–62. Margaret Spufford is notable in making an explicit attempt to investigate the religious opinions of 'the ordinary villager': Spufford, *Contrasting Communities*, ch. 13.

11 I. Luxton, 'The Reformation and popular culture', in F. Heal and R. O'Day (eds), *Church and Society in England: Henry VIII to James I* (London, 1977), pp. 73–7; P. Burke, *Popular Culture in Early Modern Europe* (London, 1978), pp. 223–9; C. Hill, *Society and Puritanism in Pre-Revolutionary England* (London, 1964).

12 The authors state that the parish was 'originally selected for the exceptional quality of its parish register': Wrightson and Levine, *Poverty and Piety*, p. ix.

13 C. Hill, 'Parliament and people in seventeenth-century England', *Past and Present*, Vol. XCII (1981), pp. 119–22. cf. J. A. Sharpe, 'The history of crime in late medieval and early modern England: a review of the field', *Social History*, Vol. VII (1982), p. 193.

14 Wrightson and Levine, *Poverty and Piety*, p. 183. See also K. Wrightson, *English Society*

1580–1680 (London, 1982), esp. pp. 212–13.

15 Population trends are exhaustively analysed in E. A. Wrigley and R. S. Schofield, *The Population History of England 1541–1871: A Reconstruction* (London, 1981). For a summary of agrarian trends, see J. Thirsk, 'Seventeenth-century agriculture and social change', in id. (ed.), *Land, Church and People: Essays Presented to Professor H. P. R. Finberg, Agricultural History Review*, Vol. XVIII, Supplement (1970), pp. 148–77.

16 Laslett *et al.*, *Bastardy and its Comparative History*, pp. 12–20 and chs 2–5 *passim*.

17 D. Cressy, *Literacy and the Social Order: Reading and Writing in Tudor and Stuart England* (Cambridge, 1980); M. Spufford, *Small Books and Pleasant Histories: Popular Fiction and its Readership in Seventeenth-Century England* (London, 1981), esp. chs 1–2.

18 For a demonstration of the increase in church court business in the dioceses of York, Chester and Norwich, see R. A. Marchant, *The Church under the Law: Justice, Administration and Discipline in the Diocese of York 1560–1640* (Cambridge, 1969), ch. 6. Further evidence will be offered in my forthcoming book on ecclesiastical justice in England 1580–1640. For the activities of county justices, see Wrightson, 'Two concepts of order'; Sharpe, 'The history of crime', pp. 191–2.

19 The literature is extensive. For two recent surveys, see Luxton, 'The reformation and popular culture', and Wrightson, *English Society*, ch. 7.

20 Wrightson, *English Society*, p. 171.

21 Hey, *An English Rural Community*.

22 Skipp, *Crisis and Development*, p. 82 and *passim*.

23 Spufford, *Contrasting Communities*, esp. chs 6–10, 13.

24 J. A. Sharpe, 'Crime and delinquency in an Essex parish 1600–1640', in J. S. Cockburn (ed.), *Crime in England 1550–1800* (London, 1977), pp. 90–109; cf. Sharpe, 'The history of crime', p. 193n.

25 P. Collinson, 'Cranbrook and the Fletchers: popular and unpopular religion in the Kentish Weald', in P. Newman Brooks (ed.), *Reformation Principle and Practice: Essays in Honour of Arthur Geoffrey Dickens* (London, 1980), pp. 173–202. For the town of Cranbrook, see P. Clark and P. Slack, *English Towns in Transition 1500–1700* (London, 1976), pp. 21–3.

26 For discussion of the relationship between religion and society in English towns generally in this period, see Clark and Slack, *English Towns in Transition*, pp. 149–51; W. J. Sheils, 'Religion in provincial towns: innovation and tradition', in Heal and O'Day, *Church and Society*, pp. 156–76. For studies of the particular towns mentioned in the text, see Collinson, 'Cranbrook and the Fletchers', pp. 194–6; Clark, *English Provincial Society, passim*; W. J. Sheils, *The Puritans in the Diocese of Peterborough 1558–1610* (Northamptonshire Record Society, Vol. XXX, 1979), ch. 8; P. Slack, 'Poverty and politics in Salisbury 1597–1666', in P. Clark and P. Slack (eds), *Crisis and Order in English Towns 1500–1700. Essays in Urban History* (London, 1972), pp. 164–203.

27 The main sources for the history of the parish in the period 1560–1640 are as follows. Public Record Office, London (hereafter PRO): Lay Subsidy Rolls (E 179); Prerogative Court of Canterbury: Will Registers (PROB 11). Wiltshire County Record Office, Trowbridge (hereafter WRO): Keevil Parish Register 1559–1664 (653/1); Keevil *cum* Bulkington Court Books, 1602–26, 1644–64 (288/1–2); Archdeaconry Court of Salisbury and Episcopal Consistory of Salisbury, Probate Records; Quarter Sessions Records (listed in M. G. Rathbone, *Guide to the Records in the Custody of the Clerk of the Peace for Wiltshire* (Wiltshire County Council, Guide to the Record Office, pt I, 1959), pp. 1–3); Salisbury Diocesan Records, especially court and visitation records of the bishop and archdeacon of Salisbury (listed in P. Stewart, *Guide to the Records of the Bishop, the Archdeacons of Salisbury and Wiltshire, and other Archidiaconal and Peculiar Jurisdictions ...* (Wiltshire County Council, Guide to the Record Offices, pt IV, 1973), esp. pp. 24–39, 57–60). Some aspects of the history of the parish are discussed in K. H. Rogers, 'Keevil', in *VCH Wilts.*, Vol. VIII, pp. 250–63, and M. J. Ingram, 'Ecclesiastical justice in Wiltshire 1600–1640, with special reference to cases concerning sex and marriage' (D.Phil. thesis, Oxford University, 1976), chs 2–11 *passim*.

28 Keevil was probably rather larger. The Compton Census figures of 463 communicants + 7 dissenters would, if accurate, indicate a total population of over 700 in 1676.

29   Hill, 'Parliament and people', p. 120.

30   For the background of trading difficulties, see G. D. Ramsay, *The Wiltshire Woollen Industry in the Sixteenth and Seventeenth Centuries* (London, 1943), ch. 5; B. E. Supple, *Commercial Crisis and Change in England 1600–1642* (Cambridge, 1959), chs 1–6 *passim*.

31   Ingram, 'Ecclesiastical justice in Wiltshire', pp. 100–1, 375–6; WRO, Quarter Sessions Great Rolls, Easter 1625/139.

32   For example, WRO, Archdeaconry Court of Salisbury Probate Records, Will of Thomas Taylour, 1639.

33   Rogers, 'Keevil', p. 263.

34   Ingram, 'Ecclesiastical justice in Wiltshire', pp. 375–6; M. J. Ingram, 'Communities and courts: law and disorder in early-seventeenth-century Wiltshire', in Cockburn, *Crime in England 1550–1800*, p. 133.

35   The very high mortality in Keevil in the late 1590s may be a relevant factor in accounting for the latter difference.

36   Ingram, 'Ecclesiastical justice in Wiltshire', pp. 198–9.

37   Wrightson and Levine, *Poverty and Piety*, p. 9.

38   For comments on the limitations of wills as evidence of religious belief and commitment, see Spufford, *Contrasting Communities*, ch. 13.

39   Rogers, 'Keevil', p. 260.

40   Spufford, *Contrasting Communities*, ch. 13.

41   ibid., p. 211; Cressy, *Literacy and the Social Order*, p. 49.

42   Cressy, *Literacy and the Social Order*, pp. 50–2; cf. Collinson, 'Cranbrook and the Fletchers', p. 188.

43   This suggestion was made to me by Margaret Spufford.

44   WRO, Archdeaconry Court of Salisbury Probate Records, Will of Christopher Gaffray, 1620.

45   WRO, Quarter Sessions Great Rolls, Trinity 1624/121; Keevil *cum* Bulkington Court Book 1602–26, View of Frankpledge 31 March 1 Car. (1625).

46   WRO, Keevil *cum* Bulkington Court Book 1602–26, View of Frankpledge 18 December 19 Jac. (1621).

47   WRO, Keevil *cum* Bulkington Court Book 1602–26, 4 September 9 Jac. (1611); Quarter Sessions Great Rolls, Michaelmas, 1611/108.

48   WRO, Salisbury Diocesan Records, Archdeaconry of Salisbury Act Book (Office) 13, 22 July 1624, *Office* v. *Aneave, Blagden, Elliot, Foote*; Episcopal Act Book (Office) 11, 23 July 1625, *Office* v. *Harris* (apparently referring to dancing, and so on, in the previous year).

49   WRO, Salisbury Diocesan Records, Episcopal Act Book (Office) 11, 31 October 1625, *Office* v. *Ford*.

50   PRO, STAC 8/59/11, membrane 2.

51   WRO, Salisbury Diocesan Records, Episcopal Act Book (Office) 2, fol. 11^V, *Office* v. *Blagden*; Episcopal Deposition Book 24, fols 60–75^V; Dean of Salisbury's Act Book 21, fol. 275, *Office* v. *Blagden*.

52   WRO, Archdeaconry Court of Salisbury Probate Records, Will of Robert Blackden, senior, 1635.

53   But some of the legacies to the ministers may have represented payment for services, for example, writing the will, and some of the bequests to Keevil church were for graves.

54   Ingram, 'Ecclesiastical justice in Wiltshire', pp. 353–5.

55   cf. Marchant, *Church under the Law*, p. 218.

56   Ingram, 'Ecclesiastical justice in Wiltshire', esp. pp. 86–90.

13 Godparenthood: the Fortunes of a Social Institution in Early Modern Christianity

JOHN BOSSY

Two years ago I published a paper on this subject in *Quaderni Storici*.[1] There the general topic of discussion was the relation of 'official' and 'popular' Christianity, and I wished to put forward the view that these were not properly to be considered as adversarial entities, either in substance, as suggested by Carlo Ginzburg, or in time, which would follow from Jean Delumeau's conception of the 'Christianisation' of the population of Europe in and after the sixteenth century. This volume is dealing specifically with early modern Europe, and I have thought it appropriate to offer a discussion of a more restricted problem, which is: For what reasons falling within the social history of Christianity did the institution of godparenthood fall into some discredit in the sixteenth century? The discredit was not universal, but it was widespread, and it placed those who maintained the institution in a markedly defensive position. It may seem a small question, though in fact I think it is a large one. At the end of this essay I shall offer some general, possibly over-general, thoughts intended to shed light on it.

I shall begin with some fairly elementary information about the theology, characteristics and earlier history of the institution, before attempting a description of its social reality in late medieval Catholicism – which is also to a large extent its social reality in early modern Catholicism, to go no farther.

Theology is our first topic. St Augustine said that it was characteristic of sacraments, as of all symbolic rites of religion, to establish relationships between people; among the sacraments of the medieval church, baptism is one of those where the relations created are expressly considered as relations of kinship. This does not seem to be a necessary fact, and some liturgical traditions, notably the Roman, have been rather nervous about it. It was not quite firmly the case in the West, as far as I can see, before the Carolingian period. Further, as the water symbolism shows, baptism represents the passage from one side of a river to the other; the child enters the rite as unredeemed and leaves it redeemed. According to St Paul, the proper analogy is of death and rebirth: we are baptised into Christ Jesus, not in him. Hence in principle we leave behind on the hither side of Jordan all the relationships, including kin relations, which we have had there: flesh and blood cannot inherit the kingdom of God. The important empirical fact, of course, was that after the early centuries of Christianity the subjects of baptism were normally infants.

These two considerations seem to me to have governed the practice of godparenthood in late medieval Christianity, which had five characteristics. First, it was a kin relation; secondly, it excluded natural parents; thirdly, it was plural, and bilateral in gender. Fourthly, the kin relation extended through the child to its natural kin, and to some extent between one godparent and another: the principle of *compaternitas* and its analogues, which in Latin languages at least provided the terms in which the institution was normally described. Last, a bar to marriage existed within the group so constituted.

This is no place to go into the historical stages through which the institution had reached this degree of elaboration, several of which seem in any case rather unclear. But three relevant points seem established. It had been worked out between roughly the seventh and the twelfth centuries, and was not therefore simply a consequence of infant baptism. Its essential characteristic, the exclusion of natural parents, was not primitive. And it had not on the whole been very congenial to Rome, which had attempted to maintain its own tradition of the single male *patrinus*.

The group into whose hands the child was delivered at the end of the complicated rites of medieval baptism, standing in for Christ as the most immediate body into which it was incorporated as a Christian, was in most cases a large one. Synods sought to restrict the number to three or four, and Boniface VIII, who tried to reaffirm the Roman tradition of the single godparent, was clearly a voice crying in the wilderness. Most baptismal registers, in so far as they were kept, recorded three, but clearly there were often many more, formally admitted or not. Joan of Arc at her trial named five, three male and two female, and said that her mother had told her that she had a lot more: at least three more seem to be mentioned incidentally.[2] Cases, perhaps aberrant, are reported from Venice of twenty or so. A would-be reformer at the Council of Basle in 1432 represented a feeling common among the clergy that the institution was getting totally out of hand: 'passim currunt in nonnullis provinciis homines catervatim ad levandum puerum de sacro fonte'.[3] Since this multiplication is the most obvious fact about godparenthood on the eve of the Reformation, my discussion will start from it.

It does not seem easy to reconcile with a view of the social function of the institution recently suggested by Pierre Chaunu that it was a form of patronage.[4] I would argue against this view on various grounds.

First, it does not seem compatible with the collapse in the West of the Roman tradition of the single male *patrinus*, despite efforts to revive it, as by the Council of Trent.

Secondly, the evidence is that the relationship of *compaternitas* was rather more prized than the godparent–child relation itself. This is certainly what one would conclude from the incidental references to the subject which come from Montaillou in the fourteenth century, from Domrémy in the fifteenth and from north-western Italy in the sixteenth. The only signs of anything resembling a patronal relation which emerge here are two cases from Friuli where women are taken by their *padrini* on night expeditions of a diabolic or similar kind, and this is hardly patronage in the sense intended.[5] The essentially egalitarian character of the relation described by Pitt-Rivers for twentieth-century Andalusia seems equally characteristic of the late medieval and early modern West; it distinguishes it sharply from the state of affairs in Spanish America, where *compadrazgo* has certainly been a patronal relation, and from the equally patronal *kumstvo* of Serbia, which may be characteristic of orthodox Christianity in general and does not seem to have existed among the Catholic south Slavs.[6]

Thirdly, it is certainly significant that godparenthood in the West seems to have risen to its highest degree of popularity at the same time as the powerful movement in the later Middle Ages towards the humanisation of the conception and iconography of the saints: the increasingly universal bestowal of saints' names brought godparents, who named the child and very commonly named it after themselves, and name-saints into an intimate relation, and led to what seems a general tendency to envisage the name-saint as him- or herself a *patrinus*. A. N. Galpern, discussing the traditional Christianity of sixteenth-century Champagne, explains that in the language of the time one must distinguish the saint as *patronus* of the parish, fraternity, or other collectivity, from the saint as *patrinus* or *parrain* of the individual who bears his name. The name-saint, like the *compadre* or *comadre* but unlike the saint-*patronus*, is voluntarily chosen, at least by the godparents, and a kinsman: hence he is a more attractive object of personal prayer than the professional or local *patronus*. The linguistic distinction seems to have been lost in later Catholic usage, though there is evidence for its popular survival, as from Portugal. Since the humanisation of the saints would seem a peculiarly Western phenomenon, there seems no difficulty in supposing that Western practice of godparenthood may have differed from that of other regions of Christendom.[7]

Finally, there is the practical question, capable in principle of an objective answer, to what extent godparents were habitually chosen from people of higher status than natural parents. This does seem to have been the case among the nobility, and possibly among those directly dependent on them like household servants. The assumption is strengthened, though to some extent counterbalanced, by the conscious adoption among the upper classes of the pious practice of picking for godparents two poor people chosen at random. Montaigne's father, who did this for his son, told him that the reason was 'que je fusse tenu de regarder plutôt vers celui qui me tend le bras que vers celui qui me tourne le dos'. The custom was condemned by Carlo Borromeo in the sixteenth century, and denounced by J.-B. Thiers at the end of the seventeenth, but seems to have been maintained by the Breton nobility until the Revolution. No doubt this was the choice of the minority, though a not insignificant one.

For the rest of the population I offer two English examples. One of the few registers of the Elizabethan Church of England to record godparents, that of the parish of Bilton near York, shows that at about a quarter of the baptisms one of the three recorded godparents was a member of the gentry (or at least called 'Mr' or 'Mrs'), more usually female than male, and that the child was quite often named after him or her. This seems a high proportion. On the other side, the early (eighteenth-century) registers of the post-Reformation English Catholic community, which was highly seigneurial in its structure, show an extremely low proportion: in the case of a congregation which had a resident family of Catholic gentry, the village of Lytham in Lancashire, the figure was 2·7 per cent and the children in question were invariably those of present or former domestic servants. Possibly something happened to English social attitudes between the sixteenth century and the eighteenth which made the gentry unwilling to countenance relationships which they had found acceptable in the century of the Reformation. If so, it also happened in Andalusia, where in modern times a godparent of higher status than the godchild seems rare. It seems more likely that outside the nobility he (or she) had never been a very common figure.[8]

My feeling that this judgement is correct is strengthened by two facts about Western godparenthood which are equally true, though they may seem contradictory. The first is that it is evident from the language in which the institution has been described, both popularly and officially, in late medieval/early modern times as in the twentieth-century Mediterranean world, that the principal preoccupation motivating the choice of godparents has been the creation of a formal state of friendship between the godparents and the natural family. Members of religious orders (though not secular priests) were forbidden to act as godparents because of the *amicitia* and *sodalitas* which would be created; an Irish synod of the seventeenth century legislated against the multiplication of godparents *amicitiae ineundae aut alia de causa*. The Irish were further alleged by William Camden to have been so strongly imbued with the connection as to have habitually chosen wolves as godparents for their children, on the grounds that the friendship so created would oblige the wolf to do them no harm. In Spain we have the institution of the *compadres/comadres de Carnaval*, whereby at the festival the young unmarried choose, or are given by lot, a certain number of others to whom they are in a relation of formal friendship.[9] In cases cited by nineteenth-century French folklorists, godparenthood and a liberally interpreted compaternity were the agents of a general state of formal amity in village communities; they may have been unusual, but it cannot be an accident that in English the word 'gossip' and in French 'commérage' have come to describe the corpus of amiable conversation within a community. All this suggests that the model of *compaternitas* as a relation of formal amity, entailing honesty, absolute mutual trust and obligatory assistance, a sacred and specifically Christian relationship, an ideal to which natural kinship aspires but perhaps rarely attains, has been in an important sense embedded in the entire history of the institution in the West; and that we should take patronal relations, where they occur, as a special case of friendship rather than vice versa.[10]

The claim may be thought to be contradicted by the extent to which godparents have been chosen from natural kin, which is perhaps statistically the most common case; though there have been occasions when it has been banned, as in late sixteenth-century France, under the influence of the social theologians of the Catholic League, anxious to defend the holiness of the institution and the Augustinian principle of the diffusion of charity by alliance.[11] At least from the sixteenth century, it has been widely held that grandparents have a special claim to the godparenthood of first-born children, and various sets of rules have been discovered for the choice of godparents from natural kin. One thing is common to them all, that they are obligatorily bilateral: a godparent on one side of the family must be balanced by a godparent of opposite sex on the other side. It is likely that the Tridentine restriction of the number of godparents to two allowed such bilateral systems to develop; but what is obvious is that the kinship-creating capacities of the sacrament were being used to reinforce the marriage alliance from which the child has been born, and what looks like an abandonment of the idea of compaternity as alliance was in fact a disguised form of it. It is true in Andalusia, and may be generally true, that where a compaternal relation is so created between people already related by marriage, it is held to be superior to the previous relationship, and takes precedence over it, for example, in forms of address. Kinship, that is, is transformed into friendship.[12]

Any significant connection between godparenthood and marriage is evidence against considering it a form of patronage, and this is not the only or perhaps the most interesting one. I should like to conclude this description with some thoughts about the incest barrier which since at least the twelfth century had been erected around the compaternal group. There is possibly something to be said here on the fundamental issue raised by Natalie Davis and Richard Trexler about the relation in late medieval/early modern social practice of the sacred and the profane. The evidence on the question seems contradictory. On one side there is strong modern evidence, mainly Spanish, that the barrier is firmly respected, more firmly indeed than the prevailing ecclesiastical legislation requires; within the group continence is regarded as a condition which both gives *compadrazgo* its sacred character and permits the absolute familiarity which the relationship entails. Signs of the same feeling, admittedly scrappy, may be found in our own period.[13] On the other side, there is a great deal of evidence from literature, law and folklore that continence might be breached. There is for example the story in Boccaccio's *Decameron* of Rinaldo who, wishing to become the lover of a wife, got himself chosen as godparent to her child in order to be able to visit her with perfect propriety and security. When the wife eventually admitted him to her bed she conceded that what they were about to do was a grave sin, but did it all the same. In another case, the man in the story died, went to Purgatory, returned and explained that he had got off lightly because it was full of people who were there expiating the same offence. If Boccaccio is thought a suspect source, one might cite the case of Pierre Clergue, priest of Montaillou, and his *commère* and mistress Beatrice de Planissoles; or, nearer home, a synodal statute of Florence dating from 1517 claiming precisely that the condition of *familiare consortium* created between two young godparents of opposite sex was likely to lead to marriage between them, and that parents had often chosen them with this object in view. This is likewise the burden of much proverbial wisdom about baptismal feasts and weddings. The relationship has been held to be 'often a sexually ambivalent one', and this ambivalence is probably implied in the Friulian stories about godfathers carrying off their daughters to sabbats and the like. It has certainly been a reliable source of jokes.[14]

Perhaps the joke-proneness of the relation is some kind of a clue to an otherwise perplexing problem: suggesting (rather like race relations, at least in Britain) a belief which in principle and in general practice is held to be sacred, but in certain precise circumstances, or when a proliferation of the sacred appears to be making impossible the continuation of normal life, or simply out of the need for human nature to blow off steam from time to time, may be breached with a particular kind of gusto. If that is true Luther, who approved of godparenthood and compaternity but rejected the bar to marriage as a nuisance invented by canon lawyers, was depriving Christendom of one of its modest pleasures. The Catholic hierarchy, responding in its own way, invented baptismal registers in order to ensure that young couples related by godparenthood should not, having it was alleged forgotten their relation, subsequently get married: a case which, to judge by ecclesiastical statutes, was pretty common. It does, however, seem improbable that a relation which parents clearly gave a good deal of thought to constructing (and which couples were apt to remember when contemplating divorce) should have been simply mislaid on a large scale, and more likely that this ecclesiastical cliché disguised a difference between a joke-prone population and a joke-resistant clergy (the difference being not whether the sacred was sacred, but how much entertainment was to be got out of the juxtaposition of the sacred and the profane).

Such juxtapositions were not to the liking of sixteenth-century reformers, Catholic or Protestant. Though most of them did not, like the Anabaptists and their sectarian descendants, abolish godparenthood along with infant baptism, they behaved towards it in an embarrassed and defensive way which indicates not only irritation with the more obvious features of late medieval baptismal practice, but a real incapacity to fathom its underlying principles. The Council of Trent tried, vainly, to revive the single Roman *patrinus*, and was finally satisfied with a pair of symbolic parents: thereafter Catholic bishops spent a century or so trying to persuade their flocks of the virtues of this system. Most magisterial reformers thought that the institution could be defended as making provision for the Christian instruction of the child, but viewed it as a substitute for the natural parents, to be activated if these were disenabled by death or otherwise from performing their natural or providential function: the first statement of this theme which I have seen is in a Hussite baptismal ritual of the fifteenth century. Among them Calvin was nearest to a complete abolitionist: the theology of the covenant seemed to require that the body into which the child was incorporated after baptism should be its natural family; his baptismal rite carefully avoided specifying who was to present the child, but implied that it should be the father. In practice, Geneva, like Rome, seems to have fallen back on the single male *patrinus*; but many English Genevans insisted that only the natural parents could present the child, or make the promises on its behalf. One refused to baptise the child of a sick father without a certificate that he would personally answer for it as soon as he was able. The general discredit of godparenthood among the clergy of the English Reformation has been illustrated from the case of the seventeenth-century parson Ralph Josselin, who did not use the word or think much of the relation.[15] Josselin's attitude was certainly not universal among Anglican clergy, and it seems that it would have been found exceedingly strange by contemporary Lutheran pastors, or at least by their wives; the pastor's wife in her capacity as godmother looks like an important agent in the diffusion of evangelical domesticity from the households of the clergy to the rest of the population. We should not exaggerate the extent to which the late medieval practice of godparenthood was actually affected during the sixteenth century, or overdo the consensus among reformers. But in so far as there was reform, it was generally the effect of a reversal of unstated assumptions about Christianity as a social system: a passage from exclusion to inclusion as the primary status of natural parents in respect of the Christian family.

If then we are looking for explanations in the general field of social history for the problem about godparents in the sixteenth century, and hence in a small way for the problem about reformation, we might consider three possibilities.

If my analysis is correct, one of them may be excluded: if godparenthood was not a system of patronage, its relative discredit cannot be explained by anti-hierarchical feelings in general, or by hostility to late medieval forms of clientage or patronage in particular.

By contrast, it seems attractive to look for explanations in the history of feelings about the family. Seen in this context, the problem about godparenthood must have had some connection with a certain shift from extensive to concentrated conceptions of the family, with a tendency to identify the family with the domestic unit and to regard its function as principally educative.

Finally, one kind of general relevance of a history of godparenthood to problems of European social history may be underlined: its acute and perhaps exceptional capacity to provide evidence about what Natalie Davis has, rightly in my view, identified as a central topic of social history: that is to say, the exact location of the boundary between the self and others. A traditional practice of godparenthood, and the traditional rite of Christian baptism upon which it was constructed, entailed a strong feeling for the permeability of these borders, for the possibility of identification between the self and others. Among those who may be cited as evidence for a rising sense in sixteenth-century Europe that any such identification was mythological are those Elizabethan Protestants who found it inconceivable that, at a Christian baptism, a newborn child, speaking through the mouths of an assorted group of its parents' relatives, friends and neighbours, should answer a question phrased in the second person singular with a singular 'I will'.

Notes: Chapter 13

1 'Padrini e madrine: un'istituzione sociale del christianesimo popolare in Occidente', trans. Gianna Pomata, in *Religioni delle classi popolari*, no. 41 of *Quaderni storici*, Vol. XIV (1979), pp. 440–9; to which, and to my previous 'Blood and baptism: kinship, community and Christianity in Western Europe, 14th–17th centuries', in D. Baker (ed.), *Studies in Church History*, Vol. X (Oxford, 1973), pp. 13–35, I refer for further annotation.

2 R. Pernoud, *Joan of Arc* (English trans., London, 1964), pp. 15 ff., 18, 32, 174.

3 *Concilium Basiliense*, ed. H. Dannenbauer, Vol. VIII (Basle, 1936), p. 33.

4 P. Chaunu, *Le Temps des Réformes* (Paris, 1975), pp. 178 ff.

5 E. Le Roy Ladurie, *Montaillou* (English translation by Barbara Bray, London, 1978), pp. 67, 206, 228, 251 ff., 310 ff.; C. Ginzburg, *I Benandanti* (Turin, 1974), pp. 101, 148.

6 J. Davis, *People of the Mediterranean* (London, 1977), pp. 223–32; J. Pitt-Rivers, *The People of the Sierra*, 2nd edn (Chicago and London, 1971), pp. 106 ff.

7 A. N. Galpern, 'The legacy of late mediaeval religion in sixteenth-century Champagne', in C. Trinkaus and H. Oberman (eds), *The Pursuit of Holiness* (Leiden, 1974), pp. 154 ff.; Davis, *People of the Mediterranean*, pp. 231 ff.

8 'Padrini e madrine', pp. 444 ff.; Pitt-Rivers, *The People of the Sierra*, p. 108.

9 J. Caro Baroja, *El Carnaval* (Madrid, 1965), p. 383.

10 Cf. J. Pitt-Rivers, 'The kith and the kin', in J. Goody (ed.), *The Character of Kinship* (Cambridge, 1973), pp. 89–105; id., *The People of the Sierra*, pp. 140 ff.

11 E. Martène and U. Durand (eds), *Thesaurus novus anecdotorum*, Vol. IV (Paris, 1717; repr. New York, 1968), p. 1002; cf. Natalie Davis, "Ghosts, kin and progeny: family life in sixteenth-century France', *Daedalus*, Vol. CVI, no. 2 (1977), pp. 87–144.

12 'Padrini e madrine', pp. 445 ff.; Pitt-Rivers, *The People of the Sierra*, pp. 98 ff., 107.

13 ibid., p. 107; Davis, *People of the Mediterranean*, pp. 230 ff.; cf. J.-L. Flandrin, *Familles: parenté, maison et sexualité dans l'ancienne société* (Paris, 1976), p. 35; and the following extract from the will of John Musgrave of Wortley, Leeds, 9 June 1534, kindly communicated to me by Dr Claire Cross (*Thoresby Society Publications*, Vol. XI, Leeds, 1904, p. 293): 'Also I will that John my son take not to his wife Agnes Bussye, for she is my god daughter . . .'

14 Boccaccio, *Decameron*, Seventh Day, Third Story, also Tenth Story (English translation by G. H. McWilliam, London, 1972), pp. 532, 580; Le Roy Ladurie, *Montaillou*, pp. 164, 245, n. 2; R. Trexler, *Synodal Law in Florence and Fiesole, 1308–1518*, Studi e Testi, no. 268 (Vatican City, 1971), p. 67; Davis, *People of the Mediterranean*, p. 231.

15 P. Collinson, *The Elizabethan Puritan Movement* (London, 1966), pp. 367 ff.; A. Macfarlane, *The Family Life of Ralph Josselin* (Cambridge, 1970), pp. 144 ff.

14 Confraternities, *Curés* and Communities in Rural Areas of the Diocese of Lyons under the Ancien Régime

JEAN-PIERRE GUTTON, translated by John Burke

The theme of 'religion and community' allows us to analyse the relations existing between resident community and parish. I have chosen to treat this question within the reference points of the old diocese of Lyons, an area in which I have undertaken or directed research in religious history. This vast enough area then included the departments of Rhône and Loire, while another part, and in some ways an important one, was comprised of Isère, Ain and the Jura. I hope to demonstrate that the ties between community and parish were very complex, considering that the parish was given life by many forces which were not necessarily convergent.

I

For the most part, *Lyonnais* resident communities under the ancien régime did not have anything more than a very loose structure. Nothing is found here to compare with the villages of Languedoc or, more markedly still, of Provence. Communities had only few possessions; in particular, there was a town hall only in exceptional cases. Few archives, or none at all, are preserved outside those in private hands, and the community's representative – the syndic – was not always a permanent institution. The essential business was to collect taxes for the king's account, and the important persons were the consuls, or consul, who were assessors-collectors. Therefore, the community remained very close to its administrative origins, which were those of the tax unit.

Nevertheless, resident communities led an intense collective life. In simple terms, the supports of this collective life were situated in an interspace, difficult to define, but situated between the resident community and the parish. Let me describe the situation which prevailed until about 1600–50. The collective life of the village was assured in the first place by confraternities of the Holy Spirit which sometimes exchanged this name for that of the patron saint of the place. The whole community was gathered together by these confraternities: living and dead, rich and poor. Certain confrères made a donation to the confraternity, asking to be maintained after their death, to benefit from the prayers of all. There were therefore living and

202

dead confrères, and at mealtimes the dead confrères were represented by the poor. One of the aims of the confraternity was mutual assistance. This was shown by a common meal and also by distributions – bread, 'lard', beans, peas, cheese, salt, wine – handed out at the time appointed for the feast of Pentecost. These distributions, although they may have been called 'aumônes' (alms), were never linked to a state of poverty, but to the confrère's rank. The confraternity generally united the whole village, rich as well as poor. And there are still more tangible signs of assimilation by the confraternity of place and community. In the *Lyonnais* region, as in others, the origin of the community seems tied, in part, to the existence of these confraternities. The first syndics of the community may have been those of the confraternity of the Holy Spirit. At Irigny, at the beginning of the fifteenth century, two 'procureurs de la ville et paroisse' censed the confraternity's vineyard in the name of the community. At the end of the same century, the 'prudhommes' of the confraternity of Saint-Cyr-au-Mont-d'Or were similarly called 'procureurs de la communauté de Saint-Cyr'. At Condrieu, the consuls of the community were rectors of the confraternity. Together with other factors (development of fiscality, the Hundred Years' War, and so on), the confraternities of the Holy Spirit facilitated the consolidation of communal autonomy in the sixteenth century. They permitted a local group to arrange and to serve an apprenticeship in municipal life.

Another characteristic of these confraternities of the Holy Spirit was the possession of often important goods, acquired through donations and bequests. This capital consisted of rents, lands, vines and houses, and these possessions were sometimes administered as goods of the community. Furthermore, the 'maison de la frairie' might be the place where the community assembled, as was the case at Ceyzériat and Rive-de-Gier, or the presbytery might have been the confraternity's property. This confusion between confraternity of the Holy Spirit and community could, finally, be carried much further. A document dating from 1601 shows that at Ceyzériat, entry into the resident community and use of common lands were tied to admission, after payment of a fee and acceptance, to the confraternity of the Holy Spirit.

One of the roles of the confraternities of the Holy Spirit lay in the organisation of the patronal feast. This was a great affair – involving organisation of the 'fête baladoire', where dancing, gaming, tournaments, sometimes a real theatrical representation took place – which demonstrates once again the role of these confraternities in giving cohesion to the community. However, in this task the confraternities of the Holy Spirit were joined by other groups to which they were attached by ties which are hard to unravel. These were the 'kingdoms' (*royaumes*) and the youth of the parish.

The *royaumes*, or *reinages*, are to be found throughout central France and particularly in the area of Lyons. A 'kingdom' consisted of the annual public auction sale of titles: king, queen, dauphin, constable, page, chamberlain, and so on. These auctions took place in the church or church porch, and sales were made in wax or oil more often than in *livres tournois*.

The proceeds would also be used for the maintenance of church lighting. For the title-holder, the 'kingdom' was a manifestation of piety, but it was also a token of belonging to the community. Newcomers sought these ephemeral and expensive titles. Above all, the 'king' was charged, at least in certain cases, with the organisation of the patronal feast, a heavy and sometimes costly task. And it is here that links with confraternities are difficult to specify. At Montarcher, a parish of upper Forez, the confraternity of St Pantaléon, patron of the parish, was in charge of the patronal feast. A *baile* of the confraternity, appointed each year, paid for musicians on the day of the feast of St Pantaléon and the following Sunday. But the parish register shows that the last nomination of the *baile* dates from 1497. Three years before that date a new organisation, a 'kingdom', had taken charge of the feast. Kings and queens of St Pantaléon and, on the other hand, of the Assumption, which name had been joined in 1496 to those of the Holy Spirit and the patron saint of the parish, were elected. Moreover, two 'septchaux' (*sénéchaux*) had more particular responsibility for the feast. This example suggests a dependence between the two institutions: a hypothesis – and a simple one – which I do not propose to extend in the absence of further proof, but which is confirmed to a small extent by an incident which happened in 1538 at l'Hôpital-sous-Rochefort. There the confrères refused to pay a contribution to the king towards the expenses of the feast, notably covering the expenses of the tambour-players.

There remains a third institution, that of youth. It can carry the name of 'abbeys of youth', 'enfants de la ville', or more simply 'garçons de paroisse'. It often represents not so much collective youth as the group of celibates, without ties, unstable persons, as against the stable world of marriage. Hence responsibility for defending and carrying high the community's honour in the brawls which so often accompanied festivities and fairs fell to this group. Its tasks also included the policing of meetings between young men and girls and of marriages. The 'garçons de paroisse' kept watch on the conduct of young girls, for misconduct could bring the community into bad repute. They watched to prevent young men from other areas or widowers from spiriting away any of the village girls of marriageable age. The demands for monetary compensation or charivaris which followed marriages in which husband and wife were of disproportionate ages are thus explained. The jurisdiction of 'garçons de paroisse' extended also to young married couples on whom strange ordeals could be imposed on the first Sunday in Lent. Finally, in many communities the responsibility for organising the patronal feast lay with the 'garçons de paroisse'. Thus it is evident that confusion over the confraternity of the place, the *royaume* and the 'garçons de paroisse' can be insoluble. In each village one or other of the three institutions was responsible for the feast; but in all cases, under different names, the same men were involved. There are, in addition, other proofs of the links between confraternities, *reinages* and 'garçons de paroisse'. At Boën, the confraternity's house included frescoes depicting the Holy Spirit, the patron of the parish, but also St Nicholas, the patron of youth. In such a village, auctions benefiting the *reinage* were split up into 'dances' and this method of appointing kings and queens corresponded to the method by which youth abbots were sometimes chosen. Elsewhere the kings had a right of jurisdiction comparable to that of the youth abbots. At Saint-Symphorien-sur-Coise, on St Symphorien's and on St Bartholomew's day (24 August) he had the right, surrounded by officers, to judge certain offences – notably adulteries – committed between 22 and 24 August. This jurisdiction is comparable to that of the youth abbots. And when, towards the mid-seventeenth century, *reinages* were suppressed, they were replaced, in the organisation of the feast of St Symphorien, by an association of young people.

Little importance can be attached to the inextricable ties between the three institutions which one continually comes up against. The important thing is that they held village society together. In fact, since community and parish did not coincide, it was really the parish which was united by these institutions. The community as a tax unit played a very insignificant part in this; and the *curé*'s role in this respect was not pre-eminent. What is important is that lay power was expressed through institutions which, being parochial, were independent of the hierarchy. This situation, however, was to change gradually over the last two centuries of the ancien régime. Under the influence of Tridentine reform, *curés*, henceforth much less close to the people, fought against these three forms of association and, at least in the case of the first two, busied themselves transforming them, even to the point of distorting their meaning.

II

Even before the Tridentine reforms were implemented, the confraternities of the Holy Spirit were to fall first victim of this development. Royal legislation in the sixteenth century, particularly the Ordonnance of Orléans, had denounced the banquets of confraternities and ordered them to be suppressed. Effective suppressions there had been. In February 1561, at Saint-Symphorien-sur-Coise, Charles IX's Letters Patent appropriated the possessions and revenues of the confraternity in order to found a college. In 1566 Letters Patent authorised the creation of a college at Boën, foreseeing that it would be set up 'in the house of the confraternity of the said place' and that it would annexe the revenues of the confraternities of Boën and of surrounding villages. The Wars of Religion, on the other hand, ensured that a certain number of rents were paid no longer. Above all, the bishops and *curés* occupied themselves in transforming these confraternities. They set out to purify them, which is to say they attacked almsgiving and the Whitsuntide banquet at the same time. Alms had to be distributed to the 'true' poor, not simply to anybody. Here is a new conception of assistance: almsgiving is no longer considered pleasing to God in all cases and conducive to the love of one's neighbour, therefore to solidarity; rather, it should not encourage idleness and sloth and therefore it should be selective. As for the banquet, it was one of the aspects of communal conviviality repudiated in favour of devotion. In one of the very rare cases where the creation of a new confraternity of the Holy Spirit was permitted, the letters of authorisation specify that the *curé* who presides over the confraternity will partake of the meal which will be 'a frugal meal in which the confrères will partake to maintain fellowship and proper understanding amongst themselves, at which meal the said *curé* assists with his vicar, during which meal the statutes and rules of the said confraternity are read and which, as much for the assembly of the said confrères as for refection, shall not last but an hour and a half or thereabouts, from which they shall not go out but to be present at Vespers'. Such an attitude was systematised by a ruling made in 1749 by the Archbishop de Tencin at a meeting with all the confraternities of the Holy Spirit: only those confrères concerned with helping the poor through the confraternity's funds might remain in the association; almsgiving and the meal were suppressed, the revenues of the confraternity were to be distributed, in money or bread, to the poor; all of these measures were to be put into operation under the *curé*'s authority. In the seventeenth and eighteenth centuries the *curé*, with the title of 'conseiller', was one of the officers of the confraternity, and even before the publication of this ruling he assisted at the Pentecostal meal, drew up the list of persons benefiting from almsgiving and occasionally oversaw the distribution of alms. In fact there are many examples, before as well as after this general ruling, of an evolution of this kind. In 1671, in the parish of Ailleux in Forez, the confraternity's house was reunited to the church, the banquet suppressed and the revenues diverted to repair of the church and poor relief. It is true that in 1705 the *curé* had to start afresh the fight against the banquet. At Saint-Germain-Laval, the confraternity's revenues were misappropriated by a person who was looking after the church buildings. It was the *curé* of the not inconsiderable village who, in 1726, made him restore the revenues and, once recovered, put them to use in the maintenance of a hospital for the poor. In 1738 he asked the residents to use these revenues to establish the nuns of Saint-Joseph-du-Puy in the parish. These religious women were at that time concerned with the sick, the poor and the instruction of children. Similarly, at Neuville-sur-Saône the confraternity of the Holy Spirit disappeared in the mid-seventeenth century and its possessions went to a 'poor-relief department' presided over by the *curé*. It is therefore clear that, in all cases, if the confraternity's goods stayed in service of the community, it was henceforth under the control of the *curé*, who acted as the administrator. That residents had perceived the danger in this dispossession is shown by the occasional instances of resistance to these changes. In 1641, at Saint-Romain-le-Puy, they boycotted an auction sale of the ruined buildings of the confraternity. The proceeds of the sale were to have been used for the construction of the presbytery. In 1671, at Rive-de-Gier, many residents were opposed to the transfer of the goods of the confraternity of the Holy Spirit to the Hôtel-Dieu and church lighting fund. In 1751 the syndics and twenty-five inhabitants of Pérouges were opposed to the suppression of alms-giving, the Pentecostal banquet and the unification of the goods of the confraternity and those devoted to the fabric of the church. All of these were rearguard actions, but they are evidence of the slowness of changes taking place in the resident community.

At the same time as they fought against old confraternities, Tridentine *curés* favoured new devotions. In particular, two types of confraternities, those of the Rosary and Holy Sacrament, were created, whether by initiative or by the encouragement of pastors. At the time of the pastoral visits of 1657 and 1662, the Archbishop Camille de Neuville declared the existence of 296 confraternities. Out of this total, 124 were confraternities of the Rosary and 48 confraternities of the Holy Sacrament. These figures merely indicate a temporary situation. In fact, the confraternities in honour of the Virgin, and notably those of the Rosary, were established at the beginning of the seventeenth century; but it was not until the second half of the seventeenth century that the confraternities of the Holy Sacrament were established, foundations which continued to be made until the mid-eighteenth century. Confraternities of the Holy Sacrament, means of eucharistic devotion, were particularly characteristic of Tridentine reform. Now, the role of the *curé* was not limited to the creation of the confraternity. In the villages the *curé* was at the head of the association, bearing the title of rector. His name was first on the list of confrères, preceding those of one or several vicars, members, like him, of the confraternity. He guided the parishioners in the choice of the feast of the confraternity, nominated the officers who directed it and, more important still, examined the accounts. He frequently possessed a key to the coffer where the confraternity's archives were preserved. When the confraternity had no premises of its own, and met in the parish church, this coffer was found in the sacristy. Control of a confraternity's finances seemed to be a guarantee of propriety in public activities. A return to the practices of the confraternities of the Holy Spirit was thus avoided. If, finally, even the reception of new members took place in the *curé*'s presence, control of the new confraternity was all the more effectively in his hands. This fashion of controlling new confraternities was, of course, a way of diffusing Counter-Reformation devotion. Altars consecrated to intercessory saints of a rural type – Blaise, Antoine, and so on – were henceforth dedicated to the Rosary or Holy Sacrament. It was also a way of controlling the leisure activities of rural folk. The synodal statutes which recommended *curés* to establish a confraternity of the *Très Saint Sacrement* specified very clearly that the feasts, supervised by them, would proceed without 'dances publiques ... vogue ou autres divertissements' (public dancing ... parades, or other entertainment). Moreover, feasts of new confraternities occasionally had the aim of competing with traditional feasts.

This last aspect is still more clear with respect to the church's attitude to 'kingdoms'. This demonstrates that the clergy not only opposed traditional culture but were also drawn at the time of the Tridentine reform into a battle for control of youth, at least celibate youth. It is hard to avoid the impression that, given the two institutions which provided for youth, *reinages* and abbeys of youth, the church decided to christianise the first and stamp out the second. A decisive choice, certainly; but perhaps the consequences were fatal, for the institution which survived, and remained for a long time the most active, was really that of the 'garçons de paroisse', abbeys of youth. And this may partly explain the church's subsequent loss of male youth. The facts are there, at all events. Tridentine sensibility was shocked by the noisy demonstrations of the *reinages*. The *Lyonnais* branch of the *Compagnie du Saint-Sacrement* decided, in 1646, to 'solliciter l'abolition de l'usage de crier les royaumes dans les églises, attendu le scandale qu'ils y causent' (request the abolition of calling *royaumes* in the churches, considering the scandal they cause there). One of the members of this same company, Noël Chomel, denounced the custom which consisted in throwing holy water by the handful over the 'king'. The work of purification was conducted with effect. The auction sale no longer took place in the church, but in the open air. New 'kingdoms' were created, under the influence of, and sometimes at the suggestion of, the *curé*. Thus, from 1638 to 1655, in the parishes of Charly and Vernaison, *reinages* were instituted in honour of St Anthony, St Vincent, *Notre-Dame d'aoust*, St Roch, St Denis, St Laurence, St Nicholas, St Mary-Magdalen, St Abdon and St Sennen. Certain 'kingdoms' were, from that time, exclusively feminine, as a sort of counterbalance to the ancient, very masculine, *royaumes*. Women or children were the most common members of village *reinages* dedicated to this or that saint. These new 'kingdoms' were *royaumes* of devotion. Someone became king or queen, and was placed under the protection of the Virgin or of a saint. The proceeds of auctions sometimes served for the maintenance of a confraternity, or to supply the church with wax or oil. Sometimes statues were commissioned with this money. And the 'kingdom's' festivities were quiet ones, even if the celebration occurred on the day of a traditional feast, the better to christianise it.

It remains to be said that new confraternities and *reinages* were not capable of constituting by themselves the framework of village social life. In what was often a loosely structured form, but a lively one, the 'garçons de paroisse' formed a pocket of resistance to the influence of Tridentine *curés*. As organisations without written statutes their archives have not come down to us. Their tangles with authorities have simply left traces in judicial documents. The brawls which accompanied village festivities, in the course of which the honour of the village was defended by the 'garçons de paroisse', ensured that the protocols of the *marechaussée* (the mounted constabulary) speak clearly of their role in these circumstances. Similarly, their conflicts with the *curés* can be encountered in the papers of ordinary jurisdiction, and occasionally in those of ecclesiastical courts. In 1683 the *curé* of a Beaujolais parish, Saint-Étienne-la-Varenne, refused to confess two boys who had danced in the *fête-baladoire*; he shunned the wax offered by the 'king' of the patronal feast. In 1777 the *curé* of Claveisolles beat a young man of the village with a stick, following a hot pursuit. The reason was apparently the theft of some cherries; in fact the youth was part of a group of young people who played music before the great door of the church. In 1779 several *curés* of the diocese supplicated the Parlement of Paris for an injunction which would prohibit young people gathering at patronal feasts. They complained, in their plea, of debauches, violent behaviour and brawls occasioned by these assemblies.

The merit of having been the first to attempt to quantify the evidence of these conflicts in judicial archives falls to an American historian, Philip Hoffman. Using criminal pleas from the bailiwick of Beaujolais, and by taking samples, he obtained the results shown in Table 14.1.

Table 14.1 *Conflicts between* Curé *and Parishioners in the Bailiwick of Beaujolais Shown as a Percentage of the Total Number of Proceedings Examined*

	Conflicts between curé *and parishioners*
	%
Before 1650	0·9
1650–1700	2·6
1701–50	2·9
1751–88	3·9

These conflicts were centred less on material problems (tithes, repairs to the presbytery, and so on) than on fundamental differences – opposition to religious reforms, resistance to the *curé*'s influence in community organisations, tensions between the *curé* and local elites or youth groups. It should also be noted that Hoffman's inquiry established two important points. First, it is the men (and notably the young people) who turn up in these proceedings. This confirms a known fact: the Counter-Reformation, which was running into difficulties where male power was concerned, was better assimilated by women. Secondly, the proportion of pleas coming from lay persons reached a notable climax from 1751 to 1788.

III

It is time to draw conclusions from all these facts, or to attempt to do so. There are a number of ways in which the increasing number of conflicts between parishioners and *curés* at the end of the ancien régime, and their being more often due to the initiative of lay persons, might be explained. Is it, perhaps, a proof of that 'dechristianisation' which historians trace at different periods? We will return to this question. In any case, it demonstrates that villagers were not happy to accept assaults by Tridentine *curés* on ancient customs and institutions. In this respect, there is a difference from the town, where proceedings involving *curé* and parishioners are almost unheard of. Catholic reform penetrated later in the countryside. Here the *curé* was a cultural intermediary, of a culture which can be qualified in general terms as that of the town. From the moment when the *curé* no longer contented himself with participating in ancient practices by blessing them but set out to play a reforming role in the parish, it was inevitable that repercussions would follow, and so much more so when the concern of the reformer led to intervention in the temporal domain, that of charity, for example. Thus the *curé* became a kind of ambassador, encouraged by the Crown which was happy to find someone on the spot to pass on its directives which to a remarkable extent lacked local officials to carry them out. The action of the *curés* favoured centralisation and the creation of more structured institutions which were likewise more dependent on central power, for example, that of oligarchically structured councils, or that controlled by *intendants*. The *curé* played a greater role when the traditional parish was obliterated in favour of the tax unit which became the new administrative framework. It was in more secular institutions that the *curé* was to play, above all in the eighteenth century, an important role.

All of this kept pace with the rise of the state, and of a classic culture suspicious of old autonomies. And when there was less fear that the misconduct of young girls and women would attract a curse on the community, the influence of youth groups could only decrease. The administrative influence of *curés* on the village level thus appears to have been linked to the progress of centralisation and, finally, to central power. The parish was formerly a way of tying the community together; at the end of the ancien régime the parish, now represented by the *curé*, could have a dissolving effect on the old ties. In summary, the Tridentine parish was integrated in the rise of a community which was traditional no longer but which, under the control of the state, became an administrative unit. This administrative unit multiplied gatherings beyond those of Sunday, named those accountable known by the *intendant* and accepted the written word and the reading of ordinances drawn up in French.

There is another conclusion which I consider important. It relates to 'dechristianisation'. The combined efforts of state and Tridentine *curés* were evidently not very favourable to the role of the parish. There was a laicisation of local life, in favour of transforming the parish into a tax unit and, above all, of central power. Urban culture imposed by the Tridentine reform did not, perhaps, favour christianisation in the country, as Jean Delumeau suggests. In the end, wishing to organise youth groups, the church chose to christianise the *reinages* and fight against the 'garçons de paroisse'. In the long term at least, this signifies that it made its choice against the structure which remained the most active and which would have the most longevity. A whole series of studies now emphasises the resurgence of youth associations in the revolutionary period and in the nineteenth century. Finally, as it did this, the church consistently favoured women above men. Might this be one of the reasons for the quicker detachment from the church of men compared to women?

In the history of the village, even more than in other fields of historical research, it is possible to understand the past only by seeing it as a whole.

Note: Chapter 14

References to the documents will be found in: J.-P. Gutton, 'Reinages, abbayes de jeunesse et confréries dans les villages de l'ancienne France', *Cahiers d'Histoire*, Vol. IV (1975), pp. 443–53; id., *Villages du Lyonnais sous la monarchie (XVIème-XVIIIème siècles)* (Lyons,

1973); id., *La Sociabilité villageoise dans l'ancienne France: Solidarités et voisinages du XVIème au XVIIIème siècles* (Paris, 1979).

The following thesis, prepared at Lyons for the degree of Ph.D., may be consulted to great advantage, particularly for its analysis of proceedings between *curés* and parishioners: Philip Hoffman, 'Church and community: the parish clergy and the Counter Reformation in the diocese of Lyon: 1500–1789' (typescript, Yale University, 1979).

15 Organisational Forms of Popular Piety in Rural Old Bavaria (Sixteenth to Nineteenth Centuries)

HERMANN HÖRGER, translated by Deborah Monroe and Lyndal Roper

'Popular piety' (*Volksfrömmigkeit*)[1] is a concept which stands in urgent need of a more precise and critical investigation than it is currently receiving. Though piety imbues society as a whole with meaning, it is embedded in a distinctly stratified social structure where each stratum experiences and forms that piety differently. Taken in its entirety, it is an expression of the life of a society and it allows us to make inferences about its concurrent, various modes and about changes in them.[2] The more complex and differentiated the structure of a society, the more subtle and difficult it is to grasp its religious life as practised by its individual groups.[3] Even in the more highly developed societal form of the city, it is impossible to avoid speaking of popular piety, if by this we mean the form and expression of religious life.

Such an investigation can best be pursued by selecting simple and surveyable societal forms which change little over time. Rural parishes in Old Bavaria, which have been studied in detail elsewhere,[4] provide the core material for this investigation, augmented by comparisons with examples from the Swabian region of Bavaria and the lower Austrian *Waldviertel*. The first point to notice is that it was not the regional character but rather the varying forms of authority and social structure in these parishes which led to differing expressions of religious life and sensibility.[5]

There is hardly any consensus about what should be understood by 'popular piety'. It is problematic either to place it as a third, independent type of devotion within Catholicism, somewhere between objective liturgy and private prayer, or to count it merely as an ornamentation of the cult and liturgy of a high religion.[6] And these difficulties arise partly because liturgy itself, *leitourgia*, is always understood as *leiton ergon*, as an act and religious expression of the people, even if the people's participation in this act seems to be restricted to a few acclamations.[7]

Neither can popular piety be understood, as Friedrich Heiler suggests, as that ancient popular belief which gives expression to a *religio innata*, that is to say, as a common property of humankind.[8] Popular piety is primarily liturgy celebrated by faithful folk, from the simplest form of private prayer to the high form of the liturgy of the mass. What is essential is that the ecclesiastical forms of worship should take up general human concerns and allow space for independent, though guided, meditation: take, for example, the problem of mortality, that is, of life and death, or of light and darkness, freedom and bondage, guilt and redemption, to suggest only a few pairs of opposites which are dealt with inside the framework of religious practice. Seen from this perspective, it is irrelevant whether non-Christian or pre-Christian elements found their way into Christianity or were accommodated within it. Every human being moves in the tension between life and death. Coming to terms with this reality is a fundamental human concern, whether within or outside the historical parameters of a religion. Thus it is almost inevitable that the liturgical celebrations centred on Christ should coincide with the natural turning-points of the solar year, and that a ritual of procreation, representing new life in God, should be built into the celebration of Easter night: the Easter candle, signifying the risen Christ, is immersed in the baptismal font, the womb of the church, to invest the church with divine life.[9]

This, however, is not to be understood as a concession to popular piety or to pagan survivals, but rather as an essential condition of the fact that people can assimilate what takes place in worship, and that worship can have concrete effects on their own lives.

Let us now turn to the organisational forms of piety as they were practised over a three hundred-year period by devout folk in the cities and countryside of Old Bavaria. These forms of piety find expression indirectly, in sources which historians have, for the most part, not considered worthy of attention.[10] We have to distinguish the formal elements of time[11] and place. To these, a further dimension can be added, which might be described as the internalisation and translation of religious values into the daily life of the individual and his or her society.

The two dominant feast-cycles[12] of the church year[13] are determined by the solar and lunar years. The fixed Christmas feast-cycle is based on the solar year: the celebration of the birth of Christ's precursor, John the Baptist, falls on the day of the summer solstice, the turning-point of the old into the new; the feast of the Annunciation, Christ's becoming flesh, falls on the day of the spring equinox; and finally, the festival of the birth of Christ falls on the day of the winter solstice, that is, the birthday celebration of the Roman *sol invictus*. The feasts of Circumcision and Epiphany belong to this narrower circle of feasts too;[14] and the feast of the Transfiguration (6 August) – that is, the manifestation of the numinous in human existence[15] – should also be classified as belonging to the Christmas feast-cycle.

In addition, there is a close, even inextricable relationship between the Christmas feast-cycle and a series of feasts of St Mary.[16] They were introduced into church life only after centuries of ecclesiastical debate; but, amazingly, their themes had been common property of the arts for centuries and they ought rather to be understood as *vox populi* expressions of popular piety. So, for example, centuries before the Immaculate Conception (1854) and Assumption (1950) were declared dogma, these feasts constituted a common property of worship by the faithful, as evidenced, inter alia, by the iconography of church interiors since the fourteenth and fifteenth centuries at least.[17]

Together with these celebrations come the very deeply rooted festivals of Purification or Candlemas (February 2), the Visitation (July 2), Mary's Nativity (September 8) and the Presentation of Mary (November 21). These are stations in an ascending path reaching its dogmatic climax in the admission of Mary into heaven in body and soul. Interpreted along mythological lines this corresponds to the deification of the female within a patriarchal religion, and it thereby represents the balance in the bipolarity of human life. C. G. Jung is said to have described this dogma of the Assumption, pronounced in 1950, as one of the most profoundly significant events of our century.[18]

The movable Easter feast-cycle, with its major celebrations of the Resurrection and Ascension of Christ, the sending of the Spirit, as well as the presence of Christ in the form of the eucharistic bread (Corpus Christi), is aligned with the lunar year.[19] In Latin Christianity, Easter is always celebrated on the Sunday after the first full moon in spring; while in certain Eastern diasporas it is celebrated on the very day of the first full moon in spring.[20] The waxing and waning moon is an image of the frailty of life, but it also implies the triumph over death and the possibility of life made spiritualised and divine.[21]

Lacking a close connection to these two feast-cycles are a series of twenty-five obligatory saints' days distributed throughout the entire church year.[22] In addition there are the individual churches' own patrons, who were usually honoured with celebrations lasting several days. It must be emphasised that most of these feasts were tied to consecrations and benedictions of wine and food, herbs, salt, the livestock and fields. Thus, practically all aspects of rural life and work were incorporated in the comprehensive framework of ecclesiastical liturgy even if, for example, at Epiphany when the house was consecrated, the father of the resident family, not the official liturgist, presided.[23]

For the whole church – or at least for the individual churches – these organisational elements of time were (and still are) the overall framework within which popular piety could find expression. The organisational elements of space, on the other hand, correspond in a far more flexible way to the local needs of popular devotion. The church interior, with its titular saint who is a legal person, the altars each with their particular saint and reliquaries,[24] the entire iconography of the church building[25] inside and out, offer a richness of possibilities of identification, realised by the individual and by the group in the act of devotion.[26] A parish with chapels, wayside shrines and field crosses extends the sacrality of the church area[27] to encompass the entire living space of the people who live and work there. Usually there were manorial relationships that bound up to ten parishes together in a sort of loose prayer association. These associations became evident in the prayer processions on the days preceding Ascension and in a series of pilgrimages to nearby shrines which commonly took place on the day of the local church patron;[28] and incidentally, the area they covered was roughly identical with the marriage field of the resident population.[29] Nowadays, we can only partly reconstruct the richness and distinctive features of these iconographic fields because so many of the churches in the countryside were removed in the secularisation of 1803. But even what little remains conveys the impression of the religious intensity which must have developed in the life of our ancestors, and which cannot be seen as separate from their daily lives.[30]

With the organisational elements of space and time we have the prerequisites for translating piety into action; for practical action as opposed to hearing the Word and viewing the image; for providing the non-living structure with organs so as to produce something capable of life – after all, this is what the word 'organisation' actually means in its deeper sense.[31]

As in the preceding paragraphs, we can only point to possible approaches and only touch on developments if we are not to risk getting lost in detail. At this point, let us attempt a definition: what is religious custom? Is there such a thing at all?[32] The consecration of water, wine, or salt, food and herbs, the benediction of the bridal chamber, of houses, workshops and stalls – are they custom or liturgy? Are the benedictions of livestock, fields and tools concessions to pagan survivals in popular piety? Or are they not rather the incorporation of daily life into the framework of worship? Are they not, therefore, *leiton ergon*, liturgy in its original sense, where naturally one might expect some degeneration or accretion over the centuries?[33]

Is it indeed possible to evaluate the different segments of liturgy (the mass, liturgy of the sacraments, liturgy for the dead, the sacramentals, and so forth)[34] in isolation from one another without attacking the very substance of liturgy itself? To what extent we can dismiss the parallel forms of popular piety which are not part of the official religious frameworks and confessions as pre-Christian, non-Christian, or magical is only an issue when we do not examine how these activities came into being. Such activities are really nothing more than the ever-new attempts of people of particular periods to control and make sense of their lives. This artificial division of liturgy into official high forms on the one hand and corrupt, popular forms on the other should by now have become a thing of the past.[35]

The basic forms of religious performance are the same whether in private, domestic devotion or in official church services: singing[36] and meditative prayer, usually linked to the contemplation of images, the forms of cultic play, usually pared down to a few characteristic gestures (and lately reactivated in various ways)[37] – the humble and receptive attitudes of kneeling or the liberating meditative walking in the procession or pilgrimage.[38] These forms, incidentally, are now being rediscovered and acclaimed for their therapeutic value.[39] All these attitudes must be practised for they inaugurate the processes of internalisation and spiritualisation.

It makes it possible for the act of worship to be taken in, expanded upon and enriched to the point where it, in turn, can affect the person's external environment in a healing and fruitful way. This is precisely what the admonitions decreed by the Augsburg Diocesan Synod of 1610 appear to be saying: under the chapter heading 'De cultu divino' we read

> Est vero duplex huiusce servitutis cultus, primarius quidem internus, quo per intellectum affectum voluntatis homo DEO conjunctus ... Alter cultus externus est, professio nimirum & testimonium interni cultus, quem externis quibusdam & visibilibus indiciis ac signis fideles proferunt ac declarant ...[40]

That is, the forms of popular piety must be actualised in such a way that they can be assimilated by the individual as well as performed by the congregation in ecclesiastical liturgy. They must touch off a movement in the person which releases inner energies into his or her participation in outer celebrations. Participation, however, itself creates internalising impulses which penetrate, sanctify and transform the daily life of the individual.[41] The central statement of late medieval mysticism, 'that which is without is within; and that which is within, is without', here becomes a practical reality.[42] We should not be misled by the considerable differences in the forms of official liturgy practised in city and countryside as well as in the numerous monasteries into trying to split the quantitative richness of liturgy into qualitatively separate compartments. By way of clarification, let us consider a few cases – for example, the sixteenth-century saint who brought the entire troubled and problematic period to expression in his own suffering and powers of healing. He was canonised as early as the beginning of the seventeenth century, certainly in part for reasons of church politics,[43] and was presented to the faithful as an example and model for identification.[44]

The Augsburg Synod of 1610 demonstrated its conformity to St Augustine when it prescribed the following with regard to the veneration of saints in general: 'Populus Christianus memorias Martyrum religiosa solemnitate concelebrat, & ad excitandam imitationem, & ut meritis eorum consocietur, atque orationibus adjuvetur.'[45] *Imitatio*, however, means more than simply mimicry or imitation – it also means adopting a given figure, seeking to approximate to it and finally becoming identical with the original image.[46] St Teresa of Avila was an example of a saint who unfolded the royal path of introspective meditation for people of the sixteenth and seventeenth centuries, not just in theory, but by conveying it to ordinary people in a way which enabled them to understand, translate and transform the images of her visions and experiences of faith into their own courses of meditation.[47] It is clear that this reinforced a wavering edifice of faith, cleared up a series of newly formulated points of disputed – because incomprehensible – dogma, and helped to close the gaps in the traditional understanding ordinary people had of their faith.

The manner in which these new ideals and the values they embodied were taken over varied greatly. This process might develop from the contemplation of the story of the saint's life and the legends which surrounded it – usually in the form of devotional pictures which made the most important points graphically visible.[48] It might take place in the various forms of devotion with all their attendant manifestations which keen observers have classed as belonging to the field of psycho-techniques.[49] It might happen when an individual was given a saint's name and thereby entered into a lifelong relationship of clientage to that saint,[50] towards whom all aspects of an individual's life might be directed. It could take the shape of service, usually within a confraternity,[51] towards living or dead kin. Or it might simply take the form of persevering obedience to the demands of life which finds its climax in inner liberation – an attitude which prayer-books and devotional literature of all periods have tried to inculcate.[52]

However, the basic structure of the practice of piety is always one and the same: the *Kenosis*, the renunciation of the self as the person moves closer to God.[53] The assistance which is offered takes many forms and extends from Christian instruction and sermons through activities in one of the many brotherhoods,[54] to the festive service in the cathedral or monastery whose iconography has been composed as an intelligible whole.[55]

We have still not addressed the question of how disturbances affected such an apparently intact and smoothly functioning system, what might have sparked off such disturbances and how the church responded.

In the seventeenth and even in the eighteenth and nineteenth centuries, we can observe changes in village piety by looking at the statistics of baptismal names. These changes suggest a shift in the canon of values. In response, new ideals and values were created – with what success cannot be discussed here. The pastoral duties carried out by enlightened monks set new accents in the prevailing moral codes and in all other areas of piety; yet by the beginning of the nineteenth century these already appeared untenable to higher church officials, and restrictive measures were passed to regulate them.[56] Measures relating to these matters, published in official notices, were immediately transferred to parish announcement books as well, though the many extant parish visitation protocols from the nineteenth century do not convey the impression that they were entirely successful.[57] When we ask why this was so, we must not forget one thing: the secularisation of 1803, closing several hundred monasteries, suddenly threw thousands of people out of work and created great material hardship for them. The cultural 'drainage' of the countryside was accompanied by the migration of this jobless workforce into the few cities where they hoped to find a living in the early, rather slowly developing industries after the attempt to start industrial enterprises in the abandoned monasteries had failed. The previously flourishing village crafts decayed; uprooted people who had been torn out of their traditional working world and everyday environment were forced to build a new existence.[58] The agrarian reforms of the Bavarian minister Montgelas, conceived after the French model and not always implemented with due care, aimed at creating employment for as many people as possible on very small farms by dissolving the large manorial units. The huge project of drying up the large moors had the same aim of getting the workforce set free by secularisation off the streets and giving them new ties in the countryside which would make them less dangerous to the state. These projects were only partly successful.[59]

The few attempts to establish industry in the countryside had a lasting effect on the environment of the rural population and greatly changed their lives within a few decades, even affecting the intimate area of generative behaviour.[60] Slowly this group lost the work rhythm based on the natural course of the year and the seven-day week; for many of its members religion, which remained tied to this natural rhythm and kept its agrarian nature, lost its support function of providing a sense of meaning and became a devalued private matter. As early as 1851, in a pastoral letter, the Archbishop Count Reisach made the resigned observation that the church had already lost the majority of the working classes.[61] And 124 years later the Würzburg Synod of 1975, in a discussion paper on 'The church and the working classes', sees itself compelled to reach the sobering conclusion that up to now it has been 'only in a limited sense possible to give the rising social group of the nineteenth century, the major group of the working people, steady roots in the church'.[62]

Close ties existed between natural time-rhythm, ecclesiastical ritual and rural religiosity. Village religiosity, hitherto supplemented by many magical and superstitious elements, lost its strength precisely when disturbances in this rhythm, the tearing away of people from their traditional environment, as well as new conditions of work, had created a new type of man. It must be added that the section of the industrial working classes which lived in the village without pursuing an incidental agrarian occupation reacted no differently from family members who operated a farm. Only in its generative behaviour did it adapt to a changed occupational world.[63]

Notes: Chapter 15

1 cf. F. Schmidt-Clausing, 'Volksfrömmigkeit', in *Religion in Geschichte und Gegenwart*, Vol. VI, 3rd edn (Tübingen, 1962), cols 1451–5; hereafter cited as *RGG*.

2 Jean Delumeau uses a pertinent point made by P. de Grandmaison: 'L'homme adore, implore, sacrifie ordinairement avec, dans et par son groupe.' See J. Delumeau, *Le Catholicisme entre Luther et Voltaire* (Paris, 1971), p. 194.

3 I have reservations regarding Peter Burke's comments on 'Sensibility and history: how to reconstitute the emotional life of the past', according to which emotions could in principle become institutionalised and thus subject to control 'in the same way as a ritual'. I have no basic objection against this. However, if I understand P. Burke correctly, he seems to overlook the fact that through the institutionalisation of emotions, which in most instances necessarily relies on force, the driving spirit of emotions is erased and buried in the letter of a regulation or law. What actually survives this process are scant remnants of the erstwhile emotion. The reconstruction of the original emotion, starting with this residuum for the purpose of historical analysis, is therefore a very questionable procedure. See P. Burke, *A New Kind of History from the Writings of Febvre* (New York, Evanston, Ill., and San Francisco, 1973), p. 15.

4 H. Hörger, *Kirche, Dorfreligion und bäuerliche Gesellschaft: Strukturanalysen zur gesellschaftsgebundenen Religiosität ländlicher Unterschichten des 17. bis 19. Jahrhunderts, aufgezeigt an bayerischen Beispielen*, pt 1 (Munich, 1978).

5 The choice of baptismal names, for example, illustrates this point. In parishes controlled by monasteries or the nobility we can observe over a period of several centuries that the population established a distance between itself and the favoured patrons of the religious orders and the nobility, and turned instead to the patrons of their trades (the patron saints

of peasants and craftsmen), whereas in the vicinity of a monastery the same names enjoyed great popularity. See H. Hörger, 'Frömmigkeit auf dem altbayerischen Dorf um 1800', *Oberbayerisches Archiv*, Vol. CII (1978), pp. 123–42.

6   *RGG*, Vol. VI, col. 1452.

7   For the notion and the meaning of 'liturgy', see A. G. Martimort (ed.), *L'Eglise en prière: Introduction à la liturgie* (Paris, Tournai, Rome and New York, 1961), pp. 3 ff.

8   Cited in *RGG*, Vol. VI, col. 1452.

9   This is certainly not meant to downgrade the role of the feasts of Christ in celebrations of human life-stations. Such a view is expressed by P. Graff, *Geschichte der Auflösung der alten gottesdienstlichen Formen* (Göttingen, 1939).

10 I am thinking of votive donations, printed or handwritten prayer-bills as used by confraternities, of parish *Verkündbücher* or *Seelenbeschriebe* with their interesting marginal notes. cf. H. Hörger, 'Stabile Strukturen und mentalitätsbindende Elemente in der dörflichen Frömmigkeit: Die pfarrlichen Verkündbücher als mentalitätsgeschichtliche Quelle', *Bayerisches Jahrbuch für Volkskunde*, 1980/1 (Munich, 1983), pp. 110–33.

11 cf. the compact and seminal article by H. B. Meyer, 'Zeit und Gottesdienst: Anthropologische Bemerkungen zur liturgischen Zeit', *Liturgisches Jahrbuch*, Vol. XXXI (1981), pp. 193–213.

12 J. Pieper, *Zustimmung zur Welt: Eine Theorie des Festes* (Munich, 1963). On this theme, cf. also H. Cox, *Das Fest der Narren: Das Gelächter ist der Hoffnung letzte Waffe*, 3rd edn (Stuttgart and Berlin, 1971), written from the point of view of American sociology.

13 See, for example, A. Löhr, *Das Herrenjahr*, 6th edn (Regensburg, 1955); J. Pascher, *Das liturgische Jahr* (Munich, 1963); A. Adam, *Das Kirchenjahr mitfeiern* (Freiburg, 1979); T. J. Talley, 'Liturgische Zeit in der Alten Kirche: Der Forschungsstand', *Liturgisches Jahrbuch*, Vol. XXXII (1982), pp. 25–45.

14 H. Frank, 'Frühgeschichte und Ursprung des römischen Weihnachtsfestes im Lichte der neueren Forschung', *Archiv für Liturgiewissenschaft*, Vol. II (1952), pp. 1–24; L. Fendt, 'Der heutige Stand der Forschung über das Geburtsfest Jesu am 25. XII. und über Epiphanias', *Theologische Literaturzeitung*, Vol. LXXVIII (1953), pp. 1–10; generally on this theme, cf. F. J. Dölger, *Sol salutis: Gebet und Gesang im christlichen Altertum; mit besonderer Rücksicht auf die Ostung in Gebet und Liturgie*, Liturgiegeschichtliche Quellen und Forschungen, Vols. XVI/XVII, 2nd edn (Münster, 1925).

15 J. Blinzler, *Die neutestamentlichen Berichte über die Verklärung Jesu* (Münster, 1937); A. M. Ramsey, *The Glory of God and the Transfiguration of Christ* (London, 1956).

16 A. M. Greeley, *Maria: Die weibliche Dimension Gottes* (Graz, Vienna and Cologne, 1979); W. Nyssen, *Maria im Festkreis der Erlösung* (Cologne, 1979).

17 A brief and clear summary of the essential aspects of mariology with a good bibliography on individual problems is in *Mysterium Salutis*, Vol. III/2: *Das Christusereignis* (Einsiedeln, Zürich and Cologne, 1969), pp. 393–510.

18 In his memoirs he calls this the 'only flash of light' (Lichtblick) for Christendom in our century. A. Jaffé (ed.), *Erinnerungen, Träume, Gedanken von C. G. Jung* (Zürich and Stuttgart, 1963), p. 334.

19 W. Huber, *Passa und Ostern* (Berlin, 1969); A. Strobel, *Ursprung und Geschichte des frühchristlichen Osterkalenders* (Berlin, 1977).

20 On the debates over the date of Easter, see M. Richard, 'La question pascale en IIe siècle', *L'Orient Syrien*, Vol. VI (1961), pp. 179–212.

21 This question is discussed within the framework of the comparative history of religions by the contributors to *Leben und Tod in den Religionen: Symbol und Wirklichkeit*, ed. G. Stephenson (Darmstadt, 1980).

22 The Augsburg calendar of saints, which partially applies to our area of investigation, lists the following feasts: Matthias (24/ii), Joseph (19/iii), George (24/iv), Philip and Jacob (1/v), Peter and Paul (29/vi), Ulrich (4/vii), Mary Magdalen (22/vii), Jacob (25/vii), Ann (26/vii), Afra (7/viii), Lawrence (10/viii), Assumption (15/viii), Bartholomew (24/viii), Guardian Angel (Sunday preceding Nativity of Mary), Mathew (21/ix), Michael (29/ix), Simon and Judas (28/x), All Saints (1/xi), Martin (11/xi), Catherine (25/xi), Andrew (30/xi), Nicolas (6/xii), Thomas (21/xii), Stephen (26/xii), John the Evangelist (27/xii), Holy Innocents (28/xii). See *Decreta Synodalia . . . Augustae Vindel. Anno Dni. MDCX*

... *promulgata* (Augsburg, 1776), caput x: 'De Festis diebus rite celebrandis', pp. 22 ff. cf. also F. A. Hoynck, *Geschichte der kirchlichen Liturgie des Bistums Augsburg* (Augsburg, 1889), pp. 235 ff.

23 A. Franz, *Die kirchlichen Benediktionen im Mittelalter*, 2 vols (reprint of 1st edn, Freiburg /Br. 1909; Graz, 1960).

24 S. Beissel, *Die Verehrung der Heiligen und ihrer Reliquien*, 2 vols. (Freiburg/Br., 1890–2); J. A. Jungmann, 'Vom Patrozinium zum Weiheakt', *Liturgisches Jahrbuch*, Vol. IV (1954), pp. 130–48.

25 A. Reinle, *Zeichensprache der Architektur: Symbol, Darstellung und Brauch in der Baukunst des Mittelalters und der Neuzeit* (Zürich and Munich, 1976).

26 I. Baumer, 'Interaktion – Zeichen – Symbol: Ansätze zu einer Deutung liturgischen und volksfrommen Tuns', *Liturgisches Jahrbuch*, Vol. XXXI (1981), pp. 9–35.

27 On the usage of 'Kirche' (church) see K. Mörsdorf, *Die Rechtssprache des CIC* (Paderborn, 1937), pp. 232 ff.

28 H. Hörger, 'Frömmigkeit', cited n. 5 above, pp. 131 ff. Based on a regionally defined statistical analysis of baptismal names covering an extended period of time we can demonstrate the extent to which popular piety underwent change, that is, intensified itself and specified its orientation. H. Hörger, 'Dorfreligion und bäuerliche Mentalité im Wandel ihrer ideologischen Grundlagen', *Zeitschrift für bayerische Landesgeschichte*, Vol. XXXVIII (1975), pp. 244–316.

29 On marriage mobility within the population of Old Bavaria of the seventeenth and eighteenth centuries, cf. Hörger, *Kirche, Dorfreligion*, pp. 99 ff.

30 Concerning the changes in society and mentality of the first half of the nineteenth century within the region under investigation, cf. H. Hörger, 'Mentale Umschichtungen im Dorf des 19. Jahrhunderts – zum Wandel bäuerlichen Namengutes und seiner gesellschaftlichen Hintergründe im südbayerischen Raum', *Zeitschrift für Agrargeschichte und Agrarsoziologie*, Vol. XXIV (1976), pp. 161–79; id., 'Kulturlandschaft im Wandel: Der oberbayerische Pfaffenwinkel in der ersten Hälfte des 19. Jahrhunderts', *Beiträge zur altbayerischen Kirchengeschichte*, Vol. XXXII (1979), pp. 11–32.

31 W. Jetter, *Symbol und Ritual: Anthropologische Elemente im Gottesdienst* (Göttingen, 1978); R. Hotz, 'Religion – Symbolhandlung – Sakrament: Die christlich-theologische Bedeutung des kultischen Symbolhandelns', *Liturgisches Jahrbuch*, Vol. XXXI (1981), pp. 36–54.

32 See the following selection of older literature written from an apologetic point of view: H. Koren, *Volksbrauch im Kirchenjahr*, 2nd edn (Salzburg, 1935); E. Fuhrmann and A. Schneider, *Kirche und Volkstum im deutschen Raum* (Paderborn, 1936); L. A. Veit, *Volksfrommes Brauchtum im Mittelalter* (Freiburg/Br., 1936); E. Fehrle, *Feste und Volksbräuche im Jahreslauf europäischer Völker* (Kassel, 1955); A. L. Veit and L. Lenhart (eds), *Kirche und Volksfrömmigkeit im Zeitalter des Barock* (Freiburg/Br., 1956).

33 There is a good survey of the broad scope of current benedictions and consecrations covering everyday life in *Benediktionale: Studienausgabe für die katholischen Bistümer des deutschen Sprachgebietes* (Einsiedeln, Zürich, Freiburg and Vienna, 1978); particular attention should be paid to the pastoral introduction, pp. 11 ff.

34 V. Thalhofer and L. Eisenhofer, *Handbuch der katholischen Liturgik*, Vol. II, 2nd edn (Freiburg/Br., 1912); A. Franz, *Die Messe im deutschen Mittelalter: Beiträge zur Geschichte der Liturgie und des religiösen Volkslebens* (reprint of 1st edn, Freiburg/Br., 1902; Darmstadt, 1963).

35 There is a noticeable attempt in the *Constitutio de Sacra Liturgia* issued by the Second Vatican Council to integrate popular forms of liturgical life into the official ecclesiastical liturgy: the church 'favourably considers that which in popular customs of peoples is not intrinsically interwoven with superstition and error, and if it is able to do so, it seeks to preserve this in an entirely unimpaired form. On occasion it [the church] even incorporates it into the liturgy, providing that it is fundamentally compatible with the true and real spirit of liturgy' (*Lexikon für Theologie und Kirche: Das Zweite Vatikanische Konzil*, Freiburg, Basle and Vienna, 1966, p. 43).

36 A. Rosenberg, *Die christliche Bildmeditation* (Munich and Planegg, 1955).

37 G. von Kujawa, *Ursprung und Sinn des Spiels*, 2nd edn (Cologne, 1949); J. Huizinga,

Homo ludens, 4th edn (Hamburg, 1956); H. Rahner, *Der spielende Mensch*, 4th edn (Einsiedeln, 1957); J. Pieper, *Musse und Kult*, 5th edn (Munich, 1962).

38 R. Guardini, *Von heiligen Zeichen* (Mainz, 1961); B. Kötting, *Peregrinatio religiosa: Wallfahrten in der Antike und das Pilgerwesen in der alten Kirche* (Münster, 1950); for an extended bibliography see the article on 'Wallfahrt' by O. A. Erich and· R. Beitl, *Wörterbuch der deutschen Volkskunde*, 3rd edn (Stuttgart, 1974), p. 932.

39 C. G. Jung, *Die Beziehungen der Psychotherapie zur Seelsorge*, 2nd edn (Zürich, 1948); J. Goldbrunner, *Sprechzimmer und Beichtstuhl: Über Religion und Psychologie* (Freiburg, Basle and Vienna, 1965).

40 *Decreta Synodalia ... MDCX ... promulgata* (Augsburg, 1776), pp. 30 ff.

41 A study of the *Verkündbücher* of the nineteenth and twentieth centuries shows that new contents of piety were spread by the schools and, above all, by way of popular devotion. See my article, 'Stabile Strukturen', cited n. 10 above.

42 On this Paracelsian expression consider the comments of E. Zippert, drawing on the comparative history of religions, on the problem of 'Die inneren Gründe für die Weltanschauungsnöte der Gegenwart', in id., *Vom Gleichgewicht der Seele: Essays zur praktischen Psychologie der religiösen Tiefe* (Ulm, 1958), pp. 11 ff.

43 On the political cult of saints, cf. G. Korff, 'Politischer "Heiligenkult" im 19. und 20. Jahrhundert', *Zeitschrift für Volkskunde*, Vol. lxxi (1975), pp. 202–20; as far as their contents are concerned, Korff's observations apply to our example as well.

44 Hörger, *Kirche, Dorfreligion*, pp. 157 ff.

45 *Decreta Synodalia*, p. 29.

46 Cf. W. Dürig, *Imago: Ein Beitrag zur Terminologie und Theologie der römischen Liturgie* (Munich, 1952), pp. 82 ff.

47 W. Nigg, *Vom Geheimnis der Mönche* (Zürich and Stuttgart, 1953), pp. 324–65.

48 R. Guardini, *Kultbild und Andachtsbild* (Würzburg, 1939); A. Spamer, *Das kleine Andachtsbild* (Munich, 1930).

49 T. Löbsack, *Die manipulierte Seele: Von der Gehirnwäsche zum gesteuerten Gefühl*, 2nd edn (Munich, 1972).

50 E. Britschgi, *Name verpflichtet*, 2nd edn (Würzburg, 1967).

51 There is no study of high quality for our area of investigation. Instead see R. Henggeler, *Die kirchlichen Bruderschaften und Zünfte der Innerschweiz* (Einsiedeln, 1955).

52 J. Hacker, *Die Messe in den deutschen Diözesangesang- und Gebetbüchern von der Aufklärungszeit bis zur Gegenwart* (Munich, 1950); F. X. Haimerl, *Mittelalterliche Frömmigkeit im Spiegel der Gebetbuch-Literatur Süddeutschlands* (Munich, 1952).

53 J. R. Geiselmann, *Jesus der Christus* (Stuttgart, 1951), pp. 130 ff.; on the *Kenosis*-passage in Phil. 2: 5–11, see E. Lohmeyer, *Die Briefe an die Philipper, an die Kolosser und an Philemon*, 13th edn (Göttingen, 1964), pp. 90 ff.

54 We need a comprehensive study of the communal-social nature of the numerous confraternities. The examination within a small, regionally limited area of the tasks they fulfilled has shown that the latter extended from the assistance to the dying, over the solution of specific problems of charity, to attempts at integrating social outcasts (the burial of executed offenders and suicides). cf. Hörger, *Kirche, Dorfreligion*, pp. 164 ff.

55 The study of the relationship between ecclesiastical iconography and the social structure of the respective parish is based on the examples of the altars in the monastery churches of Stams (Tyrol) and St Ulrich und Afra (Augsburg); cf. Hörger, ibid., pp. 148 ff.

56 The pastoral letters of the Enlightenment period circulated by the Bishop of Salzburg in 1782 and by the Bishop of Augsburg in 1783 and 1786 had a programmatic effect; cf. A. Gulielminetti, 'Klemens Wenzeslaus, der letzte Fürstbischof von Augsburg und die religiöse Reformbewegung', *Archiv für die Geschichte des Hochstifts Augsburg*, Vol. I ([Dillingen], 1909–11), pp. 493–598; G. Rückert, 'Brauchtum und Diözesanrituale im Aufklärungszeitalter: Das Rituale Augustanum vom Jahre 1764', *Volk und Volkstum*, Vol. II (1937), pp. 297–313; J. Schöttl, *Kirchliche Reformen des Salzburger Erzbischofs Hieronymus von Colloredo im Zeitalter der Aufklärung* (Jetzendorf, 1939).

57 F. M. Phayer, *Religion und das Gewöhnliche Volk in Bayern in der Zeit von 1750–1850* (Munich, 1970), pp. 64 ff.

58 Hörger, 'Kulturlandschaft im Wandel', cited n. 30 above.

59 F. Hausmann, *Die Agrarpolitik der Regierung Montgelas: Untersuchungen zum*

gesellschaftlichen Strukturwandel Bayerns um die Wende vom 18. zum 19. Jahrhundert (Bern and Frankfurt/M., 1975).

60 H. Hörger, 'Familienformen einer ländlichen Industriesiedlung im Verlauf des 19. Jahrhunderts', *Zeitschrift für bayerische Landesgeschichte*, Vol. XLI (1978), pp. 771–819; id., 'Mortalität, Krankheit und Lebenserwartung der Penzberger Bergarbeiterschaft im 19. und beginnenden 20. Jahrhundert', *Zeitschrift für bayerische Landesgeschichte*, Vol. XLIII (1980), pp. 185–222; id., 'Die Bevölkerung Penzbergs 1852 bis 1900: Gesellschaftlicher Stand und Herkunftsgebiete der Einwohnerschaft einer entstehenden Industriesiedlung', *Oberbayerisches Archiv*, Vol. CV (1980), pp. 225–36.

61 Phayer, *Religion und das Gewöhnliche Volk*, pp. 246 ff.

62 See the periodical *Synodenbeschlüsse*, no. 15: text incorporating the final decisions of the eighth plenary meeting of the synod on 21 November 1975 on 'Church and working classes: a decision of the general synod of the bishoprics in the Federal Republic of Germany'.

63 These questions are dealt with in the second part of my work (cited n. 4 above) on *Kirche, Dorfreligion und bäuerliche Gesellschaft* (Munich, 1983).

16 Religion in the Life of German and Swiss Autobiographers (Sixteenth and Early Seventeenth Centuries)

KASPAR VON GREYERZ

In recent years, autobiographical sources have been used judiciously and fruitfully by British and French social historians of the early modern period.[1] A similar claim cannot be made – with a few exceptions – for the social history of the German and Swiss Reformation and Counter-Reformation periods, perhaps because standard bibliographies quite erroneously suggest that such source material is fairly limited for the countries and epochs concerned.

In this exploratory essay I shall concentrate on a selection of autobiographies[2] covering, roughly speaking, the period from the immediate aftermath of the Reformation to the end of the Thirty Years' War. This selection consists of Protestant accounts, not least because Protestant religiosity of the later sixteenth and early seventeenth centuries, as opposed to the Tridentine popular Catholicism of the countries in question, has been neglected by research to date. The Catholic autobiographies from this period which will not be considered here are, in any case, comparatively scarce.[3] The same qualification also applies to personal accounts written by women.[4]

Most accounts surveyed here originated among the bourgeois 'higher middle' and upper classes, if one uses as a gauge the social situation or position of the author at the time he wrote his autobiography. There are only four genuine craftsmen's descriptions of their lives pertaining to the period in question. Only two of them have yet been published in full. These are: the autobiography of the Anabaptist Georg Frell of Chur (1530–97?) who was a bookbinder,[5] and the Silesian house- and family-chronicle of the goldsmith Wolfgang Vincentz of Breslau covering the years 1534–83.[6] Only fractions of an account written by a seventeenth-century shoemaker from Baden are available in print.[7] The fourth document to be mentioned here is the autobiography of Augustin Güntzer, who was an Alsatian *Kannengiesser* (that is, a pewterer) and lived from 1596 to about 1657, which I have used in the original.[8]

The omission from this study of autobiographies written by noblemen may seem somewhat arbitrary considering the permeable lines of division between contemporary urban aristocracy and landed nobility.[9] In the present connection, I am thinking in particular of the Swiss autobiographer Ludwig von Diessbach (1452–1527)[10] or of Sebastian Schertlin von Burtenbach (1496–1577),[11] or even of the Silesian nobleman Hans von Schweinichen (1552–1616),[12] who spent a good part of his life in urban surroundings. Some of these autobiographies will be considered here, although it must be added that the accounts of men of action, such as Sebastian Schertlin von Burtenbach, scarcely yield any noteworthy insights to the social historian of religion. Peasant autobiographies are practically non-existent during the period under consideration, barring one exception, which will be taken into account: Hans Heberle's *Zeytregister* covering the years 1618–72 – a chronicle written by an Upper Swabian village shoemaker and peasant containing a fair amount of autobiographical information.[13]

The following study is divided into three parts. First, I will briefly assess the value of autobiographies from the sixteenth and seventeenth centuries as a historical source. Secondly, the place of religion in the lives of the autobiographers considered will be analysed in as much detail as possible. Thirdly, in a short conclusion, I will try to place this analysis in a broader historical context.

I

Three distinct medieval autobiographical traditions have influenced the development of early modern personal accounts:[14] the tradition inspired by St Augustine's *Confessions*, the late medieval mystical tradition and travel reports written by pilgrims and merchants.[15] The early writing of urban autobiographies of the late fourteenth and fifteenth centuries chiefly grew out of this latter current, as well as out of annalistic historiography. Subjectivity, the expression of personal opinions or feelings, is a trait squarely missing in these pre-Reformation accounts. Only in Burkard Zink's (1396–1474/5) autobiography and especially in Ludwig von Diessbach's family-chronicle does a more personal style prevail, particularly in Diessbach's account of mourning over the loss of his first wife in 1487.[16] Diessbach's family-chronicle foreshadows the more individualised and more subjective autobiography of the post-Reformation period, such as the accounts written by Bartholomäus Sastrow,[17] Thomas[18] and Felix Platter.[19] There is no German or Swiss urban upper-class auto-biography from the first half of the seventeenth century that matches the fullness of expression in these and other sixteenth-century accounts, except perhaps for Johann Valentin Andreae's self-portrayal which, particularly in its mystical elements, already is a forerunner of the Pietist tradition.[20] This tradition of the later seventeenth century and beyond will not be considered here.

In the light of the influence literary tradition could exert on the writing of early modern autobiography, we are compelled to call into question the historical authenticity of such personal accounts. It is important to point out, therefore, that for the social historian autobiographical sources can only have relevance if they are placed within a social and collective frame of reference. Although comparative analysis of a sufficient number of auto-biographical accounts alone can yield such a framework, it cannot, of course, replace more broadly based investigations.

In most autobiographies considered here there is a certain inclination of the author to justify his actions of the past for the benefit of his immediate descendants to whom he entrusts his personal account. Rarely does the author turn to a wider public.[21] This element of self-justification can naturally result in tendentious misrepresentation, as well as in omissions and the suppression of important but uncomfortable facts.[22] In addition, the author's debt to literary tradition and the exigencies of genre can impair the historical value of his presentation, although we must add that this dependency is noticeably weaker during the period under consideration than during the late Middle Ages or, again, in the autobiographical tradition of Pietism.

Having said this, I will now briefly turn to what I regard as the positive historical value of early modern autobiographical accounts. In the social history of religion the sources commonly used are the acts and protocols of notaries and of secular and ecclesiastical courts, acts of ecclesiastical visitations, funeral sermons, last wills and testaments, epitaphs, as well as broadsheets and popular literature. Autobiographical sources generally speaking surpass the quality of this material in the *immediate* connection with the individual as the centre of everyday life which they establish.[23] Although, in discussing the commonly used sources listed above, Alan Macfarlane perhaps overstated the case in claiming that 'using such records one gains only a very partial picture of some very delimited areas of the past', it is nevertheless true that autobiographies and diaries can have an important corrective function and, in some cases, play the role of a substitute source.[24] The experience of everyday life as mirrored by auto-biographical accounts assumes a particularly relevant corrective function within the context of the theme of this volume, for more recent social history of the early modern period has concentrated especially on *collective* and ritual expressions of religion, such as on confraternities, the cult of saints, pilgrimage and religious-moral social control, to name only a few aspects.[25] Against this background, the study of autobiographies enhances our understanding of the place of religion in the attitudes, actions and experiences of individuals. However, as my concluding remarks will show, such individual aspects can only assume historical weight as part of an interpretation that focuses on society as a whole.

II

One of the striking features of sixteenth- and early seventeenth-century German and Swiss autobiographies is the obvious concern of most authors to document their own social and religious conformity. This concern comes across most clearly in the autobiographer's reflections about his childhood and adolescence. The Basle physician Felix Platter recalls the Bible-reading sessions at home before the family attended the Sunday service,[26] and the Alsatian pewterer Augustin Güntzer remembers vividly his lengthy Sunday walks enabling him to attend Calvinist catechetical instruction in a neighbouring town.[27] As children and adolescents both Felix Platter and Augustin Güntzer often resented their fathers for the strict and sometimes heavy-handed upbringing they had to suffer. Their later thankfulness towards their fathers makes a case for the long-lasting effects of the moral and religious indoctrination received at home.[28] This conditioning could be so strong and long-lasting as to preoccupy Thomas Platter continually about how he should join the priesthood – which is what his family and native community wanted him to turn to – when he sat among the listeners of Huldrych Zwingli's first reformed sermons in Zürich.[29] School and catechism naturally strengthened the commitments fostered by the family, although the autobiographical evidence considered is more equivocal in this respect, compared to the adult writer's positive assessment of the education and upbringing received at home.[30]

The religious orientation thus formed referred to a world similar to that which the history of science has called a 'closed world'.[31] Within this world sacred spaces and times were distinguished from the profane, and the experience of the sacred was seen as different from the experience of the profane. The 'manifestations of the sacred' (M. Eliade) could either strengthen or radically weaken this cosmological conception of order. The family and the community were able to channel the religious experience of the individual only within the framework of this order. The irruption of elementary disorder thus resulted in a very direct and personal experience of sacred power, which family and community were unable to mediate. In the case of our authors, the experience of illness and disease, particularly of ravaging plague, constituted such a direct irruption of the sacred into daily life. God was directly experienced as a punishing father. Augustin Güntzer, for example, describes in detail all the illnesses that have beset him since his early years. His simple rhyme, 'O Lord, you have wounded me; please, Lord, let me recover through your grace', sums up these experiences.[32]

Perhaps more clearly than the Middle Ages, the Protestants of the sixteenth and early seventeenth centuries regarded the plague as a punishment instituted directly by God.[33] Although the experience of the plague may have created chiliastic hopes on the part of the few,[34] it certainly inspired widespread fear among the many.[35] It was seen as God's punishment, not only because it constituted a disruption of natural order, but also because it resulted in the temporary dissolution of religiously sanctioned social order, such as the family and the community.[36] This is born out by Wolfgang Vincentz's account of the plague epidemics experienced by the inhabitants of Breslau in 1514, 1525 and 1542.[37] Traces of the fear generated by the plague can also be found in the deep grief felt by Felix Platter as he recalls the death of his sister Ursula during the plague of 1551, or in Lucas Geizkofler's account of his difficult and dangerous journey through plague-stricken northern Italy to South Tyrol in 1577.[38]

Manifestations of the sacred were an integral and almost calculable part of urban daily life.[39] Sacred power, on the other hand, could manifest itself in an extraordinary way as disruption of natural and social order. This in turn could result in a particularly strong feeling of exposure. Such feelings are mirrored in autobiographical accounts of the travels of journeymen and students. Far from home, the religious education earlier received at home and within the native community helped to stabilise the traveller's identity and to counteract the sense of exposure.

The sixteenth- and early seventeenth-century traveller experienced the presence of the sacred regularly and intensively, as summed up by Bartholomäus Sastrow regarding his journey from Mainz to Rome in 1546: 'I relied plainly on the gracious protection and shelter offered by the good Lord, whose gracious presence I certainly have felt.'[40] The autobiographers among these travellers lavished God with praise and thankful prayers for his protection and benevolence once a journey had successfully been accomplished. In returning to Silesia from the Rhineland in 1577, Hans von Schweinichen praises the Lord for the fatherly protection granted 'during this extended, dangerous, hard and fastidious journey, particularly against the manifold snares of the devil',[41] and such examples could easily be multiplied. In the conviction of the respective authors, it was God's very direct interference that saved Bartholomäus Sastrow and Augustin Güntzer from the claws and teeth of wolves encountered on their travels to Italy,[42] the Swiss minister Josua Mahler in a storm on the English Channel in 1547, and Augustin Güntzer from the hands of robbers encountered in the Haguenau forest.[43]

Confessionalism, too, helped to reassert one's social and religious identity while abroad. In the material discussed here, this comes about most strongly in negative terms, as when the traveller found himself in a Catholic area or country. This was invariably experienced as a potentially and some-times openly hostile environment. More vividly than by any other of our authors, this point is driven home by the observations recorded by the Calvinist Augustin Güntzer, clearly because his childhood and adolescence in the Catholic Alsatian city of Obernai had hardened him in this respect. His recollection that 'I experienced my misery, wretchedness, fear and distress already in my youth from morning to night, when the Papist boys rebuked me as a young Lutheran heretic' is a case in point.[44]

Confessionalism, however, only appears in an attenuated form in the autobiographies of authors whose wider family and so-called 'Freundschaft' encompassed Protestants and Catholics alike. This was certainly the case with Thomas and Felix Platter and even, in some respects, with the Reformed minister Josua Mahler.[45] The process of increasing confessionali-sation of the sixteenth century must have rendered the maintenance of such cross-confessional ties of kinship and friendship ever more precarious, as when Catholics as godparents were excluded from Protestant baptismal ceremonies, an event approvingly recorded for Basle in the diary kept by the minister Johannes Gast.[46]

Similar forms of social control were vividly experienced by contemporary German and Swiss Protestant autobiographers recalling their stays in Catholic Italy and France – again with the notable exception of Felix Platter. This is highlighted by the Lutheran Lucas Geizkofler's unease felt in Padua in 1576 about the rumours circulating in this city alleging that the contemporary outbreak of the plague had been caused by the presence of German Protestant students.[47] Further examples are Augustin Güntzer's repeated flight from Italian priests who insisted that he confess, as well as Bartholomäus Sastrow's hasty departure from Rome for fear his Lutheran leanings might cause him bodily harm.[48]

The travels of students and journeymen were an important rite of passage initiating them into adulthood.[49] Adulthood for the autobiographers examined here was synonymous with 'Ehestand', the state of matrimony, which was in most cases preceded by the acquisition of masterhood, or of a doctorate or ministry. Life now took on a more orderly pace, punctuated at fairly regular intervals by the experience of birth and death.

Having thus traced the biographical process during which religion constitutes itself for the individual as a general *Weltansicht*,[50] we shall not continue to pursue this line of inquiry here. Little has been said so far about the actual contents of religion as it was experienced, practised and professed by German and Swiss autobiographers of the Reformation and Counter-Reformation periods. This is the question I will now turn to.

Some of the autobiographies in question contain lengthy *Glaubens-bekenntnisse*, statements of creed, faithfully adhering to official Lutheran or Calvinist confessions.[51] All of them reflect a concern to document one's religious conformity. There is a striking contrast between the relative sobriety of such pursuits and the personal or even emotional ways in which our autobiographers describe their own religious experiences and document the religious motivations of their daily behaviour. At first this is a purely external contrast, to be sure. What needs to be looked at more closely, therefore, is the inner coherence of this religion.

God, according to Genesis 1:7, 'made the firmament, and divided the waters which were above the firmament'. In the case of torrential rain, hail, or storms on sea – so ran the belief in sixteenth- and seventeenth-century Europe – God allowed the original chaos temporarily to reconstitute itself. There was no doubt that he did so to warn or punish humanity from or for digression from his commandments. The sense of guilt which contemporary Protestants felt in the face of such extraordinary elementary events was intense. The material in question suggests that this was by no means the preserve of the upper classes alone, for such feelings are a particularly prominent element in Hans Heberle's *Zeytregister*. As a villager, Heberle was perhaps more exposed to nature's idiosyncrasies than were the city dwellers. But a sense of apprehension is also detectable in Felix Platter's account of extreme weather conditions prevailing in the south of France in 1556, which caused some Provençals to prepare themselves for the last judgement.[52] And for Josua Mahler there was no doubt that, if he did not survive the storm he experienced on the English Channel, he, as well as all the other passengers on board, would end up in hell.[53]

As the magical means of popular pre-Tridentine Catholicism, by which communities, in an attempt to manipulate nature, sometimes almost literally speaking tried to stem the tide, were officially unavailable to Protestants due to the lack of co-operation or outright prohibition on the part of their church, their attention focused instead on prognostics and divine signs. Although I would not like to infer that their church's attitude was emulated faithfully by all Protestants, it is nevertheless clear that the Reformation led to a shift away from the attention previously given to collective, and often magical rituals towards the individual preoccupation with prognostics and prodigies.[54] Such signs were thought to hint at the course of providence. They could thus alleviate the shock of unannounced divine punishment. Heeding prognostics offered at least a chance to amend one's ways before it was too late to do so.[55] The belief in prognostics helped to take the edge off the feeling of individual and collective guilt generated by the reformer's insistence on man's fundamental corruption. This is implied in the words of Johannes Stumpf in his mid sixteenth-century Swiss chronicle: 'The pagans let themselves be introduced to religion and the fear of God through dreams and idle appearances. We, as Christians, however, are not moved by any benevolence and not even by any signs of impending punishment that God places before our eyes, such as epidemics, illness, famine, dearth, war, earthquakes, comets and eclipses.'[56]

All personal accounts examined here testify to the wide dissemination of such beliefs among all but the Protestant lower classes which are not represented by the material in question. Among learned Protestants, it is true, this could combine with a 'pre-scientific' outlook, that is, with naturalistic observation, in which an attempt was made to distinguish between the workings of nature and the sacred. This is most apparent in the physician Johann Morhard's diary. He cited Pliny, Cornelius Gemma and other authorities to the effect that, even though prodigies had natural causes, they were nevertheless harbingers of impending evil (Pliny) and divine wrath (Gemma).[57] This may also apply to the case of the Basle theologian and mathematician Christian Wurstisen who carefully, but very briefly, listed in his diary events such as those catalogued above by Johannes Stumpf.[58] But it must be added that the rise of a naturalistic preoccupation with prodigies did not play an important role during the period considered here.[59] This is indicated, for example, by Wolfgang Vincentz's scepticism as to whether the lack of prodigies announcing the plague of 1523 legitimised a naturalistic explanation of the event.[60]

The interpretation of prodigies as prognostics also often combined with the widespread fear of the Turks. Christian Wurstisen as well as Josua Mahler, for example, noted the red colour of the sun which announced the imminent victory over the infidel at Lepanto in 1571.[61] In 1640 Johann Valentin Andreae tried to underline his call for a thorough reform of moral conduct within Württemberg's Lutheran church by referring to divine signs, which had appeared in the sky, as well as flooding and a miraculous birth that occurred in the same year.[62] He notes that he saw with his own eyes how blood rained from the firmament on 15 November 1642.[63] A similar convergence of belief in the miraculous and experience of the sacred cannot be ascertained in the case of authors who did not record their role as direct witnesses of prodigial events, or who did not leave us sufficient evidence as to the authenticity of their belief in the sacred meaning of prodigies. Like many other autobiographers of his day, Hans Heberle, for instance, regularly copied pamphlets covering the appearance of prognostics.[64] Such pamphlets enjoyed a remarkable level of circulation. Among them, those focusing on recently observed comets as signs announcing divine retribution were very numerous indeed. The comet's tail was invariably interpreted as a symbol of God's 'Zuchtrute' or punishing stick, and it was important to observe in which direction of the compass it would point.[65]

'Kein Komet ist je gesehen, drauff nicht Böses ist geschehen' (1655) – 'No comet was ever seen, which was not followed by pernicious events' – declared a seventeenth-century broadsheet. German and Swiss autobiographies from the period in question abundantly reflect this concern. It was a comet appearing in 1618 that prompted Hans Heberle to start writing his family-chronicle, and the same comet appears in one of the few illustrations contained in Augustin Güntzer's account.[66] The caption at the bottom of Güntzer's picture is an appeal to God's mercy, beginning with the words: 'O Lord, I cannot imagine anything else or find a different explanation than that You will punish us severely in our German lands by this comet and rod. Discipline us with restraint and not in your scorn; Lord, be merciful.'[67]

Not all such signs, however, could be considered as sent by God. It was thus important to distinguish between divine portents and devilish trickery, according to Luther's admonition that 'God's signs and the angels' warnings are mixed up with Satan's insinuations and hints, as the world deserves it'. Luther added that a distinction between these two kinds of signs, if at all possible, could only be based on personal experience rather than on religious teaching.[68] The authors considered here were far less discriminating than Luther, not least in their confessional polemic. Lucas Geizkofler's polemics against the cult of saints is a case in point. In 1572, when an old woman had allegedly induced a statue of St Mary at St Hilaire's Church in Paris to weep, Geizkofler, then in Paris, was quick to point out that this was the work of the Devil.[69] He implied, of course, that the old woman had used black magic. Likewise, he dismissed as sheer idolatry the claim that a statue of the Virgin in Padua had miraculously stopped the plague in that city. This claim was made in conversation by the Franciscan Johannes Nas from Ingolstadt, a prolific confessional polemicist who, between 1565 and 1568, published no less than six anti-Protestant works on miracles and prodigies.[70] Belief in miracles was not a Catholic monopoly. But for Protestants it was important to be able to prove that the miraculous prodigies, which caught their interest, were signs that stemmed directly from God. This principle applied likewise to the interpretation of dreams which were faithfully recorded by the authors in question.[71]

While dreams could only communicate a relatively vague sense of what divine providence had in store, popularised astrology was capable of providing more detailed information. The autobiographers studied here frequently refer to the signs of the zodiac and to Galen's theory of the four temperaments, especially in recording their own and their children's births. The theory of temperaments was closely linked to astrology in that contemporary astrologers considered the main planets of the Ptolemaic system to be endowed with human temperaments and elementary properties. Thus days as well as hours were thought to be governed by different planets.[72] Many among the authors considered faithfully recorded the exact date and hour of their own and their children's births. In the case of Augustin Güntzer this meant that he was of a melancholy nature, cold and dry like earth.[73] Wolfgang Vincentz, who otherwise felt very sceptical about the legitimacy of astrological predictions, discovered with some surprise that his fellow journeyman-traveller on the route from Venice to Augsburg in 1547 was, in fact, a very witty man, although, as Vincentz adds, he was born under the sign of Pisces, as a phlegmatic, cold, wet and watery sort of person.[74]

Closely linked to this practice was the interest in nativities or horoscopes. This finds only partial expression in our material. But we know, for example, that Lucas Geizkofler had two lengthy nativities established for himself in 1569 and 1606, although he does not record the first one in his autobiography which ends in 1590.[75] Hans von Schweinichen, however, reports in detail the horoscope composed for him by an old monk in Cologne.[76] Amongst straightforward advice regarding his heavy drinking, it also contained instructions as to how he had better avoid contact with cats and be careful about eating boiled eggs, for they might encapsulate a love charm. Hans von Schweinichen's comments about his nativity underline the staunch Lutheran's ambiguous relationship to magic. Although he points out that he has since tried to keep out of the way of cats at all costs and to crack the shell of a boiled egg only at its tip, he concludes his observation by saying: 'I commend all this to God whom I trust. He will do as he pleases, and I shall follow such things [that is, his nativity] barely or not at all. I only wish that this prophecy would swim in the water, so that nobody could find it. But God may see to it that all is well. Have given the monk four crowns.'[77]

The most detailed account of a nativity comes from the goldsmith Wolfgang Vincentz regarding a horoscope drawn up for him by a companion while working as a journeyman at Nuremberg in 1552. It is also the most sceptical account and ends with the observation: 'Several points he has written down about me are quite accurate and literally true. However, as for the rest, I abstain from any judgement. It is also fair to assume that such speculation was for him [Vincentz's companion] above all a source of entertainment and a brush with which to stroke the coat of the superstitious.'[78]

The belief in spirits, ghosts and sympathetic magic played an obvious role in the life of the autobiographers concerned. A few examples must suffice here. Both Lucas Geizkofler and Hans von Schweinichen faithfully record their respective encounters with spirits and ghosts, and even a minister like Johann Valentin Andreae allowed himself to wonder whether his brother Jacob, who passed away in 1631, had died at the hands of robbers or ghosts.[79] Confessionalism and the belief in magic could be combined in the explanation of illness and disease. Josua Mahler was convinced that his sister was ultimately driven into a state of permanent insanity due to her overexposure to popery while living in the bi-confessional Swiss town of Bischofszell.[80] Augustin Güntzer, in turn, attributed the grave illness that beset him on the journey to Rome to the stench of garlic and the smoke of candles he had inhaled in the pilgrimage church of San Loreto. In Rome, he feared that kissing the pope's statue at St Peter's might bring renewed disease upon him.[81] This is an extreme form of confessionalism that cannot be found in other personal accounts, it is true. However, even if one excludes here the autobiographies and diaries written by Protestant ministers, the example of the strongly confessionalist attitude of the burgomaster of Stralsund, Bartholomäus Sastrow, forbids the hasty conclusion that this kind of confessionalism was above all the preserve of lower strata of Protestant society.

In the material examined here social differentiation, and perhaps also significant differences between elite and popular culture, become especially apparent in references made to the role of magic in the treatment of illnesses. The pewterer Augustin Güntzer reports about an illness he had in 1607: 'In Obernai there was an executioner's wife who handled medication well. She prescribed human and dog's fat and other medicine. She treated me during half a year. I finally recovered through God's might.'[82] On another occasion he is treated by 'a peasant with a goitre called Deischtger'.[83] The Basle physician Felix Platter, on the other hand, complained about the competition he suffered from magical healers. In the list he provides of them, he mentions a man named 'Amman, who is called the peasant from Utzendorf, who was visited by surprisingly many people; he could soothsay based on a urine sample and used strange arts during many years.' Felix Platter also mentions the two Basle executioners of his time.[84] Certainly, the social and cultural differentiation which surfaces here should not be exaggerated, because Felix Platter likewise practised the speculation over urine samples, 'wherefrom I had to prophecy, an art which I mastered well enough, so that many were astonished and began to consult me'.[85]

It is tempting, of course, to categorise the particular religious outlook of an Augustin Güntzer as that later to be found in the German *Klein-bürgertum* or petty bourgeoisie.[86] There is a degree of this-worldly asceticism and a preoccupation with original sin and with patience as the prime virtue in the face of suffering that cannot be found to the same extent in any of the other autobiographical accounts discussed here.[87] However, although the material in question provides much more information for an exploration of the relationship between elite and popular religion than could be considered here, it does not lend itself adequately to an analysis of religion in terms of social class. Apart from functionalist fallacies that such a line of inquiry might easily entail, there is one main reason for this: the social origin of the majority of authors is too homogeneous before the production of craftsmen's autobiographies reaches greater proportions in the later seventeenth century. Furthermore, I believe that the historical analysis of religion, taking into account such factors as social status and class, must first of all be tackled in the form of local case studies, of which little has been done for Germany and Switzerland. Autobiographical evidence, in turn, can help to give a heuristical framework to such an undertaking and can have a corrective function as far as the interpretation of local material is concerned.

III

I hope that the preceding analysis has shown that it is not easy to apply the notion of 'popular religion' to early modern daily life in its *urban* setting. These difficulties result from the fact that the notion of 'popular religion' primarily is a product of the study of medieval and early modern *agrarian* society. The accentuation of divisions between the religion of the peasant, the 'common man' in sixteenth-century Germany, and that of a village or neighbouring urban elite is part and parcel of this notion.[88] It could, of course, be argued that the majority of German and Swiss towns of the sixteenth and seventeenth centuries were so-called *Ackerbürgerstädte* whose inhabitants chiefly worked in the agrarian sector of the economy. However, this argument would scarcely do justice to the complex social functions of religion, nor to the relatively differentiated social structure and organisation of towns of a middling size, which A. G. Dickens has labelled the 'typical German city' of the period in question.[89] Richard Trexler is right in criticising the fact that social historians of religion to date have rarely considered the sociology of the city.[90]

The material we have examined here pertains mainly, barring a few exceptions, to the urban middle and upper classes. But it should be clear from the above discussion that the autobiographers considered cannot be regarded simply as representatives of learned or elite religion alone, and that the question of the effect of the Reformation on urban Protestant religion cannot be answered based on an overschematised division between popular and elite religion.

In a recent article William Bouwsma argues that medieval cosmology, modelled on the exigencies of agrarian communities, gave intelligibility to the universe in bounding and distinguishing the sacred from the profane.[91] He points out that 'as a fully articulated system of boundaries, medieval culture was admirably suited to the management of anxiety'. He interprets the rise of anxiety among Renaissance men as the result of the growing inability of medieval cosmology to cater for the complex social and ethical needs of urban populations 'no longer inhibited by the pressures of traditional community'.[92] I am not sure, however, whether this is not based on an all too mythological view of the medieval agrarian community. Yet I agree with Bouwsma that the cultural meaning of the Reformation, at least on the face of it, lies in the reformers' insistence on the ontological basis of human culture, as a culture essentially created by men and thus subject to change, rather than being based on transcendental notions.[93]

The Reformation was a radical transformation of culture in that it attempted to do away with most medieval communal and individual means of managing the sacred within the profane, such as processions, pilgrimages, the cult of saints and the veneration of the dead.[94] And, most importantly, it tried to destroy power that popular belief had previously invested in sacraments and sacramentals. Apart from an appeal to faith and prayer, the reformers had no new ritual to offer, which could replace the immediate efficacy of the medieval management of anxiety. Their insistence on man's fundamental corruption could in fact create new forms of anxiety and fear. A look at Wolfgang Vincentz's observations on the plagues of 1514 and 1542 in the Silesian city of Breslau illustrates this point. Referring to the latter plague year he notes that many fled the town and that others gave themselves 'to prayers, spiritual recollection and fear of God and repented their unseemly way of life. There were also daily prayers in the churches, so that the human race would not have to suffer this dangerous epidemic for too long or even perish through it.' In his account of the plague of 1514 he observes that the city dwellers refused to buy the hitherto popular pictures of plague-saints from the monks, and goes on to state: 'This time there was such great fear, that the blood-letting letters ... were again attached to the doors of many houses.'[95]

Research on Protestant visitation records, certainly, has made us sceptical as to the reformers' success in driving home the new doctrine on a broad scale, particularly as far as rural society is concerned.[96] It is important to note, however, that these records scarcely account for the spread of the Reformation in the cities.[97] The predominantly urban autobiographies examined here underline this scepticism in regard to the prominence of magical beliefs among their Protestant middle- and upper-class authors. Yet this role of magic does not constitute the whole story. The same material strongly suggests that the Reformation message had a relatively broad appeal within the urban environment. This appeal did not so much consist of spreading a new certainty of forthcoming salvation, but rather of lending a new and cosmic dimension to the individual fears of disorder caused by irruptions of sacred power. The preoccupation, if not obsession, with prodigies and prognostics found in the autobiographical material in question was a new way of channelling anxiety, of ordering the sacred within the profane, which strongly emphasised the cosmic importance of morality in daily life.

Notes: Chapter 16

I should like to thank the audiences to whom earlier versions or parts of this paper have been read in Bern, London and Wolfenbüttel for their helpful comments. I am particularly indebted for his valuable suggestions to Michael Hunter who has read an earlier draft of this article, and to Hans-Christoph Rublack who has generously forwarded copies of material not readily available to me.

1   For Britain, see A. Macfarlane, *The Family Life of Ralph Josselin* (Cambridge, 1970) and M. Spufford, 'First steps in literacy: the reading and writing experiences of the humblest seventeenth-century autobiographers', *Social History*, Vol. IV, no. 3 (October 1979), pp. 407–35. For French historiography, see J. Delumeau, *Le Catholicisme entre Luther et Voltaire*, Nouvelle Clio, Vol. XXXbis, 2nd edn (Paris, 1979), pp. 215–16 (and the studies quoted there), and E. François' unpublished 'Mémoire ... du Diplôme d'Etudes Supérieures' entitled: 'Mémoires et chroniques familiales dans l'Allemagne d'entre la Paix

d'Augsbourg et la Guerre de Trente Ans (Images familiales et religieuses)' (Paris, 1967). I should like to thank Étienne François for making a copy of his thesis available to me for the revision of this paper. In complete independence from each other, we have reached some remarkably similar conclusions regarding the role of prodigies in German Protestant autobiographies of the later sixteenth and early seventeenth centuries.

2 The term 'autobiography' used here also includes diaries.

3 Probably the best-known Catholic urban account from the period in question is the voluminous diary written by Hermann Weinsberg of Cologne: *Das Buch Weinsberg: Kölner Denkwürdigkeiten aus dem 16. Jahrhundert*, ed. K. Höhlbaum, 5 vols (Bonn and Leipzig, 1886–1926).

4 I am aware of only two accounts written by women and pertaining to the period in question. Both were written by Catholic nuns, contain little genuinely autobiographical information and should rather be classified as chronicles: C. Höfler (ed.), *Der hochberühmten Charitas Pirkheimer, Äbtissin von S. Clara zu Nürnberg, Denkwürdigkeiten* ..., Quellensammlung für fränkische Geschichte, Vol. IV (Bamberg, 1852); and G. Meier (ed.), 'Bericht über das Frauenkloster St. Leonhard in St. Gallen von der Frau Mutter Wiborada Fluri', *Anzeiger für Schweizer Geschichte und Altertumskunde* (1915), pp. 14 ff.

5 S. Rageth (ed.), 'Die Autobiographie des Täufers Georg Frell von Chur' (with an introduction by O. Vasella), *Zwingliana*, Vol. VII, no. 7 (1942), pp. 444–69.

6 C. R. Vincentz (ed.), *Die Goldschmiede-Chronik: Die Erlebnisse der ehrbaren Goldschmiede-Ältesten Martin und Wolfgang, auch Mag. Peters Vincentz* (Hanover, [1918]).

7 This is the diary of Emanuel Groos (b. 1618). See W. Groos, 'Wanderschaft eines jungen Handwerkers zur Zeit des Dreissigjährigen Krieges', *Die Pyramide: Wochenschrift zum Karlsruher Tagblatt*, Vol. IX, no. 26 (27 June 1920), pp. 177–9. I wish to thank Dr Schwarzmaier, Director of the Generallandesarchiv in Karlsruhe, for kindly providing me with a copy of this article. Sections thereof are reprinted in W. Fischer (ed.), *Quellen zur Geschichte des deutschen Handwerks: Selbstzeugnisse seit der Reformationszeit*, Quellensammlung zur Kulturgeschichte, Vol. XIII (Göttingen, Berlin and Frankfurt, 1957), pp. 62–4.

8 The manuscript version of A. Güntzer's autobiography used here is kept at the Universitätsbibliothek Basel, Handschriften-Abteilung. A modernised and severely abridged version, which leaves much to be desired, was published in 1896: *Augustin Güntzers merkwürdige Lebensgeschichte: Ein Kulturbild aus dem Jahrhundert des 30jährigen Krieges*, Barmer Bücherschatz, Vols III and IV (in one vol.) (Barmen, [1896]).

9 See, for example, the remarks in T. A. Brady, *Ruling Class, Regime and Reformation at Strasbourg, 1520–1555*, Studies in Medieval and Reformation Thought, Vol. XXII (Leiden, 1978), pp. 123–40.

10 *Ludwig von Diesbach, Herrn zu Landshut und Diesbach, Chronik und Selbstbiographie*, Der schweizerische Geschichtsforscher, Vol. VIII, Heft no. 1 (Bern, 1830). Reprinted in H. Wenzel (ed.), *Die Autobiographie des späten Mittelalters und der frühen Neuzeit*, Vol. I, Spätmittelalterliche Texte, Vol. III (Munich, 1980), pp. 92–152. See also the editor's comments, ibid., esp. pp. 94–5.

11 E. Hegaur (ed.), *Leben und Taten des weiland wohledlen Ritters Sebastian Schertlin von Burtenbach: Durch ihn selbst deutsch beschrieben* (Munich, [1910]).

12 H. Oesterley (ed.), *Denkwürdigkeiten des Hans von Schweinichen* (Breslau, 1878).

13 G. Zillhardt (ed.), *Der Dreissigjährige Krieg in zeitgenössischer Darstellung: Hans Heberles 'Zeytregister' (1618–1672), Aufzeichnungen aus dem Ulmer Territorium*, Forschungen zur Geschichte der Stadt Ulm, Vol. XIII (Ulm, 1975). The Swiss equivalent of Heberle's 'Zeytregister', the chronicle written by the well-to-do peasant Jost von Brechershäusern, contains very few autobiographical elements. See A. Bärtschi (ed.), 'Die Chronik des Josts von Brechershäusern', *Burgdorfer Jahrbuch*, Vol. XXV (1958), pp. 79–132.

14 For a recent, succinct survey, see G. A. Benrath, 'Autobiographie, christliche', *Theologische Realenzyklopädie*, Vol. IV (Berlin and New York, 1979), pp. 772–89.

15 See T. Klaiber, *Die deutsche Selbstbiographie: Beschreibungen des eigenen Lebens, Memoiren, Tagebücher* (Stuttgart, 1921), pp. 5–14.

16 For Diessbach, cf. n. 10 above; for Zink, Wenzel, *Die Autobiographie des späten Mittelalters*, Vol. II, pp. 44 ff. cf. also ibid., Vol. I, p. 9 (characterising the late medieval autobiography): 'Das dargestellte Ich ist eher definiert durch seine Partizipation an äusseren Begebenheiten als durch subjektive Brechung des Geschehens in der Dimension persönlicher Erfahrung.' A similar view is also expressed by G. Misch, *Geschichte der Autobiographie*, Vol. IV, pt 2 (Frankfurt/M., 1969), pp. 583–4.

17 G. C. F. Mohnike (ed.), *Bartholomei Sastrowen Herkommen, Geburt und Lauff seines gantzen Lebens ...*, 3 pts (Greifswald, 1823–4). See also Misch, *Geschichte der Autobiographie*, p. 619.

18 A. Hartmann (ed.), *Thomas Platter: Lebensbeschreibung*, Sammlung Klosterberg (Basle, 1944).

19 V. Loetscher (ed.), *Felix Platter: Tagebuch (Lebensbeschreibung) 1536–1567*, Basler Chroniken, Vol. X (Basle and Stuttgart, 1976). For the German sixteenth-century autobiography in general, see Klaiber, *Die deutsche Selbstbiographie*, pp. 15–16, and Misch, *Geschichte der Autobiographie*, Vol. IV/2, pp. 616–25.

20 J. V. Andreae, *Selbstbiographie*, ed. and trans. D. C. Seybold, in id. (ed.), *Selbstbiographien berühmter Männer*, Vol. II (Winterthur, 1799). For a survey of German seventeenth-century urban autobiographies, see Klaiber, *Die deutsche Selbstbiographie*, pp. 54–6.

21 The Calvinist minister A. Scultetus' account and the Lutheran theologian J. V. Andreae's autobiography are cases in point. See G. A. Benrath (ed. and trans.), *Die Selbstbiographie des Heidelberger Theologen und Hofpredigers Abraham Scultetus (1566–1624)*, Veröffentlichungen des Vereins für Kirchengeschichte in der evangelischen Landeskirche in Baden, Vol. XXIV (Karlsruhe, 1966); and J. V. Andreae, op. cit. Götz von Berlichingen's autobiography is a well-known earlier example of this genre. For this and further reference, see W. Mahrholz, *Deutsche Selbstbekenntnisse: Ein Beitrag zur Geschichte der Selbstbiographie von der Mystik zum Pietismus* (Berlin, 1919), pp. 60–9.

22 For a list of the pitfalls that can present themselves to the historian using autobiographical source material, see Klaiber, *Die deutsche Selbstbiographie*, pp. 335–9, and for a more recent assessment, focusing primarily on eighteenth-century craftsmen's accounts: A. Griessinger, *Das symbolische Kapital der Ehre: Streikbewegungen und kollektives Bewusstsein deutscher Handwerksgesellen im 18. Jahrhundert*, Ullstein tb, no. 35080 (Frankfurt/M., Berlin and Vienna, 1981), pp. 52–7.

23 See Klaiber, *Die deutsche Selbstbiographie*, pp. 342–4. Misch, *Geschichte der Autobiographie*, Vol. IV/2, p. 587. Mahrholz, *Deutsche Selbstbekenntnisse*, pp. 7–9. H. Stratenwerth, 'Selbstbekenntnisse als Quellen zur Sozialgeschichte des 16. Jahrhunderts', in H. Rabe *et al.* (eds), *Festgabe für Ernst Walter Zeeden*, Reformationsgeschichtliche Studien und Texte, Supplementary Vol. II (Münster 1976), pp. 21–35, here p. 31.

24 For a discussion of these and other uses of this source material, see Stratenwerth, op. cit. n. 23 above.

25 See H. Hörger, *Kirche, Dorfreligion und bäuerliche Gesellschaft ...*, pt 1, Studien zur altbayerischen Kirchengeschichte, Vol. V (Munich, 1978), p. 20, n. 23.

26 Loetscher, *Felix Platter*, p. 79.

27 Güntzer, op. cit. n. 8 above, fol. 22r.

28 Loetscher, *Felix Platter*, pp. 80–1. Güntzer, op. cit., fol. 22v. See also Rageth, 'Die Autobiographie des Täufers Georg Frell', cited n. 6 above, p. 458.

29 Hartmann, *Thomas Platter*, pp. 61–4.

30 See, for example, the strong criticism of the Latin school of Sterzing (Tyrol) by Lucas Geizkofler in *Lucas Geizkofler und seine Selbstbiographie, 1550–1620*, ed. A. Wolf (Vienna, 1873), pp. 24–6.

31 See R. Horton, 'African traditional thought and Western science', pt 2: 'The "closed" and "open" predicaments', *Africa*, Vol. XXXVII (April 1967), pp. 155–86. I should like to thank Michael Hunter for drawing my attention to this article.

32 Güntzer, op. cit. n. 8 above, fol. 25r: 'Sie Her, du hast mich verwundt. Ach Her, mach mich aus genade widerumb gesundt.'

33 This differentiation is suggested by the fact that the odious late medieval legend imputing responsibility for plague epidemics to the Jews had lost much of its earlier appeal by the

time of the Reformation. For this legend, see L. Zehnder, *Volkskundliches in der älteren schweizerischen Chronistik*, Schriften der Schweizerischen Gesellschaft für Volkskunde, Vol. LV (Basle, 1976), pp. 377–8.

34 R. E. Lerner, 'The Black Death and Western European eschatological mentalities', *American Historical Review*, Vol. 86, no. 3 (June 1981), pp. 533–52.

35 C. Cipolla, *Faith, Reason and the Plague in Seventeenth-Century Tuscany*, trans. M. Kittel (Ithaca, NY, 1979).

36 See, for example, Wolfgang Vincentz's observation on the plague of 1542 in Breslau: 'It attacked the most well-to-do people. In many houses father and mother both died, leaving behind small children. Long thereafter those who recovered had to carry a white walking stick in the streets, so that they could be recognised.' Vincentz, *Die Goldschmiede-Chronik*, p. 118. cf. also the *Thanner Chronik* (regarding the Black Death): 'Die Elteren achten keine Kinder, die Kinder keine Elteren mehr; Herren, Frawen, Knecht and Mägdt war alles gleich, dan niemand ehret oder observierte das andere, jedermann gab nur auf sich selbsten acht.' M. Tschamser (ed.), *Annales oder Jahrs-Geschichten der Baarfüseren ... zu Thann*, Vol. I (Colmar, 1864), p. 362.

37 Vincentz, *Die Goldschmiede-Chronik*, pp. 12, 53, 116–18. cf. also below, n. 95.

38 Loetscher, *Felix Platter*, pp. 115–17. Wolf, *Lucas Geizkofler*, pp. 113–19.

39 See J. Chiffoleau, *La Comptabilité de l'au-delà: Les hommes, la mort et la religion dans la région d'Avignon à la fin du Moyen-Age (vers 1320–vers 1480)*, Collection de l'École française de Rome, Vol. XLVII (Paris, 1980).

40 Mohnike, *Bartholomei Sastrowen Herkommen*, pt 1, p. 302: 'allein begab ich mich auf meine Apostellpferde, den langen weiten Weg verliess mich schlechtes auf genedige Beschutzunge und Beschirmunge meines lieben Gottes, dessen gnedige Gegenwerdigkeit ich auch entpfunden hab.'

41 H. Oesterley (ed.), *Denkwürdigkeiten des Hans von Schweinichen* (Breslau, 1878), p. 144.

42 Mohnike, *Bartholomei Sastrowen Herkommen*, pt 1, pp. 304–5. A Güntzer, op. cit. n. 8 above, fol. 54v.

43 Güntzer, op. cit., fol. 41r–44r; and J. Mahler [Maaler], 'Usszug und kurze Verzeichnung ...', in *Bekenntnisse merkwürdiger Männer*, Vol. IV, ed. J. G. Müller (Winterthur, 1810), pp. 187–464, esp. pp. 244–5. I have been unable to consult the more recent edition of J. Mahler's account: 'Selbstbiographie eines zürcherischen Pfarrers aus der zweiten Hälfte des 16. Jahrhunderts', *Zürcher Taschenbuch* (1885) and (1886).

44 Güntzer, op. cit. n. 8 above, fol. 8v: 'Mein Elendt, jamer, angst undt nodt erfuhre ich schon in meiner jugendt frie und spadt. Von den Babisten, jungen und alten, werdt ich als ein junger laudterischer ketzer gescholten.' For Obernai's politico-religious situation in the late sixteenth and early seventeenth centuries, see J. Gyss, *Histoire de la ville d'Obernai*, Vol. I (Strasburg, 1866), pp. 470–504.

45 Born and raised in Upper Valais, Thomas Platter entertained uninterrupted connections with Catholics there, long after his departure and his conversion to Protestantism. Josua Mahler had close Catholic relatives in the Breisgau and Black Forest.

46 *Das Tagebuch des Johannes Gast*, ed. and trans. P. Burckhardt, Basler Chroniken, Vol. VIII (Basle, 1945), p. 169. It must be added, however, that such confessionalism attracted increasing learned criticism in the course of the seventeenth century. An early example thereof can be found in the physician Johann Morhard's anger expressed over the intransigent funeral sermon preached by a Lutheran minister on the occasion of the death in 1610 of a close colleague and friend of Morhard's who had converted to Catholicism. See J. Morhard, *Haller Haus-Chronik*, ed. Historischer Verein für Württembergisch Franken (Schwäbisch Hall, 1962), p. 97. I should like to thank Christopher Friedrichs for drawing my attention to this source.

47 Wolf, *Lucas Geizkofler*, p. 120. On the phenomenon of communal 'pollution' alluded to by Geizkofler, see N. Z. Davis, 'The rites of violence', in id., *Society and Culture in Early Modern France* (Stanford, Calif., 1975), pp. 152–87, esp. p. 159, and Ph. Benedict, 'The Catholic response to Protestantism: church activity and popular piety in Rouen, 1560–1600', in J. Obelkevich (ed.), *Religion and the People, 800–1700* (Chapel Hill, NC, 1979), pp. 168–90, esp. pp. 170–1.

48 Mohnike, *Bartholomei Sastrowen Herkommen*, pt 1, pp. 373, 302.

49 I am not convinced by Philippe Ariès's argument that no noticeable distinction was made

between age-groups during the period concerned. See P. Ariès, *L'Enfant et la vie familiale sous l'Ancien Régime*, Collection 'Points Histoire', Vol. XX (Paris, 1973), pp. 13, 312.

50 See V. Drehsen and H. J. Helle, 'Religiösität und Bewusstsein: Ansätze zu einer wissensoziologischen Typologie von Sinnsystemen', in W. Fischer and W. Marhold (eds), *Religionssoziologie als Wissenssoziologie* (Stuttgart, Berlin, Cologne and Mainz, 1978), pp. 38–51, here p. 45.

51 See Andreae, *Selbstbiographie*, pp. 205–7. H. Oesterley (ed.), *Denkwürdigkeiten des Hans von Schweinichen* (Breslau, 1878), pp. 1–5. A Güntzer, op. cit. n. 8 above, fols 28r–29r and fols 165r–192r.

52 Loetscher, *Felix Platter*, pp. 246–7. Likewise, the seventeenth-century Swabian physician Johann Morhard repeatedly refers to the manifestation of divine providence in good and bad weather, such as when the favourable weather prevailing in 1610 is praised as 'mirum ... et sapientiae Dei insigne testimonium'. cf. Morhard, *Haller Haus-Chronik*, p. 96 and *passim*.

53 Mahler, 'Usszug und kurze Verzeichnung ...', cited n. 43 above, pp. 244–5. Hieronymus Köhler (1507–73) sums up the point made here: 'Also ein gwaltiger herr ist unser Gott, dan das gross wüten des meeres wellen, die starken wind kan der herr in nöten mit einem wort stillen und weren, im sey lob und eher.' See H. S. M. Amburger, 'Die Familiengeschichte der Koeler: Ein Beitrag zur Autobiographie des 16. Jahrhunderts', *Mitteilungen des Vereins für Geschichte der Stadt Nürnberg*, Vol. XXX (1931), p. 230.

54 The recent article by K. Park and L. J. Daston, 'Unnatural conceptions: the study of monsters in sixteenth- and seventeenth-century France and England', *Past and Present*, Vol. XCII (August 1981), pp. 20–54, bears this out.

55 H. Lehmann, *Das Zeitalter des Absolutismus: Gottesgnadentum und Kriegsnot, Christentum und Gesellschaft*, Vol. IX (Stuttgart, Berlin, Cologne and Mainz, 1980), pp. 124–5, who emphasises the strong eschatological connotation this preoccupation assumed in the course of the seventeenth century.

56 Cited after Zehnder, *Volkskundliches*, p. 498.

57 Morhard, *Haller Haus-Chronik*, pp. 66–7. See also ibid., p. 44: '5. Novembris vesperi hora octava prodigium Halae ante portam novam in caelo visum ao.99 [= 1599]. Ego pro chasmate aut trabibus volantibus habeo *qualia in talibus autumnalibus non sunt infrequentia*' (my italics). It is evident here that, although Morhard tried to systematise his observation of prodigies, he did not go so far as to question the miraculous and sacred workings of nature. cf. also ibid., p. 105, where Morhard briefly refers to caterpillars which fell from heaven on 27 February 1614.

58 See R. Luginbühl (ed.), 'Diarium des Christian Wurstisen, 1557–1581', *Basler Zeitschrift für Geschichte und Altertumskunde*, Vol. I (1902), pp. 53–145.

59 The old argument by H. Bächtold-Stäubli (ed.), *Handwörterbuch des deutschen Aberglaubens*, Vol. V (Berlin and Leipzig, 1932/3), cols 113–15, that the scholarly and 'scientific' tradition of astrological preoccupation with prognostics (as represented by Cardano, Bonatti and others) owed its spread *in Germany* to its transformation by popular astrology, is still valid. See also J. Céard, *La Nature et les prodiges: l'insolite au XVIe siècle, en France*, Travaux d'Humanisme et Renaissance, Vol. CLVIII (Geneva, 1977), which also covers important German material, and the article by Park and Daston, cited n. 54 above.

60 Vincentz, *Die Goldschmiede-Chronik*, p. 52: 'Because at this time no punishing comet had admonished them, people thought it [the plague of 1523] came from deep wells fallen into disuse, from which the putrid vapours arose, or from great and strong earthquakes in other countries ...'

61 Luginbühl, 'Diarium des C. Wurstisen', cited n. 58 above, p. 119; Mahler, 'Usszug und kurze Verzeichnung ...', cited n. 43 above, p. 324.

62 Andreae, *Selbstbiographie*, p. 221.

63 ibid., p. 256.

64 Another such case is that of the Pomeranian nobleman Joachim von Wedel (1552–1609). See J. Freiherr von Bohlen-Bohlendorf (ed.), *Hausbuch des Joachim von Wedel ...*, Bibliothek des Litterarischen Vereins in Stuttgart, Vol. CLXI (Tübingen, 1882), for example pp. 155, 160, 173, where the author repeatedly refers to the *Wunderbücher* written by Job Fincel and Kaspar Goldwurm. Regarding the Protestant production of such

books, see W. Brückner (ed.), *Volkserzählung und Reformation: Ein Handbuch zur Tradierung und Funktion von Erzählstoffen und Erzählliteratur im Protestantismus* (Berlin, 1974). See also R. W. Scribner, *For the Sake of Simple Folk: Popular Propaganda for the German Reformation* (Cambridge, 1981), pp. 126–7.

65 W. Hess, *Himmels- und Naturerscheinungen in Einblattdrucken des XV. bis XVIII. Jahrhunderts* (Leipzig, 1911), pp. 51–2.

66 See Zillhardt, *Hans Heberles 'Zeytregister'*, pp. 86–7, 93. Heberle also took careful note of the comets of 1652 and 1664: cf. ibid., pp. 249, 264.

67 A. Güntzer, op. cit. n. 8 above, illustration inserted between fol. 64r and 63[a]r.

68 See H. Schilling, 'Job Fincel und die Zeichen der Endzeit', in Brückner, *Volkserzählung und Reformation*, pp. 326–92, here p. 365. The quotation is from Martin Luther's foreword to the 1527 Wittenberg edition of Johann Lichtenberger's late fifteenth-century prophecies. cf. A. Warburg, *Heidnisch-antike Weissagung in Wort und Bild zu Luthers Zeiten*, Sitzungsberichte der Heidelberger Akademie der Wissenschaften, Phil.-hist. Klasse, 26. Abhandlung (Heidelberg, 1920), pp. 36, 46. cf. also ibid., pp. 81–6, for the complete text of Luther's foreword.

69 A. Wolf (ed.), *Lucas Geizkofler und seine Selbstbiographie, 1550–1620* (Vienna, 1873), pp. 65–6.

70 ibid., pp. 119–20. On Johannes Nas, see R. Schenda, 'Hieronymus Rauscher und die protestantisch-katholische Legendenpolemik', in Brückner, *Volkserzählung und Reformation*, pp. 179–259, here pp. 196–7.

71 For records of dreams see, for example, Andreae, *Selbstbiographie*, p. 22; Lötscher, *Felix Platter*, p. 202; Güntzer, op. cit. n. 8 above, fol. 63[a]v.

72 See Hess, *Himmels- und Naturerscheinungen*, pp. 42–3. Only in a few of the Protestant accounts in question one finds mirrored Martin Luther's outlook, who believed in the sacred nature of prodigies and portents, but rejected astrological prediction as a product of arrogant human reasoning. Thus, Wolfgang Vincentz noted for the year 1539 that only God knew 'whether the planets also were a cause of the advantage gained by the Turks'; and Johann Morhard later added to his earlier reference to the sombre astrological predictions occasioned by the solar eclipse of 1605: 'Fools are those who let themselves be scared by the astrologers.' See Vincentz, *Die Goldschmiede-Chronik*, p. 102; Morhard, *Haller Haus-Chronik*, p. 64. For Luther's view, see Warburg, *Heidnisch-antike Weissagung*.

73 Güntzer, op. cit. n. 8 above, fol. 4r: 'Bin auff dise welt gebohren worden im Jahr ano. 1.5.9.6. den 4 dag May alten kallenders, Zinstag in der nacht zwischen i undt 2 uhren, so dass Midwochs dagsstunden anfahen im Planeten Luna, der 12 himlischen zeichen nach im steinbocke, gahr Melancolisch[er] Nadtuhr, kalt undt trucken [wie] die Erdt.'

74 Vincentz, *Die Goldschmiede-Chronik*, p. 140.

75 See Wolf, *Lucas Geizkofler*, p. 157.

76 H. Oesterley (ed.), *Denkwürdigkeiten des Hans von Schweinichen* (Breslau, 1878), pp. 118–20.

77 ibid., p. 120.

78 Vincentz, *Die Goldschmiede-Chronik*, pp. 224–8, esp. p. 228: 'Etliches, was er von mir ausgeschrieben hat, ist ganz richtig und buchstäblich wahr. Wie aber das Ganze beschaffen ist, stelle ich an seinen Ort. Es ist auch zu glauben, solches Deuten sei ihm vorab eine Kurzweil gewesen und ein Striegel, abergläubigen Leuten damit das Fell zu streichen...' For Wolfgang Vincentz's rational and naturalistic view of the aims of astrology, see ibid., pp. 150–2. cf. also above n. 72.

79 ibid., pp. 131–2. See also Andreae, *Selbstbiographie*, pp. 131–2. Lucas Geizkofler's case is probably an exception in this respect, for he refers to ghosts and spirits with some scepticism, although he concedes that the Bible mentions some examples. He has no doubts, however, as to the Devil's use of such apparitions: Wolf, *Lucas Geizkofler*, pp. 54–5, 73–5. For the contemporary attack launched by the Protestant churches against the popular belief in ghosts, see J. Delumeau, *La Peur en occident (XIVe–XVIIIe siecle): Une cité assiégée* (Paris, 1978), p. 78. For the relatively long time it took these attacks to have any effect, see N. Z. Davis, 'Ghosts, kin and progeny: some features of family life in early modern France', *Daedalus* (April 1977), pp. 87–114, esp. p. 95.

80 Mahler, 'Usszug und kurze Verzeichnung...', cited n. 43 above, p. 323.

81 Güntzer, op. cit. n. 8 above, fols 60v–61r (on his visit to St Peter in Rome), and fol. 58v (on the aftermath of his stay in San Loreto): 'In der zeitt stiess mich die hitzige ungerische kranckheitt an wegen des starken, hitzigen weins und des gestanckes des knobloch und wax, so ich in mich geschlucket habe in der Capel zu Loreto durch den Atem.'

82 ibid., unnumbered folio (between fols 16r and 17r).

83 ibid., fol. 52r.

84 Lötscher, *Felix Platter*, pp. 337–8.

85 ibid.

86 Regarding this outlook see P. Burke, *Popular Culture in Early Modern Europe* (New York, 1978), p. 213. See also H. Möller, *Die kleinbürgerliche Familie im 18. Jahrhundert: Verhalten und Gruppenkultur*, Schriften zur Volksforschung, Vol. III (Berlin, 1969), esp. pp. 203–78, and, for the rise of the *Kleinbürgertum* in German history: C. R. Friedrichs, 'Capitalism, mobility and class formation in the early modern German city', *Past and Present*, Vol. LXIX (November 1975), pp. 24–49.

87 For the notion of 'patience' in German Protestant autobiographies of the later sixteenth century, see E. François' salient observations in id., 'Mémoires et chroniques', cited n. 1 above, esp. p. 98.

88 See my Introduction above.

89 A. G. Dickens, *The German Nation and Martin Luther* (London, 1974), pp. 177–9.

90 See R. Trexler's contribution to this volume.

91 W. J. Bouwsma, 'Anxiety and the formation of early modern culture', in *After the Reformation: Essays in Honor of J. H. Hexter*, ed. B. C. Malament (Manchester, 1980), pp. 215–46.

92 W. J. Bouwsma's use of the notion of 'anxiety' calls for the following comments:

    (a) It is certainly much more difficult for the historian to distinguish 'anxiety' from 'fear' than J. Delumeau would have it; cf. id., *La Peur*, pp. 13–17. As W. J. Bouwsma, op. cit., p. 222, points out, 'fear' is often but a subjective, individual or collective reification of 'anxiety': 'The relationship between anxiety and fear remains close, for behind the fear of a particular danger always lurks, again, uncertainty about its eventual outcome.'

    (b) The attempt to view 'anxiety' as a cause of certain religious beliefs, as tentatively suggested by A. Macfarlane, *The Family Life of Ralph Josselin*, p. 193, involves conceptual problems; cf. the discussion of a functional understanding of religion in my Introduction above. If I opt here for W. J. Bouwsma's use of the notion of 'anxiety' it is not from an inclination to define religion as a kind of psychological need-fulfilment, for 'the force behind faith in astrological predictions or in curing by spells lies not in the severity of danger in the situation, nor in an anxious need to believe in an illusory solution to it, but in a conviction of their truth...' (H. Geertz, 'An anthropology of religion and magic, I', *Journal of Interdisciplinary History*, Vol. VI, Summer 1975, pp. 71–89, esp. p. 83). cf. also B. Scribner's discussion of the two-way flow between sacred place or object and its devotees in id., 'Interpreting religion in early modern Europe', *European Studies Review*, Vol. XIII (1983), pp. 89–105, esp. pp. 94–5.

    (c) The notion of 'anxiety' as used by the social historian of religion is clearly in need of further refinement, particularly concerning its relationship to change over time. A notable attempt in this direction has been undertaken by H. Lehmann, *Das Zeitalter des Absolutismus*, pp. 105–69. However, I am not sure whether Lehmann's approach does not involve too strong a contrast between the sixteenth and seventeenth centuries, as when he argues that the faith in human progress dominating the sixteenth century broke down in the seventeenth century, which was marked by worries and anxiety, in contrast to the atmosphere of confidence and hope prevailing in the Reformation century (ibid., p. 111). Compare this with W. J. Bouwsma, op. cit., p. 222: 'The personal intensity of both Protestant and Catholic piety in the age of the Reformation can only be understood against the background of the peculiar anxiety that it sought to assuage.' For H. Lehmann's earlier discussion of the historical notion of 'anxiety', cf. id., '"Absonderung" und "Gemeinschaft" im frühen Pietismus...', *Pietismus und Neuzeit*, Vol. IV (Göttingen, 1979), pp. 54–82, esp. pp. 65–7.

93 W. J. Bouwsma's argument must be assessed in connection with his earlier suggestive article, 'The Renaissance and the drama of Western history', *American Historical Review*, Vol. LXXXIV, no. 1 (February 1979), pp. 1–15, in which he opposes E. Le Roy Ladurie's

view of the 'motionless history' of the masses of pre-industrial Europe and maintains that the Renaissance was an age of cultural transition. He relies on an anthropological concept of 'culture' and proposes (ibid., pp. 11–12) that 'this conception of culture is perhaps the contemporary world's most generous legacy from the Renaissance: the recognition that culture is a product of the creative adjustment of the human race to its varying historical circumstances rather than a function of universal and changeless nature, and the perception that culture accordingly differs from time to time and group to group'. This is a useful reminder that Bouwsma's view of the cultural meaning of the Reformation may not necessarily apply to the outlook of all social groups involved in that process. It does, however, largely apply to the beliefs expressed by the urban middle- and upper-class authors examined here.

94 Although formulated with polemical intention, the Bernese chronicler Valerius Anshelm's description of a storm which occurred in 1532 provides a good illustration for this point: 'Zuo miten Meien kam ein dicker hagel, eiergross steinen über ein stat Bern, one sundren schaden, wiewol etliche wib und man umb die glocken und Heiligen kläglich schruwent.' Cited after L. Zehnder, *Volkskundliches*, p. 199.

95 Vincentz, *Die Goldschmiede-Chronik*, pp. 12, 116. Wolfgang Vincentz was born in 1525 (ibid., p. 53). His account of the plague of 1514 is based on a diary left by his father (ibid., pp. 52, and esp. p. 164).

96 See G. Strauss, *Luther's House of Learning: Indoctrination of the Young in the German Reformation* (Baltimore, Md, and London, 1978).

97 See id., 'Success and failure in the German Reformation', *Past and Present*, Vol. LXVII (May 1975), pp. 30–63, esp. p. 48.

Part Five

Historiography, Sacred or Profane?

17 Reverence and Profanity in the Study of Early Modern Religion

RICHARD C. TREXLER

> There are limits that one cannot
> cross even if there is no barrier.
> Sovetskaya Rossiya[1]

Social historians' fascination with the idea of popular culture and popular religion is surprising in the light of folk ideology's destructive role in recent history. The concepts of *Volk* and *peuple* had come to a bad end in Europe, not least because of their evocative rather than actual content. The people was a chimera, we learned. Yet from the 1960s until today, a profusion of scholarly conferences and writings has raised this alleged culture and its religion to new heights.[2] Not without criticism, to be sure: various scholars have convincingly argued that to this day neither cultural forms nor social groups have been isolated which can exclusively be identified as popular.[3]

For this reason, the title of this volume, 'Religion and Society in Early Modern Europe', represents a hopeful sign for a future social history of religion. In the last generation great storehouses of the religious artefacts of the past have been retrieved and studied with a seriousness and ingenuity few would have thought possible a generation ago, and no one would doubt the fruitfulness of that work or that it has enriched our understanding of humanity's material and spiritual heritage. Yet rich as the quality and quantity of religious studies inspired by the focus on popularity has been, that very concept has perpetuated serious biases, and not the least of these has been the focus on defining popularity rather than religion. The search can have a Grail-like intensity: 'I was born of the people', Jacques Le Goff cites Michelet; 'I have the people in my heart. But its language is inaccessible to me, and I have not been able to speak it.'[4]

The insatiable search for popular essence has meant two things for the study of religion before the French Revolution. First, religion usually remains undefined by historians. Secondly, the emphasis on 'popular' rather than on 'religion' has led us to think of 'popular religion' as essentially different from what is variously called high, elite, or learned religion. Indeed, elite religion is more likely to be called something else, like 'spirituality', and books on spirituality exclude 'the people' as a matter of course. The absence of a book, conference, or field called 'high' or 'elite religion', or even 'clerical religion', suggests that religion has become by definition popular. It will be worthwhile, I think, to go back to the question of what religion is.

This chapter has three purposes. First, I want to relate our understanding of religion to the development of the modern European intelligentsia. Arguing that conventional definitions have crippling disadvantages for its study, I will suggest a definition of religion which, I think, proves particularly appropriate for the social historian of early modern Europe. Finally, I want to explore the relation between religion and historical writing and discourse, and argue their procedural and affective similarity. In the course of this contribution I will suggest tactics and strategies for the historian wishing to write a profane rather than a reverential history of religion. Before plunging into early modern period history – taking for granted what religion is – we should re-examine what we are doing when we talk and write about religion.

Our Religion and their Religion

A survey of what Western historians mean by religion reveals one pervasive assumption: religion in the West was either identical with or the reverse of meaningful activities of formal ecclesiastical or state institutions. Whatever practitioners have said religion was, their historians have defined it *with reference to* the real and idealised behaviour and reflections of a corporate division of labour, the clergy. Perhaps this is most evident in the German academic tradition, where a discrete confessional approach to the discipline of religious and theological studies remains in place to this day. What religions have in common, that is, religion, is discovered in the relation of each to its clergy.

Yet the institutionally focused study of religion is but part of a larger propensity of the West's complex societies. If in medieval Europe the idea of religion was limited by reference to the exemplary actions and reflections of an institutionalised clergy, reduced into norms, so today the pursuit of knowledge is associated with the university, and power is usually described with exclusive reference to the state. Now if it is true that in Western practice such fundamental human activities or states are normally referred to institutions, it is reasonable to ask if this corporate thrust is related to the institutional character of those who formally define what religions were and were not. The social historian more than any other must begin the study of past religions by examining the corporate paradigms of intellectual, moral and fideistic constructs.[5]

The sacramental and lay clerical groups that have normatively defined and limited religion have clashed since the Renaissance on defining religion, its social location and on who the 'people' are who practised it. Before a corporate lay intelligentsia appeared in the Renaissance, the sacramental clergy said that religion consisted of lay and clerical liturgical behaviour as well as in clerical reflection on the divine, that is, on order and disorder and their meaning. Pointing to itself as that social body which behaved in a graced or particularly efficacious form and which contemplated, the sacramental clergy defined all non-ordained or non-ecclesiastical persons as the *populus*, even if the clergy in the interest of its finances co-opted its patrons out of 'the people' by ambivalently associating them with itself, for example by clothing the merchant or king in religious habit for burial, allowing their presence in the choir, and so on. As Roger Chartier recently noted, the people was not a social group but a status;[6] in the view of the clergy, that *populus* did not reflect, but its liturgical behaviour, however inadequate, was 'religious'. The people had religion in certain of its activities.

The lay (non-sacerdotal or -ministerial) intelligentsia of the early modern period increasingly rejected this concept of religion and of the people. Generally not wealthy or powerful patrons, who might be co-opted into grace by the clergy, they rejected a concept of the people which embraced them and, competing for patronage with the sacramental clergy before their princes, they increasingly disputed the centrality of graced behaviour to a definition of religion.[7] Beginning with conventional attacks on participatory acts like processions, pilgrimages, and the like, which for the laity at large were observably the most significant liturgical acts, some of these lay intellectuals ended by questioning what some called clerical magic, that is, sacramental activities in which the clergy's intervention was said to be decisive.[8] The essence of religion for the *Schriftgelehrten* or humanists became contemplation or reflection on a single world or cosmic order. Behaviour was relatively unimportant to religion, and the simpler the behaviour, the better.[9]

Thus in this view the sacramental clergy was religious mainly to the extent that it was reflective; depending on the power of the local clergy, the cosmic efficacy of its liturgy was thrown into question more or less radically. More important, this emphasis on reflection excluded 'the people' from religion, for everyone agreed that they did not reflect. One has only to read Erasmus or Pico della Mirandola among a host of writers of the age to see that lay scholars were even more determined to separate themselves from the vulgar than they were to attack clerical pretensions.[10] On the one side this intelligentsia attacked the religious activism of the 'people', while on the other it questioned the liturgical activities of the clergy. Its socially passive definition of religions was ready made for its patrons, the territorialising princes of early modern Europe.

In the courts, these laymen now turned their attention to the assertedly non-liturgical behaviour called courtesy, and gave it a religious aura. In the Middle Ages 'good manners and religion' were two sides of the same behavioural coin, and bad manners were a type of sin. One and the same system of bodily comportment, for example, was considered appropriate and efficacious in dealing with princes and gods, actions towards the latter being legitimated through biblical authority and actions towards the former by custom and by natural law transference from divine to human princes.[11] This symbiosis was muted in the Renaissance, especially by those lay intellectuals like Von Hutten and Pomponazzi, Montaigne and More, Vivés and Guazzo, who increasingly doubted the efficacy of liturgical behaviour. A group of terms like courtesy, regality, urbanity and civility, classicised later in the term *civilisation*, came to the fore, and the princes became their mirror. Challenging the liturgical efficacy of the sacramental clergy, the lay intelligentsia offered the prince their services in creating a system of princely behaviour which would guide and legitimate, and render efficacious, *human* communications. Though sometimes viewed as thaumaturgic in those actions, the prince of early modern Europe became the predominant model for a binding *social* behaviour developed by his intellectual masters of ceremonies and emanating from his court.[12] The 'religion' of gentlemen was spawned in a 'sacred' ambience. Irreverence remained outlawed and profane, only now, decorum went by different names and was defined by different clergies.

This early corporate history of definitions of religion helps us to understand how the social history of religion has been written in modern times, and what have been the focuses of its various practitioners. In the modern age the ordained clergy's monopoly of the historiography of European religion has been broken, and clerical historians have almost everywhere been supplemented by lay scholars committed to clerical leadership who share with the sacramental clergy the view of religion as a reflective and a behavioural phenomenon. This body of committed historians studies historically conditioned behaviour, their writing chronicles changing lay behaviours and beliefs in terms of how closely they approach or depart from ideal clerical states or norms. Secondly, historians following Gabriel Le Bras, himself a 'religious sociologist', are comfortable with sociological categories in studying the people of the gods. Indices of class, residence, age, occupation and sex have been used not only by pastors to discover how to get today's people to church, but by historians studying ages as far removed as that of the Merovingians.[13] This clerical approach remains remorselessly moralistic, to be sure, yet that makes it critical of past and present political authority; the behaviour of 'the people' can still be the *vox dei* for committed historians. The immutable gods of Christianity, surprisingly, allow a history, sociology and critical philosophy to their historiographic devotees.

If infinitely more complex, the assertedly secular intelligentsia's study of lay religion, descended from the Renaissance, also betrays a corporate character. Generally speaking, this historiographical tradition in the study of Western religion has proven less concerned with change than the church tradition, in part because it privileges static models derived from social anthropologists studying distant tribal societies. Secondly, the anthropologists' emphasis on overarching tribal unity has discouraged the historiographic application of trans-tribal sociological indices like age, sex, status and class to European societies, resulting in a model of social operation that is non-conflictual with regard to the relation between 'tribes' and which identifies the 'tribe' with its mature males. Finally, modern secular historians' criticisms of the biases of the committed intelligentsia and their own commitment to value-free scholarship notwithstanding, they tend to conceptualise the study of religion in such a way as to accept and perpetuate rather than to view critically both the states whose religions they study and those they themselves live in, not unlike some of the anthropologists who inspired them.[14] Applying tribal models to the European 'popular' world, they have converted the old clergy–*populus* distinction into a sociologically amorphous, quasi-cosmic Manicheanism pitting mental light against mental darkness, a religious world in which the state does not figure as a religious structure and thus cannot undergo a critical review in religious terms. The state has become power, not religion. The problem is rooted in this intelligentsia's group-interested definition of religion as reflection.

Since the nineteenth century, this secular intelligentsia has had three stances towards Western religion. The most remarkable has been to ignore it. Just as many anthropologists turned towards Africa and Asia and thus avoided studying Western religion in the same fashion used in distant parts, so historians of the 'secular' Renaissance long ignored its religion, which presumably could not be studied in the same way as its 'modern' political and artistic institutions could be.[15] The other two stances have examined the subject, but diverged from each other in their attitudes towards non-reflective or 'false religion', identified, as we have seen, with 'the people'. The first group of historians are the linear descendants of the Renaissance intellectuals I have mentioned, and they have viewed this false religion as dangerous to 'true religion' but even more to 'civilisation', that is, to that paraliturgical theatre of manners earlier mirrored in the prince, but in post-revolutionary Europe hypostatised in the bureaucratic structures of the modern state and in the 'businesslike' behaviour of its employees.[16]

The most recent stance towards non-reflective religion has been positive, its adherents' ancestral opposition to the sacramental clergy often being supplemented by an opposition to the modern bourgeois state, that is, to their patrons. Such historians generally agree with their civilisational colleagues that the beliefs of the people are false, and that actions based on them are 'irrational'. But behaviour like industrialisation which the civil-isationalists ridicule, the populists praise as a spiritual and social force which gave 'the people' identity and solidarity against the modernising state from which these intellectuals themselves are alienated.[17] Impressed by the wealth of behavioural information gathered by folklorists like Van Gennep and by committed historians like Delaruelle, these secular historians, thinking they were secularly reflecting instead of religiously acting on the past, believed that they could recover from a functionally useful behaviour an actual intellectual coherence inaccessible to the unreflective people. Mental darkness became for scholars like Bakhtin a type of liturgical inner light, and 'popular religion' became a good reversal of the meaningful if baneful behaviour of the clergy and state.[18]

Thus among secular social historians of religion, the behaviour of the 'people' has steadily come to the fore as a matter of serious intellectual inquiry. To historians like Mandrou and Laslett, popular religion is basically a rural behavioural world lost through some cosmic event like the industrialisation, whose reflective meaning persists only as a mental light among the historians of those religions. To others like Edward Thompson, this active 'plebeian religion' tends to lose all chronological or locative reference and so lives on despite social change, a force ready to resist the modern state especially if 'the people' heed the ideal role and essence the historians assign them.[19] Both approaches are acts of faith. With little clear reference in group sociology, 'the people' easily become a victimised fancy produced by pop-psychological characterisations among historians who, even as they defend or attack 'the people', do not consider themselves behaving towards the religions they study. Paradoxically, the result has often been a gulf between past peoples and their elites, between the same social groups and their historians, between the study of religion and the study of power.

From the earliest days of cultural classifications, apologists have distinguished between irrational and rational, external and internal, collective and individual, routine and spontaneous religions, and until recently such conceptual territorialisations passed unchallenged for science. Romans used the former quality of each set to brand Christians, Christians to label Jews, Protestants to dismiss Catholics and Westerners to characterise natives; then the same irrationality, externality, collectivism and routine were applied first by sixteenth-century internal missionaries 'christianising' 'our [European] Indians' and last by secular intellectuals to condemn and then to praise 'the people'. In my analysis, secular historians could apply these marginalising conventions even less ambivalently than committed ones. If committed historians condemned religious externality, for example, they did so only because the behaviour they observed seemed to them to lack interiority, or what Savonarola once called 'enamorative *virtù*'.[20] External, collective and routine, yes even irrational behaviour ('holy madness'), remained in itself an essential part of religion. For the secular historians, however, religion was essentially reflective and its terminology psychological, so their use of such labels was the more fatal. We shall see that, paradoxically, the use of these categories lends the secular historiography of religion its own particular religious character.

These categories are distinctly ideological rather than intellectual in quality. Distinguishing between inside and outside in this fashion bestows an a priori unity upon 'popular religion' which contrasts sharply with the diffuseness of contemporary life experienced by the working historian. These categories certainly do help the historian to assemble a persuasive portrait of past religions. Yet when rooted in such categories, these portraits can be so devoid of scholarly rigour as to make the reader wince. Keith Thomas's by now well-known retort that historians do not have the time to get straight what it is they are doing has just such an effect. Thus Stuart Clark has noted that Jean Delumeau, for example, argues that the irrationality of 'the people' causes their acts, but does not notice that such an aetiology is tautological.[21] The ideological component in such an approach becomes particularly glaring when the spell is considered irrational and pre-religious, but prayer, at least private prayer, is reckoned as good common sense, eminently rational.[22]

The ideological content of the other standard polarisations is no less evident. Without asking if it is theoretically sound to oppose externality and internality, recent students have argued that Martin Luther more or less discovered internal religion, that Protestantism appealed to merchants because it avoided the time consumed by 'external apparatus', that 'magic' has been in decline since then and that the history of religion records the slow victory of internality over externality, that is, of reflection over action.[23] Before questioning whether individual identity is describable or observable apart from collective frames of reference like societal rites *and* the historian's language, sympathetic historians of 'the people' conspire in the deindividuation of their subjects by rooting their behaviour in timeless ritual or mythic structures. Instead of recognising that under the rubric of 'routine ceremony' lie legions of individual lives changed decisively by participation in ceremonies, historians like Le Roy Ladurie speak of villages 'without a state and without politics', where the dynamic conflicts and contracts of 'routine', which produce memory and identity for individuals and groups, find no constitutive significance.[24]

Historians' unwillingness to deal with such conceptual problems is not new, of course, but their persistent use of such psychological categorisations, themselves functions of the scholars' own ambivalent social position, ensures that history remains in part what it was for our clerical and humanistic ancestors, an edifying science. Reverence lives, whether it be one of respect or rancour. Beneath the asserted secularity of much of the profession resides a structural reverence for the past and present functionally quite as forceful as that which others bestow on personal gods. The cosmic dualism between psychologically but not sociologically defined high and low cultures, and between the subject and object of the historical discourse, is what produces that reverence. Reverence lives through the very absence of exchange, that is of politics, between these worlds.

Thus the problems associated with the concept of popular religion are not soluble by the editorial elimination of words like 'superstition', 'gläubiges Volk', 'magic', and the like. These marginalising characterisations of religions are in part the result of a particular historically developed corporate identity, and they will persist in other guises until a behavioural and reflective strategy of negation challenges the established image of the historical scholar.[25] To counter either respectful or rancorous reverence for 'the people', therefore, one should directly attack the source of the problem in those who 'are not of the people'. Short of redefining religion itself, the most negating or profane approach to the study of religion would be to examine the high culture with which historians identify themselves with the same methods and modes of discourse used now to study 'popular culture'.

If historians of religion were to take seriously those unsettling similes which compare scientists to priests, academic departments to tribes, scholarly conferences to collective rituals and professional journals to folklore, the results might be not only therapeutic and amusing but of significant methodological and epistemological value. I have noted that there are no books called 'elite religion' to match the many on popular religion, so with a methodology in place and the elite certainly a more specific or determinable social entity than 'the people', the abundant sources for such a study are inviting. The profanity of studying the behaviour of the elite, its externality, collectivism and routines, when the intellectuals within that elite fundamentally identify themselves as a rational reflective division of labour, would have three important results. Erstwhile students of popular religion would soon discover that, for evident reasons of corporate interest, historians know almost nothing about past elite religious behaviour.[26] Secondly, they would quickly understand that in comparing non-elite to elite religions, one must compare behaviour to behaviour and not to ideas. Finally, this approach would have the great benefit of ultimately ascribing to the non-elite the same measure of internality, individualism and spontaneity as the inside has always reserved for itself.[27]

Doubtless, scarcity of sources will always complicate the historians' ability to study reflection among non-elites, impressive as has been the progress of the Menocchios of that world in recent years.[28] This is but one more reason why the social history of religion must be founded upon the study of behaviour if that study hopes to examine all social groups without a priori psychological assumptions. The task is not to dismiss ideas, but to gain the behavioural foundation to begin to understand them. The following definition of religion could not only decrease the evident ideological functions of an association of the intelligentsia with reflection and of reflection with religion. It may also prove useful in conceptualising the history of early modern Europe.

Religion Reformed

Reverence or decorum, *pietas*, is, I would argue, the foundation of social life.[29] Many incorporated or fleeting groups in society are persuaded to swear to systems of bodily and verbal behaviours labelled appropriate by statutes or customs, and these systems are said to be efficacious in internal bonding and in distinguishing one group from another. Such a group is called a religion when it practises this sworn behaviour in the context of operational and nominal classifications of sacrality and profanity. A religion's sacred activity is that rigid or formalised motion around certain times, places and objects named sacred during that activity, while that same religion's profane activity consists of insults toward the *sacra* of outsiders done with non-rigid and sometimes unprescribed behaviours.[30] The memory of such behaviours is called religious experience, and is distinguished from ordinary social exchange.[31] A religion's profane activity also includes similar activities directed towards its own *sacra*, but these activities, though described as religious experience at the time, are rarely remembered and then labelled sacrilege or irreverence.[32]

Isolated tribal entities already possess several such religions for their different sexes, ages and clans, and such tribes commonly have masters of ceremony who are also masters of the meanings of the various groups' sacred and profane activities, which may or may not be ceremonially integrated. Contacts with other tribes produce the conditions of religions in societies: the sacred and profane times, places and objects of different tribes are increasingly irreconcilable. The enforcement by the tribal masters of ceremony of the behavioural patterns of their religions' living and dead members fails, in part because of the development of voluntary associations that can unite sexes, occupations and even cohorts across tribal lines.[33]

To regulate religions within complex societies, rulers, through their public activities as precedence-setters, propagate an overarching classification of sacred and profane times, places and objects, which it is the duty of their masters of ceremony to actualise and justify. Rulers and their clerks call reverence within this classification 'religion' in the singular, and they identify its practice with authenticity. In complex societies, religion and an absence of deceit become normatively identical. Yet deceit and authenticity only being determinable through behaviour, contending groups *testify* so as to prove their own religion or piety.[34] Beliefs, in short, exist only in performance. Groups and individuals perform bodily and verbal imitations of their codified past before the masters. They claim these testimonies are authentic within the classification of sacred and profane established by the precedence and thus precedent-setting ruler.

Understanding religions primarily as plural communities of behaviour seems at first particularly inappropriate for early modern European history, which is renowned for its doctrinal disputes. These disputes are of undeniable importance for social historians of this period, who rightly view the debates as glossing fundamental questions of social organisation. Let us realise, however, that the verbal articulation of such doctrines can be studied as behavioural systems of aural and visual semiotics uttered within specific social and political contexts, and that the most pressing task of new religions was not the articulation of clear intellectual differences from Catholicism and among each other, but the establishment of new sacred times, spaces and objects for meaningful behaviour.[35] Once the imperativeness of these needs is recognised, our approach permits the social historian to understand the religious strife of the period partially in terms of its general behavioural history. I refer, of course, to the intense process of casting social behaviour into a framework of norms, which took place between the fifteenth and seventeenth centuries.

Long ignored as 'mere externality' or dismissed as pathologic, the attention early modern Europeans gave to questions of precedence, manners and social rituals has recently become a focus of historical research. We are far from fully understanding why Burgundian and Italian rulers of the late fourteenth and fifteenth centuries, guided by their new masters of ceremony, increasingly turned their public and private actions into displays of meticulously arranged precedence and extraordinarily detailed bodily and verbal language.[36] The movement seems to have started in the monarchical and republican courts, and especially in the context of diplomatic receptions, where the new ceremonialism emphasised the majesty of princes in relation to their noble retinues as well as in their status relations with visitors.[37] From the courts, this enormous attention to organised public display spread downwards into society, producing in the end hundreds of tracts enjoining specific behaviours for men, youth, adolescents, boys, women, girls, widows, distinct occupations, and so on.

The post-Schism papacy joined the parade, and churchmen at large recognised the trend before the Reformation, and later significantly entitled some of their works on prayer modes and preaching 'Christian rhetoric'.[38] The Renaissance was the ceremonial age *par excellence*, and it is particularly interesting that contemporaries charged official historiographers with the responsibility of organising and recording such 'externalities'. The rhetoric of modern historical writing and discourse has its deep roots in the organising and the recording of public representations by historian-masters of ceremony.[39]

This new liturgical fervour, antedating the Reformation, helps explain what happened after its outbreak. Beforehand, Savonarola protested against excessive ceremonialism, while after 1517 Luther, unable to do the ceremonies right, wished he could pass one day without thus communicating with his god.[40] The Ferrarese friar wanted to replace many short masses with one affective ceremony lasting three hours! The German monk and the Protestants, beginning precisely with attacks on excessive ceremonialism, structured new devotional worlds. There could be no direction without expression. At Münster the Anabaptists at first forbade flags as idolatrous, but once surrounded by the enemy they received illumination through the visions of a minister and quickly hoisted standards: defence of their community imposed the organisation of space, and organising units in space required figured banners.[41] Comparable in this respect to the French Revolution as studied by Soboul, Ozouf and in the present volume by Michel Vovelle, the revolutionary struggles of the early modern period occurred in a hypertense world of anxiety in which different behavioural systems competed with each other so as to define binding organisations of time, space and objects.

Where to meet? Various reformers chose rural hedges and had them sanctified before moving to closed quarters, which were either purified Catholic churches or new divine houses reverentially sealed off from profanity. The process of establishing new sacred places proceeded with protests against the very idea of doing so, with the tension and uncertainty presumably being the more pressing in those border areas of repeatedly changing testimonial commitments studied by Trevor-Roper.[42] Sacred time too was not eliminated but transformed, old festive calendars being challenged by new ones through calculated profanities on old sacred days. Protestants as well as Catholics quickly incorporated the celebrations of princely births, victories, marriages and deaths, a calendrical integration which was the major innovation in the sacred time of the early modern period.[43]

Objects were modified and remodelled by the turmoil, and it is not surprising that in these religions of the book, the printed word would first be stripped of its rich authenticating bindings and then rebound with new jewels and relics. If Luther burned the books of the law, he did so to bring men and women to their knees before the Bible. Yet the object of worship was not just any Bible, but the Word in the national language, and reverence to the one was commonly engendered by profanation of the other language. Nor would just any Bible in the national language engender the awe reserved for the locally revered volume of the particular church, square, meeting house, or for the Bible revered precisely because it came from a distant court or had been touched by a fabulous preacher. The Bible, the soon-refurbished law and the polemical tracts of this period were in the first place privileged objects used to restructure behaviour.

The elites of the new religions quickly produced a mass of printed norms to regulate distinct behaviours, and the Catholics followed suit. The myriad Confessions, Books of Discipline, Prayer and Ritual of the early modern Christian world first must be understood as behavioural phenomena, means through which, in public contexts, the actions of the faithful could be compared to the inspiring lives of their leaders to determine election or salvation, damnation or purgatorial status. Weapons in the battle for religious primacy, these tracts stimulated literacy because in them one could learn the verbal and behavioural codes which would pass the Christian through the fire of testimony.[44] Beginning with the engravings in these books, which furnished new devotional images – for example, the icons of reformation heroes – and then instruction in bodily behaviour, one moved to the captions and then to the text to learn the way.

Testimony was a condition of the time. If I found 'memorisation' a feature of the humanistic education of adolescents in pre-Reformation Florence, a learning meant for public performance, Gerald Strauss has studied a strife-torn Germany in which children learned by heart formulas of 'good manners and religion' while their parents also prepared themselves for testimonial performances in the public visitations of the time. After centuries of decline, public confessions rose to renewed prominence.[45] Similar patterns of testimonial public behaviour are found in the New World, the missionaries being quite as determined to uncover through public performances the deceits of the Antichrist and 'Lutherans' as were the ministers and lords in Europe.[46] The new worlds, times and objects of awe and profanation were central contexts for these meaningful performances and thus creation of individual and group identities. The Americans who suffered the violence of these radically new contexts and, as Natalie Davis has shrewdly noted, the Protestants who denied their relevance regarding salvation, had no less a decorum or behavioural reverence for such things than did Catholics.[47]

Thus a series of behavioural facts conventionally defined as being within the religious sphere take on a new life once they are placed alongside the ceremonial facts of the court, which are not so defined even though they have all the earmarks of religious activities as we have defined them above. Is this definition of religion too broad? I do not think so. Our definition is in fact close to the terminology used in traditional Europe, where religions as plural were defined as sets of social behaviours rather than as communities of doctrine, while religion in the singular meant something akin to the behavioural piety of a group as found in the affected individual.[48] If the modern usage of religion as reflection represented an epistemological advance over the traditional one, that definition would, of course, be preferable. But such is not the case. Putatively, 'religion' is the result of reflection as well as its essence, but in modern usage it actually has ideological institutional foci. The modern definition's victory over the traditional one is linked more to the victory of the state, which controls the ritual stage and says faith is private but behaviour a public matter. It is also linked to the supremacy of an intelligentsia which has celebrated a mind-body dualism in which symbols are made to seem factual rather than facts being made to seem symbolic. That modern definition's victory is much less due to historical observation.[49] Instead of greater methodological or conceptual clarity, the modern approach features ideological convenience.

Sharing in that fatal disciplinary tendency to cauterise human experience so as to conform to academic departments of knowledge, the modern idea of religion permits the historian as the apostle of conceptual progress to decide what was religious and what not, and allows her or him to root 'real religion' in, when it is not derived from, elite institutions. The concept of christianisation is exemplary in this regard. At its least occult, the term designates the clerical effort during the early modern period to cast lay behaviour into a normative framework. Many historians try to measure the success of such campaigns by studying lay performances in institutionally authenticated 'Christian' contexts. For confessional historians, the approach presents no problems: either a Catholic or a particular Protestant practice *is* Christian. For less engaged historians, the concept is problematical, since these scholars are increasingly realising that what they call christianisation, but what I see as a ceaseless search for group-identifying sets of behaviour permitting religious experience, was common to all Christian religions of early modern Europe.[50] Those who call this ubiquitous process christianisation become enmeshed in the passions of their sources, for each group labelled its behaviour Christian and others devilish; those despised practices which moderns may label non-Christian, pagan, or traditional vestiges, their sources commonly recognise as satanic performances by their so-called Christian adversaries. Recognising there-fore that two committed historians studying two different religions may find both being successfully christianised, even though the practices of the groups are quite incomparable, these historians rely upon internalisation to bridge the behavioural problems and to discover the reality beneath the mask. This process can also be found in their sources, where the thought dominates that transparency, authenticity, or internality are Christian, and deceit or 'mere externality' non-Christian.

Those historians who descend directly from the Renaissance view of religion as reflection have meanwhile reached the same point by more direct means. For them no behaviour but only internality is *really* religious in the first place, and since internality is by definition unobservable if describable, these historians simply intuit which christianisation was successful and which not, which ages were Christian and which not.[51] This fatal link between institutions and internality, epitomised in the idea of christian-isation but linked to the broader modern link between power and virtue, ends by requiring or allowing the historian to uncover the deceit of others, and thus leads her or him implicitly to denounce that deceit as an irreverent profanation. In this process, sincerity is recognisably modern and actualised in the words of the historian, the past is deceptive to the extent it varies from the written word of its resurrector.

Instead of opting for this approach with its blissful ignorance of current deceit theory, we should imagine the early modern village as synonymous with procession, the court as associated with the parade, the city blending the two.[52] Contemporaries called both processions and parades sacred, and the groups in them religions. Both marched beneath crosses and flags with similar figures, and processions and parades could be occasions for violence, even if the stated purpose of both was to display the community of behaviour at certain times around certain objects. A behavioural approach warns us not to define the one as religious, the other as secular, not to tell the reader that instead of having a religious intent, Richelieu, for example, 'used religion as a pretext'. The authority for such censorial assurances is often nothing more solid than our own association of procession with religion more than with parade. The denunciations of Richelieu by contemporaries for using religion as a pretext tell us something about their strategy for constructing their own sacred co-ordinates, but not necessarily anything about the cardinal; our judgement requires other supporting evidence. The historian's presumptive judgement on what was a religious and political strategy of his subjects only raises the suspicion that that presumption is part of an historiographical strategy with the comparable end of establishing sacred co-ordinates in historical writing.

If we watch what happens instead of plumbing the internality of our elite, we may determine that the procession and parade were certainly not identical: the procession was linked to established sacred places, while the parade in the same places augured the defilement of the sacred places of the internal or external enemy. Then, once carried abroad out of sacrally defined spaces, the two forms remain associated but distinct: parading besiegers staged processions as if the land were already theirs, as if the spaces to be conquered already were redefined within the sacred–profane structures of the conquerors.[53] Whether those contested spaces were neighbourhoods or kingdoms, the historical observer notes that before the combatants forgot, they have used deceit not only as a military but as a processional strategy to produce victory through various types of conjurations, exorcisms, threats, prayers and insults stimulating through tricking themselves and their gods. The victor remembers smashing the images of others but suppresses the memory of his sly challenge to his own gods, parading them as if their identity had never been doubted by deceitful offerants. A behavioural approach to religion recognises deceit as essential to religious experience in both the parade and procession. The social history of sacralisation through profanation, and profanation through sacralisation, is a key to understanding the politics of religion.

The institutional biases of our contemporary understanding of religion is nowhere more evident than in the study of early modern iconoclasm, that phenomenon which, while beckoning us to admit the relation between the profane and the sacred, most powerfully seduces historians into imposing their modern concepts of the sacred as non-violent, non-political, non-dynamic and non-deceitful. Sure that 'true religion' is reflective and immaterial, historians sometimes consider iconoclasm either a vestigial phenomenon of Christian animism or as a necessary recurrent attack on fetishism.[54] Defining religious representations as those which churches say they are, many historians emphasise the ecclesiastical impact of iconoclasm to the exclusion of the impact such destruction had on the honour and property rights of the objects' lay as well as ecclesiastical owners. But it is perhaps the most telling reflection of the historians' own depoliticised understanding of religion that iconoclasm is regarded as pre-eminently a crisis phenomenon and not as a secular one, the result of parade violence, so to speak, rather than of processional stability.

A behavioural study proceeds differently, beginning by laying aside the presumption that there has been a decline in conceptual animism and leaving the question open whether such an eventual decline has been accompanied by a secular decline in iconoclasm itself. It notes first that the verbal and bodily behaviour used against the most varied material objects is remarkably similar in past and present, and it would appear that the common element in these attacks is the inimical status of the objects, which are 'in the way'. Iconoclasm is a general historical phenomenon.

Secondly, the observer will conclude that to distinguish between images which are religious and those which are not is abstract, for in practice, iconoclasm against figures conventionally defined as religious, like Virgins, has been regularly approved by those who worship 'the Virgin' when a particular Virgin was said to be but a shape of the Devil. Conversely, colours (for example, the Levellers'), shapes (such as eucharistic hosts) and images which are not representations of divinities (like coats of arms) have commonly been viewed by the authorities as godly or devilish or, more precisely, they have claimed for such objects the same behavioural reverence or profanation as that accorded to divine figures.

Thus, thirdly, to insist on the relation between the behaviour and belief of iconoclasts is to miss the fundamental nature of the behaviour itself. When a Jesuit missionary forced Indians publicly to smash a particular image, the belief of the missionary might be as complex (the image as devil *and* as mere matter) as that of the natives, but the significance of the event was behavioural.[55] There is in fact no reason to believe that iconoclasm necessarily presupposes beliefs about animism at all, but only interpersonal associations extended through objects.

Historians' emphasis upon iconoclasm against pictures of gods is comparable to the verbal manner with which the iconologists among art historians have traditionally examined art for its meaning: both assume a certain canonical meaning of a picture and fail to consider the questions of who owned the picture, in whose chapel it resided and, most important perhaps, whose occupational or noble or confraternal coat of arms was painted on or otherwise associated with it. Yet if anything is characteristic of early modern iconoclasm in Europe or in the European dependencies, it is that the iconoclasts attacked particular property rights, and that the massive assaults on those conventionally sacred objects during the period in question were attempts to redistribute property.[56] Property was and is secured within and in part through the sacred and profane behavioural classifications in a society, and iconoclasm is an historically widespread behaviour when societies redistribute property. No more than iconologists can historians understand this other image of the image when they isolate the picture from its context.

A close behavioural emphasis in studies of iconoclasm, finally, shows that breaking, reshaping, or ignoring previously venerated representations are central parts of ongoing religious behaviour, and are in no way limited to the political crises which draw such actions to our attention. Religions continually test the utility of their objects, and then apologise to the figure or relic; they change divine representations to increase their utility; they discard or store away those proved useless and, since objects harm as well as heal, these various modes of ongoing group iconoclasms are practised against both gods and devils to prevent harm as well as cause good. Precious metal objects of worship may be melted when fiscal needs require, and contrarily, icons may be put back together, like Osiris or St Bartholomew, a scattered polyptych or a flooded pastiche of fresco flecks, a fragmented ancient scroll.

This little-studied phenomenon is evidently not limited to hosts, relics and icons, but is a procedure of any group dealing with the objects around which it organises its behaviour. Just as certainly, there is a difference in scale and publicity between the iconoclasm of politically stable and revolutionary times. But once this complex topic receives the attention it deserves, iconoclasm in both times will be found to rest on the same fundamental principles of group and individual identity formation and transformation. The competition within a particular religion changes its images, and the competition within a given body politic for images such as flags accomplishes similar ends. Iconoclasm in the great revolts of the early modern period was part of a fundamental, ongoing social process involving the modification and transformation of existing religious order.

The turmoil of behavioural order in early modern Europe involves profanations that, when directed against 'false gods', are called religious experiences.[57] Far from being an understanding of order, the sacred is often not even its experience, but rather an exhilaration in disorder resolved through action. When one reads diaries and letters rather than official group histories, where forgetfulness edifies memory,[58] one uncovers religious experience in an iconoclasm towards one's own *sacra* which reflects the inherent disorder of the changing identities of religions. The historian's willingness to accept at face value a group memory which invariably emphasises group solidarity amounts to a depoliticisation of social processes going on inside a group and to a deindividuation of the persons involved in this competitive face-to-face behaviour towards each other and towards their changing gods.

Across early modern Europe and its dependencies, peasants and Indians, monarchs and missionaries experienced the sacred in the act of profaning their own and others' gods by attacking properties. These were sacred times, to be sure, remembered and relived as an age of aweful, efficacious behaviour, in which, in Hegel's formulation, heaven came to earth. Call its widespread testimonial iconoclasms a world-historical event if one likes, yet understand it not as the reverse but as the mirror of 'routine' times. When watching not just the parade but also the procession, profanation appears as a condition of sacrality.

Historiographical Rhetoric and Religious Experience

To the sound of Brahms, historians still annually march in uniform beneath the truncheon, as did their ancestors in cities and courts. A mere tradition, even historians might argue, but the social historian of religion knows by now that the *survivances vivent*. In the academic procession of commencement, the historian who wants to study 'popular religion' will begin by studying this elite. Colleagues' rigidity increases as the procession, including one's self, comes into view of the audience: at this moment, scholars in cap and gown use bodily and vocal persuasion – the more sculptured the more powerful – upon parents and students in a sacral setting. Beneath those grave academic robes one may wear levis and read articles and exams as the commencement speaker drones on. Yet who can dismiss the rhetoric? The rhetoric of academics at commencement mirrors the persuasions they use to communicate at a conference, in a classroom, in writing. Reverential forms are no mere sacrament of simple folk; on the contrary, the elites have historically been called 'the solemn persons'. In concluding, I want to examine the relation between historiographical rhetoric and religion, and suggest elements of a behavioural strategy for combating the deceit that there is none.

Societies record religious experience in two different fashions, we have said. In his diary, the individual includes his profanation of his own gods, and thus of his living associates; in the history, on the other hand, the group forgets its self-profanations, and religious experience becomes our memory of individuation as we revere our group and its gods while profaning some other group.[59] Historical writing is not dissimilar. Beginning with insight, during which the images are subject to iconoclasm, we proceed to written communications, a type of open social behaviour in which the imperatives of linguistic convention and the corporate intellective paradigms of the historian's colleagues make their reverential influences felt. Charles Tilly has found that most historians of the United States express their findings in terms of a limited number of recognisable questions.[60] The study of early modern religion is no exception to such behaviour. Like Françoise Zonabend's peasant woman, the religious experience of the 'old days' flattens out into predictable patterns.[61] Recalling idols which did not change and creating ones that did not exist can become the condition of identity for the historian and the peasant.

All historians evoke ancestors, as do most religions; once stated, this simile highlights the difference between the historian of religion and other historians, and the difference between past religions and historiographical evocation. It is a question of exchange and its objects in present and past. In the present, all historians exchange with colleagues and patrons recognisable formations of past behaviours and ideas, but the student of a past religion deals with social formations which created affective, meaningful solidarities in the past, and those solidarities are on their face quite as imperious as those the patronised historians themselves obey in their present world.

When that historian of religion looks to the object of his or her study, the nature of these conflicting exchanges becomes clear. The historical religion had as a condition of its solidarity making *its* ancestors its own; its legitimacy was rooted in giving the behavioural ghosts of its past an 'aura of factuality'.[62] Separated from that religion by time and usually place, the historian of that religion tries to raise up for present colleagues a religion part of whose essence was the ongoing resurrection of its specific dead. This difficult task calls for the historian to successively affect his or her religion, so as to evoke its specific dead, and it requires that he or she be affected by those individual generations of a past religion. At such distances from the objects, the historian's results, achieved under the pressure of his or her own colleagues and patrons, are not shocking. Concepts like 'popular religion' eliminate the line between past life and death and the specifics of time and place, while psychological characterisations distance the past from the present. The fact that the historian evokes the past for a decorous exchange with the living, while the historical religion evoked a specific past that was behaviourally exchanged with its living, amounts to a fundamental obstacle in the study of religion. It explains in part why the religious actors of early modern Europe, though dead, often are made to behave without thinking, while their historians, though alive, seem at times to breathe only thoughts.

Awareness of the ideological dangers this complex exchange system poses for the study of religions cannot in itself dissolve them; the fact that the language through which we communicate has inherent structures of sacrality and profanity alone negates that possibility. Yet exactly this insight does, I believe, offer a way of alleviating the danger: language as used by the historian *is* a political behaviour, and if the language of reverence makes it seem that it is not, the language of profanation allows us to maintain awareness of deceit and to constantly subvert an instrument of communication that is essentially sacred in its significations for the present.

The ongoing profanations I would recommend for the study of past religions, that is, for the affective exchanges the historian seeks with the past and present, might take many different forms, of which I want to single out four. The first approach profanes the present, and involves avoiding all distancing and marginalising linguistic conventions which are demonstrably modern and violations of past linguistic usages. I shall limit myself to the phenomenon of capitalisation, almost unknown until adopted with a vengeance in the sixteenth century in evident relation to an explosion of authoritarian ideology. Today's scholars use an admittedly narrowed range of capitalisation with a certain flexibility: if it is not unusual to encounter 'King', 'Church', 'Pontiff', 'Him' (*sic*!), and so on, perhaps most historians no longer capitalise such words. But a non-scientific survey of my library shows that all historians preserve the capitalisation of the

Judeo-Christian 'God', though many of the same writers speak of 'god' or 'the god' when referring to non-Christian deities, and almost all these writers render references to more than one god in the lower-case 'the gods'. It is unnecessary to spell out the conceptual assumptions such usages preserve, or to insist that explaining this as 'mere convention' only makes the point that conventions are powerful and that writers, not editors, are the ones who exercise that power. In capitalisation the concept of ideal conceptual and political unity is encapsulated, while the plural gods on the margins are rendered small. The rational Western present is preserved for exchange among the living, but the quality of the exchanges past religions made with their living, and especially with their dead, is unavoidably contorted.

The second usage would profane the religion we study by refusing to adopt those past characterisations of the objects of religious exchange which at the time had self-evident marginalising or exclusionary functions. I refer only to the use of the terms 'image' and 'idol'. We know that in the immediate context of religious experience, one group of Christian contemporaries opposed to another group did call the latter's images, such as a certain Virgin or Bible, 'idols', but the historian recognises that passion as marginalising, so he or she refers to any Christian image as just that, even if it is not unusual to find Protestant historians still verbally smashing Catholic images. Yet how are we to explain that when either committed or uncommitted historians deal with images of non-Christian religions, they regularly refer to them as 'idols', as in 'the idol of Huitzilopochtli'? In the past this and similar distinctions were evidently signs by which devotees testified as to those objects one exchanged with and those which one avoided. For the historian wishing to analyse instead of judging the ubiquitous social phenomenon of religion, the injunction is apparent: refer to such objects as images, and drop the word idol with all its ideological baggage. The alternative is historiographical idolatry.

A third usage returns to the profanation of the present, and involves adopting all those linguistic usages of past religions which characterised religious exchange without the evident function of marginalising the persons and objects of those exchanges. I refer to exchange terminologies historians of religion are familiar with but usually do not use. Consciously or unconsciously, such terms are now considered irreverent as character-isations of the exchanges most historians understand to underlie the phenomenon of religion; religion as reciprocity is one thing to say but, as we noted regarding the use of the words 'spell' and 'prayer', another to communicate. Thus contemporaries called a secular priest who sold exchanges between heaven and earth without benefice a mercenary; we mention the fact but do not integrate the word. In their account books if not in their histories, members of religions kept what they called 'accounts of god'; what was a matter-of-fact usage for them is a curiosity to us.[63] Contemporaries expected to be 'paid' by their gods, to receive 'interest', and so on; we avoid integrating such business terminology into our analysis. A painting of the Adoration of the Magi which showed the infant with his hand in the jar of gold pieces is taken as evidence of the famous 'mixing of the sacred and profane' of those ages, often with the clear implication that we moderns have got them straightened out, especially by not using the language of *do ut des* in our analysis.[64] Precisely because of our embarrassment with past exchange language, the result not of a better but of a more controlled practice of religion, incorporating such language into analysis would be not only true to the primary sources of religious life, but disruptive of the segregation of the decommercialised holy the present expects of its historians.

My last suggestion profanes both the past and present, and involves applying the systematic language of economics to the portrayal of past religious behaviour. The practice might be dangerously anachronistic if it were not for the fact that the late Middle Ages came so close to a systematic mathematisation of the business of salvation. The phenomenon is not unknown: contemporaries moved from investments based on calculations of life expectancies to calculating the solidarity they could expect from their living friends and relatives once they had died; armed with the church's estimations of the value of different indulgences, they then proceeded to calculate the length of purgatory and to arrange their testaments on that basis. Rarely mentioned except in the context of Protestant attacks on Catholic 'superstition', pride, and rationalism, the phenomenon has now been studied by Jacques Chiffoleau in a book on Avignonese testaments significantly titled *La Comptabilité de l'au delà*.[65]

Chiffoleau has drawn the systematic consequences from his sources' common but unsystematised use of the economic terminology referred to above, and casts these usages into an economic framework. Thus the author speaks of the 'economy of salvation' and of its 'mathematics'; his contemporaries are made to reckon the 'price of passage', the laws of 'spiritual supply and demand' in constructing a 'budget of the beyond'. The author presumably chose this terminology to drive home what he took to be the essence of the religious behaviour he was studying.

But the procedure has other benefits. It provides the type of affective aesthetic unity moderns rightly expect from their historians without doing irreparable violence to the images of the past, since that systematic terminology is implied in the sources. Incompatible though it might seem with my insistence on the specificity of each community of behaviour I have called a religion, such terminology yet evokes that behavioural process of individuation within social codes which is religion itself. By materialising past affects, it may also challenge historians of religion to consider their own tenaciously defended identity-in-reflection as a strategy for rendering the body of their work incorrupt in death.

Less preachily and more to the point, systematising the language of religious exchange, and the other linguistic procedures I have suggested, drive home the point that the historian does behave towards the past: Chiffoleau's judgements, for example, are the more apparent because of the systemic language of exchange he chose to describe the religious experience of composing a testament.[66] Historians too testify. Like our religious ancestors, and like the operators of today's computers, experimenting with body and verbal language can produce facts, new insights and concepts.

This essay has tried to critique the language and concepts we use to study past religion by relating them to our own corporate identity, for I believe that this is a precondition for an improved approach to the religions of early modern Europe. I pointed to an association of historians with reflection and of 'the people' with behaviour as a sound reason for emphasising religious behaviour in our studies.

It would be counterproductive, I argued, to create a new marginalisation between ideas and behaviour to replace those psychological marginalisations I faulted. Emphasising the behaviour of elites would, I thought, lead historians of religion to recognise the behavioural aspects of their own work, but becoming familiar with the ethology and semiotics of verbalisation would help us understand the nature of ideas better, including their deceit. To that end I offered a behavioural definition of religion.

Such an approach seems on examination to be particularly appropriate to the study of religion in early modern Europe. It allows us to study its parades and processions as intimately related and intimately religious. It is clear that the religions of the time all faced the common task of classifying times, spaces and objects into systems of sacrality and profanity, though the solutions were individual, indeed the very identity of each religion.[67] That process was not, finally, limited to the institutions conventionally defined as religions. One result of a behavioural approach to religion was to note the fundamentally similar formal and affective characteristics of the contemporary mass *and* court, and I suggested that to ignore these similarities was to calcify the study of religion and of the religious experience of past individuals and groups.

Early modern Europe began and ended in great waves of iconoclasm, and surely the historian inevitably recreates a more or less reverential, more or less profane picture of those times. It is therefore not a question of historians being objective or dropping their beliefs and prejudices, but of interminably profaning the past and themselves in the face of ever-new linguistic authoritarianism and corporate orthodoxies. Reverence is the enemy as it is the condition of social life and historical writing. Loath to consider St Anne as a witch, as Jean Wirth has profanely done,[68] we prefer our sacred–profane organisation to that of the past. We have been understandably slow, therefore, to study that most Christian, most iconoclastic of all activities and ideas of European religion, the eating of the god . . . then, and now.

Notes: Chapter 17

1   Criticising C. Vermorelle's 'Lenin, Stalin and Trotsky', as performed in Belgrade; cited in the *New York Times*, 30 May 1982. I thank Roger Chartier and especially Robert Seaberg for reading two different versions of this paper. The views and errors are mine; some comparative English materials were furnished by Professor Seaberg.

2   F.-A. Isambert lists several conferences in his 'Religion populaire, sociologie, histoire et folklore', *Archives de sciences sociales des religions*, Vol. XLIII (1977), pp. 162–3.

3   Most recently R. Chartier in his 'La "culture populaire": un découpage questionné', in S. Kaplan (ed.), *Understanding Popular Culture: Europe from the Middle Ages to the Nineteenth Century* (The Hague, 1984). The absence of social specificity has been a criticism of the important work of P. Burke, *Popular Culture in Early Modern Europe* (London, 1978). See also D. Rei, 'Note sul concetto di "religione popolare"', *Lares*, Vol. XL (1974), pp. 264–80; J.-C. Schmitt, 'Les traditions folkloriques dans la culture médiévale. Quelques réflexions de méthode', *Archives de sciences sociales des religions*, Vol. LII (1981), pp. 5–8, with accompanying bibliography; N. Zemon Davis, 'Some tasks and themes in the study of popular religion', in C. Trinkaus and H. Oberman (eds), *The Pursuit of Holiness in Late Medieval and Renaissance Religion* (Leiden, 1974), pp. 307–36. W. Christian, Jr, *Local Religion in Sixteenth Century Spain* (Princeton, NJ, 1981). The range of objects and patrons labelled popular is wide in *Religion et traditions populaires (Musée national des arts et traditions populaires 4 déc. 1979–3 mars 1980)* (Paris, 1979).

4   Michelet is cited in J. Le Goff, *Pour un autre Moyen Age* (Paris, 1977), p. 8. See the round table allegedly on 'les interprétations de la notion de "religion populaire"', but actually only on the word 'popular', in the volume *La Religion populaire (Paris 17–19 oct. 1977)* (CNRS Colloque 576) (Paris, 1979), pp. 394 ff. In his intervention, C. Ginzburg recommended putting the word 'popular' in prolonged hibernation: ibid., p. 399.

5   T. Kuhn has suggested that intellectual historians must do the same thing: *The Structure of Scientific Revolutions* (Chicago, 1962). Opposition to a social history of the hard sciences is currently lively; a social history of humanist historians does not seem to exist.

6   See his paper cited n. 2. J. Le Goff finds status implying domination whatever the actual wealth or power relations: the 'people' or laity was 'subordinate to the clerks in religious matters'; *Religion populaire*, p. 403.

7   In northern Europe, I am thinking of certain strands of the Common Life, and thus of the pre-Reformation. Though Erasmus insisted on the value of acts in the free-will debate with Luther, his *philosophia Christi*, already reflected in the *Praise of Folly*, is built on criticism of clerical action; the neo-Platonism of Florence had earlier carved out an area for its own 'magic' by similar criticisms.

8   D. P. Walker, *Spiritual and Demonic Magic from Ficino to Campanella* (London, 1958).

9   The attack on behaviour in religion was part of a larger distancing of this new intelligentsia from manual activities at large; F. Yates's brilliant attempt to relate a neo-Platonic 'magic' – essentially a mental operation or reflection – to the artistic work of the Italian Renaissance was ultimately undemonstrable; *Giordano Bruni and the Hermetic Tradition* (London, 1964).

10 The pages of such writers are full of admonitions for the 'vulgar' to better themselves, to be sure, but such sentiments are perfectly congruous with despising the 'brutes' who did not hire a teacher. 'Man' in Mirandola's *Dignity* did not include such 'beasts'. For a different reading, see M. Venard, 'Dans l'affrontement des réformes du XVIe siècle: regard et jugements portés sur la religion populaire', in *Religion populaire*, pp. 115 ff.

11 R. Trexler, *Public Life in Renaissance Florence* (New York, 1980), ch. 3; R. Trexler, 'Aztec priests for Christian altars. The theory and practice of reverence in New Spain', in *Scienze. Credenze occulte. Livelli di cultura. Convegno Internazionale di Studi (Firenze, 26–30 giugno 1980)* (Florence, 1982), pp. 175–96 (another valuable conference on the 'relation between popular culture and elite culture': ibid., p. v); R. C. Trexler, 'Legitimating prayer gestures in the twelfth century. The *De Penitentia* of Peter the Chanter', forthcoming in *History and Anthropology*.

12 Castiglione's *Courtier* and Della Casa's *Galateo* are innocent of such structural considerations of manners; the neglected Stefano Guazzo's *De civili conversatione* is a masterpiece along these lines. N. Elias, *Die höfische Gesellschaft* (Darmstadt, 1979), ch. VI, notes the gradual limitations placed on kings through such courtesy systems. It is significant that Elias's book on court etiquette scarcely mentions the thaumaturgic powers associated to some of these kings, and M. Bloch's *Les Rois thaumaturges* (Paris, 1961) hardly mentions etiquette, though the two are deeply related.

13 This type of work is encountered in the series *Histoire et sociologie de l'église* (Sirey), which was edited by Le Bras. See also the pioneering work of J. Toussaert, *Le Sentiment*

religieux en Flandre à la fin du Moyen-Age (Paris, 1963), with *nihil obstat*. Especially characteristic is Le Bras, 'Le clergé dans les derniers siècles du Moyen Age', *Unam Sanctam*, Vol. XXVIII (Paris, 1954), pp. 153–81, in an issue on 'Priests of yesterday and today' edited by J.-F. Lemarignier. Criticism of this tradition is in F. Isambert, 'Autour du catholicisme populaire. Réflexions sociologiques sur un débat', *Social Compass*, Vol. XXII (1975), pp. 193–210. On 'historical religious sociology' as against sociology of religion, see C. Langlois' contribution to *Religion Populaire*, pp. 325 ff.

14 For the ongoing anthropological debate, see the articles in 'Towards an ethics for anthropologists', in *Current Anthropology*, Vol. XII (1971), pp. 321 ff., and the debate over C. Turnbull's *The Mountain People*, ibid., Vol. XVI (1975), pp. 343 ff. Similarly, see B. Lewis, 'The attack on orientalism', *The New York Review of Books* (24 June 1982), pp. 49 ff. Evidently, historians are as variegated as anthropologists, and the striking absence of political considerations in the literature on popular religion at large is merely more impressive than the presence of historians of 'plebeian culture'. Still, the latter historians *accept* their states, since they describe relations between the latter and 'popular culture' in terms of resistance not revolt; see further below. A structured exclusion of the state from 'popular religion' is available in E. Le Roy Ladurie's *Montaillou, village occitan de 1294 à 1324* (Paris, 1975). Religion and politics are reintegrated in R. Firth's important 'Spiritual aroma: religion and politics', *American Anthropologist*, Vol. LXXXIII (1981), pp. 582–601.

15 Not until C. Trinkaus' *In our Image and Likeness. Humanity and Divinity in Italian Humanist Thought*, 2 vols (Chicago, 1970), was the Burckhardtian 'secularisation' of thought fundamentally put into doubt. Until very recently, religion has played no significant role in explaining Renaissance politics. N. Elias's works, including *Über den Prozess der Zivilisation* (Bern, 1969), have remarkably little to say about religion.

16 The link between a 'civilisation' of unquestioned manners and bureaucratic structures is best understood by S. Freud in his *Civilisation and its Discontents* (New York, 1962), and by R. Sennett, *The Fall of Public Man* (New York, 1977). Elias, *Prozess*, does not mention it; see his ch. I on the specifically French and English emphasis on behaviour as *civilisation*.

17 Such a crude typology does not justly describe any one historian, of course, nor is it meant to; I found myself in all the categories I describe. But it is fair to suggest that Michelet was a type of godfather to this latter group and in its most brilliant form that spiritual cognation is evident in the work of E. P. Thompson. Thompson's own reading of his progeny is in an interview in the *Radical History Review*, Vol. IV (1976), pp. 4–25. Such historians, including myself, tend to replace class considerations with emphases on age and sex; see the interview with N. Zemon Davis, ibid., Vol. XXIV (1980), pp. 115–39. A critique of this approach is provided by E. Fox-Genovese and E. Genovese, 'The political crisis of social history: a Marxian perspective', *Journal of Social History*, Vol. X (1976), pp. 205–21.

18 *Rabelais and his World* (Cambridge, Mass., 1968).

19 For the equation rural-collective, see R. Mandrou, *Introduction à la France moderne; essai de psychologie historique 1500–1640* (Paris, 1974), ch. 16; P. Laslett, *The World We Have Lost* (New York, 1965). The observation on Thompson could also fairly be made of my *Public Life*, cited n. 11 above.

20 ibid., p. 471. The comparison of Europeans to Indians is studied by A. Prosperi, '"Otras Indias": missionari della contrariforma tra contadini e selvaggi', in *Scienze*, cited n. 11 above, pp. 205–34.

21 S. Clark, 'French historians and early modern popular culture', *Past and Present*, Vol. C (1983), pp. 62–99. See K. Thomas citing Dyce in 'An anthropology of religion and magic, II', *Journal of Interdisciplinary History*, Vol. VI (1975), p. 91.

22 As in Thomas's epochal *Religion and the Decline of Magic* (London, 1971), p. 41. When prayer alone of human actions toward the gods is considered efficacious, the results are curious; see my review of R. Manselli, *La Religion populaire au moyen âge* (Montreal, 1975), in *Speculum*, Vol. LII (1977), pp. 1019–22.

23 Respectively M. Ruel, 'Christians as believers', in J. Davis (ed.), *Religious Organisation and Religious Experience* (London, 1982), pp. 9–31; H. Trevor-Roper, *The Crisis of the Seventeenth Century* (New York, 1956), p. 24; K. Thomas, *Religion*; N. Belmont,

'Superstition et religion populaire dans les sociétés occidentales', in M. Izard and P. Smith (eds), *La Fonction symbolique. Essais d'anthropologie* (Paris, 1979), pp. 53–70.

24 Le Roy Ladurie, *Montaillou*, ch. 22. This deindividuation is particularly marked in R. Muchembled, *Culture populaire et culture des élites* (Paris, 1978), esp. pp. 127 ff. I have examined contract and competition combined in ritual in my *Public Life*, ch. 8. The classic treatment of social identity are the papers of the 1974–5 seminar conducted by C. Lévi-Strauss, *L'Identité* (Paris, 1977).

25 The process of interpreting the past as 'not us' must, I believe, include an understanding of the interpreters as simultaneously negating the present as 'not us'. Assessments of this 'critical philosophy' are in *The Critical Spirit. Essays in Honour of Herbert Marcuse*, ed. K. Wolff and B. Moore, Jr (Boston, Mass., 1967).

26 This is despite the fact that church attendance today, and probably in the past, is directly related to wealth and status: academicians go to church more often than workers or rural peoples; see, for example, M. Argyle, *Religious Behaviour* (London, 1958).

27 The absence of mediation when such psychological characterisations are used is epitomised in the title of H. Dedieu, 'Quelques traces de religion populaire autour des frères mineurs de la province d'Aquitaine', in *La Religion populaire en Languedoc du XIIIe à la moitié du XIVe siècle* (Toulouse, 1976), pp. 227–49, where the behaviour of friars becomes vestigial 'popular religion'.

28 C. Ginzburg, *Il formaggio e i vermi* (Turin, 1976). In *Religion populaire*, p. 399, Ginzburg insists historians place religion within social contexts; this essentially corrects his handling of Menocchio, whose mental gymnastics are excellently described but whose occupation as a miller takes on no significance until the last part of the book. Le Roy Ladurie's *Montaillou* is, of course, another successful individuation of village characters. See also Giovanni Morelli's experiences edited by R. Trexler, 'In search of father: the experience of abandonment in the recollections of Giovanni di Pagolo Morelli', *History of Childhood Quarterly*, Vol. III (1975), pp. 225–52.

29 Besides Elias's *Prozess*, cited n. 15, see E. Shils, *The Constitution of Society* (Chicago, 1972), pp. 143–75, on deference.

30 C. Geertz warns against associating gravity with reverence; *The Interpretation of Cultures* (New York, 1973), p. 97. I am not aware of a definition of religious behaviour which attempts to integrate profanation. See recently, F.-A. Isambert, 'L'élaboration de la notion de sacré dans l'école durkheimienne', *Archives de sciences sociales des religions*, Vol. XXVI (1976), pp. 35–76. On the problem of reconciling the socially defined state of rigid reverence with ecstasy or 'excessive gestures' viewed as an instrumentalisation of humans by the gods, see my *Public Life*, cited n. 11, pp. 104 ff.

31 The process of memorising through a mental architecture that profanes the outside is studied by F. Yates, *The Art of Memory* (Chicago, 1966).

32 More on these different descriptions of religious experience below. This approach tries to exorcise an inadequate interpretation of carnival as inversion and anti-religious behaviour, or as *intervallum mundi*: J. Caro Baroja, *El carnaval* (Madrid, 1979), Introduction. By my definition, carnival is religious; see R. Scribner's richly documented attempt to link carnival as inversion to Protestant propagandisation of beliefs in 'Reformation, carnival and the world turned upside-down', *Social History*, Vol. III (1978), pp. 303–29.

33 This irreconcilability, I suggest, arises first in the area of behavioural diplomacy, only much later as a question of meaning or theology.

34 Imposed behaviours, a precondition of order and affect, complicate the discovery of transparently 'true sentiment'. See W. Christian, Jr's important study on using tears as such an indicator, even though a technology for inducing them and thus the presence of deceit had long existed: 'Provoked religious weeping in early modern Spain', in Davis, *Religious Organisation*, pp. 97–114.

35 As is shown by N. Zemon Davis, 'The sacred and the body social in sixteenth-century Lyon', *Past and Present*, Vol. XC (1981), pp. 40–70.

36 See my introduction to *The Libro Cerimoniale of the Florentine Republic by Francesco Filarete and Angelo Manfidi* (Geneva, 1978). To date there is no modern work on Burgundy to supplant O. Cartellieri, *The Court of Burgundy* (New York, 1929); E. Muir, *Civic Ritual in Renaissance Venice* (Princeton, NJ, 1981); links between diplomacy and everyday rituals are in the three volumes of J. Jacquot and E. Konigson (eds), *Les Fêtes de*

la Renaissance, esp. Vol. III (Paris, 1975). On confraternal rituals, R. Weissman, *Ritual Brotherhood in Renaissance Florence* (New York, 1982). My view is not that there was more 'external behaviour' in this age, but rather greater attention to more organised behaviour.

37 See my *Public Life*, cited n. 11, ch. 9.

38 See for example Diego Valvades, *Rhetorica christiana ad concionandi et orandi usum accommodata* (Perugia, 1579). Earlier churchmen had been known to scorn rhetoric; Trexler, 'Legitimating prayer gestures', cited n. 11.

39 Trexler, *Libro Cerimoniale*, pp. 20–31.

40 Trexler, *Public Life*, p. 474; J. Wirth, *Luther. Étude d'histoire religieuse* (Geneva, 1981).

41 M. Rocke, 'Ritual, identity and social order in the New Jerusalem. Münster, 1534–1535', read at the conference on Persons in Groups. Social Behavior as Identity Formation (Binghamton, New York: 14–16 October 1982).

42 In his *The Crisis*, cited n. 23, pp. 90 ff.

43 Elizabeth of England as an example had the *Acts and Monuments* of John Foxe, a work incorporating all these new sacred times, places and objects, put up in every church in England: W. Haller, *Foxe's Book of Martyrs and the Elect Nation* (London, 1963), p. 13.

44 The primarily religious causes of increasing literacy are emphasised in F. Furet and J. Ozouf, *Lire et écrire*, 2 vols (Paris, 1977).

45 R. Trexler, 'Ritual in Florence: adolescence and salvation in the Renaissance', in Trinkaus and Oberman, *The Pursuit of Holiness*, pp. 200–64; G. Strauss, *Luther's House of Learning. Indoctrination of the Young in the German Reformation* (Baltimore, Md, 1978). Public confessing was, of course, a feature of certain Protestant confessions; it was fostered by the late medieval confraternity system; the use of public punishment was on the upswing, the punishment identifying the crime. The medieval decline of public confession did not lead up to 'internal' Lutheranism; see my review of T. Tentler, *Sin and Confession on the Eve of the Reformation* (Princeton, NJ, 1977), in *Speculum*, Vol. LIII (1978), pp. 862–5.

46 See, for example, R. Padden, *The Hummingbird and the Hawk* (New York, 1967) esp. ch. 13.

47 *Society and Culture in Early Modern France* (Stanford, Calif., 1975), p. 174.

48 Thus the hospitallers were a religion or a *doctrina*, both words referring to sets of behaviours, clothing, and so on, summarised in statutes. A person who 'had religion', in Geertz's excellent formulation, had 'liabilities to perform particular classes of acts or have particular classes of feelings'; see Geertz, *Interpretation*, p. 97. On the other hand, those like Geertz who view religion as a system of interpretative symbols are at odds with those many interpreters of traditional Europe who argued that the less one knew the holier one might be (*sancta rusticitas*). Note that, with no special word for religion, Chinese speaks of doctrine – of the litterati – and rites. Like me it does not distinguish *a priori* between church and secular rites; M. Weber, *The Religion of China*, ed. H. Gerth (New York, 1951), p. 144.

49 See Geertz's interpretive definition of religion in *Interpretation*, cited n. 30, pp. 90 ff.

50 J. Delumeau, *Le Catholicisme entre Luther et Voltaire* (Paris, 1971); id., *La Mort des pays de Cocagne* (Paris, 1976), chs 6–7. Vovelle's thesis of modern dechristianisation has predictably aroused hackles among the faithful; see B. Plongeron (ed.), *La Religion populaire dans l'occident chrétien* (Paris, 1976), p. 17.

51 See my review mentioned above, n. 22. See also S. Kierkegaard, *Fear and Trembling* (Princeton, NJ, 1974), pp. 81–2, and esp. p. 89 for the 'Knight of Faith' whose internality was not recognisable, even to another such knight.

52 A recent issue of *Daedalus* (Summer 1979) on *Hypocrisy, Illusion and Evasion* completely avoided the scientific literature on animal deceit and its implications for the human question; see R. Dawkins, *The Selfish Gene* (Oxford, 1976), pp. 171 ff.

53 See examples in my *Public Life*, cited n. 11, pp. 3–6 and 'insults and ridicule' in the index.

54 See the critique of this position in P. Geary, 'La coercition des saints dans la pratique religieuse médiévale', in P. Boglioni (ed.), *La Culture populaire au moyen âge* (Quebec, 1979), pp. 145–60. On English iconoclasm as 'lamentable ... but not without its compensations', see G. Elton, *England under the Tudors* (London, 1960), p. 149. Thomas, *Religion*, cited n. 22, pp. 75 ff., sees Protestant iconoclasm as part of an attempt

to take magic out of religion. The tendency to empty iconoclasm of iconoclasts is particularly marked in England, where the state had an important hand in it; see J. Phillips, *The Reformation of Images: Destruction of Art in England, 1535–1660* (Berkeley, Calif., 1973), where the actual actor when unguided by the state becomes irrational. P. Mack Crew's *Calvinist Preaching and Iconoclasm in the Netherlands 1544–1569* (Cambridge, 1978) identifies the iconoclasts and judiciously evaluates their motivations.

55 Notoriously, the statement that an object is lifeless is a means of making it so: R. Trexler, 'Florentine religious experience: the sacred image', *Studies in the Renaissance*, Vol. XIX (1972), pp. 7–41. W. Brückner's important *Bildnis und Brauch* (Berlin, 1966) spends inordinate time on showing that belief in *Bildmagie* was less widespread than art historians assume, and not enough on the behaviour towards the 'shame-effigies' he richly documents. The distinction between planned and unpremeditated iconoclasm, between conscious and unconscious behaviour (see Phillips, *Destruction*, p. 4), between belief and non-belief in animism (Brückner) should not divert one from recognising the fundamentally antagonous nature of the behaviour and of the object attacked.

56 As brought out in M. Warnke (ed.), *Bildersturm. Die Zerstörung der Kunstwerke* (Munich, 1973); see also Phillips, *Destruction*, pp. 201 ff., and pp. 90–4 for some telling contemporary sources.

57 I have only to call attention to the searing religious convictions of N. Davis, 'Rites of violence', in her *Society*, cited n. 47, pp. 152–87.

58 On the differences in these sources, see my *Public Life*, cited n. 11, ch. 2.

59 This distinction does not apply where, as in the Puritan diaries, they were written for future testimony or printing: see W. Haller, *The Rise of Puritanism* (New York, 1947), pp. 97, 101 ff.

60 C. Tilly, *As Sociology Meets History* (New York, 1981), pp. 18–21.

61 F. Zonabend, *La Mémoire longue: temps et histoires au village* (Paris, 1980); cf. Le Roy Ladurie, *Montaillou*, cited n. 14, pp. 419–31.

62 For C. Geertz, ritual clothes conceptions with this aura: *Interpretation*, cited n. 30, pp. 109–19.

63 Trexler, *Public Life*, cited n. 11, ch. 3, on exchange. On Puritans who 'posted [their] account with god' and spoke of 'incomes and profits received in spiritual traffic', see Haller, *The Rise of Puritanism*, p. 100.

64 See, for example, Muchembled, *Culture*, cited n. 24, p. 129. On the Adoration, E. Gombrich, 'The evidence of images', in C. Singleton (ed.), *Interpretation* (Baltimore, Md, 1969), pp. 90–1.

65 *La Comptabilité de l'au-delà: les hommes, la mort et la religion dans la région d'Avignon à la fin du moyen âge* (Rome, 1980), esp. pt ii.

66 He repeatedly judges whether testators were 'sincere' or not, whether they clothed themselves in friars' habits for burial because of 'magic', or because of 'true piety', and so on.

67 N. Davis, 'Sacred', and 'Rites' in her *Society*, cited n. 47, attempts to distinguish between Reformed and Catholic solutions on the basis of what she occasionally calls 'style'; I am suggesting that to the extent that one religion identifies another, it is done on the basis of observed behavioural characters, whether the observations are right or wrong.

68 'Sainte Anne est une sorcière', *Bibliothèque d'Humanisme et Renaissance*, Vol. XL (1978), pp. 449–80.

Appendix

German, French and Italian Works Cited Above Available in English Translations

Blickle, P.
Die Revolution von 1525, Munich and Vienna, 1975 (2nd rev. edn, 1981)

The Revolution of 1525: The German Peasants' War from a New Perspective, trans. H. C. E. Midelfort and T. A. Brady, Jr, Baltimore, Md, 1982

Bloch, M.
Les Rois thaumaturges, Paris, 1961

The Royal Touch: Sacred Monarchy and Scrofula in England and France, trans. J. E. Anderson, London, 1973

Delumeau, J.
Le Catholicisme entre Luther et Voltaire, Paris, 1971

Catholicism between Luther and Voltaire: A New View of the Counter-reformation, trans. J. Moiser, London, 1977

Elias, N.
Über den Prozess der Zivilisation, 2 vols, Bern, 1969

The Civilising Process, trans. E. Jephcott, New York (Pantheon Books), 1982

Elias, N.
Die höfische Gesellschaft, Darmstadt, 1979

Courtly Society, New York (Urizen Books), forthcoming

Fanon, F.
Les Damnés de la terre, Paris, 1961

Wretched of the Earth, trans. C. Farrington, New York, 1965

Ginzburg, C.
Il formaggio e i vermi: Il cosmo di un mugnaio del 1500, Turin, 1976

The Cheese and the Worms: The Cosmos of a Sixteenth-Century Miller, trans. J. Tedeschi and A. Tedeschi, Harmondsworth, 1982

also cited above in the German translation as:

Ginzburg, C.
Der Käse und die Würmer: Die Welt des Müllers um 1600, Frankfurt am Main, 1979

Halbwachs, M.
Das Gedächtnis und seine sozialen Bedingungen (1925), Berlin and Neuwied, 1966

The Social Framework of Memory, European Sociology Series, reprint, New York, 1975

Le Roy Ladurie, E.
Montaillou, village occitan de 1294 à 1324, Paris, 1975

Montaillou, trans. B. Bray, London, 1978

Mandrou, R.
Introduction à la France moderne: Essai de psychologie historique, 1500–1640, Paris, 1974

Introduction to Modern France, 1500–1640: An Essay in Historical Psychology, trans. R. E. Hallmark, London, 1976

Moeller, B.
'Die deutschen Humanisten und die Anfänge der Reformation', *Zeitschrift für Kirchengeschichte*, Vol. LXX (1959), pp. 46–61

'The German Humanists and the beginnings of the Reformation', in id., *Imperial Cities and the Reformation* (see below), pp. 19–38

Moeller, B.
Reichsstadt und Reformation, Schriften des Vereins für Reformationsgeschichte, no. 180, Gütersloh, 1962

'Imperial cities and the Reformation', in id., *Imperial Cities and the Reformation*, trans. and ed. H. C. E. Midelfort and M. U. Edwards, Jr, Philadelphia, Pa, 1972, pp. 41–115

also cited above in the French translation as:

Moeller, B.
Villes d'empire et Réformation, Geneva, 1966

Troeltsch, E.
Die Soziallehren der christlichen Kirchen und Gruppen, Tübingen, 1912

The Social Teaching of the Christian Churches, 2 vols, trans. O. Wyon, Chicago, 1981

Weber, M.
Wirtschaft und Gesellschaft: Grundriss der verstehenden Soziologie, Tübingen, 1956

Economy and Society: An Outline of Interpretive Sociology, 2 vols, ed. G. Roth and C. Wittich, Berkeley, Calif., 1978

Notes on Contributors

Bob Scribner is Lecturer in Modern History at the University of Cambridge and a Fellow of Clare College. He is the author of *For the Sake of Simple Folk: Popular Propaganda for the German Reformation* (1981) and of several important articles, notably on the social history of the German Reformation, as well as co-editor (with Gerhard Benecke) of *The German Peasant War 1525: New Viewpoints* (1979).

Hartmut Lehmann is Professor of History at the University of Kiel. His major publications include *Pietismus und weltliche Ordnung in Württemberg vom 17. bis zum 20. Jahrhundert* (1969) and *Das Zeitalter des Absolutismus: Gottesgnadentum und Kriegsnot*, Christentum und Gesellschaft, Vol. IX (1980). He is also the author of numerous articles mainly on the social history of German Pietism.

Peter Burke is Lecturer in Modern History at the University of Cambridge and a Fellow of Emmanuel College. His publications include *Venice and Amsterdam: A Study of Seventeenth-century Elites* (1974), *Popular Culture in Early Modern Europe* (1979), and *Sociology and History* (1980). He is the editor of Vol. XIII (Companion Volume) of *The New Cambridge Modern History* (1979) and author of many articles concerned with Italian history of the Renaissance and early modern periods and, more generally, with social and intellectual aspects of early modern Europe.

Robert Muchembled is a Lecturer in History at the University of Lille III. His publications include *Culture Populaire et Culture des Elites dans la France Moderne (XVe-XVIIIe siècles)* (1978), *La Sorcière au Village (XVe-XVIIIe siècle)* (1979) and *Les Derniers Bûchers: Un Village de Flandre et ses Sorcières sous Louis XIV* (1981). He has also published several articles on the social history of early modern France and is co-author (with M.-S. Dupont-Bouchat and W. Frijhoff) of *Prophètes et Sorciers dan les Pays-Bas, XVIe-XVIIIe siècle* (1978).

Jean Wirth is a Lecturer in Art History at the University of Strasburg. He is the author of 'La jeune fille et la mort: recherches sur les thèmes macabres dans l'art germanique de la Renaissance', *Hautes Etudes Mediévales et Modernes*, Vol. XXXVI (1979) and of *Luther: Etude d'Histoire Religieuse* (1981), as well as of articles in the art history and the social history of religion in the late medieval and Reformation periods.

Michel Vovelle is Professor of Modern History at the University of Provence at Aix-en-Provence. His many books and articles on the history of seventeenth- and eighteenth-century France include *Piété Baroque et Déchristianisation en Provence au XVIIIe siècle* (1963), *Mourir Autrefois: Attitudes Collectives Devant la Mort aux XVIIe et XVIIIe siècles* (1974), *Les Métamorphoses de la Fête en Provence (1750-1820)* (1976) and *Religion et Révolution: La Déchristianisation de l'An II* (1976).

Klaus Deppermann is Professor of History at the University of Freiburg im Breisgau. Among his publications, which include several articles on the history of German and Swiss Anabaptism and German Pietism, are *Der Hallesische Pietismus und der preussische Staat unter Friedrich III (I.)* (1961) and *Melchior Hoffman: Soziale Unruhen und apokalyptische Visionen im Zeitalter der Reformation* (1979).

Gerald Strauss is Professor of History at Indiana University. He has published many articles mainly on the history of humanism and the German Reformation. His more recent, book-length publications include *Nuremberg in the Sixteenth Century* (1966) and *Luther's House of Learning: Indoctrination of the Young in the German Reformation* (1978). He is also the editor of *Manifestations of Discontent in Germany on the Eve of the Reformation* (1971).

Bruce Lenman is Reader in Modern History at the University of St Andrews. His more recent publications include *The Economic History of Modern Scotland 1660–1976* (1977) and *The Jacobite Risings in Britain 1689–1746* (1980). He is also a co-editor (with V. A. C. Gatrell and G. Parker) of *Crime and the Law: The Social History of Crime in Western Europe since 1500* (1980) and has published many articles, mainly on Scottish history.

Mary Fulbrook is a sociologist and a Lecturer in History in the Department of German, University College, London. Her major publication to date is *Piety and Politics: Religion and the Rise of Absolutism in England, Württemberg and Prussia* (1983). She is also the author of several articles in sociology and history.

Martin Scharfe is a folklorist and a lecturer at the University of Tübingen. His more recent publications are *Evangelische Andachtsbilder: Studien zu Intention und Funktion des Bildes in der Frömmigkeitsgeschichte vornehmlich des schwäbischen Raumes* (1968) and *Die Religion des Volkes: Kleine Kultur- und Sozialgeschichte des Pietismus* (1980). He is also a co-author (with H. Bausinger, U. Jeggle and G. Korff) of *Grundzüge der Volkskunde* (1978) and has published many articles, especially on the historical aspects of German folklore and popular religion.

Martin Ingram is a Lecturer in Modern History at the Queen's University, Belfast. His Oxford University D.Phil. thesis (1976) concerned ecclesiastical justice in Wiltshire 1600–1640, with special reference to cases concerning sex and marriage and he contributed an article based on this research to *Crime in England 1550–1800*, ed. J. S. Cockburn (1977).

John Bossy is Professor of Modern History at the University of York. He has published numerous articles (notably in *Past and Present* and *Annales E. S. C.*), some of them of a seminal nature, on the history of the English Catholic community and the social history of Catholic Europe in the early modern period. His major book-length study to date is *The English Catholic Community 1570–1850* (1975). He is also a co-editor (with Peter Jupp) of *Essays Presented to Michael Roberts* (1976).

Hermann Hörger is a theologian and historian. Formerly at the University of Munich, he now serves a Bavarian parish as a priest. He has published many articles on aspects of rural religion in early modern and nineteenth-century Upper Bavaria, as well as 'Kirche, Dorfreligion und bäuerliche Gesellschaft: Strukturanalysen zur gesellschaftsgebundenen Religiosität ländlicher Unterschichten des 17. bis 19. Jahrhunderts, aufgezeigt an bayerischen Beispielen', *Studien zur altbayerischen Kirchengeschichte*, Vols. V and VII (1978 and 1983).

Jean-Pierre Gutton is Professor of History at the University of Lyons II. He is the author of many articles on the social history of the Lyonnais and early modern France. His several book-length publications include *La Société et les Pauvres: L'exemple de la Généralité de Lyon, 1534–1789* (1971), *La Société et les Pauvres en Europe (XVIe-XVIIIe siècles)* (1974), *Villages du Lyonnais sous la Monarchie (XVIe-XVIIIe siècles)* (1973), *La Sociabilité Villageoise dans l'Ancienne France: Solidarités et Voisinages du XVIe au XVIIIe siècles* (1979) and *Domestiques et Serviteurs dans la France de l'Ancien Régime* (1981).

Richard Trexler is Professor of History at the State University of New York at Binghamton. His publications include 'The spiritual power: republican Florence under interdict', *Studies in Medieval and Reformation Thought*, Vol. IX (1974), *Public Life in Renaissance Florence* (1980) and numerous articles, notably on the social history of Renaissance Florence.

Kaspar von Greyerz is currently Research Fellow at the German Historical Institute. His major publication to date is 'The Late City Reformation in Germany: The Case of Colmar, 1522–1628, *Veröffentlichungen des Instituts für Europäische Geschichte Mainz*, Vol. XCVIII (1980).

Index